Reading Philosophy of Language

Selected Texts with Interactive Commentary

Jennifer Hornsby
and
Guy Longworth

Blackwell
Publishing

© 2006 by Jennifer Hornsby and Guy Longworth

BLACKWELL PUBLISHING
350 Main Street, Malden, MA 02148-5020, USA
9600 Garsington Road, Oxford OX4 2DQ, UK
550 Swanston Street, Carlton, Victoria 3053, Australia

The right of Jennifer Hornsby and Guy Longworth to be identified as the Authors of this Work has been asserted in accordance with the UK Copyright, Designs, and Patents Act 1988.

First published 2006 by Blackwell Publishing Ltd

1   2006

Library of Congress Cataloging-in-Publication Data

Reading philosophy of language : selected texts with interactive commentary/Jennifer Hornsby and Guy Longworth.
   p. cm. – (Reading philosophy)
Includes bibliographical references and index.
  ISBN-13: 978-1-4051-2484-3 (hardcover : alk. paper)
  ISBN-10: 1-4051-2484-9 (hardcover : alk. paper)
  ISBN-13: 978-1-4051-2485-0 (pbk. : alk. paper)
  ISBN-10: 1-4051-2485-7 (pbk. : alk. paper)
  1. Language and languages–Philosophy. I. Hornsby, Jennifer.
II. Longworth, Guy. III. Series.
  P107.R4 2005
  401–dc22

                          2005003246

A catalogue record for this title is available from the British Library.

Set in 10.5/12.5 pt Sabon
by SPI Publisher Services, Pondicherry, India
Printed and bound in India
by Replika Press Pvt Ltd, Kundli

The publisher's policy is to use permanent paper from mills that operate a sustainable forestry policy, and which has been manufactured from pulp processed using acid-free and elementary chlorine-free practices. Furthermore, the publisher ensures that the text paper and cover board used have met acceptable environmental accreditation standards.

For further information on
Blackwell Publishing, visit our website:
www.blackwellpublishing.com

Contents

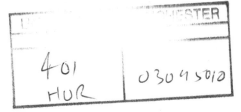

Sources and Acknowledgements

The authors and publisher gratefully acknowledge the permission granted to reproduce the copyright material in this book:

Gottlob Frege, 'On Sense and Reference', pp. 56–78 from Peter Geach and Max Black, *Translations from the Philosophical Writings of Gottlob Frege*, 3rd edn. Oxford: Blackwell, 1980. Copyright © 1980 by Blackwell Publishing. Reprinted by permission of Blackwell Publishing Ltd.

J. L. Austin, 'Performative Utterances', pp. 234–52 from *Philosophical Papers*, 3rd edn. Oxford: Oxford University Press, 1979. Copyright © 1973 by J. L. Austin. Reprinted by permission of the Estate of J. L. Austin.

William P. Alston, 'Meaning and Use', pp. 107–24 from *Philosophical Quarterly* 13, 1963. Copyright © 1963 by *Philosophical Quarterly*. Reprinted by permission of Blackwell Publishing Ltd.

John R. Searle, 'Meaning', pp. 42–50 from *Speech Acts* (Section 2.6). Cambridge: Cambridge University Press, 1969. Copyright © 1969 by Cambridge University Press. Reprinted by permission of Cambridge University Press.

Donald Davidson, 'Radical Interpretation', pp. 313–28 from *Dialectica* 27. Oxford: Dialectica, 1973. Copyright © 1973 by Dialectica. Reprinted by permission of Dialectica.

Scott Soames, 'Semantics and Semantic Competence', pp. 575–96 from *Philosophical Perspectives* 3, 1989. Copyright © 1989 by *Philosophical Perspectives*. Reprinted by permission of Blackwell Publishing Ltd.

Crispin Wright, 'Theories of Meaning and Speakers', pp. 204–38 from *Realism, Meaning, and Truth*. Oxford: Blackwell, 1987. Copyright © 1987 by Blackwell Publishing. Reprinted by permission of Blackwell Publishing Ltd.

Noam Chomsky, 'Knowledge of Language as a Focus of Inquiry', pp. 1–14 from *Knowledge of Language: Its Nature, Origin, and Use* (Ch. 1). Westport, CT: Praeger, 1986. Copyright © 1986 by Greenwood Publishing Group. Reproduced with permission of Greenwood Publishing Group, Inc., Westport, CT.

Michael Dummett, 'What Do I Know When I Know a Language?', pp. 94–105 from *The Seas of Language*. Oxford: Oxford University Press, 1993. Copyright © 1993 by Michael Dummett.

John Campbell, 'Knowledge and Understanding', pp. 17–29 from *Philosophical Quarterly* 32, 1982. Copyright © 1982 by *Philosophical Quarterly*. Reprinted by permission of Blackwell Publishing Ltd.

Paul Horwich, 'The Composition of Meanings', pp. 154–83 from *Meaning* (Ch. 7). Oxford: Oxford University Press, 1998. Copyright © 1998 by Paul Horwich. Reprinted by permission of Oxford University Press.

James Higginbotham, 'A Perspective on Truth and Meaning', pp. 671–86 from *The Philosophy of Donald Davidson*, XXVII. Illinois, IL: Open Court, 1999. Copyright © 1999 by Open Court Publishing. Reprinted by permission of Open Court Publishing Company, a division of Carus Publishing Company, Peru, IL.

Paul Pietroski, 'The Undeflated Domain of Semantics', pp. 161–76 from *Sats: The Nordic Journal of Philosophy* 1, 2000. Copyright © 2000 by *Sats: The Nordic Journal of Philosophy*.

Merrie Bergmann, 'Metaphorical Assertions', pp. 229–45 from *Philosophical Review* 91, 1982. Copyright © 1982 by *Philosophical Review*. Reprinted by permission of *Philosophical Review* and the author, Merrie Bergmann.

Martin Davies, 'Idiom and Metaphor', pp. 67–86 from *Proceedings of the Aristotelian Society* 83, 1983. Copyright © 1983 by *Proceedings of the Aristotelian Society*. Reprinted by permission of Blackwell Publishing Ltd.

Kent Bach, 'Speaking Loosely: Sentence Non-literality', pp. 249–63 from P. French and H. K. Wettstein, *Figurative Language*, Midwest Studies in Philosophy XXV. Oxford: Blackwell, 2001. Copyright © 2001 by Blackwell Publishing. Reprinted by permission of Blackwell Publishing Ltd.

Every effort has been made to trace copyright holders and to obtain their permission for the use of copyright material. The publisher apologizes for any errors or omissions in the above list and would be grateful if notified of any corrections that should be incorporated in future reprints or editions of this book.

Primary Sources

Locke, J., *An Essay Concerning Human Understanding*, Book III, Ch. 1, §§1–4 and Ch. 2, §§2 and 4–8 (1690).
Mill, J. S., *System of Logic, Ratiocinative and Inductive*, Vol. I, Book 1, Ch. 2, 'Of Names' (1865).

Introduction

Language plays a central role in human life. Much that we do depends on it: shopping for food, chatting to family and friends, reading this book. Indeed, language is so central, and so familiar, that it only rarely engages our attention. Rather, our attention is directed to what we say, to the things we speak about, and to the various activities that our speaking facilitates. When we do focus specifically on language, it is usually because something has interrupted the smooth flow of ordinary communication, as when we find ourselves having to work out what someone means by what we heard them say.[1] Speaking and understanding are so easy that we don't ordinarily think about the means by which we get our thoughts across to one another.

In order to start to think about how language works, it can be instructive to turn to cases where it doesn't work – cases where understanding fails. Think about the situation we face when we travel to countries whose language we don't know. We hear unfamiliar sounds all around us. Simple activities, like buying food, become bothersome chores. We are forced to rely much more on gesturing and pantomiming – and, indeed, good will – than we did in our linguistically familiar clime. For many of us, it is difficult not to try using our native language, pointless as that has become. We may become envious of the people around us happily engaging in fluent conversation, and wish that we'd made the effort needed to acquire their skills. As those initial reactions

---

[1]   Here and throughout we follow conventional philosophical practice and talk as if linguistic communication always took place between a speaker and hearer. But of course some people use sign language; and sign languages are not excluded from our theories. You can think of *speech* broadly so that it encompasses the use of sign language, spoken language, and indeed written language.

subside, we might begin to think about the skills we lack. Of what precisely are we envious? What are the abilities we wish we possessed?

There is, of course, a straightforward answer. The people around us know something that we don't: they know the local language. Familiar and correct as that answer is, it is unsatisfying. What exactly is it that the people around us know? Anyone who has attempted to learn a second language will recognize that this is not a matter merely of learning some new words. As well as words, one has to learn new ways of putting those words together into sentences, and of adjusting the words to their contexts, as when Italian *la* becomes *l'* if it precedes a vowel. Moreover, and crucially, one has to learn what the words mean. Sometimes one learns what words mean by matching them with words one already understands, for instance when one learns that what 'ananas' means in Italian is the same as what 'pineapple' means in English. What is the property that 'ananas' shares with 'pineapple'? And how is it that that property can also be revealed by someone's pointing to a pineapple and saying 'ananas'?

Although these properties of words can be revealed to us, they are not available to superficial inspection. It is usually impossible to figure out what foreign speakers are talking about by simply observing their noises and gestures. What are the properties in virtue of which their words are meaningful? And how are those properties made available to those who know the language? What distinguishes the meaningful sounds and gestures made by speakers from the meaningless sounds and gestures that they also produce – for instance, their humming or leg tapping? From the perspective of a linguistic outsider, it can be difficult to tell the significant apart from the meaningless. But for the linguistic insiders there is all the difference in the world.

When you begin to think about these questions, you are engaging in the philosophy of language. *Reading Philosophy of Language* is designed to help you. Our commentary aims to give you a head start in taking on some readings in the area. It situates these readings in an argumentative context; it explains unfamiliar or difficult ideas in them; and it presents specific questions to think about while reading. The first of the book's chapters is broadly historical, with extracts from works by Locke, Mill, and Frege. The pieces in the following five chapters have all been published in the last 40-odd years, and most are by leading figures, e.g. Austin, Chomsky, Davidson, Dummett, Searle. Our selection and arrangement has been intended both to ensure that readers become acquainted with some principal writings, and also to encourage a thoughtful approach to questions about language and meaning.

Doing philosophy involves more than simply learning what philosophers think. It involves actively engaging with what they think and with why they think it. This can be daunting. It is not always easy to fathom what a philosopher thinks or to determine their reasons for thinking it. Having done so, one is sometimes left with little more than a feeling of unease, a vague sense that one agrees or disagrees with what one has read. Our aim has been to help you to sharpen that initial response, to pinpoint your agreements and disagreements with the texts, and to articulate your reasons for agreeing or disagreeing. We hope that by working through the commentaries on the texts, you will deepen your understanding, not only of the views they express but also of your own answers to the questions they raise.

Let us now consider some of these questions, in a preliminary way.

It is natural to think that what differentiates meaningful speech from mere noise has something to do with what speakers are able to make of it. Perhaps the reason why the special properties of language are not apparent to superficial inspection is that what makes language special resides in the minds of speakers. The natural thought is plausible, but it has to be handled with care. The idea that word meaning has something to do with speakers' minds needs to be squared with the fact that words are used to talk about the world. If the meaning of 'pineapple' resides in facts about the minds of people who speak English, how can 'pineapple' be a word that they can use, for instance, to ask for a pineapple? The readings in Chapter 1 are concerned with what we should say about meaning, starting from the case of individual words.

A second natural thought about word meaning is that it has something to do with speakers' *activities*. Perhaps the meaning of 'pineapple' is a matter of what the word can be used to do. We can use 'pineapple' not only to ask for a pineapple, but also to ask about pineapples, to swap opinions about tastes, to answer questions about fruit, and so forth. These are just some of the things that English speakers find easy to do with the word 'pineapple', but are unable to do in Italy if they don't understand 'ananas' and other Italian words. Perhaps what distinguishes meaningless noise from meaningful speech is the variety of uses to which speech can be put. The readings in Chapter 2 develop that plausible thought, and engage with questions that arise out of the great variety of different ways in which language is used.

As well as using language to ask and answer questions, to make statements, to issue requests, we use it to warn people of things, to make promises, to amuse, among many other things. How could my various uses of 'pineapple' – to warn you that pineapples are afoot, to promise to give you a pineapple, to amuse you with pineapple anecdotes, etc. – arise from recognition of a simple property of the word 'pineapple'? A proposal that emerges in Chapter 2 is that any adequate answer to that question will invoke a distinction among speakers' abilities, between (on the one hand) general communicative abilities, common to speakers of any language whatever, and (on the other hand) abilities specific to the understanding of a particular language. That is, a distinction should be drawn between abilities shared by speakers of English and Italian, and abilities that they don't share but possess only by virtue of speaking the particular language they do – whether English or Italian. Word meaning will then be seen as connected with abilities of the latter kind.

In Chapter 3 we turn to an attempt to say more about word meanings – about the special properties of words that are recognized by speakers of the language they belong to. Consideration of what speakers do with words encourages a new perspective on word meanings: speakers typically do things using sentences, not individual words. To convey a piece of information about the world (for instance) takes a whole sentence. While it might be plausible to think that some individual words carry information about the world by standing for things, it is difficult to see what sentences might stand for. If sentences stood for things in the way individual words did, then there would be no distinction between a sentence such as 'Jo likes pineapple' and a list such as 'Jo, pineapple, likes'. Thus we need an account of what sentences mean that is able to sustain the fact that they carry information about the world. And we need that account to explain how the meanings of sentences arise from the meanings of the words that make them up. In Chapter 3, such an account is presented and discussed.

Suppose that we had an adequate account of meaning for words and sentences. Would that quell our philosophical puzzlement about language? No. For we should still want to understand how the facts about linguistic meaning are related to facts about speakers. We noted the commonplace that speakers of English are said to know English. But is this ordinary knowledge, like that involved in knowing that pineapples are fruits? We noted also that anyone who has attempted to learn a second language recognizes that this is not a matter merely of learning some new words. We might have added that it seems not to be a matter merely of learning new facts. Knowledge of a language can seem to be a special form of knowledge. Think again about an experience you may have while abroad. The peaceful background babble of what is, for you, meaningless noise can be suddenly broken by hearing speech in your own tongue and by the consequent invasion of your mind by another's thoughts. We might wonder how someone's coming to know a language could have the sort of effect it does on their experience of their surroundings.[2]

---

[2]   Some people will object to the sentence we have just used in the text. These people think that, since the word 'someone' is singular, grammar requires that it be followed with 'his' or 'her' or 'his or her': they think that 'their' cannot be singular. (They also think that 'them' and 'they' cannot be singular: these people would object to our sentence in the text above where the first footnote was flagged, and to 'Anyone can understand this, if they try'.) Well, we accept that using 'they' etc. as singulars has been proscribed by prescriptive grammarians who have had an influence on English usage. But we don't think that they are authoritative. Also we doubt that 'he' is the sex-indefinite pronoun that some say it is; and we find that in many contexts 'he or she' and 'his or hers' can be clumsy. So we actually have a reason for sometimes using 'they' and 'their' as singulars. You will find this usage – alongside singular 'he' and singular 'she' – elsewhere in this book.

For an account of the change in English pronominal usage over the centuries, see Ann Bodine, 'Androcentrism in Prescriptive Grammar', in *Language in Society* 4 (1975), reprinted in *The Feminist Critique of Language*, ed. Deborah Cameron (London and New York, 1990 and 1998). This is a good place to start if you are interested in questions about language change.

Chapter 4 further investigates these and other issues concerning the special nature of linguistic knowledge.

Chapter 5 examines in more detail how the meanings of words can serve to fix the meanings of sentences in which they occur. One important feature of language is that understanding some parts of a language enables one to understand other parts. So, for example, if you understand a sentence involving 'pineapple' – e.g., 'Jo eats pineapple' – then you can understand every other sentence involving 'pineapple', as long as you understand the other words in those sentences. Explanation of that feature of language seems to depend on individual words having the same meaning in every occurrence. In Chapter 5, we will confront arguments for and against the claim that this fact about word meaning dictates a particular kind of account of linguistic meaning.

Suppose, as seems plausible, that words carry the same meaning in all their occurrences, and that sentence meaning is fully determined by word meaning. The question then arises of how we are to explain uses of sentences in which they appear to enable the transmission of information not determinable just on the basis of knowing what occurrences of their constituent words elsewhere mean. For example, if asked about the weather, I might say 'It's raining'. But the understanding of my words you can achieve just by knowing what these words mean in other utterances will not enable you to figure out where I have said it to be raining. So far as the actual words I have used goes, I might be commenting on the weather where I am, where you are, or indeed elsewhere. The fact, of course, is that you ordinarily would know where I've said it to be raining. But we need an account of that fact. Similar but even more striking effects are achieved through the use of metaphor. In a suitable context I can convey something to you with 'Life is a yo-yo'. But what I convey is presumably not something you know just because you know the literal meanings of 'life' and 'yo-yo'. (Life could hardly be literally a yo-yo.) Chapter 6 looks at some different ways of thinking about how speakers communicate so much more in using sentences than is predictable simply on the basis of their standing knowledge of the sentences' constituents. In explaining what goes on in cases of metaphor and the like, one is forced to think about how exactly to draw the distinction between general abilities of language users and the abilities that are specific to the speakers of a particular language. How do abilities of the two sorts work together in actual cases of linguistic communication?

Each of our chapters contains its own Introduction and Conclusion, and its three texts, each preceded by a short introduction and followed by a commentary using arrow markers. The system of arrow markers – $\boxed{a} \mapsto$, $\boxed{b} \mapsto$ and so on – enables us to link our commentaries with specific passages in the texts.

We envisage the reader using a chapter in something like the following way. Start with the chapter's introduction. Then read the introduction to each text before you tackle it. But take the texts one at a time. First read it through to gain a general idea of the argument, then read it a second time more carefully, pausing and taking a few notes if that is helpful. Then turn to the commentary on that text, and take it slowly, stopping at the boxed questions or tasks. 'Zoom in' on each question or task in its own right, and work on it before moving on.

Where texts are difficult, we hope that the commentaries will help with understanding. But the purpose of the commentaries is *not* to summarize texts. They have two main purposes. The first is to make you think. The second is to make connections – connections between pieces within the book, and between the pieces here and a wider literature – so that the book as a whole can impart some overall feel for a range of the concerns of the philosophy of language.

If you want to deepen or broaden your knowledge, then the Further Reading lists at the end of the book will point your way. Some of these lists provide more material on topics covered in the book, others on topics only alluded to here. We make reference to all the reading lists in the course of our commentary, so that you can follow up on a subject as you go, if you feel so inclined.

1

Reference and Meaning

Introduction

The words of English, indeed the words of any language which people speak, have meaning. This is a mundane fact. Every day there are countless interactions between people which rely on it – on the fact that when people interrelate with one another by producing and hearing sounds, they are using words which have meanings. But however mundane this fact, it is very far from obvious how to account for it. How can sounds achieve so much? What account should we give of words having meaning? In reading the extracts in this first chapter, from three classic sources – Locke, Mill, and Frege – we shall see that this question has been approached in some very different ways in the last three centuries.

Let us think now about how one might start on the question. Two thoughts that one might have, when wondering how to account for the facts about words having meaning, are, first, that words *stand for* things; and second, that words are used to *communicate*.

If words stand for things, then presumably they often stand for real things. So the first thought connects language with reality. There is surely something right in the idea that words make connections with reality. Yet a simple idea of words as standing for things seems actually to be well suited only to the words that are proper names. 'Guy' stands for Guy (that person); 'Fido' stands for Fido (that dog); 'Rome' stands for Rome (that city); and so on. When it comes to words like 'run' or 'dog' or 'green', a simple idea of 'standing for' does not appear to work quite so straightforwardly. And when it comes to other words, such as 'particularly' or 'and' or 'by', the idea that words stand for things may strike us as plain wrong. At the end of the present chapter, we shall try to pinpoint a difference in the way in which 'Guy' or 'Fido' or 'Rome' make connections with things in reality and the way in which 'run' or 'dog' or 'green' do. In later chapters, we shall come to understand better why one should want to say different things about different sorts of words: in accounting for words' meaningfulness, the best approach is to think about words in relation to one another – to think of words as combining one with another to make up meaningful sentences. This was the approach of Frege, and we get a glimpse of it in the reading from him here. But it was not the approach of Locke or Mill. As we shall see, Locke, for his part, did not accept that it is the role of words to stand for real things. And Mill, although he has plenty to say about the different behaviours of different sorts of words, did not envisage the kind of systematic theory of words' combination that Frege introduced.

The second thought – that words are used to communicate – is surely correct. When you use words, you get your thoughts across to others, and when others use words, they get their thoughts across to you. On its own, however, the idea of communication may not appear to take us very far with questions about words and their meanings. The reason is that it seems as if words can be used to communicate *because* they have meaning. And then it can seem as though we need to have something to say about what words mean in order to think about how they are used in communication. Well, not everyone agrees with this. But we shall wait until Chapter 2 to think about approaches in which questions about what speakers do or intend are treated as more fundamental than questions about what words do.

Whether or not linguistic meaning might be explained in terms of communication, an account of words having meaning cannot lose sight of human beings as thinkers who can convey their thoughts to one another. In the course of this book, we shall see that one of the most difficult tasks for philosophy of language is to bring the fact that people use words and sentences to convey their thoughts to one another into the right relation with the fact that words and sentences make connections with reality. In the present chapter, in reading Locke, we shall discover some of the difficulties there are in finding appropriate connections between words and real things when words are treated as if they got their meanings in the minds of individual thinkers. In reading Mill and Frege, we shall discover that even when it comes to proper names, which can seem to be words of which a very simple account might be given, there are questions about their role in communication.

Questions about meaning and communication in general recur in this chapter, then. But by the end, we shall come to focus on the particular case of proper names, and the question of how they should be treated. Proper names, as we saw above, very plausibly do stand for things. But is that all there is to be said about them?

Introduction to Locke

John Locke (1632–1704) is the first of the three philosophers often collectively known as the British empiricists (the others are Berkeley and Hume). Empiricism is a doctrine that holds that experience is the source of all our knowledge. Locke's *Essay Concerning Human Understanding* presents views on traditional topics, such as the nature of the self, the world, God, and the grounds of our knowledge of them. But Locke comes to these topics only in the fourth and last book of the *Essay*, having set out his empiricist stall. The *Essay*'s first book argues against the doctrine of innate principles and ideas, the second deals with ideas, and the third, from which the extracts below are taken, with words.

Locke ends Book II by saying that 'it is impossible to speak clearly and distinctly of our knowledge...without considering, first, the nature, use and signification of language' (II, Ch. 23, §19). A recurrent theme of Book III, and the principal claim in these extracts (which comprise less than one twentieth of the whole Book), is that words signify ideas. Under the heading of 'ideas', Locke subsumed every kind of content of the mind, from concrete impressions got in sense perception through to abstract intellectual concepts. He explains, in the *Essay*'s Introduction, that he will use the word 'idea' with great frequency, it being the word best suited to stand for 'whatsoever is the object of understanding when a man thinks' (I, Ch. 1, §8). Ideas, in Locke's parlance, are 'in the mind', where this includes both what is consciously present and what resides in memory. As you read Locke, you might consider whether you can find in your own mind the 'ideas' in terms of which Locke explains the meanings of the words you use.

John Locke, 'Of Words' (extracts from Book III of *An Essay Concerning Human Understanding*)

Ch. 1   Of Words or Language in General

1. *Man fitted to form articulate sounds.* God, having designed man for a sociable creature, made him not only with an inclination, and under a necessity to have fellowship with those of his own kind, but furnished him also with language, which was to be the great instrument and common tie of society. Man, therefore, had by nature his organs so fashioned, as to be fit to frame articulate sounds, which we

call words. But this was not enough to produce language; for parrots, and several other birds, will be taught to make articulate sounds distinct enough, which yet by no means are capable of language.

2. *To use these sounds as signs of ideas.* Besides articulate sounds, therefore, it was further necessary that he should be able to use these sounds as signs of internal conceptions; and to make them stand as marks for the ideas within his own mind, whereby they might be made known to others, and the thoughts of men's minds be conveyed from one to another.

3. *To make them general signs.* But neither was this sufficient to make words so useful as they ought to be. It is not enough for the perfection of language, that sounds can be made signs of ideas, unless those signs can be so made use of as to comprehend several particular things: for the multiplication of words would have perplexed their use, had every particular thing need of a distinct name to be signified by. To remedy this inconvenience, language had yet a further improvement in the use of general terms, whereby one word was made to mark a multitude of particular existences: which advantageous use of sounds was obtained only by the difference of the ideas they were made signs of: those names becoming general, which are made to stand for general ideas, and those remaining particular, where the ideas they are used for are particular.

a→ 4. *To make them signify the absence of positive ideas.* Besides these names which stand for ideas, there be other words which men make use of, not to signify any idea, but the want or absence of some ideas, simple or complex, or all ideas together; such as are nihil in Latin, and in English, ignorance and barrenness. All which negative or privative words cannot be said properly to belong to, or signify no ideas: for then they would be perfectly insignificant sounds; but they relate to positive ideas, and signify their absence. [. . .]

Ch. 2   Of the Signification of Words

2. *Words, in their immediate signification, are the sensible signs of his ideas who uses them.* The use men have of these marks being either to record their own thoughts, for the assistance of their own memory or, as it were, to bring out their ideas, and lay them before the view of others: words, in their primary or immediate signification, stand for nothing but the ideas in the mind of him that uses them, how imperfectly soever or carelessly those ideas are collected from the things

b→ which they are supposed to represent. When a man speaks to another, it is that he may be understood: and the end of speech is, that those sounds, as marks, may make known his ideas to the hearer. That then which words are the marks of are the ideas of the speaker: nor can any one apply them as marks, immediately, to anything else but the ideas that he himself hath: for this would be to make them signs of his own conceptions, and yet apply them to other ideas; which would be to make them signs and not signs of his ideas at the same time, and so in effect to have no signification at all. Words being voluntary signs, they cannot be voluntary signs imposed by him on things he knows not. That would be to make them signs of nothing, sounds without signification. A man cannot make his words the signs either of qualities in things, or of conceptions in the mind of another, whereof he has none in his own. Till he has some ideas of his own, he cannot suppose them to correspond with the conceptions of another man; nor can he use any signs for them: for thus they would be the signs of he knows not what, which is in truth to be the signs of nothing. But when he represents to himself other men's ideas by some of his own, if he consent to give them the same names that other men do, it is still to his own ideas; to ideas that he has, and not to ideas that he has not. [...]

4. *Words are often secretly referred first to the ideas supposed to be in other men's minds.* But though words, as they are used by men, can properly and immediately signify nothing but the ideas that are in the mind of the speaker; yet they in their thoughts give them a secret reference to two other things.

c→   First, They suppose their words to be marks of the ideas in the minds also of other men, with whom they communicate: for else they should talk in vain, and could not be understood, if the sounds they applied to one idea were such as by the hearer were applied to another, which is to speak two languages. But in this men stand not usually to examine, whether the idea they, and those they discourse with have in their minds be the same: but think it enough that they use the word, as they imagine, in the common acceptation of that language; in which they suppose that the idea they make it a sign of is precisely the same to which the understanding men of that country apply that name.

5. *To the reality of things.* Secondly, because men would not be thought to talk barely of their own imagination, but of things as really they are; therefore they often suppose the words to stand also for the reality of things. But this relating more particularly to substances and their names, as perhaps the former does to simple ideas and modes, we shall speak of these two different ways of

applying words more at large, when we come to treat of the names of mixed modes and substances in particular: though give me leave here to say, that it is a perverting the use of words, and brings unavoidable obscurity and confusion into their signification whenever we make them stand for anything but those ideas we have in our own minds.

6. *Words by use readily excite ideas of their objects.* Concerning words, also, it is further to be considered:

First, that they being immediately the signs of men's ideas, and by that means the instruments whereby men communicate their conceptions, and express to one another those thoughts and imaginations they have within their own breasts; there comes, by constant use, to be such a connexion between certain sounds and the ideas they stand for, that the names heard, almost as readily excite certain ideas as if the objects themselves, which are apt to produce them, did actually affect the senses. Which is manifestly so in all obvious sensible qualities, and in all substances that frequently and familiarly occur to us.

[d]→ 7. *Words are often used without signification, and why.* Secondly, That though the proper and immediate signification of words are ideas in the mind of the speaker, yet, because by familiar use from our cradles, we come to learn certain articulate sounds very perfectly, and have them readily on our tongues, and always at hand in our memories, but yet are not always careful to examine or settle their significations perfectly; it often happens that men, even when they would apply themselves to an attentive consideration, do set their thoughts more on words than things. Nay, because words are many of them learned before the ideas are known for which they stand: therefore some, not only children but men, speak several words no otherwise than parrots do, only because they have learned them, and [e]→ have been accustomed to those sounds. But so far as words are of use and signification, so far is there a constant connexion between the sound and the idea, and a designation that the one stands for the other; without which application of them, they are nothing but so much insignificant noise.

8. *Their signification perfectly arbitrary, not the consequence of a natural connexion.* Words, by long and familiar use, as has been said, come to excite in men certain ideas so constantly and readily, that they are apt to suppose a natural connexion between them. But that [f]→ they signify only men's peculiar ideas, and that by a perfect arbitrary imposition, is evident, in that they often fail to excite in others (even that use the same language) the same ideas we take them to be signs

of: and every man has so inviolable a liberty to make words stand for what ideas he pleases, that no one hath the power to make others have the same ideas in their minds that he has, when they use the same words that he does. And therefore the great Augustus himself, in the possession of that power which ruled the world, acknowledged he could not make a new Latin word: which was as much as to say, that he could not arbitrarily appoint what idea any sound should be a sign of, in the mouths and common language of his subjects. It is true, common use, by a tacit consent, appropriates certain sounds to certain ideas in all languages, which so far limits the signification of that sound, that unless a man applies it to the same idea, he does not speak properly: and let me add, that unless a man's words excite the same ideas in the hearer which he makes them stand for in speaking, he does not speak intelligibly. But whatever be the consequence of any man's using of words differently, either from their general meaning, or the particular sense of the person to whom he addresses them; this is certain, their signification, in his use of them, is limited to his ideas, and they can be signs of nothing else.

Commentary on Locke

Locke aimed for an account of words that explains how, as 'sociable crea-tures', we achieve our communicative goals. A person's ideas are not access-ible to other people, Locke thought; but a person can communicate her thoughts to others using the sounds of speech: her words are signs standing for her ideas, and others can hear her words.

In what follows, we shall consider whether Locke's account is adequate to his aim. Locke's view of words is not popular with philosophers today. So it seems appropriate to focus on two main questions here. A: Does Locke have a good argument for his view? B: What problems are there for it? Under B, we shall see that things that Locke said himself can be suggestive of problems.

A. Locke's argument

An argument for the claim that the words a speaker uses are signs of their ideas starts at ⟨b⟩→ and continues to the end of the section.

Can you spell out the argument following ⟨b⟩→? Why does Locke take it to be ruled out that words should stand for something other than the speaker's ideas?

Locke thinks that words *must* be signs of the speaker's ideas, because words are significant, and there is nothing else in which their significance could reside. The argument here appears to rely upon two claims: (1) that words are 'voluntary signs'; (2) that one can make a word a sign for something only if that something is *immediately* present to one and *known* to one. Both of these claims might be challenged.

(1) Locke spells out the first claim further at §8 when he says 'every man has [an] inviolable liberty to make words stand for what ideas he pleases'.

In order to think about this, 'make the following experiment: [suggested by Wittgenstein[1]] *Say* "It's cold here" and *mean* "It's warm here".'

Probably you don't find it easy to come out with the sound of the word 'cold' and use it to mean anything except *cold*. You might try to imagine yourself speaking ironically; but even in that case it doesn't seem as if you straightforwardly mean *warm* when you say 'cold'.[2] Perhaps the difficulty here stems from the fact that 'cold' is a word of English whose meaning you and others know, and which you cannot do whatever you please with. If so, then the words that belong to spoken languages are not 'voluntary'. Humpty Dumpty said, 'When *I* use a word, it means just what I choose it to mean, neither more nor less'; and this seems ridiculous.[3]

Even if words are not voluntary, it might still be allowed that they are 'arbitrary', which is how Locke describes them at [f]↦. You should think about the difference between voluntariness and arbitrariness.

To say that words are 'arbitrarily imposed' is to say that one sound (say 'red') could have signified what another (say 'green') actually does. 'Red' actually applies to red things (or, in Locke's view, to an idea of red), but it could have been that 'red' applied to the green things. Locke thinks that speakers of English have 'tacitly consented' to using 'red' as a sign of their ideas of red. And he acknowledges that one wouldn't speak intelligibly if one made the word 'red' signify something different from other people. So Locke might acknowledge that there is one respect in which one isn't free to use words exactly as one pleases: one must use them as others do if one is going to be understood.

(2) To contest Locke's second claim is to start to contest his empiricism itself. So one would need to read much more than Book III of Locke's *Essay* properly to evaluate it. But we can notice here that the claim certainly can be questioned. One might think that a person could have immediate knowledge

---

[1] Wittgenstein, §510, *Philosophical Investigations* (Oxford: Blackwell, 1953).
[2] Irony, which is a sort of non-literalness, is touched on in Chapter 6.
[3] This is in Ch. 6 of Lewis Carroll's *Alice Through the Looking Glass* (1871).

of something in the world (as opposed to the mind). And/or one might think that some of the contents of a person's mind need to be explained not just in terms of the person's own individual sense experience but of their interactions with other people. Thus someone who took a different view from Locke might say that a child's mind is formed, and its contents are gained, as the child grows up and learns a language. It would then seem appropriate to think about words' meanings in connection with concepts people share with one another rather than in connection with the ideas of each isolated speaker.

B. *Problems for Locke*

There are problems with Locke's treatment of 'general signs'. These are problems that Mill recognized, so that we postpone discussion of them to the Commentary on Mill below.

1. At $\boxed{a}\vdash$ we come across an exception to Locke's general principle about words, that they stand for ideas.[4]

> Locke gives 'ignorance' and 'barrenness' as examples of words belonging in the category of words signifying the absence of positive ideas. What other words do you think belong in this category?

You may not find this exercise straightforward. Perhaps 'rejection' belongs in the category? Perhaps 'fruitless' does? The question is difficult to answer. The point of the exercise is to show that it may be harder than Locke allowed to know what, exactly, is involved in some word's signifying the absence of one of your ideas.

Indeed, you may be puzzled even about what it is for a word to stand for a positive idea. If you choose a word whose meaning you know – 'cold', for instance – then you might say, 'I know what "cold" means: it means *cold*, and this is the idea that the word "cold" signifies for me.' But here it seems that in isolating an idea you rely upon knowing what the English word 'cold' means; if so, then you have not isolated an idea in Locke's sense. In Locke's sense, an idea is something that you can discover in your mind, so that, by attaching a sound to it, you can go on to mean something using that sound. Such an idea could evidently not be one that you relied upon knowledge of word meaning to find in your mind. We may well wonder quite what Locke thinks *is* in our minds when we take our words to be meaningful.

---

[4]   Locke did not think that *all* words stand for ideas. He made a definite exception of words which, following seventeenth-century English usage, he called 'particles' – such as 'and' and 'not' and 'but'. These signify neither ideas nor their absence but 'the connection that the Mind gives to ideas, one with another' (Book III, Ch.7, §1).

2. At $\boxed{c}{\mapsto}$ Locke talks about people supposing that words might stand for ideas in other people's minds, or stand for things outside of any mind. Locke thinks that people *wrongly* suppose both these things. The problem for Locke is that it is hard to see how people could get it so wrong.

Take the case of a proper name. The reason why it seems only right to say that 'Guy' stands for Guy (for the man, as opposed to an idea) is that a speaker will only get across her thought that Guy is in London when she says 'Guy is in London' if the hearer knows that she is talking about Guy. If both speaker and hearer know whom 'Guy' stands for, then it is easy to see how her thought can be communicated. But on Locke's account, it is not at all easy. It looks as if the hearer could only surmise that the idea he has when he hears the word is an idea of the same sort as the one whom the speaker chose to attach the word 'Guy' to. And it looks as if he would need further to surmise that it is Guy (that man) whom both the speaker and himself then have an idea of. If we really did have to guess, in the case of every word we hear, what idea the speaker signified by it, and whether our idea is an idea of the same thing as the speaker's, then would it not be a great deal harder to understand people than actually it is? And would we ever be right in thinking that we knew what had been said to us?

3. At $\boxed{d}{\mapsto}$ Locke talks of words as often used without signification.

> What would be examples of 'speaking words no otherwise than parrots do'? Are words used 'without signification' in such cases?

One sort of example might be of someone acting as a mouthpiece. You pass on a telephone message, 'Andrew needs the book', but you don't know who Andrew is or which book he needs. Another sort of example might be of someone who doesn't fully understand some words. I say, 'Quarks come in six flavours', and a physicist who hears me concurs; but I am not certain what quarks are, and don't really know what 'flavour' means when it is used to differentiate between quarks. Examples of these sorts apparently fit Locke's idea of words used by a speaker who has not 'settled their significations perfectly'. But it is doubtful whether we should agree with Locke that the words in these cases are 'nothing but ... insignificant noise'. When you pass on the message, the person you speak to knows exactly what you are saying if they know which person called Andrew and which book are in question. The physicist who concurs with me finds what I say perfectly meaningful.

When Locke speaks of 'insignificant noise', he is speaking of words applied without any 'constant connection' between sound and idea (see $\boxed{e}{\mapsto}$). Locke takes it for granted that usually, when a particular word is used from occasion to occasion, there is a regular match between the idea of its speaker and the idea of those who hear the speaker. The examples we have just looked at are ones where speakers' and hearers' ideas would seem to be mismatched, but without necessarily destroying the words' significance.

We have already questioned whether the existence of the regular matches that Locke takes for granted can really be taken for granted by someone who thinks that it is up to people in the role of speakers to make a sound a mark of their own idea. But it is important to recognize that Locke wants to allow that there are regularities of meaning; and that what he says about the arbitrariness of the relation between sounds and meanings seems correct.[5] When we examined Locke's argument, we saw that it may be tempting to think that the words of a language someone learns as a child and speaks as an adult are common currency among those who also speak that language. What has been at issue here is not so much whether Locke actually rejected this tempting thought, as whether the account he gave of words entitles him to embrace it.

We noted at the outset that Locke's account of words is no longer popular. Certainly his view that words are names of *ideas* no longer finds favour. Mill, whom we come to next, had no truck with it. 'When I use a name for the purpose of expressing a belief, it is a belief concerning the thing itself, not concerning my idea of it', he said.[6]

Introduction to Mill

John Stuart Mill (1806–73) is probably best known for his work in political and moral and philosophy. His *On Liberty* was published in 1859, and *Utilitarianism* in 1863. *System of Logic, Ratiocinative and Inductive* was Mill's first major work. It was published in 1843, and went through eight editions in Mill's lifetime; it is in two volumes, amounting to about eleven hundred pages. 'Logic', said Mill in his introduction, 'comprises the science of reasoning, as well as an art, founded in that science'. And Mill used 'reasoning' in its most general sense. The final part of *System of Logic* is concerned with the right method of thinking for constructing a 'science of human nature' that would include psychology, sociology, and economics.

The first chapter of *System of Logic* is devoted to explaining why an analysis of language should precede the rest of Mill's enquiries. 'Of Names' is the second chapter.

In keeping with the usage of his contemporaries, Mill used the word 'name' broadly. Probably, when asked to think of names, we think of words such as 'Jane' and 'John', i.e. of proper names. But so far as Mill was concerned, 'woman' and 'man' are equally names, and, for that matter so are 'white' and 'brave', and 'John Nokes, who was mayor of the town' (this last, Mill called a

---

[5] Philosophers have sometimes wanted to capture the idea of there being arbitrary regularities between words and what those words stand for (regularities which Locke would have said speakers 'tacitly consent to') using the notion of a convention. For more about convention, see Commentary on Wright in Chapter 3, and the reading list on Language and Convention.

[6] Mill, *System of Logic*, Book I, Ch. 2, §1.

'many-worded name'). Mill thought that all words were either names or parts of names. He worked with a historically long-standing division between categorematic words and syncategorematic words. Categorematic words or phrases are meaningful when they stand alone, and these are all names for Mill; syncategorematic words or phrases convey no meaning until they are joined with other words or phrases. It may be controversial exactly how we should understand the idea of something that has meaning when it stands alone, and thus controversial what belongs in Mill's category of 'name'. Suffice it here to say that Mill did not think that all words are names, but that in treating all the words that he termed names, he covered an enormous amount of ground.

Mill's purpose, in the following extracts, is to establish a classification of names. He made three principal divisions among them. Presupposed to these divisions is a distinction between things and attributes of things – a distinction that can be understood by reference to simple subject-predicate sentences. Thus in the sentence, 'Socrates is wise', the attribute wisdom is predicated of the thing Socrates; in 'That book is red', the attribute redness is predicated of the thing which is that book. (Some philosophers would use the word 'property' or 'quality' rather than 'attribute' here.) Mill's classification of names is of interest for two main reasons. First, when we know what different kinds of names there are, we can go on to say something about the different kinds of *things* there are; this is the topic of Mill's subsequent chapter. Second, the differences between names of different sorts correspond to differences in the workings of different sorts of words. Although Mill's way of thinking about these differences has largely been overtaken by work in compositional semantics (see Chapters 3 and 5), it can be instructive to think about individual words and the various ways in which they behave, or have meaning. The divisions, Mill said, were 'according to their signification'.

J. S. Mill, 'Of Names' (extracts from *System of Logic*, Book 1, Ch. 2)

§3. All names are names of something, real or imaginary; but all things have not names appropriated to them individually. For some individual objects we require, and consequently have, separate distinguishing names; there is a name for every person, and for every remarkable place. Other objects, of which we have not occasion to speak so frequently, we do not designate by a name of their own; but when, the necessity arises for naming them, we do so by putting together several words, each of which, by itself, might be and is used for an indefinite number of other objects; as when I say, *this ston*e: "this" and "stone" being, each of them, names that may be used of many other objects besides the particular one meant, though the only object of which they can both be used at the given moment, consistently with their signification, may be the one of which I wish to speak.

Were this the sole purpose for which names, that are common to more things than one, could be employed; if they only served, by mutually limiting each other, to afford a designation for such individual objects as have no names of their own; they could only be ranked among contrivances for economizing the use of language. But it is evident that this is not their sole function. It is by their means that we are enabled to assert *general* propositions; to affirm or deny any predicate of an indefinite number of things at once. The distinction, therefore, between *general* names, and *individual* or *singular* names, is fundamental; and may be considered as the first grand division of names.

A general name is familiarly defined, a name which is capable of being truly affirmed, in the same sense, of each of an indefinite number of things. An individual or singular name is a name which is only capable of being truly affirmed, in the same sense, of one thing.

Thus, *man* is capable of being truly affirmed of John, George, Mary, and other persons without assignable limit; and it is affirmed of all of them in the same sense; for the word man expresses certain qualities, and when we predicate it of those persons, we assert that they all possess those qualities. But *John* is only capable of being truly affirmed of one single person, at least in the same sense. For though there are many persons who bear that name, it is not conferred upon them to indicate any qualities, or anything which belongs to them in common; and cannot be said to be affirmed of them in any *sense* at all, consequently not in the same sense. "The king who succeeded William the Conqueror," is also an individual name. For, that there cannot be more than one person of whom it can be truly affirmed, is implied in the meaning of the words. Even "*the* king," when the occasion or the context defines the individual of whom it is to be understood, may justly be regarded as an individual name.

It is not unusual, by way of explaining what is meant by a general name, to say that it is the name of a class. But this, though a convenient mode of expression for some purposes, is objectionable as a definition, since it explains the clearer of two things by the more obscure. It would be more logical to reverse the proposition, and turn it into a definition of the word *class*: "A class is the indefinite multitude of individuals denoted by a general name."

It is necessary to distinguish general from collective names. A general name is one which can be predicated of each individual of a multitude; a collective name cannot be predicated of each separately, but only of all taken together. "The 76th regiment of foot in the British army," which is a collective name, is not a general but an individual name; for though it can be predicated of a multitude of individual soldiers taken jointly, it cannot be predicated of them severally. We may say, Jones is a soldier, and Thompson is a soldier, and Smith is a soldier, but we cannot say, Jones is the 76th regiment, and Thompson is the 76th regiment, and Smith is the 76th regiment. We can only say, Jones, and Thompson, and Smith, and Brown, and so forth (enumerating all the soldiers), are the 76th regiment.

"The 76th regiment" is a collective name, but not a general one: "a regiment" is both a collective and a general name. General with respect to all individual regiments, of each of which separately it can be affirmed; collective with respect to the individual soldiers, of whom any regiment is composed.

§4. The second general division of names is into *concrete* and *abstract*. A concrete name is a name which stands for a thing; an abstract name is a name which stands for an attribute of a thing. Thus, *John, the sea, this table*, are names of things. White, also, is a name of a thing, or rather of things. Whiteness, again, is the name of a quality or attribute of those things. Man is a name of many things; humanity is a name of an attribute of those things. *Old* is a name of things; *old age* is a name of one of their attributes.

I have used the words concrete and abstract in the sense annexed to them by the schoolmen, who, notwithstanding the imperfections of their philosophy, were unrivalled in the construction of technical language, and whose definitions, in logic at least, though they never went more than a little way into the subject, have seldom, I think, been altered but to be spoiled. A practice, however, has grown up in more modern times, which, if not introduced by Locke, has gained currency chiefly from his example, of applying the expression "abstract name" to all names which are the result of abstraction or generalization, and consequently to all general names, instead of confining it to the names of attributes. The metaphysicians of the Condillac school, – whose admiration of Locke, passing over the profoundest speculations of that truly original genius, usually fastens with peculiar eagerness upon his weakest points, – have gone on imitating him in this abuse of language, until there is now some difficulty in restoring the word to its original signification. A more wanton alteration in the meaning of a word is rarely to be met with;

for the expression *general name*, the exact equivalent of which exists in all languages I am acquainted with, was already available for the purpose to which *abstract* has been misappropriated, while the misappropriation leaves that important class of words, the names of attributes, without any compact distinctive appellation. The old acceptation, however, has not gone so completely out of use, as to deprive those who still adhere to it of all chance of being understood. By *abstract*, then, I shall always mean the opposite of *concrete*: by an abstract name, the name of an attribute; by a concrete name, the name of an object.

Do abstract names belong to the class of general, or to that of singular names? Some of them are certainly general. I mean those which are names not of one single and definite attribute, but of a class of attributes. Such is the word *colour*, which is a name common to whiteness, redness, &c. Such is even the word whiteness, in respect of the different shades of whiteness to which it is applied in common; the word magnitude, in respect of the various degrees of magnitude and the various dimensions of space; the word weight, in respect of the various degrees of weight. Such also is the word *attribute* itself, the common name of all particular attributes. But when only one attribute, neither variable in degree nor in kind, is designated by the name; as visibleness; tangibleness; equality; squareness; milkwhiteness; then the name can hardly be considered general; for though it denotes an attribute of many different objects, the attribute itself is always conceived as one, not many. To avoid needless logomachies, the best course would probably be to consider these names as neither general nor individual, but to place them in a class apart.

It may be objected to our definition of an abstract name, that not only the names which we have called abstract, but adjectives, which we have placed in the concrete class, are names of attributes; that *white*, for example, is as much the name of the colour as *whiteness* is. But (as before remarked) a word ought to be considered as the name of that which we intend to be understood by it when we put it to its principal use, that is, when we employ it in predication. When we say snow is white, milk is white, linen is white, we do not mean it to be understood that snow, or linen, or milk, is a colour. We mean that they are things having the colour. The reverse is the case with the word whiteness; what we affirm to *be* whiteness is not snow, but the colour of snow. Whiteness, therefore, is the name of the colour exclusively: white is a name of all things whatever having the colour; a name, not of the quality whiteness, but of every white object. It is true, this name was given to all those various objects on account of the quality; and we may therefore say, without impropriety, that the quality forms part of its signification; but a name can only be said to stand for, or to be a name of, the things of which it can be predicated. We shall presently see that all names which can be said to have any signification, all names by applying which to an individual we give any information respecting that individual, may be said to *imply* an attribute of some sort; but they are not names of the attribute; it has its own proper abstract name.

§5. This leads to the consideration of a third great division of names, into *connotative* and *non-connotative*, the latter sometimes, but improperly, called *absolute*. This is one of the most important distinctions which we shall have occasion to point out, and one of those which go deepest into the nature of language.

A non-connotative term is one which signifies a subject only, or an attribute only. A connotative term is one which denotes a subject, and implies an attribute. By a subject is here meant anything which possesses attributes. Thus John, or London, or England, are names which signify a subject only. Whiteness, length, virtue, signify an attribute only. None of these names, therefore, are connotative. But *white, long, virtuous*, are connotative. The word white, denotes all white things, as snow, paper, the foam of the sea, &c., and implies, or as it was termed by the schoolmen, *connotes*,[1] the attribute *whiteness*. The word white is not predicated of the attribute, but of the subjects, snow, &c.; but when we predicate it of them, we imply or connote, that the attribute whiteness belongs to them. The same may be said of the other words above cited. Virtuous, for example, is the name of its class, which includes Socrates, Howard, the man of Ross, and an undefinable number of other individuals, past, present, and to come. These individuals, collectively and severally, can alone be said with propriety to be denoted by the word: of them alone can it properly be said to be a name. But it is a name applied to all of them in consequence of an attribute which they are supposed to possess in common, the attribute which has received the name of virtue. It is applied to all beings that are considered to possess this attribute; and to none which are not so considered.

All concrete general names are connotative. The word man, for example, denotes Peter, Jane, John, and an indefinite number of other individuals, of whom, taken as a class, it is the name. But it is applied to them, because they possess, and to signify that they possess, certain attributes. These seem to be, corporeity, animal life, rationality, and a certain external form, which for distinction we call the human. Every

---

[1] *Notare*, to mark; *connotare*, to mark *along with*; to mark *with* or *in addition to* another.

existing thing, which possessed all these attributes, would be called a man; and anything which possessed none of them, or only one, or two, or even three of them without the fourth, would not be so called. For example, if in the interior of Africa there were to be discovered a race of animals possessing reason equal to that of human beings, but with the form of an elephant, they would not be called men. Swift's Houyhnhnms* were not so called. Or if such newly-discovered beings possessed the form of man without any vestige of reason, it is probable that some other name than that of man would be found for them. How it happens that there can be any doubt about the matter, will appear hereafter. The word man, therefore, signifies all these attributes, and all subjects which possess these attributes. But it can be predicated only of the subjects. What we call men, are the subjects, the individual Stiles and Nokes; not the qualities by which their humanity is constituted. The name, therefore, is said to signify the subjects *directly*, the attributes *indirectly*; it denotes the subjects, and implies, or involves, or indicates, or as we shall say henceforth *connotes*, the attributes. It is a connotative name.

Connotative names have hence been also called *denominative*, because the subject which they denote is denominated by, or receives a name from, the attribute which they connote. Snow, and other objects, receive the name white, because they possess the attribute which is called whiteness; Peter, James, and others receive the name man, because they possess the attributes which are considered to constitute humanity. The attribute, or attributes, may therefore be said to denominate those objects, or to give them a common name.

It has been seen that all concrete general names are connotative. Even abstract names, though the names only of attributes, may in some instances be justly considered as connotative; for attributes themselves may have attributes ascribed to them; and a word which denotes attributes may connote an attribute of those attributes. Of this description, for example, is such a word as *fault*; equivalent to *bad* or *hurtful quality*. This word is a name common to many attributes, and connotes hurtfulness, an attribute of those various attributes. When for example, we say that slowness, in a horse, is a fault, we do not mean that the slow movement, the actual change of pace of the slow horse, is a bad thing, but that the property or peculiarity of the horse, from which it derives that name, the quality of being a slow mover, is an undesirable peculiarity.

---

* **Editors' note:** The Houyhnhnms are one of the nations of creatures that Gulliver encounters in Jonathan Swift's 1726 satirical novel *Gulliver's Travels*.

In regard to those concrete names which are not general but individual, a distinction must be made.

Proper names are not connotative: they denote the individuals who are called by them; but they do not indicate or imply any attributes as belonging to those individuals. When we name a child by the name Paul, or a dog by the name Cæsar, these names are simply marks used to enable those individuals to be made subjects of discourse. It maybe said, indeed, that we must have had some reason for giving them those names rather than any others; and this is true; but the name, once given, is independent of the reason. A man may have been named John, because that was the name of his father; a town may have been named Dartmouth, because it is situated at the mouth of the Dart. But it is no part of the signification of the word John, that the father of the person so called bore the same name; nor even of the word Dartmouth, to be situated at the mouth of the Dart. If sand should choke up the mouth of the river, or an earthquake change its course, and remove it to a distance from the town, the name of the town would not necessarily be changed. That fact, therefore, can form no part of the signification of the word; for otherwise, when the fact confessedly ceased to be true, no one would any longer think of applying the name. Proper names are attached to the objects themselves and are not dependent on the continuance of any attribute of the object.

But there is another kind of names, which, although they are individual names, that is, predicable only of one object, are really connotative. For, though we may give to an individual a name utterly unmeaning, which we call a proper name, – a word which answers the purpose of showing what thing it is we are talking about, but not of telling anything about it; yet a name peculiar to an individual is not necessarily of this description. It may be significant of some attribute, or some union of attributes, which, being possessed by no object but one, determines the name exclusively to that individual. "The sun" is a name of this description; "God," when used by a monotheist, is another. These, however, are scarcely examples of what we are now attempting to illustrate, being, in strictness of language, general, not individual names: for, however they may be *in fact* predicable only of one object, there is nothing in the meaning of the words themselves which implies this: and, accordingly, when we are imagining and not affirming, we may speak of many suns; and the majority of mankind have believed, and still believe, that there are many gods. But it is easy to produce words which are real instances of connotative individual names. It may be part of the meaning of the connotative name itself, that there can exist but one individual possessing the attribute which it connotes: as, for instance, "the *only* son of John Stiles;" "the *first* emperor of Rome." Or the attribute connoted may be a connexion with some determinate event, and the connexion may be of such a kind as only one individual could have; or may at least be such as only one individual actually had; and this may be implied in the form of the expression. "The father of Socrates" is an example of the one kind (since Socrates could not have had two fathers); "the author of the Iliad," "the murderer of Henri Quatre," of the second. For, though it is conceivable that more persons than one might have participated in the authorship of the Iliad, or in the murder of Henri Quatre, the employment of the article *the* implies that, in fact, this was not the case. What is here done by the word *the*, is done in other cases by the context: thus, "Cæsar's army" is an individual name, if it appears from the context that the army meant is that which Cæsar commanded in a particular battle. The still more general expressions, "the Roman army," or "the Christian army," may be individualized in a similar manner. Another case of frequent occurrence has already been noticed; it is the following. The name, being a many-worded one, may consist, in the first place, of a *general* name capable therefore in itself of being affirmed of more things than one, but which is, in the second place, so limited by other words joined with it, that the entire expression can only be predicated of one object, consistently with the meaning of the general term. This is exemplified in such an instance as the following: "the present prime minister of England." Prime Minister of England is a general name; the attributes which it connotes may be possessed by an indefinite number of persons: in succession however, not simultaneously; since the meaning of the word itself imports (among other things) that there can be only one such person at a time. This being the case, and the application of the name being afterwards limited by the article and the word *present*, to such individuals as possess the attributes at one indivisible point of time, it becomes applicable only to one individual. And as this appears from the meaning of the name, without any extrinsic proof, it is strictly an individual name.

From the preceding observations it will easily be collected, that whenever the names given to objects convey any information, that is, whenever they have properly any meaning, the meaning resides not in what they *denote*, but in what they connote. The only names of objects which *connote* nothing are *proper* names; and these have, strictly speaking, no signification.[2]

---

[2] Archbishop Whately, who in the later editions of his *Elements of Logic* aided in reviving the important distinction treated of in the text, proposes the term "Attributive" as a substitute for "Connotative," (p. 22, 9th ed.). The expression is, in itself, appropriate; but as it has not the advantage of being connected with any verb, of so markedly distinctive a character as "to connote," it is not, I think, fitted to supply the place of the word Connotative in scientific use.

g→   If, like the robber in the Arabian Nights, we make a mark with chalk on a house to enable us to know it again, the mark has a purpose, but it has not properly any meaning. The chalk does not declare anything about the house; it does not mean, This is such a person's house, or This is a house which contains booty. The object of making the mark is merely distinction. I say to myself, All these houses are so nearly alike that if I lose sight of them I shall not again be able to distinguish that which I am now looking at, from any of the others; I must therefore contrive to make the appearance of this one house unlike that of the others, that I may hereafter know, when I see the mark – not indeed any attribute of the house – but simply that it is the same house which I am now looking at. Morgiana chalked all the other houses in a similar manner, and defeated the scheme: how? simply by obliterating the difference of appearance between that house and the others. The chalk was still there, but it no longer served the purpose of a distinctive mark.

When we impose a proper name, we perform an operation in some degree analogous to what the robber intended in chalking the house. We put a mark, not indeed upon the object itself, but, so to speak, upon the idea of the object. A proper name is but an unmeaning mark which we connect in our minds with the idea of the object, in order that whenever the mark meets our eyes or occurs to our thoughts, we may think of that individual object. Not being attached to the thing itself, it does not, like the chalk, enable us to distinguish the object when we see it; but it enables us to distinguish it when it is spoken of, either in the records of our own experience, or in the discourse of others; to know that what we find asserted in any proposition of which it is the subject, is asserted of the individual thing with which we were previously acquainted.

[...]

Commentary on Mill

We shall focus on two matters in this commentary: first, Mill's treatment of general names, which contrasts with Locke's treatment of them; secondly, Mill's treatment of proper names, which we shall come to see contrasts with Frege's.

But first we should take stock, and consider Mill's classification of names.

How did Mill characterize the three principal divisions among names that he makes in the extract?

A name is *singular* or *general* according to whether it is the name of *one thing* or is capable of being applied to *many things*.[1] A name is *concrete* or *abstract* according to whether it is a name of a *thing* or of an *attribute*. A name is *connotative or non-connotative* according to whether or not it *implies – that is, indirectly signifies – an attribute*.

What distinction did Mill make within the category of singular names?

Mill makes a distinction between proper names and other singular (or individual) names in the sentences following [b]→, and he elaborates this further at [f]→. The examples Mill gives of names that are singular but not proper come into a category known as definite descriptions – 'the king who succeeded William the Conqueror', 'the Prime Minister', 'Caesar's army', etc. The topic of definite descriptions is something we set aside here;[2] the discussion under 'proper names' below concerns only one sub-species of Mill's own category of singular names.

General names

When Mill takes exception to Locke's terminology at [c]→, his quarrel is over more than Locke's choice of the word 'abstract' for general signs. So far as Locke is concerned, the only reason for our having general signs is convenience: it would be inconvenient to give a different name to every single object (see §3 of his Ch. 1 above). For Locke the difference between a particular sign and a general one – between 'Fido' and 'dog', say – is a difference between ideas of two sorts: speakers attach a particular idea to the word 'Fido', an abstract one to the word 'dog'. Whereas Locke treats singular and general names as behaving in the same way (names of both sorts attach to an idea, and stand for it), Mill thinks that singular and general names behave differently from one another. In Mill's treatment of them, the difference between 'Fido' and 'dog' is that 'Fido' denotes Fido alone, but 'dog', denotes all the things that are dogs.[3]

---

[1] Mill usually uses 'thing' so that things are not abstract, indeed so as to make a distinction between things and attributes. But Mill sometimes needs to use the word 'thing' with a broad application, so that attributes are included among things – they are then abstract things. There is an example of the broad use of 'thing' here: it enables Mill to treat the singular/general distinction as having application to abstract names as well as to concrete ones.

[2] Bertrand Russell put forward a theory about definite descriptions: Russell rejects Mill's assumption that definite descriptions should be treated as categorematic (cf. Introduction to Mill above). An enormous amount of philosophical attention has been devoted to the question of whether Russell was right. We supply a reading list on Definite Descriptions.

[3] Here we pick up on the word 'denote', which is the word Mill most commonly uses for the relation between names and things. In the Conclusion to this chapter, there is something about the variety of terms used for word/thing relations.

Mill's distinction between abstractness and generality surely represents an advance on Locke. Of course dogs are not abstract things; and this is recorded when a distinction is made between the question of whether a name is general and the question of whether the name denotes something abstract. Such a distinction is excluded in Locke's way of thinking about words.

Mill's treatment of general names has two further advantages over Locke's. First, it enables a distinction to be made between words like 'doghood' or 'whiteness' and words like 'dog' or 'white'. 'Whiteness' is a singular name denoting an attribute possessed by white things, whereas 'white' is a general name denoting white things. Secondly, Mill is able to think of general names as allowing us to assert general propositions: see [a]→. When Mill recognizes that speakers may want to say something about more than one object, there is an implicit criticism of Locke: it could not be the sole rationale for the presence in language of general terms that speakers want to avoid the inconvenience of giving a separate name to each object.

Nevertheless, it is hard to leave matters where Mill left them: it is hard to rest content with the idea that 'dog' denotes dogs and that it can occur in generalizations. Mill speaks of the 'principal use' of a general name as its use 'in predication' (see [d]→). But it seems that we need to understand how the same word 'dog' which occurs in 'Fido is a dog' – where it is employed simply in predicating an attribute of Fido – can also occur in 'All dogs are four-legged' and in 'A dog barked at John'. It seems that we ought to be able to find something to say about general terms that will enable us to understand how they combine with a variety of other terms. Well, the development of the predicate calculus has provided a way of treating predication and generality hand in hand. This calculus relies upon a notation of quantifiers and variables, which Frege discovered (you have probably encountered it if you have done some elementary logic). In the wake of Frege's discovery, the category of predicate has supplanted Mill's category of general names. (This may be part of the explanation why the word 'name' is nowadays seldom given the broad application that it had among Mill and his predecessors and contemporaries.)

One consequence of Mill's recognizing a class of general words that are not abstract is that there are two dimensions in his account of meaning where there was only one in Locke's. Mill saw that there was more to be said about the meaning of the word 'dog' than could be said using the idea of denotation. An explanation of what a word like 'dog' means will allude to an attribute, Mill thought. 'Dog' denotes, or is truly attributable to, all and only the things that are dogs, but it is so attributable in virtue of an attribute of those things. It connotes that attribute: it indirectly signifies the attribute of doghood.

Proper names

We spoke of the difference between 'Fido' and 'dog' as a difference between a word that denotes one thing, and a word that is such as to denote many things. Mill allows that many things may have the same proper name as one another: see b⟩→. There could be many things called 'Fido', but in any ordinary use of 'Fido' as a name it stands for just one thing. Mill says that when 'Fido' is used to stand for some particular thing, it does so simply because the name has been given to that thing, and not because of any of its attributes. Here Mill sows the seeds of his view that proper names are not connotative. The view comes to be stated in various ways later on: proper names are 'without signification'; they are 'unmeaning marks'.

Mill gives arguments in support of his view that proper names lack connotation at e⟩→ and g⟩→. Do you find these arguments forceful?

Mill's first argument is that even where a proper name might seem to depend upon an attribute of the thing named, still the name's continued functioning does not depend upon the attribute. In Mill's second argument, he invites us to compare a chalk mark attached to a house in order to single it out with a proper name attached to an object. He suggests that we should no more think of a proper name as working through knowledge of some attribute of what it singles out than we think of the chalk mark as working through such knowledge.

We shall return to proper names in connection with Frege. What we should notice now is that in Mill's scheme of things, crediting a word with a connotation is the only way, besides attributing a denotation to the word, of registering the word's significance. This is why the claim for which Mill argues – that proper names do not indirectly signify any attribute – boils down to the claim that proper names are 'not affirmed in any sense at all', are 'without signification', are 'unmeaning'. Whether or not we agree with Mill, his claim about the difference between 'dog' and 'Fido' – that 'dog' has connotation, whereas 'Fido' lacks it – perhaps explains why we should find ourselves saying (what was suggested in the Introduction) that a simple idea of words as standing for things seems well suited to the words that are proper names, but that a simple idea of 'standing for' does not work quite so straightforwardly for 'run' or 'dog' or 'green'.

Introduction to Frege

Gottlob Frege (1848–1925) was a German mathematician, logician, and philosopher who worked at the University of Jena. In mentioning the predicate calculus above, we have already spoken of one of Frege's great achievements. The notation that Frege devised for this calculus was first outlined in his *Begriffsschrift* (1879), to which Frege refers in the extract below. Frege's aim, in devising the notation, was to find a way of regimenting thought and reasoning so as to make it possible to formalize proofs used in mathematics.

In the course of providing a foundation for views about the relationship of logic and mathematics, Frege came up with a comprehensive theory of language. The main ideas of that theory are presented in 'On Sense and Reference' (1892).

The first paragraph of 'On Sense and Reference' has assumed enormous importance in the history of twentieth-century philosophy. It presents what is known as 'Frege's Puzzle about Identity'. Frege's first examples of statements of identity there are '$a = a$' and '$a = b$'. Here Frege uses the '$=$' sign, in a way familiar in arithmetic, to express identity. In everyday English, the word 'is' sometimes expresses identity; where it does, it can be replaced with 'is the same as' or 'is identical to'. Thus if I say that Ruth Rendell is Barbara Vine, I mean that Ruth Rendell is the same person as Barbara Vine. So the contrast Frege intends – between '$a = a$' and '$a = b$' – is a contrast between statements such as:

> $125 = 125$
> The morning star is identical to the morning star
> Peter Parker is Peter Parker

and statements such as:

> $78 + 47 = 125$
> The morning star is identical to the evening star
> Peter Parker is Spider-Man

It is a good idea to think of examples when reading Frege. (You could work with these, or think up examples of your own.)

It is worth noticing at the outset that Frege uses 'proper names' for all of the signs in statements such as these. (He says that he calls them all proper names 'for brevity'.) Thus in Frege's usage 'proper name' covers the entire category of Mill's singular names: it includes definite descriptions along with proper names proper. In order to compare Frege with Mill, we shall need to think about cases where Mill and Frege would have agreed on calling an expression a proper name. Thus, to the list above, we can add the example:

> Phosphorus is [identical to] Phosphorus

and

> Hesperus is [identical to] Phosphorus

This example is very famous, and widely used in discussions of Frege. The planet Venus can be seen from Earth just before sunrise (at some times of the year) and just after sunset (at other times). There were early Greeks who thought that the morning and evening appearances of Venus were appearances of two different objects, calling it 'Phosphorus' when it appeared in the eastern morning sky and 'Hesperus' when it appeared in the western evening sky (cf. 'the morning star' and 'the evening star' of Frege's own example). The identity – the fact that Hesperus is Phosphorus – has been known for a very long time, having been first discovered by the ancient Babylonians.

Gottlob Frege, 'On Sense and Reference' (extract)

Identity[1] gives rise to challenging questions which are not altogether easy to answer. Is it a relation? A relation between objects, or between names or signs of objects? In my *Begriffsschrift*[2] I assumed the latter. The reasons which seem to favour this are the following: $a = a$ and $a = b$ are obviously statements of differing cognitive value; $a = a$ holds a priori and, according to Kant, is to be labelled analytic, while statements of the form $a = b$ often contain very valuable extensions of our knowledge and cannot always be established a priori. The discovery that the rising sun is not new every morning, but always the same, was one of the most fertile astronomical discoveries. Even today the identification of a small planet or a comet is not always a matter of course. Now if we were to regard identity as a relation between that which the names 'a' and 'b' designate, it would seem that $a = b$ could not differ from $a = a$ (i.e. provided $a = b$ is true). A relation would thereby be expressed of a thing to itself, and indeed one in which each thing stands to itself but to no other thing. What is intended to be said by $a = b$ seems to be that the signs or names 'a' and 'b' designate the same thing, so that those signs themselves would be under discussion; a relation between them would be asserted. But

---

[1]   I use this word strictly and understand '$a = b$' to have the sense of 'a is the same as b' or 'a and b coincide'.
Editors' note: We have replaced the translators' word 'equality' with 'identity' here: this brings the translation into line with current English-language philosophers' usage.
[2]   **Translators' note:** The reference is to Frege's *Begriffsschrift, eine der arithmetischen nachgebildete Formelsprache des reinen Denkens* (Halle, 1879).

this relation would hold between the names or signs only in so far as they named or designated something. It would be mediated by the connexion of each of the two signs with the same designated thing. But this is arbitrary. Nobody can be forbidden to use any arbitrarily producible event or object as a sign for something. In that case the *sentence a = b* would no longer refer to the subject matter, but only to its mode of designation; we would express no proper knowledge by its means. But in many cases this is just what we want to do. If the sign '*a*' is distinguished from the sign '*b*' only as object (here, by means of its shape), not as sign (i.e. not by the manner in which it designates something), the cognitive value of $a = a$ becomes essentially equal to

$\boxed{c} \mapsto$ that of $a = b$, provided $a = b$ is true. A difference can arise only if the difference between the signs corresponds to a difference in the mode of presentation of that which is designated. Let *a*, *b*, *c* be the lines connecting the vertices of a triangle with the midpoints of the opposite sides. The point of intersection of *a* and *b* is then the same as the point of intersection of *b* and *c*. So we have different designations for the same point, and these names ('point of intersection of *a* and *b*', and 'point of intersection of *b* and *c*') likewise indicate the mode of presentation; and hence the statement contains actual knowledge.

It is natural, now, to think of there being connected with a sign (name, combination of words, letter), besides that to which the sign refers, which may be called the reference of the sign, also what I should like to call the sense of the sign, wherein the mode of presentation is contained. In our example, accordingly, the reference of the expressions 'the point of intersection of *a* and *b*' and 'the point of intersection of *b* and *c*' would be the same, but not their senses. The reference of 'evening star' would be the same as that of 'morning star', but not the sense.

It is clear from the context that by 'sign' and 'name' I have here understood any designation representing a proper name, which thus has as its reference a definite object [. . .]. The designation of a single object can also consist of several words or other signs. For brevity, let every such designation be called a proper name.

$\boxed{d} \mapsto$ The sense of a proper name is grasped by everybody who is sufficiently familiar with the language or totality of designations to which it belongs;[3] but this serves to illuminate only a single aspect of the

---

[3]   In the case of an actual proper name such as 'Aristotle' opinions as to the sense may differ. It might, for instance, be taken to be the following: the pupil of Plato and teacher of Alexander the Great. Anybody who does this will attach another sense to the sentence 'Aristotle was born in Stagira' than will a man who takes as the sense of the name: the teacher of Alexander the Great who was born in Stagira. So long as the reference remains the same, such variations of sense may be tolerated, although they are to be avoided in the theoretical structure of a demonstrative science and ought not to occur in a perfect language.

reference, supposing it to have one. Comprehensive knowledge of the reference would require us to be able to say immediately whether any given sense belongs to it. To such knowledge we never attain.

The regular connexion between a sign, its sense, and its reference is of such a kind that to the sign there corresponds a definite sense and to that in turn a definite reference, while to a given reference (an object) there does not belong only a single sign. The same sense has different expressions in different languages or even in the same language. To be sure, exceptions to this regular behaviour occur. To every expression belonging to a complete totality of signs, there should certainly corres- pond a definite sense; but natural languages often do not satisfy this condition, and one must be content if the same word has the same sense in the same context. It may perhaps be granted that every grammat- ically well-formed expression representing a proper name always has a sense. But this is not to say that to the sense there also corresponds a reference. The words 'the celestial body most distant from the Earth' have a sense, but it is very doubtful if they also have a reference. The expression 'the least rapidly convergent series' has a sense; but it is known to have no reference, since for every given convergent series, another convergent, but less rapidly convergent, series can be found. In grasping a sense, one is not certainly assured of a reference.

If words are used in the ordinary way, what one intends to speak of is their reference. It can also happen, however, that one wishes to talk about the words themselves or their sense. This happens, for instance, when the words of another are quoted. One's own words then first designate words of the other speaker, and only the latter have their usual reference. We then have signs of signs. In writing, the words are in this case enclosed in quotation marks. Accordingly, a word standing between quotation marks must not be taken as having its ordinary reference.

In order to speak of the sense of an expression 'A' one may simply use the phrase 'the sense of the expression "A" '. In reported speech one talks about the sense, e.g., of another person's remarks. It is quite clear that in this way of speaking words do not have their customary reference but designate what is usually their sense. In order to have a short expression, we will say: In reported speech, words are used *indirectly* or have their *indirect* reference. We distin- guish accordingly the *customary* from the *indirect* reference of a word; and its *customary* sense from its *indirect* sense. The indirect reference of a word is accordingly its customary sense. Such excep- tions must always be borne in mind if the mode of connexion between sign, sense, and reference in particular cases is to be correctly under- stood.

The reference and sense of a sign are to be distinguished from the associated idea. If the reference of a sign is an object perceivable by the senses, my idea of it is an internal image,[4] arising from memories of sense impressions which I have had and acts, both internal and external, which I have performed. Such an idea is often saturated with feeling; the clarity of its separate parts varies and oscillates. The same sense is not always connected, even in the same man, with the same idea. The idea is subjective: one man's idea is not that of another. There result, as a matter of course, a variety of differences in the ideas associated with the same sense. A painter, a horseman, and a zoologist will probably connect different ideas with the name 'Bucephalus'. This constitutes an essential distinction between the idea and the sign's sense, which may be the common property of many and therefore is not a part of a mode of the individual mind. For one can hardly deny that mankind has a common store of thoughts which is transmitted from one generation to another.[5]

In the light of this, one need have no scruples in speaking simply of the sense, whereas in the case of an idea one must, strictly speaking, add to whom it belongs and at what time. It might perhaps be said: Just as one man connects this idea, and another that idea, with the same word, so also one man can associate this sense and another that sense. But there still remains a difference in the mode of connexion. They are not prevented from grasping the same sense; but they cannot have the same idea. *Si duo idem faciunt, non est idem.* If two persons picture the same thing, each still has his own idea. It is indeed sometimes possible to establish differences in the ideas, or even in the sensations, of different men; but an exact comparison is not possible, because we cannot have both ideas together in the same consciousness.

The reference of a proper name is the object itself which we designate by its means; the idea, which we have in that case, is wholly subjective; in between lies the sense, which is indeed no longer subjective like the idea, but is yet not the object itself. The following analogy will perhaps clarify these relationships. Somebody observes the Moon through a telescope. I compare the Moon itself to the reference; it is the object of the observation, mediated by the real image projected by the object glass in the interior of the telescope, and by the retinal image of the observer. The former I compare to the sense, the latter is like the idea or experience. The optical image in

---

[4]   We can include with ideas the direct experiences in which sense-impressions and acts themselves take the place of the traces which they have left in the mind. The distinction is unimportant for our purpose, especially since memories of sense-impressions and acts always help to complete the perceptual image. One can also understand direct experience as including any object, in so far as it is sensibly perceptible or spatial.

[5]   Hence it is inadvisable to use the word 'idea' to designate something so basically different.

the telescope is indeed one-sided and dependent upon the standpoint of observation; but it is still objective, inasmuch as it can be used by several observers. At any rate it could be arranged for several to use it simultaneously. But each one would have his own retinal image. On account of the diverse shapes of the observers' eyes, even a geometrical congruence could hardly be achieved, and an actual coincidence would be out of the question. This analogy might be developed still further, by assuming A's retinal image made visible to B; or A might also see his own retinal image in a mirror. In this way we might perhaps show how an idea can itself be taken as an object, but as such is not for the observer what it directly is for the person having the idea. But to pursue this would take us too far afield.

i→   We can now recognize three levels of difference between words, expressions, or whole sentences. The difference may concern at most the ideas, or the sense but not the reference, or, finally, the reference as well. With respect to the first level, it is to be noted that on account of the uncertain connexion of ideas with words, a difference may hold for one person, which another does not find. The difference between a translation and the original text should properly not overstep the first level. To the possible differences here belong also the colouring and shading which poetic eloquence seeks to give to the sense. Such colouring and shading are not objective, and must be evoked by each hearer or reader according to the hints of the poet or the speaker. Without some affinity in human ideas art would certainly be impossible; but it can never be exactly determined how far the intentions of the poet are realized.

In what follows there will be no further discussion of ideas and experiences; they have been mentioned here only to ensure that the idea aroused in the hearer by a word shall not be confused with its sense or its reference.

To make short and exact expressions possible, let the following phraseology be established:

j→   A proper name (word, sign, sign combination, expression) expresses its sense, stands for or designates its reference. By means of a sign we express its sense and designate its reference.

Commentary on Frege

Frege's theory of sense and reference is the mainstay of his very influential account of meaning. We comment on aspects of the theory in the second of the three sections that follow. The first section is devoted to Frege's puzzle, and the final one to his treatment of proper names.

The puzzle about identity

Frege's puzzle concerns how '$a = a$' can convey anything different from '$a = b$'. What treatment of identity statements will explain the difference?

At the outset Frege distinguishes two views of identity. On the first, identity is a relation between objects, on the second, a relation between names (or signs) of objects.

> Read from $\boxed{a}\rightarrow$ to $\boxed{b}\rightarrow$. What reasons does Frege see as seeming to count against treating identity as a relation between objects and favouring a treatment of it as a relation between signs?

Frege's reasons turn on the difference between (say) the statements that Hesperus = Hesperus and that Hesperus = Phosphorus. (Here we use 'Hesperus' and 'Phosphorus' in place of Frege's 'a' and 'b': see Introduction above.) The difference is that the former statement is *a priori*, i.e. (roughly) can be known independently of experience, whereas the latter is not. Astronomers discovered that Hesperus is Phosphorus, so that this is obviously not an *a priori* truth. Frege calls the difference between two such statements a difference in their cognitive value. And he says that the difference appears to be unaccountable if identity is a relation between objects. If identity were a relation between objects, then both statements alike would seem only to record the fact that some thing is the same as itself. It can then seem as though, in the case where something is learned from an identity statement, it is learned because the two *names* in it are different. And thus it could seem as though what the statement really tells us about is a relation holding between the names/signs.

> Read from $\boxed{b}\rightarrow$ to $\boxed{c}\rightarrow$. Why does the view of identity as a relation between signs fare no better than the view of it as a relation between objects?

If we took identity statements to speak merely about names, then the cognitive difference between the statements that Hesperus = Hesperus and that Hesperus = Phosphorus would again not be apparent. Obviously 'Hesperus' and 'Phosphorus' are different signs, but that isn't what the statement that Hesperus is Phosphorus conveys. *Any* sign might designate the object Hesperus (it is arbitrary which signs designate which things); so that being told that this, that, or the other sign designates Hesperus could not convey the sort of knowledge which can be expressed with the statement that Hesperus is Phosphorus.

At $\boxed{c}\rightarrow$ Frege gives his account of how '$a = b$' may record a real discovery. There can be a difference between 'a' and 'b' in respect of how they present the objects that they name – a difference in their mode of presentation. Thus a certain object may be presented in different ways according to whether '*a*' or '*b*' is used to refer to it. Calling attention to such a difference can explain the difference in cognitive value between '*a* = *a*' and '*a* = *b*', which is the very difference that Frege wanted to explain.

Where '*a* = *b*' is informative and true, '*a*' and '*b*' differ in sense – which accounts for its informativeness – and they have the same reference – which accounts for its truth. Here we start to see that Frege's notion of reference can work hand in hand both with his notion of sense and also with the notion of truth.

> Do you agree with Frege that 'Hesperus is Phosphorus' conveys 'proper knowledge' which is not conveyed by saying that the names 'Hesperus' and 'Phosophorus' refer to the same thing?

The account of identity as a relation between names is sometimes known as the metalinguistic account. It is actually not at all attractive. For a person appears to talk about Hesperus, not about the name 'Hesperus', when she says that it is (the same as) Phosphorus, just as much as she talks about Hesperus when she says that Hesperus is visible. (Certainly one can talk about names in saying what is required for the sentence 'Hesperus is Phosphorus' to be true. Thus one might say that 'Hesperus is Phosphorus' is true only if what the name 'Hesperus' refers to is Phosphorus; or – talking now about both names – that it is true only if 'Hesperus' and 'Phosphorus' refer to the same thing. But then one could just as well say that 'Hesperus is visible' is true only if what the name 'Hesperus' refers to is visible. It is not a special feature of identity statements that we can talk about the names that occur within them in saying what their truth requires.)

Sense and reference

Here we shall think both **A**, about how Frege conceives of sense, and **B**, about what else, besides solving the identity puzzle, his account of sense and reference is supposed to achieve.

> **A.** How does Frege tell us to think about sense? Read the whole of d ⟩→ to i ⟩→.

Although Frege allows for variations between the sense of a word across different contexts (see e ⟩→), he is eager to distance his notion of sense from anything like a Lockean notion of idea, in which an idea is the property of an individual speaker. Senses are not subjective, but are 'the common property of many'. This is spelt out in the paragraph beginning at g ⟩→, and elaborated further in the telescope analogy at ⬚h⬚→. Frege compares the sense of an expression with the real image on the glass of the telescope (perceptible by any observer), and compares an idea with a retinal image (belonging to some particular person). Sense, being 'common property', grasped by those who know the language, evidently belongs in an account of language as it is used to communicate: see ⬚d⬚→.

B. What does Frege have to say about how his notions of sense and reference might work in an account of language?

1. At ⬚f⬚→ Frege applies his sense/reference distinction to an account of indirect reported speech. By this, he means something of which 'She said that Hesperus is visible' is an example. This contrasts with a direct, quotational report, such as 'She said "Hesperus is visible" '. In the direct report, we may take the quoted words to refer to themselves – to 'Hesperus is visible'. But what are the words which follow 'that' doing in the indirect report? Frege's account has it that we should take such words as referring to their sense, that is to what would customarily – outside the context of indirect speech – be the sense of 'Hesperus is visible'. A consequence of this account is that sameness of sense, not mere sameness of reference, will be required of truth-preserving substitutions of words occurring inside a context of indirect speech.[1] (When we noted above how unattractive a metalinguistic view of identity statements is, we saw, in effect, that there could be a puzzle about how someone might know that Hesperus is visible without knowing that Phosphorus is visible [just as there can be a puzzle about how someone might know that Hesperus is Hesperus without knowing that Hesperus is Phosphorus]. When words following 'knows that' are treated as Frege proposed that words following 'says that' should be treated, the puzzle seems to be solved.)

2. 'Reference' and 'sense' are not the only dimensions of significance that a theorist of language may discern in words and sentences. At ⬚i⬚→ Frege alludes to 'colouring and shading', which he connects with poetic aura and relegates to the subjective realm of ideas. (There is much more to be said about 'colouring and shading' [which is often called *tone*]. Some people think that many of the differences which Frege would himself have recorded as differences of 'colouring and shading' [or tone] might appropriately be treated as differences of sense. Such a treatment might enable a range of emotive uses of language to be seen as communicative, and not as merely subjective.)

---

[1] The last sentence here gives a quick indication of what Frege's account of indirect speech may be supposed to achieve. We supply a reading list on Indirect Speech and Propositional Attitude Ascriptions, and in the Commentary on Soames in Chapter 3 below, there is something about the importance, for theories of meaning, of differences of sense.

3. Frege makes it clear that his account of sense and reference has a very general application. The notion of sense has been introduced in solving the puzzle about identity. But the connection of sense with what is *expressed* (and indeed what is *understood*, although Frege does not mention this here) ensures that it has a role to play in an account of every piece of language. We saw above that the notion of reference works hand in hand with the notion of truth. Working as such, it is an indispensable ingredient in Frege's account of how language functions.[2] Fregean reference, like Fregean sense, is a feature of all 'words, expressions and whole sentences'. Frege's idea, which he begins to convey at $\boxed{j}\mapsto$ is that, by thinking about the case of proper names, we can fix notions of sense and of reference, and that these notions can then be applied to expressions of all sorts.

Proper names

Let us confine attention now to the category of proper names recognized by Mill. Then we can think of proper names as those words to which Mill denied connotation and to which Frege attributed sense. Of course, Frege attributed sense to all words, and, as we noted, he included definite descriptions among his so-called proper names. But proper names in Mill's sense are the words we usually think of as proper names.[3] And by thinking about proper names in Mill's sense, we can contrast Fregean sense with Millian connotation. We can also make a connexion between Mill's claims about proper names and Frege's identity puzzle.

Frege's puzzle about identity is a real puzzle for Mill. According to Mill's account, a proper name functions 'to show what it is that we are talking about', and that that is *all* there is to be said about its function. Well, when we use the name 'Hesperus' we are talking about a certain heavenly body, and when we use the word 'Phosphorus' we are talking about a certain heavenly body. In fact, of course, we are talking about the same heavenly body in both cases. So if we say 'Hesperus is Phosphorus', then, on Mill's account, we have merely recorded that a certain heavenly body is the same as itself. Although our statement has the form '$a = b$', given what Mill said about how 'a' and 'b' behave, it seems that we might just as well have used a statement of the form

---

[2]   See Chapters 3 and 5 for more about employing the notion of *truth* in an account of *meaning*.
[3]   This may not be quite right, because Mill excluded words which lack a denotation from his category of proper names, whereas we may include some words which lack a denotation among proper names: 'Santa Claus' might be an example.
  A singular term which lacks a denotation/reference is often called an *empty* term. And Frege certainly thought that proper names in *his* sense could be empty: he gives an example. But, as we have noted, Frege's own way of using 'proper name' conflates the categories of definite descriptions and proper names; and the example he gives of a 'proper name' which lacks a denotation is of a definite description.

'$a = a$'. But of course we could not have said anything informative if we had used such a statement. Yet 'Hesperus is Phosphorus' *can* be used informatively.

One does not need to consider identity statements in order to bring this problem for Mill to light. Consider 'Hesperus is visible' and 'Phosphorus is visible'. These two statements have, as Frege would put it, a different cognitive value: someone might understand both statements and know that one of them was true and not know that the other was. An account of these statements which is suited to showing how they can be used in communication between people is bound to take their cognitive value into account, this being just what is conveyed from one person to another. Frege will explain the difference between 'Hesperus is visible' and 'Phosphorus is visible' by saying that the sense of 'Hesperus' is different from the sense of 'Phosphorus'. But if 'Hesperus' and 'Phosphorus' played exactly the same role in the language, as Mill thought, then it would be impossible to find any difference between the two. It would seem impossible to take account of their communicative use. It would be impossible that someone should have said that Hesperus is visible unless she had said that Phosphorus is visible. (Here one sees one of the points of Frege's treatment of indirect reported speech.)

Mill did not recognize different cognitive values for statements containing different names. And it could then seem as though Mill held a view about names that is totally opposed to Frege's. But there is actually no need for Frege to disagree with two of Mill's main points about proper names. Firstly, when Mill denied that proper names have connotation, he was getting at something that could have been acceptable to Frege. Mill's point was that a proper name does not 'tell us anything' about the object that it names, and Frege could agree. For Frege's notion of 'mode of presentation' as it applies to a name is evidently not the notion of something that we are told about the object when the name is used. In the second place, Frege could agree with Mill when Mill speaks of a proper name as 'showing what it is that we are talking about'. The fact that 'Hesperus' and 'Phosphorus' differ in sense ensures that one employs a different way of showing what one is talking about in using 'Hesperus' from the way one employs in using 'Phosphorus'. But still, when one uses either of these names, one shows what it is that one is talking about.

It now looks as though the disagreement between Mill and Frege might be explained by pointing out that Frege's notion of sense was not available to Mill, who had only the apparatus of denotation and connotation to work with.

> Were you convinced by Mill's arguments against crediting names with connotation? Do you accept that there are informative identity statements whose informativeness Mill's apparatus fails to explain?

If you answer *Yes* to both these questions, then you will probably think that the introduction of Frege's notion of sense constitutes a significant advance. Not all philosophers think this, however! Accounts of proper names have been proposed which the present discussion of Mill and Frege has not even touched on.[4]

Conclusion

Think of semantic vocabulary as vocabulary used to speak about how words behave – about their meaning. We have come across a great range of semantic vocabulary in this chapter. It may be useful now to take stock. In Locke, we find 'sign of', 'stand for', and 'make reference to'. In Mill, we find 'name of', 'stand for', 'designate', 'meaning', 'can be truly affirmed of', as well, of course, as 'denote' and 'connote'. And in Frege, we find 'designate', and, of course, 'have sense', 'have reference', and 'colouring and shading'.

It would be nice if we could give definitions of all of this vocabulary, so as to be able to come up with a fixed set of notions to use to talk about the various views there have been about linguistic meaning. But although this would be nice, it isn't possible. For when an author holds a certain view, he will use certain terms to convey that view, and his use of his terms may then not match that of those who take a different view. We have seen some examples of this. Most philosophers use 'refer to' as a relation between a word and a thing; but Locke uses 'refer to' only to speak of our words as *supposedly* making a *secret* reference to things – to things which, in his own view, they are not really (or anyway not directly) signs of. Again, Mill's claim that proper names are 'not affirmed in any sense at all' might look like a flat contradiction of Frege; but we have seen that insofar as Mill meant something different from Frege by 'sense', there may be no contradiction here at all. In the case of Frege, it is very clear that he deliberately departs from the ordinary understandings of the terms he uses when he introduces his own semantic vocabulary. His 'sense' and 'reference' (German: *Sinn* and *Bedeutung*) belong in a systematic theory of meaning for a language. We shall come back to the idea of such a systematic theory in Chapter 3. The point to notice now is that our ordinary, everyday terms for talking about language and meaning may be unsuited to systematic theory. We started with the question, 'What account should we give of words having meaning?'. Perhaps we can see already that in order to answer this question in an illuminating way, we shall need to avail ourselves of other notions than an everyday notion of 'the meaning of a word'.

In the Introduction to this chapter we suggested that a simple idea of individual words as standing for things seems actually to be well suited only to the words that are proper names. You may or may not have agreed.

---

[4] You will encounter other views if you use the reading list on Proper Names.

However that may be, it has seemed important to many philosophers to mark out a distinctive semantic role for expressions that work like proper names. Mill usually uses 'designate' when he is speaking about the semantic function of his singular names; and many philosophers have used 'designate' in such a way as to confine it to words whose role is just to latch onto an object to be talked about. By contrast, the word 'denote' is typically used more generally, so that an expression (a word, or series of words) may have a denotation even if the relation between the expression and what it denotes is not simply to latch onto a single thing. Other words that are often used to work in the manner of 'denote' are 'apply to', 'is true of', and (echoing Frege's special usage) 'refer to'.

For the reasons gestured at above, it is not possible to set out once and for all exactly how semantic vocabulary has been used by philosophers over the years. But a distinction such as that indicated here between 'designate' and 'denote' will be important if one thinks that latching onto a single thing is a special function of some expressions. Some of the interest in the way that proper names work derives from their apparently having this special function. Which other expressions may also have this function is controversial. And it is also controversial how this special function might best be characterized (our 'latching onto' serves simply as a gesture towards the idea of an especially direct relation between a word and a thing). Some of the debate about definite descriptions is involved with this controversy.[5]

---

[5]   Again see the reading list on Definite Descriptions. We also supply a reading list on Indexicals, among which are included demonstratives such as 'that man' or 'this book'. Demonstratives certainly do seem to have the 'special function'.

2

Speech and Action

Introduction

The last chapter was concerned with some ideas about what *words* do – with what account we should give of words having meaning. This chapter is concerned more specifically with ideas about what *speakers* do – with the action that is speech. We reviewed some of the notions that may be brought into a word-based account of language in the Conclusion to the last chapter; and we shall encounter some of the notions that may be brought into a speaker-based account of language in the present one. One such notion, and a central one, is that of a speech act. If you think of an *act* as something a person does, you can think of a *speech act* as something a person does when she speaks. Speech acts, then, are things done with words. A whole area of philosophy of language has come to be known as speech act theory. This chapter's three authors – Austin, Alston, and Searle – have all been leading players in its development.

Of course, speakers were not left completely out of account in the previous chapter. We saw that Frege's notion of sense, as what speakers grasp, plays a role in accounting for how thoughts are transmitted between people. Still, Frege and philosophers following him tend to treat linguistic meaning in abstraction from actual speech situations. And some people have objected to such abstraction. They think that a language cannot be isolated as a semantic system divorced from the conditions in which speech takes place. Speech act theory has been developed in part in response to the thought that explanations of how bits of language work ought not to be detached from people's *use* of those bits of language.

Actually, everyone would agree that a correct account of meaning for a language has somehow to fit into an account of the use of that language. An account of the meaning of English words and sentences has to fit into an account of what speakers of English do when they use their language. An account of the meaning of Farsi words and sentences has to fit into an account of what speakers of Farsi do when they use their language. Inasmuch as accounts of the use of English, Farsi, German, etc. would all draw on the same sorts of notion – though not, of course, on the same account of meaning for the language in question – it seems obvious that there are questions about language which are simply not broached by thinking about word and sentence meaning. There is a great deal more, then, to an account of the use of language than an account of word and sentence meaning: there is speech act theory.

One line of opposition to the Fregean approach goes beyond thinking that we must fit explanations of how bits of language work into an account of people's use of them in speech acts. Some opponents of Frege and his followers think that an idea of what speakers do when they use words is more fundamental than any idea employed in an account of what words and sentences do. They think that an account of linguistic meaning must be *founded* in speech act theoretic ideas: ideas about what speakers do are the fundamental ones in terms of which linguistic meaning is to be explicated. We shall see one example of this sort of thinking in Alston, and another example (associated with the name of Grice) when we come to the Commentary on the extract from Searle.

Introduction to Austin

John Langshaw Austin (1911–60) studied classics at Oxford, and it was at Oxford that he taught philosophy. Austin gained fame for his particular method of approaching philosophical questions: he advocated paying careful attention to the subtleties of ordinary language, and he has sometimes been called 'an ordinary language philosopher'. Austin's work covered ancient Greek philosophy, epistemology (including, especially, perception), philosophy of action, and philosophy of language. He published little during his relatively brief lifetime. After his death, two books derived from lecture series he gave were published – *How to Do Things with Words* (1961) and *Sense and Sensibilia* (1962) – and his articles were collected in *Philosophical Papers* (1961, reprinted with additions in 1969 and in 1979).

The piece from his *Philosophical Papers* that we reprint here was written for a radio talk. It contains many of the main ideas of *How to Do Things with Words*. In both places, Austin wants to get us away from an idea of language as something that simply serves a statement-making function. He wants to call our attention to the fact that the use of language is a sort of human *action*, and to the very great variety of things that people do with words. Austin was the founder of what has come to be known as 'speech act theory', and introduced various notions that are central to the theory.

J. L. Austin, 'Performative Utterances'

I

You are more than entitled not to know what the word 'performative' means. It is a new word and an ugly word, and perhaps it does not mean anything very much. But at any rate there is one thing in its favour, it is not a profound word. I remember once when I had been talking on this subject that somebody afterwards said: 'You know, I haven't the least idea what he means, unless it could be that he simply means what he says'. Well, that is what I should like to mean.

Let us consider first how this affair arises. We have not got to go very far back in the history of philosophy to find philosophers assuming more or less as a matter of course that the sole business, the sole interesting business, of any utterance – that is, of anything we say – is to be true or at least false. Of course they had always known that there are other kinds of things which we say – things like imperatives, the expressions of wishes, and exclamations – some of which had even been classified by grammarians, though it wasn't perhaps too easy to tell always which was which. But still philosophers have assumed that the only things that they are interested in are utterances which report facts or which describe situations truly or falsely. In recent times this kind of approach has been questioned – in two stages, I think. First of all people began to say: 'Well, if these things are true or false it ought to be possible to decide which they are, and if we can't decide which they are they aren't any good but are, in short, nonsense'. And this new approach did a great deal of good; a great many things which probably are nonsense were found to be such. It is not the case, I think, that all kinds of nonsense have been adequately classified yet, and perhaps some things have been dismissed as nonsense which really are not; but still this movement, the verification movement, was, in its way, excellent.

However, we then come to the second stage. After all, we set some limits to the amount of nonsense that we talk, or at least the amount of nonsense that we are prepared to admit we talk; and so people began to ask whether after all some of those things which, treated as statements, were in danger of being dismissed as nonsense did after all really set out to be statements at all. Mightn't they perhaps be intended not to report facts but to influence people in this way or that, or to let off steam in this way or that? Or perhaps at any rate some elements in these utterances performed such functions, or, for example, drew attention in some way (without actually reporting it) to some important feature of the circumstances in which the utterance was being made. On these lines people have now adopted a new slogan, the slogan of the 'different uses of language'. The old approach, the old statemental approach, is sometimes called even a fallacy, the descriptive fallacy.

Certainly there are a great many uses of language. It's rather a pity that people are apt to invoke a new use of language whenever they feel so inclined, to help them out of this, that, or the other well-known philosophical tangle; we need more of a framework in which to discuss these uses of language; and also I think we should not despair too easily and talk, as people are apt to do, about the infinite uses of language. Philosophers will do this when they have listed as many, let us say, as seventeen; but even if there were something like ten thousand uses of language, surely we could list them all in time. This, after all, is no larger than the number of species of beetle that entomologists have taken the pains to list. But whatever the defects of either of these movements – the 'verification' movement or the 'use of language' movement – at any rate they have effected, nobody could deny, a great revolution in philosophy and, many would say, the most salutary in its history. (Not, if you come to think of it, a very immodest claim.)

Now it is one such sort of use of language that I want to examine here. I want to discuss a kind of utterance which looks like a statement and grammatically, I suppose, would be classed as a statement, which is not nonsensical, and yet is not true or false. These are not going to be utterances which contain curious verbs like 'could' or 'might', or curious words like 'good', which many philosophers regard nowadays simply as danger signals. They will be perfectly straightforward utterances, with ordinary verbs in the first person singular present indicative active, and yet we shall see at once that they couldn't possibly be true or false. Furthermore, if a person makes an utterance of this sort we should say that he is doing something rather than merely saying something. This may sound a little odd, but the examples I shall give will in fact not be odd at all, and may even seem decidedly dull. Here are three or four. Suppose, for example, that in the course of a marriage ceremony I say, as people will, 'I do' – (sc. take this woman to be my lawful wedded wife). Or again, suppose that I tread on your toe and say 'I apologize'. Or again, suppose that I have the bottle of champagne in my hand and say 'I name this ship the Queen Elizabeth'. Or suppose I say 'I bet you sixpence it will rain tomorrow'. In all these cases it would be absurd to regard the thing that I say as a report of the performance of the action which is undoubtedly done – the action of betting, or christening, or apologizing. We should say rather that, in saying what I do, I actually perform that action. When I say 'I name this ship the Queen Elizabeth' I do not describe the christening ceremony, I actually perform the christening; and when I say 'I do' (sc. take this woman to be my lawful wedded wife), I am not reporting on a marriage, I am indulging in it.

Now these kinds of utterance are the ones that we call performative utterances. This is rather an ugly word, and a new word, but there seems to be no word already in existence to do the job. [...]

At this point one might protest, perhaps even with some alarm, that I seem to be suggesting that marrying is simply saying a few words, that just saying a few words is marrying. Well, that certainly is not the case. The words have to be said in the appropriate circumstances, and this is a matter that will come up again later. [...]

Although these utterances do not themselves report facts and are not themselves true or false, saying these things does very often imply that certain things are true and not false, in some sense at least of that rather woolly word 'imply'. For example, when I say 'I do take this woman to be my lawful wedded wife', or some other formula in the marriage ceremony, I do imply that I'm not already married, with wife living, sane, undivorced, and the rest of it. But still it is very important to realize that to imply that something or other is true, is not at all the same as saying something which is true itself.

These performative utterances are not true or false, then. But they do suffer from certain disabilities of their own. They can fail to come off in special ways, and that is what 1 want to consider next. The various ways in which a performative utterance may be unsatisfactory we call, for the sake of a name, the infelicities; and an infelicity arises – that is to say, the utterance is unhappy – if certain rules, transparently simple rules, are broken. I will mention some of these rules and then give examples of some infringements.

d→ First of all, it is obvious that the conventional procedure which by our utterance we are purporting to use must actually exist. In the examples given here this procedure will be a verbal one, a verbal procedure for marrying or giving or whatever it may be; but it should be borne in mind that there are many non-verbal procedures by which we can perform exactly the same acts as we perform by these verbal means. It's worth remembering too that a great many of the things we do are at least in part of this conventional kind. Philosophers at least are too apt to assume that an action is always in the last resort the making of a physical movement, whereas it's usually, at least in part, a matter of convention.

The first rule is, then, that the convention invoked must exist and be accepted. And the second rule, also a very obvious one, is that the circumstances in which we purport to invoke this procedure must be appropriate for its invocation. If this is not observed, then the act that we purport to perform would not come off – it will be, one might say, a misfire. This will also be the case if, for example, we do not carry through the procedure – whatever it may be – correctly and completely, without a flaw and without a hitch. If any of these rules are not observed, we say that the act which we purported to perform is void, without effect. If, for example, the purported act was an act of marrying, then we should say that we 'went through a form' of marriage, but we did not actually succeed in marrying.

Here are some examples of this kind of misfire. Suppose that, living in a country like our own, we wish to divorce our wife. We may try standing her in front of us squarely in the room and saying, in a voice loud enough for all to hear, 'I divorce you'. Now this procedure is not accepted. We shall not thereby have succeeded in divorcing our wife, at least in this country and others like it. This is a case where the convention, we should say, does not exist or is not accepted. Again, suppose that, picking sides at a children's party, I say 'I pick George'. But George turns red in the face and says 'Not playing'. In that case I plainly, for some reason or another, have not picked George – whether because there is no convention that you can pick people who aren't playing, or because George in the circumstances is an inappropriate object for the procedure of picking. Or consider the case in which I say 'I appoint you Consul', and it turns out that you have been appointed already – or perhaps it may even transpire that you are a horse; here again we have the infelicity of inappropriate circumstances, inappropriate objects, or what not. Examples of flaws and hitches are perhaps scarcely necessary – one party in the marriage ceremony says 'I will', the other says 'I won't'; I say 'I bet sixpence', but nobody says 'Done', nobody takes up the offer. In all these and other such cases, the act which we purport to perform, or set out to perform, is not achieved.

e→ But there is another and a rather different way in which this kind of utterance may go wrong. A good many of these verbal procedures are designed for use by people who hold certain beliefs or have certain feelings or intentions. And if you use one of these formulae when you do not have the requisite thoughts or feelings or intentions then there is an abuse of the procedure, there is insincerity. Take, for example, the expression, 'I congratulate you'. This is designed for use by people who are glad that the person addressed has achieved a certain feat, believe that he was personally responsible for the success, and so on. If I say 'I congratulate you' when I'm not pleased or when I don't believe that the credit was yours, then there is insincerity. Likewise if I say I promise to do something, without having the least intention of doing it or without believing it feasible. In these cases there is something wrong certainly, but it is not like a misfire. We should not say that I didn't in fact promise, but rather that I did promise but promised insincerely; I did congratulate you but the congratulations were hollow. And there may be an infelicity of a somewhat similar kind when the performative utterance commits the speaker to future conduct of a certain description and then in the future he does not in fact behave in the expected way. This is very obvious, of course, if I promise to do something and then break my promise, but there are many kinds of commitment of a rather less tangible form than that in the case of promising. For instance, I may say 'I welcome you', bidding you welcome to my home or wherever it may be, but then I proceed to treat you as though you were exceedingly unwelcome. In this case the procedure of saying 'I welcome you' has been abused in a way rather different from that of simple insincerity. [...]

One further way in which things may go wrong is, for example, through what in general may be called misunderstanding. You may not hear what I say, or you may understand me to refer to something different from what I intended to refer to, and so on. And apart from further additions which we might make to the list, there is the general over-riding consideration that, as we are performing an act when we issue these performative utterances, we may of course be doing so under duress or in some other circumstances which make us not entirely responsible for doing what we are doing. That would certainly be an unhappiness of a kind – any kind of nonresponsibility might be called an unhappiness; but of course it is a quite different kind of thing from what we have been talking about. And I might mention that, quite differently again, we could be issuing any of these utterances, as we can issue an utterance of any kind whatsoever, in the course, for example, of acting a play or making a joke or writing a poem, in which case of course it would not be seriously meant and we shall not be able to say that we seriously performed the act concerned. If the poet says 'Go and catch a falling star' or whatever it may be, he doesn't seriously issue an order. Considerations of this kind apply to any utterance at all, not merely to performatives.

That, then, is perhaps enough to be going on with. We have discussed the performative utterance and its infelicities. That equips us, we may suppose, with two shining new tools to crack the crib of reality maybe. It also equips us – it always does – with two shining new skids under our metaphysical feet. The question is how we use them.

II

So far we have been going firmly ahead, feeling the firm ground of prejudice glide away beneath our feet which is always rather exhilarating, but what next? You will be waiting for the bit when we bog down, the bit where we take it all back, and sure enough that's going to come but it will take time. First of all let us ask a rather simple question. How can we be sure, how can we tell, whether any utterance is to be classed as a performative or not? Surely, we feel, we ought to be able to do that. And we should obviously very much like to be able to say that there is a grammatical criterion for this, some grammatical means of deciding whether an utterance is performative. All the examples I have given hitherto do in fact have the same grammatical form; they all of them begin with the verb in the first person singular present indicative active – not just any kind of verb of course, but still they all are in fact of that form. Furthermore, with these verbs that I have used there is a typical asymmetry between the use of this person and tense of the verb and the use of the same verb in other persons and other tenses, and this asymmetry is rather an important clue.

For example, when we say 'I promise that...', the case is very different from when we say 'He promises that...', or in the past tense 'I promised that...'. For when we say 'I promise that...' we do perform an act of promising – we give a promise. What we do not do is to report on somebody's performing an act of promising – in particular, we do not report on somebody's use of the expression 'I promise'. We actually do use it and do the promising. But if I say 'He promises', or in the past tense 'I promised', I precisely do report on an act of promising, that is to say an act of using this formula 'I promise' – I report on a present act of promising by him, or on a past act of my own. There is thus a clear difference between our first person singular present indicative active, and other persons and tenses. This is brought out by the typical incident of little Willie whose uncle says he'll give him half-a-crown if he promises never to smoke till he's 55. Little Willie's anxious parent will say 'Of course he promises, don't you. Willie?' giving him a nudge, and little Willie just doesn't vouchsafe. The point here is that he must do the promising himself by saying 'I promise', and his parent is going too fast in saying he promises.

That, then, is a bit of a test for whether an utterance is performative or not, but it would not do to suppose that every performative utterance has to take this standard form. There is at least one other standard form, every bit as common as this one, where the verb is in the passive voice and in the second or third person, not in the first.

The sort of case I mean is that of a notice inscribed 'Passengers are warned to cross the line by the bridge only', or of a document reading 'You are hereby authorized' to do so-and-so. These are undoubtedly performative, and in fact a signature is often required in order to show who it is that is doing the act of warning, or authorizing, or whatever it may be. Very typical of this kind of performative – especially liable to occur in written documents of course – is that the little word 'hereby' either actually occurs or might naturally be inserted.

g ⇒ Unfortunately, however, we still can't possibly suggest that every utterance which is to be classed as a performative has to take one or another of these two, as we might call them, standard forms. After all it would be a very typical performative utterance to say 'I order you to shut the door'. This satisfies all the criteria. It is performing the act of ordering you to shut the door, and it is not true or false. But in the appropriate circumstances surely we could perform exactly the same act by simply saying 'Shut the door', in the imperative. Or again, suppose that somebody sticks up a notice 'This bull is dangerous', or simply 'Dangerous bull', or simply 'Bull'. Does this necessarily differ from sticking up a notice, appropriately signed, saying 'You are hereby warned that this bull is dangerous'? It seems that the simple notice 'Bull' can do just the same job as the more elaborate formula. Of course the difference is that if we just stick up 'Bull' it would not be quite clear that it is a warning; it might be there just for interest or information, like 'Wallaby' on the cage at the zoo, or 'Ancient Monument'. No doubt we should know from the nature of the case that it was a warning, but it would not be explicit.

h ⇒ Well, in view of this break-down of grammatical criteria, what we should like to suppose – and there is a good deal in this – is that any utterance which is performative could be reduced or expanded or analysed into one of these two standard forms beginning 'I...' so and so or beginning 'You (or he) hereby...' so and so. If there was any justification for this hope, as to some extent there is, then we might hope to make a list of all the verbs which can appear in these standard forms, and then we might classify the kinds of acts that can be performed by performative utterances. We might do this with the aid of a dictionary, using such a test as that already mentioned – whether there is the characteristic asymmetry between the first person singular present indicative active and the other persons and tenses – in order to decide whether a verb is to go into our list or not. Now if we make such a list of verbs we do in fact find that they fall into certain fairly well-marked classes. There is the class of cases where we deliver verdicts and make estimates and appraisals of various kinds. There is the class where we give undertakings, commit ourselves in various ways by saying something. There is the class where by saying something we exercise various rights and powers, such as appointing and voting and so on. And there are one or two other fairly well-marked classes.

Suppose this task accomplished. Then we could call these verbs in our list explicit performative verbs, and any utterance that was reduced to one or the other of our standard forms we could call an explicit performative utterance. 'I order you to shut the door' would be an explicit performative utterance, whereas 'Shut the door' would not – that is simply a 'primary' performative utterance or whatever we like to call it. In using the imperative we may be ordering you to shut the door, but it just isn't made clear whether we are ordering you or entreating you or imploring you or beseeching you or inciting you or tempting you, or one or another of many other subtly different acts which, in an unsophisticated primitive language, are very likely not yet discriminated. But we need not overestimate the unsophistication of primitive languages. There are a great many devices that can be used for making clear, even at the primitive level, what act it is we are performing when we say something – the tone of voice, cadence, gesture – and above all we can rely upon the nature of the circumstances, the context in which the utterance is issued. This very often makes it quite unmistakable whether it is an order that is being given or whether, say, I am simply urging you or entreating you. We may, for instance, say something like this: 'Coming from him I was bound to take it as an order'. Still, in spite of all these devices, there is an unfortunate amount of ambiguity and lack of discrimination in default of our explicit performative verbs. If I say something like 'I shall be there', it may not be certain whether it is a promise, or an expression of intention, or perhaps even a forecast of my future behaviour, of what is going to happen to me; and it may matter a good deal, at least in developed societies, precisely which of these things it is. And that is why the explicit performative verb is evolved – to make clear exactly which it is, how far it commits me and in what way, and so forth.

This is just one way in which language develops in tune with the society of which it is the language. The social habits of the society may considerably affect the question of which performative verbs are evolved and which, sometimes for rather irrelevant reasons, are not. For example, if I say 'You are a poltroon', it might be that I am censuring you or it might be that I am insulting you. Now since apparently society approves of censuring or reprimanding, we have here evolved a formula 'I reprimand you', or 'I censure you', which enables us expeditiously to get this desirable business over. But on the other hand, since apparently we don't approve of insulting, we have not evolved a simple formula 'I insult you', which might have done just as well.

By means of these explicit performative verbs and some other devices, then, we make explicit what precise act it is that we are performing when we issue our utterance. But here I would like to put in a word of warning. We must distinguish between the function of making explicit what act it is we are performing, and the quite different matter of stating what act it is we are performing. In issuing an explicit performative utterance we are not stating what act it is, we are showing or making explicit what act it is. We can draw a helpful parallel here with another case in which the act, the conventional act that we perform, is not a speech-act but a physical performance. Suppose I appear before you one day and bow deeply from the waist. Well, this is ambiguous. I may be simply observing the local flora, tying my shoe-lace, something of that kind; on the other hand, conceivably I might be doing obeisance to you. Well, to clear up this ambiguity we have some device such as raising the hat, saying 'Salaam', or something of that kind, to make it quite plain that the act being performed is the conventional one of doing obeisance rather than some other act. Now nobody would want to say that lifting your hat was stating that you were performing an act of obeisance; it certainly is not, but it does make it quite plain that you are. And so in the same way to say 'I warn you that...' or 'I order you to...' or 'I promise that...' is not to state that you are doing something, but makes it plain that you are – it does constitute your verbal performance, a performance of a particular kind.

So far we have been going along as though there was a quite clear difference between our performative utterances and what we have contrasted them with, statements or reports or descriptions. But now we begin to find that this distinction is not as clear as it might be. It's now that we begin to sink in a little. In the first place, of course, we may feel doubts as to how widely our performatives extend. If we think up some odd kinds of expression we use in odd cases, we might very well wonder whether or not they satisfy our rather vague criteria for being performative utterances. Suppose, for example, somebody says 'Hurrah'. Well, not true or false; he is performing the act of cheering. Does that make it a performative utterance in our sense or not? Or suppose he says 'Damn'; he is performing the act of swearing, and it is not true or false. Does that make it performative? We feel that in a way it does and yet it's rather different. Again, consider cases of 'suiting the action to the words'; these too may make us wonder whether perhaps the utterance should be classed as performative. Or sometimes, if somebody says 'I am sorry', we wonder whether this is just the same as 'I apologize' – in which case of course we have said it's a performative utterance – or whether perhaps it's to be taken as a description, true or false, of the state of his feelings. If he had said 'I feel perfectly awful about it', then we should think it must be meant to be a description of the state of his feelings. If he had said 'I apologize', we should feel this was clearly a performative utterance, going through the ritual of apologizing. But if he says 'I am sorry' there is an unfortunate hovering between the two. This phenomenon is quite common. We often find cases in which there is an obvious pure performative utterance and obvious other utterances connected with it which are not performative but descriptive, but on the other hand a good many in between where we're not quite sure which they are. On some occasions of course they are obviously used the one way, on some occasions the other way, but on some occasions they seem positively to revel in ambiguity.

Again, consider the case of the umpire when he says 'Out' or 'Over', or the jury's utterance when they say that they find the prisoner guilty. Of course, we say, these are cases of giving verdicts, performing the act of appraising and so forth, but still in a way they have some connexion with the facts. They seem to have something like the duty to be true or false, and seem not to be so very remote from statements. If the umpire says 'Over', this surely has at least something to do with six balls in fact having been delivered rather than seven, and so on. In fact in general we may remind ourselves that 'I state that...' does not look so very different from 'I warn you that...' or 'I promise to...'. It makes clear surely that the act that we are performing is an act of stating, and so functions just like 'I warn' or 'I order'. So isn't 'I state that...' a performative utterance? But then one may feel that utterances beginning 'I state that...' do have to be true or false, that they are statements.

Considerations of this sort, then, may well make us feel pretty unhappy. If we look back for a moment at our contrast between statements and performative utterances, we realize that we were taking statements very much on trust from, as we said, the traditional treatment. Statements, we had it, were to be true or false; performative utterances on the other hand were to be felicitous or infelicitous. They were the doing of something, whereas for all we said making statements was not doing something. Now this contrast surely, if we look back at it, is unsatisfactory. Of course statements are liable to be assessed in this matter of their correspondence or failure to correspond with the facts, that is, being true or false. But they are also liable to infelicity every bit as much as are performative utterances. In fact some troubles that have arisen in the study of statements recently can be shown to be simply troubles of infelicity. For example, it has been pointed out that there is something very odd about saying something like this: 'The cat is on the mat but I don't believe it is'. Now this is an outrageous thing to say, but it is not self-contradictory. There is no reason why the cat shouldn't be on the mat without my believing that it is. So how are we to classify what's wrong with this peculiar statement? If we remember now the doctrine of infelicity we shall see that the person who makes this remark about the cat is in much the same position as somebody who says something like this: 'I promise that I shall be there, but I haven't the least intention of being there'. Once again you can of course perfectly well promise to be there without having the least intention of being there, but there is something outrageous about saying it, about actually avowing the insincerity of the promise you give. In the same way there is insincerity in the case of the person who says 'The cat is on the mat but I don't believe it is', and he is actually avowing that insincerity – which makes a peculiar kind of nonsense.

A second case that has come to light is the one about John's children – the case where somebody is supposed to say 'All John's children are bald but John hasn't got any children'. Or perhaps somebody says 'All John's children are bald', when as a matter of fact – he doesn't say so – John has no children. Now those who study statements have worried about this; ought they to say that the statement 'All John's children are bald' is meaningless in this case? Well, if it is, it is not a bit like a great many other more standard kinds of meaninglessness; and we see, if we look back at our list of infelicities, that what is going wrong here is much the same as what goes wrong in, say, the case of a contract for the sale of a piece of land when the piece of land referred to does not exist. Now what we say in the case of this sale of land, which of course would be effected by a performative utterance, is that the sale is void – void for lack of reference or ambiguity of reference; and so we can see that the statement about all John's children is likewise void for lack of reference. And if the man actually says that John has no children in the same breath as saying they're all bald, he is making the same kind of outrageous utterance as the man who says 'The cat is on the mat and I don't believe it is', or the man who says 'I promise to but I don't intend to'.

In this way, then, ills that have been found to afflict statements can be precisely paralleled with ills that are characteristic of performative utterances. And after all when we state something or describe something or report something, we do perform an act which is every bit as much an act as an act of ordering or warning. There seems no good reason why stating should be given a specially unique position. Of course philosophers have been wont to talk as though you or I or anybody could just go round stating anything about anything and that would be perfectly in order, only there's just a little question: is it true or false? But besides the little question, is it true or false, there is surely the question: is it in order? Can you go round just making statements about anything? Suppose for example you say to me 'I'm feeling pretty mouldy this morning'. Well, I say to you 'You're not'; and you say 'What the devil do you mean, I'm not?' I say 'Oh nothing – I'm just stating you're not, is it true or false?' And you say 'Wait a bit about whether it's true or false, the question is what did you mean by making statements about somebody else's feelings? I told you I'm feeling pretty mouldy. You're just not in a position to say, to state that I'm not.' This brings out that you can't just make statements about other people's feelings (though you can make guesses if you like); and there are very many things which, having no knowledge of, not being in a position to pronounce about, you just can't state. What we need to do for the case of stating, and by the same token describing and reporting, is to take them a bit off their pedestal, to realize that they are speech-acts no less than all these other speech-acts that we have been mentioning and talking about as performative.

Then let us look for a moment at our original contrast between the performative and the statement from the other side. In handling performatives we have been putting it all the time as though the only thing that a performative utterance had to do was to be felicitous, to come off, not to be a misfire, not to be an abuse. Yes, but that's not the end of the matter. At least in the case of many utterances which, on what we have said, we should have to class as performative – cases where we say 'I warn you to . . .', 'I advise you to . . .' and so on – there will be other questions besides simply: was it in order, was it all right, as a piece of advice or a warning, did it come off? After that surely there will be the question: was it good or sound advice? Was it a justified warning? Or in the case, let us say, of a verdict or an estimate: was it a good estimate, or a sound verdict? And these are questions that can only be decided by considering how the content of the verdict or estimate is related in some way to fact, or to evidence available about the facts. This is to say that we do require to assess at least a great many performative utterances in a general dimension of correspondence with fact. It may still be said, of course, that this does not make them very like statements because still they are not true or false, and that's a little black and white speciality that distinguishes statements as a class apart. But actually – though it would take too long to go on about this – the more you think about truth and falsity the more you find that very few statements that we ever utter are just true or just false. Usually there is the question are they fair or are they not fair, are they adequate or not adequate, are they exaggerated or not exaggerated? Are they too rough, or are they perfectly precise, accurate, and so on? 'True' and 'false' are just general labels for a whole dimension of different appraisals which have something or other to do with the relation between what we say and the facts. If, then, we loosen up our ideas of truth and falsity we shall see that statements, when assessed in relation to the facts, are not so very different after all from pieces of advice, warnings, verdicts, and so on.

We see then that stating something is performing an act just as much as is giving an order or giving a warning; and we see, on the other hand, that, when we give an order or a warning or a piece of advice, there is a question about how this is related to fact which is not perhaps so very different from the kind of question that arises when we discuss how a statement is related to fact. Well, this seems to mean that in its original form our distinction between the performative and the statement is considerably weakened, and indeed breaks down. I will just make a suggestion as to how to handle this matter. We need to go very much farther back, to consider all the ways and senses in which saying anything at all is doing this or that – because of course it is always doing a good many different things. And one thing that emerges when we do do this is that, besides the question that has been very much studied in the past as to what a certain utterance means, there is a further question distinct from this as to what was the force, as we may call it, of the utterance. We may be quite clear what 'Shut the door' means, but not yet at all clear on the further point as to whether as uttered at a certain time it was an order, an entreaty or whatnot. What we need besides the old doctrine about meanings is a new doctrine about all the possible forces of utterances, towards the discovery of which our proposed list of explicit performative verbs would be a very great help; and then, going on from there, an investigation of the various terms of appraisal that we use in discussing speech-acts of this, that or the other precise kind – orders, warnings, and the like.

The notions that we have considered then, are the performative, the infelicity, the explicit performative, and lastly, rather hurriedly, the notion of the forces of utterances. I dare say that all this seems a little unremunerative, a little complicated. Well, I suppose in some ways it is unremunerative, and I suppose it ought to be remunerative. At least, though, I think that if we pay attention to these matters we can clear up some mistakes in philosophy; and after all philosophy is used as a scapegoat, it parades mistakes which are really the mistakes of every-body. We might even clear up some mistakes in grammar, which perhaps is a little more respectable.

And is it complicated? Well, it is complicated a bit; but life and truth and things do tend to be complicated. It's not things, it's philo-sophers that are simple. You will have heard it said, I expect, that over-simplification is the occupational disease of philosophers, and in a way one might agree with that. But for a sneaking suspicion that it's their occupation.

Commentary on Austin

A baffling feature of Austin's piece is that it appears both to make a great deal of the distinction between performatives and statements, but also to tell us that the distinction seems to break down (see [j]→). In order to try to understand this, we should look critically at the basis of the performative/statement distinction. Austin apparently equates a statement with that which is true or false – that is, with something truth-evaluable. We should look at the idea of truth-evaluability, before discussing the four notions which Austin lists (in his summary at [1]→). And we should finish with the idea of *illocutionary acts*. Illocutionary acts are central in speech act theory, and although Austin does not use the word 'illocutionary' in the present paper, it originates with him.

Truth-evaluability

Austin starts from an assumed contrast between utterances that may be true or false, and utterances like imperatives, expressions of wishes, exclamations. The contrast is between the indicative mood – which is found, for instance, in 'The door is shut' – and non-indicative moods – which are found, for instance, in 'Shut the door!' (which is imperative in mood) and 'Would that the door were shut' (which is optative in mood; its use is to express a wish). Notice that it can seem natural to equate the indicative/non-indicative contrast with the truth-evaluable/not-truth-evaluable one. For we can say that it's true that the door is shut; but we cannot say that it's true that shut the door. 'Shut the door!', being a non-indicative, is not truth-evaluable.[1]

---

[1]   Austin is not much interested in how to treat non-indicative sentences in the present paper. But questions about their treatment are pressing for those who advocate using the notion of *truth* as a central notion in semantic theory (see Chapter 3). We supply a reading list on Non-indicatives.

At $\boxed{a}\mapsto$ Austin tells us that adherents of the verification movement rejected the idea that indicative sentences are always truth-evaluable.[2] They held that some sentences which look grammatically to be statements (given their indicative mood) are not really statements (given they are claimed not to be truth-evaluable). Such sentences may be thought to have a different role from statements. Statements, Austin thinks, are used to report facts or to describe situations truly or falsely; those indicative utterances which are held not to be truth-evaluable have a different use (see $\boxed{b}\mapsto$). It is clear, then, from the way that Austin sets things up, that Austin himself thinks of statements as having a particular use – a use which connects with their being truth-evaluable.

Performatives

What are Austin's examples of performatives in section I? What does Austin think the principal features of performatives are?

Austin's four examples of performatives are at $\boxed{c}\mapsto$. They are introduced as utterances, which 'couldn't possibly be true or false'. And Austin characterizes them as a sort of utterance that we report by saying what the utterer *did*.

In the last forty years many philosophers have taken exception to the claim that Austin finds completely obvious – that performatives are not true or false. We shall say more about this below.

Infelicity

What kinds of infelicity do performatives suffer from? Why does the idea of felicity/infelicity matter to Austin?

Although Austin introduces subtleties, and goes into details of sub-categories, the infelicities that interest him seem to be of two basic sorts. (1) The person uttering the performatives is to be thought of as making use of a conventional procedure, governed by various rules. When the rules aren't kept to, infelicity results. See from $\boxed{d}\mapsto$ to $\boxed{e}\mapsto$. (2) The person uttering the performative lacks sincerity, or can't be held responsible; or the utterance is not understood by the hearer. Again, infelicity results. See from $\boxed{e}\mapsto$ to $\boxed{f}\mapsto$.

---

[2] Verificationists held that a sentence's meaning was a matter of its verification conditions. Thinking that the things we say when we use ethical language (for example) are not verifiable or falsifiable – or, as Austin puts it, that it is not possible to *decide* whether they are true or false – the verificationists held that such things are not truth-evaluable. (You may have encountered non-cognitivism in ethics: this is a doctrine that may be held for reasons of verificationism.)

Presumably a notion of infelicity is important to Austin because it makes a contrast with falsehood. The idea may be that whereas statements aspire to being true, performatives aspire to being felicitous.

> Ask yourself whether both sorts of infelicity we have distinguished [(1) and (2)] have application to *all* of Austin's examples of performatives.

Many writers on Austin have suggested that only some of Austin's examples can be thought of as utterances which make use of a particular conventional procedure. They would suggest that 'I do' said at a marriage ceremony might be infelicitous in way (1) but not in way (2), whereas 'I apologize' might be infelicitous in way (2) but not in way (1). (Think about this, and consider other examples.)

Explicit performatives

> Why does Austin find it difficult to find a criterion for an utterance being a performative? Read the paragraph starting at [g]→.

A criterion of performativity which Austin considers here is that the main verb of the sentence should be a word for what the speaker can be reported as having done in uttering the sentence. (Example: a speaker who says 'I warn you the bull is dangerous' can be reported as having warned of a dangerous bull.) What then gives trouble, so far as Austin is concerned, is that a speaker might use a sentence which does not meet this criterion and yet still be reported as having done what someone who had uttered a performative according to the criterion had done. (Example: a speaker who says 'Danger! Bull!' can be reported as having warned of a dangerous bull.) Previously Austin had thought of performatives as utterances that we report by saying what the utterer *did*. Austin now finds he cannot square that with a grammatical criterion.

> What does Austin mean by 'explicit performative'?

An explicit performative is an utterance in which a speaker makes it explicit which act (s)he is performing. The sort of criterion which Austin found troublesome for performatives in general apparently serves now to mark out *explicit* performatives.

At this point, we can perhaps understand why Austin's claim that performatives lack truth-values should have struck many people as wrong. Someone makes explicit what act she is performing when she says 'I promise'. In that case, when she says this, she performs the act of promising. Put more simply: she promises. But does this not mean that when she says 'I promise', she speaks truly? Someone who says 'I am cold' speaks truly if she is cold. Doesn't someone who says 'I promise' speak truly if she promises? Of course there is a difference between the sentences 'I promise' and 'I am cold'. Someone who says 'I promise' does not state that she promises, whereas someone who says 'I am cold' does state that she is cold. But this difference between the two sentences need not count against their both being truth-evaluable – not if we distinguish between (a) the question whether an utterance is a statement and (b) the question whether it is truth-evaluable.[3]

When Austin points out that statements can suffer from kinds of infelicity, he recognizes that a division between what is evaluable for truth and what is evaluable for felicity will not work to distinguish statements from performatives. And here he sees his statement/performative distinction as starting to collapse. Austin's discussion of infelicity is nevertheless important in showing us that a realistic description of language use will introduce a variety of different ways of evaluating people's utterances, and not treat them merely as true or false.

> What idea does Austin convey with 'primary' peformative: see $\boxed{i}\!\!\mapsto$?

'Shut the door' evidently qualifies as a *primary* performative (or 'whatever we like to call it') because it is used to do something – to do one of a range of things, in fact. But it is evidently not an explicit performative in Austin's sense. It seems, then, that we might say that there is a primary performative, whenever some act is performed using language, and that would seem to be *whenever* any piece of language is used communicatively. (Perhaps Austin himself would have said that there is a primary performative when someone uses a sentence to do something, so long as they don't make a truth-evaluable utterance.) Philosophers for the most part have confined the use of the word 'performative' to what Austin called explicit performatives. But many writers who have welcomed Austin's recognition that language use belongs in the domain of human agency have taken over an idea of *performativity*, and they have used this to cover a wider range of phenomena than the explicit performative.

Force

> What does Austin mean by force at $\boxed{k}\!\!\mapsto$? How might the notion of force help to explain the breakdown of the statement/performative distinction?

---

[3] No doubt there is much more to be said. We supply a reading list on Performatives and Speech Acts.

One knows the force of an utterance if one knows what point the speaker had in making the utterance, and that is a matter of knowing something about what the speaker did – what she was up to. It is, then, no wonder then that we cannot mark off performatives as a sort of utterance that gets reported by saying what the speaker did. For there can be a question about the force of *any* utterance, or at least of any which achieves any sort of purpose. Even someone who makes a statement does something: she states such-and-such; her utterance, we might say, has the force of a statement.

If we think that the question whether an utterance is a statement is a question about its force, then we shall probably resist a claim that Austin put in place at the outset – that statementhood and truth-evaluability always go hand in hand. Austin is clear that a question about the force of an utterance is distinct from a question about its meaning. And we might think that the issue of whether an utterance is truth-evaluable is a question about the meaning of the sentence uttered, not about the force with which the speaker uttered the sentence. Here we need to appreciate that in order to know what force an utterance has, one has to know about the circumstances, and not just which sentence it was an utterance of. Even though Austin speaks of performative *utterances*, he often writes as if we could mark out performatives by thinking simply about which *sentences* are uttered. Although an utterance is always of some sentence, an utterance is something made by a particular speaker at a particular time; and a single sentence uttered by different speakers at different times might be used to do different things.

Illocutionary acts

When Austin speaks of force, and distinguishes it from meaning, he is opening up the realm of speech act theory. For the force of an utterance is what we know when we know what its speaker did – specifically which illocutionary act she performed. Although Austin does not use the word 'illocutionary' in the present paper, he is thinking of verbs for what he called illocutionary acts, when he imagines drawing up a list of verbs which might occur in explicit performatives at $\boxed{\text{h}}\!\!\rightarrow$.

Austin has only a little to say here about the classification of such verbs – of illocutionary acts. One can get a flavour of the sort of thing he has in mind by looking at a classification that Alston has recently proposed.[4]

Assertives, e.g. assert, allege, report, answer, deny, predict, complain.
Directives, e.g. ask, request, implore, tell, suggest, recommend, propose.
Commissives, e.g. promise, bet, guarantee, invite, offer.

---

[4] In his *Illocutionary Acts and Sentence Meaning* (Cornell University Press, 2000). Austin proposed a classification himself in *How To Do Things with Words*.

Expressives, e.g. thank, apologize, commiserate, compliment, express such-
and-such – where such-and-such may be enthusiasm, interest, relief, intention, delight.

Exercitives, e.g. adjourn, appoint, pardon, name, hire, fire, approve.

This classification helps to bring out something that Austin wanted to emphasize – the great variety of things that people do with words. And it gives an
idea of some of what is covered in speech act theory. In providing classifica-
tions, speech act theorists hope to organize and simplify the range of purposes
that language may be put to. You should consider examples. That will give
you a sense of some of the different functions that language has among human
agents. Speech act theory has a continuing influence not only in philosophy
and linguistics, but also, for example, in literary studies and, fifty years on
from Austin, in agent-based communication systems developed in computer
science.

Introduction to Alston

William P. Alston is Professor Emeritus at Syracuse University (in the state of
New York). He has done important work in metaphysics, epistemology,
history of philosophy and philosophy of religion, as well as in philosophy of
language. His many books include *Perceiving God* (1991), *The Reliability of
Sense Perception* (1993), and *A Realist Conception of Truth* (1996).

Alston's elementary text, *Philosophy of Language*, was published in
1964. His *Illocutionary Acts and Sentence Meaning* (2000) presents a theory
that Alston has developed over forty years. Alston thinks that a sentence's
having a certain meaning consists in its being usable to play a certain role in
communication, and that a sentence's having such a role is a matter of the
illocutionary acts that could be performed in using the sentence. When one
learns of Austin's distinction between meaning and force, it can seem as
if a sentence's meaning is one thing, and the force it is used with is something quite else. (That indeed is how many philosophers think of the matter.)
But Alston's idea is that instead of treating meaning and force as quite
separate notions, we should refine notions of force in order to provide an
account of meaning: we should say what words do by saying what speakers
do when they use them. The seeds of this idea were sown in the 1963
paper reprinted below. Here Alston starts from the question of how we
should think about the *use* of a bit of language if we want a conception of
use that is suited to explaining linguistic meaning. A helpful feature of
this paper is that it takes off from notions of meaning and use that we
may find intuitive even before we try to think about meaning in a theoretical,
systematic way.

William P. Alston, 'Meaning and Use'

There is a certain conviction about linguistic meaning that is widely shared today. This conviction might be expressed as follows. Somehow the concept of the meaning of a linguistic expression is to be elucidated in terms of the use of that expression, in terms of the way it is employed by the users of the language. To wit:

> ...to know what an expression means is to know how it may and may not be employed.
>
> Gilbert Ryle, "The Theory of Meaning", in *British
> Philosophy in the Mid-Century*, p. 255

> To give the meaning of an expression is to give *general direction* for its use to refer to or mention particular objects or persons; to give the meaning of a sentence is to give *general direction* for its use in making true or false assertions.
>
> P. F. Strawson, "On Referring", *Mind*, LIX, p. 327

> ...to know the meaning of a sentence is to know how to use it, to know in what circumstances its use is correct or incorrect.... A sentence is meaningful if it has a use; we know its meaning if we *know* its use.
>
> G. J. Warnock, "Verification and the Use of Language",
> *Revue Internationale de Philosophie*, V, p. 318

And this conviction is not only held in the abstract. In the past fifteen years or so it has often been put into practice by way of investigating the use of one or another fundamental term, and a great deal of philosophical illumination has come out of these enterprises.

But despite the wide currency of the general conviction, and despite the numerous and wide-ranging investigations that have gone on under its aegis, no one has made a serious attempt to say, explicitly and in detail, what is to be meant by 'use' in these contexts, i.e., what is and what is not to count as revealing the *use* of a term. And still less has any serious attempt been made to say just how meaning is to be analysed in terms of use as so conceived. [...I]t is only too obvious that many sorts of rules which govern linguistic activity have nothing to do with use in any sense of that term in which meaning could conceivably be a function of use. For example, many speakers recognize rules forbidding them to use certain racy or obscene words in certain circumstances, or rules forbidding them to use crude or vernacular locutions in certain social circles; and such rules could be said to define a certain mode of correctness. And yet the consideration of such rules does nothing to bring out the meaning of such words.

In this essay I want to make a beginning at elucidating a suitable sense for 'use' and indicating the way in which meaning is to be understood as a function of use in this sense. I think it may serve to clear the air somewhat if I first indicate some directions from which no help is to be expected. In view of the apparently widespread impression that when one says that meaning is a function of use he is using 'use' in a quite ordinary sense, it may repay us to examine the most prominent contexts in which 'use' is used in a relatively unproblematical and unpuzzling way in connection with linguistic expressions, in order to satisfy ourselves that none of them furnishes anything which will meet our present needs.

I

First consider the fact that the phrase, 'the use of x', as it is ordinarily used, fails to identify anything which an expression *has*, or which two expressions could be said to have in common. Ordinarily we speak of the use of a word, as of anything else, in the course of saying something about the fact of its employment – when, where, how frequent, etc.

> The use of 'presumably' is inappropriate at this point.
> The use of 'whom' at the beginning of a sentence is gradually dying out.
> The use of 'by crackey' is largely confined to rustics.

Compare:

> The use of sedatives is not indicated in his case.
> The use of the hand plough is dying out all over Europe.
> The use of automobiles in Russia is mostly limited to important officials.

It is clear that in such contexts 'The use of E' fails to designate anything which E has, and which it would share with any expression which had the same meaning, but fail to share with any expression which had a different meaning. If I were to ask one who had uttered the second sentence in the first list: 'What is this use of "whom" which is dying out, and what other expressions have the same use?', I would be missing the point of what he had said. In making that statement, he was not talking about something called 'the use of whom', which could then be looked for in other surroundings, he was simply saying that people are using 'whom' at the beginning of a sentence less and less. Nor is the question, 'What is the use of E?' any more fruitful. I suppose that 'What is the use of "sanguine"?' would mean, if anything, 'What is the point of using "sanguine"?', just as 'What is the use of a typewriter?' would ordinarily be understood, if at all, as an awkward way of asking 'What is the point of having (using) a typewriter?'; and this does not help.

Let us now look at some contexts in which we talk of the *way* an expression is used, or of *how* it is used. And let us consider what counts as a way of using an expression. Look at the adverbs we use to qualify 'A used E',

A used 'Communist' effectively.
A used 'Yes sir' very insolently.
A uses 'Presumably' frequently.

Clearly none of these ways has an important bearing on meaning. The fact that two words are both used frequently, effectively, or insolently does nothing to show that they have the same meaning. Looking at the corresponding question, 'How is E used?', we might take anything which could serve as an answer to be a specification of a way of using E. It seems that such a question is normally concerned with the grammatical function of E. 'How is "albeit" used?' 'As a conjunction.' 'How is "ce" used?' 'With forms of "être" under certain conditions.' Thus we could reasonably call 'as a conjunction', 'as a transitive verb', etc., ways of using expressions. But this won't do. Two words can both be used as a conjunction, or as a transitive verb, without having the same meaning, We also speak of 'what E is used for', 'the use to which E is put', or 'the job E is used to perform'. But how do we specify what a word is used to do? It seems that the only cases in which we ordinarily make such specifications are of a rather special sort.

'And' is used to conjoin expressions of the same rank.
'Amen' is used to close a prayer.
'Ugh' is used to express disgust.

These are all cases in which it is impossible to teach someone the word by saying what it means, either because there is no approximately equivalent expression in the language ('and'), or because the exhibition of that expression would not be very helpful. (We might say '"Amen" means *so be it*' but this would be misleading at best; for it would give no hint as to the special circumstances in which 'Amen' is appropriately used.)

II

From this survey I draw the conclusion that in non-technical talk about using words we are most unlikely to discover a sense of 'use' which is even a plausible candidate for a fundamental rôle in semantics. And if so, a technical sense will have to be constructed. If we consider some of the arguments which have led, or might lead, people to embrace the use-analysis, they might contain some clue to a sense of 'use' which one could use in carrying out the analysis. I shall consider three such arguments.

[a]→ (1) 'Since the meaning of a word is not a function of the physical properties of the word, and since a given pattern of sounds can have different meanings in different language-communities, or in the same language-community at different times, the meaning of a word must somehow be a function of the activity of language users, of what they do in their employments of the word.' This argument may well lead us to suppose that meaning is a function of use in some sense but in itself it will not help us to pin down that sense.

(2) 'Specifications of meaning are commonly provided when we want to teach someone how to use the expression whose meaning we are specifying. Teaching someone how to use an expression is the native soil from which talk about meaning has grown. It is not, of course, the only sort of context in which one says what the meaning of a word is; there are also examinations, crossword puzzles, and many others. But it is the primary occasion for saying what a word means, and I would suppose that the other occasions are somehow derivative from it.' Now this does strongly suggest that in telling someone what a word means we are putting him in a position to be able to use it, hence that knowing what it means is being able to use it, and hence that the meaning of the word is a function of how it is used. But all this, I fear, goes on the assumption that we already have an adequate understanding of what is involved in knowing how to use a word. I do not see how we could derive such an understanding from these considerations.

(3) 'Ultimately a meaning-statement (a statement as to what a linguistic expression means) is to be tested by determining what people do in their employment of the expression in question. For in saying what the meaning of an expression is, what we do is not to

designate some entity which could becalled the meaning of the expression, but rather to exhibit another expression which has some sort of equivalence with the first.[1]

For example:

'Procrastinate' means *put things off*.[2]
'Prognosis' means forecast of the course and termination of a disease.
'Redundant' means *superfluous*.
'Notwithstanding' means *in spite of*.

If this is granted, the next question obviously is: what sort of equivalence must two expressions have in order that one can be thus exhibited in specifying the meaning of the other?[3] It seems plausible to say that it is equivalence in the way they are used that is crucial, for reasons similar to those put forward in the first argument. And this suggests that a meaning statement is to be tested by examining people's employment of the expressions in question, to determine whether they are employed in the same way.'

From this line of thought we can at least derive a suggestion as to how meaning is related to use, whatever use might turn out to be. We can sum up what has just been said in the following formula.

'x' means *y* (the meaning of 'x' is *y*) = df. 'x' and 'y' have the same use.

---

[1] Arguments in support of this thesis are put forward in my essay, 'The Quest for Meanings', *Mind*, Vol. LXX11, No. 285 (Jan. 1963).

[2] I should say something in explanation of my notation. I italicize what follows the word 'means' in order to indicate that there is something special about this occurrence of the expression. This is clear from the fact that we are neither using 'put things off', e.g., in the ordinary way (it is not functioning as a verb), nor are we referring to it in a way that would be marked by enclosing it in quotes. (This latter point can be seen by noting that we could not expand the sentence into: ' "Procrastinate" means the phrase, "put things off" '.) This type of occurrence, which I more or less arbitrarily call 'exhibiting', I take to be unique; and I believe that the only way to say what it is to give the sort of elucidation of meaning-statements towards which I am working in this essay.

[3] 'Having the same meaning' or 'synonymous' seem to me to be naturally employed wherever, as in the foregoing, I would speak of 'having the sort of equivalence which enables one to be exhibited in specifying the meaning of the other'. However, one must be careful not to expect more from these phrases than they are intended to express. In using them I am not presupposing that I have specified, or can specify, something called 'a meaning' which they have in common. I shall freely avail myself of these phrases, but only as convenient and intuitively plausible abbreviations for the more cumbersome phrase.

From this formula alone we get no help in trying to decide what meaning we should attach to 'use'. However, if we could make explicit just what we would look for if we set out to determine whether two expressions are used in the same way, that might give us a clue to a proper interpretation for 'use'.

[b]→ Consider the statement, ' "Procrastinate" means *put things off*'. I can test this statement, at least for my speech, as follows.[4] I review cases in which I would say 'You're always procrastinating', and determine whether I would use the sentence 'You're always putting things off' to make just the same complaint. I think of cases in which I would say 'Please don't put things off so much' and determine whether I would use the sentence 'Please don't procrastinate so much' to make the same plea. I consider cases in which I say 'Is he still procrastinating all the time?' and I determine whether I would use the sentence 'Is he still putting things off all the time?' to ask the same question. And so on.

This suggests that a meaning-statement of the form, ' "x" means "y" ' is to be tested by determining whether 'x' and 'y' can be substituted for each other in a wide variety of sentences without, in each case, changing the job(s) which the sentence is used to do, or, more precisely, without changing the suitability or potentiality of the sentence for performing whatever job(s) it was used to perform before the alteration. And since the 'suitability' or 'potentiality' of a sentence for the performance of a certain linguistic act is ultimately a function of the dispositions of the members of the community, a still more exact formulation would be this. The meaning-statement is justified to the extent that when 'x' is substituted for 'y' in a wide variety of sentences, and vice versa, the dispositions of members of the linguistic community with respect to employing sentences for the performance of linguistic actions is, in each case, roughly the same for the sentence produced by the alteration as for the sentence which was altered.

[c]→ This in turn suggests the following way of conceiving use. First of all we shift our initial focus of attention from word-sized units to sentences. Even apart from the above considerations this is not an implausible move. The jobs which one might speak of using words to do, such as referring, denoting, and conjoining, have the status of incomplete aspects of actions, rather than of actions in their own right. One cannot, after bursting into a room, simply refer, denote, or

---

[4]   For the present I am limiting myself to investigations of the meaning the investigator himself attaches to expressions, or the way the investigator himself uses expressions. [...] Of course, ultimately we should have to consider how statements of meaning and use, as we shall have analysed these terms, stand with respect to the possibility of inter-subjective testing.

conjoin, and then hastily depart. Referring or denoting is something one does in the course of performing a larger action unit, such as making a request, admission, or prediction. It is therefore natural that we should begin the treatment of use with units the employment of each of which is sufficiently isolable to be treated as a complete action. I think it will be discovered that the smallest linguistic actions which are isolable in the concrete are all normally performed with the use of sentences. (Of course, we have to take into account the fact that any linguistic element can function, for the nonce, as a sentence-surrogate, as in one-word answers to questions, e.g., 'John' in answer to 'Who was it that called?'.)

Having decided to begin with sentences, we can then define the notion of the use of a sentence as follows. ('s' and 't' will be used as sentence variables.)

> The use of 's' = df. The linguistic act for the performance of which 's' is uttered.[5]

Thus the use of 'Please pass the salt' is to request someone to pass some salt to the speaker; the use of 'My battery is dead' is to tell someone that the speaker's battery is out of operation; the use of 'How wonderful' is to express enthusiasm; and so on. Then if we recall the general formula relating meaning to use,

> IA. 'x' means y = df. 'x' and 'y' have the same use.

We can expand this for sentences, in terms of the above definition of the use of a sentence, as follows.

> IB. 's' means 't' = df. 's' and 't' are uttered for the performance of the same linguistic act.

For example, 'A haint caint haint a haint' means *it is impossible for one supernatural spirit to inhabit another supernatural spirit*. This is to say that the sentences 'A haint caint haint a haint' and 'It is impossible for one supernatural spirit to inhabit another supernatural spirit' have the same use in the sense that they are employed to make the same assertion.

---

[5] This formulation, and those on the next few pages, are vastly oversimplified by the pretence that each expression has only one use and only one meaning. This pretence has been adopted in order to enable us to concentrate on other problems first.

d→   Some writers on this subject object to speaking of the meaning of
a sentence.[6] They point out that sentences are not dictionary items, that
one does not learn a new language sentence by sentence, etc. I think they
are being over-scrupulous. One can understand the infrequency of talk
about the meaning of sentences simply in terms of the fact that it is
much more economical to present the semantics of a language in terms
of word-sized units with their meanings, plus rules for combining them
into sentences. And if this is the explanation, there is neither need nor
justification for denying that talk about the meaning of a sentence makes
sense on those, admittedly rare, occasions when it comes up. Inciden-
tally, the example given above is taken from one such occasion. A friend
was playing for me a record of some Kentucky mountain ballads in
which the sentence 'A haint caint haint a haint' occurred, and my friend
asked whether I knew what that meant. However, anyone who finds
such talk distasteful can simply ignore the definition of sentential meaning. Nothing that is said about the meaning of words depends on it.
(Although the discussion of word-meaning does depend on the notion of
a sentence being used to perform a certain linguistic act.)

Focusing back down on words and other sentence-components[7]
and continuing to follow the lead of the testing procedures outlined
earlier, we can define having the same use for such units as follows
(using 'u' and 'v' as variables for sentence-components):

'u' has the same use as 'v' = df. 'u' and 'v' can be substituted for
each other in sentences without changing the linguistic act potentials of each of those sentences.

Substituting into the initial meaning-use formula, we get

IC. 'u' means v = df. 'u' and 'v' can he substituted for each other
in sentences without changing the linguistic act potentials of
each of those sentences.

III

I must pause at this point to consider two objections to these formulations, the consideration of which will reveal important aspects of
our subject matter. First, it is possible for you to tell me that

[6] See, e.g., Gilbert Ryle, 'Use, Usage and Meaning', *Ar. Soc. Suppl.* Vol. XXXV (1961).
[7] For the sake of brevity I shall use the term 'word' alone, even where I intend what I am saying
to apply to all meaningful sentence-components. I believe it will be clear where the addition is to
be understood.

e→ two expressions have the same use (or the same meaning) without thereby telling me what either of them means. For example, you, as a native speaker of Japanese, might tell me that two expressions in that language have the same use without telling me what either of them means. Similarly I could know, at least on authority, that two expressions have the same use without knowing what either of them means. But then something is wrong with our formula, according to which to say that 'u' and 'v' have the same use is to say what 'u' means.

I do not believe that this objection is as formidable as it appears at first sight, although in order to meet it we shall have to sacrifice the classic simplicity of the analysis. It seems to me that when one tells someone what an expression means, he is in effect telling him that two expressions have the same use; but he uses the meaning formulation only when he supposes that his hearer already knows how to use the second expression. Thus the meaning statement is subject to a presupposition which distinguishes it from the statement of equivalence of use. The ultimate reason for the presence of this presupposition is the fact, noted earlier, that specifications of meaning have the primary function of teaching someone how to use an expression. Pointing out that 'u' has the same use as 'v' will do nothing to help you master the use of 'u' unless you already know how to use 'v'. Once we make this complication explicit the difficulty vanishes. Rather than explicitly indicating this kind of presupposition on each occasion, I shall simply serve notice once for all that in each case the meaning-statement is to be taken to be equivalent to the use-statement only when the use statement is taken with the presupposition that the hearer already knows how to use the second expression.

f→ The second difficulty could be stated as follows. The sentences 'I have just been to dinner at the White House' and 'Heisenberg just asked me to write a preface to his latest book' would both be employed to impress the hearer; but one certainly would not say that they have the same meaning, nor would one exhibit one of these sentences in order to say what the other means. Nor would the fact that 'call' can be substituted for 'dinner' in the first sentence without altering its suitability for being used to impress the hearer, do anything to show that 'call' and 'dinner' have, even in part, the same meaning.

In reflecting on this difficulty one comes to recognize a fundamental distinction between two sorts of acts one could be said to perform by uttering a sentence (for the performance of which one could utter a sentence), one of which is usable in our definitions, the other of which is not. Consider the following lists.

I	II
report	bring x to learn that...
announce	persuade
predict	deceive
admit	encourage
opine	irritate
ask	frighten
reprimand	amuse
request	get x to do...
suggest	inspire
order	impress
propose	distract
express	get x to think about...
congratulate	relieve tension
promise	embarrass
thank	attract attention
exhort	bore

I am going to use the term 'illocutionary' to denote acts of the sort we have in the first list and 'perlocutionary' to denote acts of the sort we have in the second list. I borrow these terms from the late Professor John Austin's William James lectures, *How To Do Things With Words*. Austin chose these terms because he thought of the first sort of art as done *in* uttering a sentence, the second sort as done *by* uttering a sentence. Although I put less stock in this prepositional test than did Austin (who, indeed, put it forward only with many qualifications), the terms seem felicitous. However, it will be clear to readers of Austin that my distinction does not precisely parallel his; and it would he unfortunate if my terminological appropriation should lead anyone mistakenly to hold Austin responsible for my analysis.

g→ These two classes of acts seem to me to differ in the following important ways.

(1) It is a necessary condition for the performance of a perlocutionary, but not an illocutionary, act, that the utterance have had a certain sort of result. I cannot be said to have brought you to learn something, to have moved you, frightened you, or irritated you, unless as a result of my utterance you have acquired some knowledge, have had certain feelings aroused, etc. But I could be said to have made a report, request, or admission, asked a question or offered congratulations, no matter what resulted from my utterance. I have still asked a question whether you answer it or not, or

for that matter, whether or not you pay any attention to me or understand me.[8]

(2) A perlocutionary, but not an illocutionary, act can be performed without the use of language, or any other conventional device. I can bring you to learn that my battery is dead by manoeuvring you into trying to start the car yourself, and I can get you to pass the salt by simply looking around for it. But there is no way in which I can report that my battery is dead, or request you to pass the salt, without uttering a sentence or using some other conventional device, e.g., waving a flag according to a prearranged signal. This difference is closely connected with the first. It is because a perlocutionary act is logically dependent on the production of a state of affairs which is identifiable apart from the movements which produced it, that I can be said to perform that action whenever I do anything which results in that state of affairs. The result provides a sufficient distinguishing mark.

(3) Illocutionary acts are more fundamental than perlocutionary acts in the means-end hierarchy. I can request you to pass the salt in order to get you to pass the salt, or in order to irritate, distract, or amuse you. But I could hardly amuse you in order to request you to pass the salt, or get you to know that my battery is dead in order to report that my battery is dead.

A convenient rule-of-thumb (but no more than a rule-of-thumb) is provided by the fact that an illocutionary, but not a perlocutionary, act can in general be performed by the use of a sentence which includes a specification of the action performed. I can admit doing x by saying 'I admit doing x'. I can propose that we go to the concert by saying 'I propose that we go to the concert'. But perlocutionary acts resist this mould. In uttering 'You're fine, how am I?', I may be amusing you; but I couldn't do the same thing by saying 'I amuse you that you're fine, how am I?'. If you were a fastidious and proud cook I might irritate you by saying 'Please pass the salt', but I could not do the same thing (of a perlocutionary sort) by saying 'I irritate you to please pass the salt' (though this last utterance might irritate you in some way.)

⟨h⟩→ The examples given earlier should make it clear that sameness of meaning cannot hang on sameness of perlocutionary act. On the other

---

[8] It may be an arguable point whether I can be said to have made a request of you if you have failed to understand what I said. But even if I am wrong in supposing that I can, there would still remain a sharp difference between the two sorts of actions with respect to effects. For even if that particular sort of effect is necessary for illocutionaries, it is a general blanket requirement that does nothing to distinguish between one illocutionary and another. Whereas a perlocutionary act is made the particular act it is by the condition that a certain sort of result has occurred. It is the specific character of the result that distinguishes it from other perlocutionary acts.

hand, I can find no cases in which sameness of meaning does not hang on sameness of illocutionary act. I therefore propose that the term 'linguistic act' in our definitions be restricted to illocutionary acts.

The notion of an illocutionary act is left in a rough state in this essay. [...]

IV

Having attained a measure of clarity concerning the sorts of acts involved, we can now turn to the task of correcting the oversimplification imposed on our definitions by the fiction that each expression has only one meaning and only one use. This is quite often not the case. 'Can you reach the salt?' sometimes means please pass the salt, sometimes are you able to reach as far as the salt?, and perhaps sometimes I challenge you to try to reach as far as the salt. 'Sound' has a great many different meanings – audible phenomenon, in good condition, long stretch of water, measure the depth of, etc. Moreover, this unrealistic note in our definienda is reflected in the definiens. It is rarely the case that two sentences are used alike in every context without altering linguistic act potentials. Thus corresponding to the above case of sentence-multivocality we have the fact that 'Can you reach the salt?' and 'Please pass the salt' are used to perform the same linguistic act in many contexts but not in all. And corresponding to the case of word-multivocality cited above, we have the fact that 'sound' and 'audible phenomenon' can be substituted for each other in some sentential contexts without changing linguistic act potentials, e.g. in 'Did you hear that...?' but not in others, e.g. in 'I've been sailing on the...'. [...]

In the rest of this section, Alston refines his definitions in an attempt (not wholly successful, he admits) to remove the oversimplification.

V

At the start of this section, Alston points towards some further difficulties with his definitions. *

---

* **Editors' note:** We have felt free to cut Alston's attempts to improve on his definitions, and to drop the pretence that he mentions at note 5, because in more recent work Alston finds other means of solving problems, and thus of providing a more satisfactory account than the one he presented here. See his *Sentence Meaning and Illocutionary Acts*.

[...] The general trend of the [foregoing] considerations...is to exhibit various respects in which talk about meaning, as it actually goes on, is vague, rough, and lacking in resources for reflecting all the significant distinctions within its subject-matter. It is clear that meaning-statements are dealing with sameness and difference of use among expressions, but it is also clear that they are dealing with this in a relatively unsubtle fashion. If we want analyses of meaning-statements which closely reflect their actual use, we are not going to get anything very fine-grained. If we want to talk in a more precise way about the facts that we are getting at in meaning-talk, the sameness of use idiom, as here developed, provides a more adequate instrument. [...]

We should now be in a position to see that meaning-talk is a practically convenient approximation of the theoretically more fundamental statement in terms of sameness of use. In helping someone to learn to use an expression we find another which is approximately equivalent in use, and then, neglecting the various respects in which the two are or are not identical, and degrees of equivalence in each of these respects, we simply present the second expression as an equivalent, recognizing the complexity only to the extent of making some crude distinctions between *the* meaning, the chief meaning, and *a* meaning. It is clear why this is a useful procedure, but it is important to see that the very complexities which make the equivalence of use idiom unsuitable for everyday language learning make it vastly superior for semantic theory.

However, the sameness of use idiom has deficiencies of its own. For one thing, there are expressions for which, within the language, there are no synonyms, not even approximate ones, e.g., 'is' and 'and'. And this means that within the language we can neither say what they mean nor that they have the same use as some other expression. And yet we want to say that these words are meaningful or have a meaning; each of them plays an important and relatively consistent rôle in our talk, as much as other expressions which are not subject to this disability, e.g., 'albeit' or 'lid'. No doubt it is always, or almost always, possible to find some expression in another language which is approximately synonymous. But it seems odd that we should be forced to go outside the language to make explicit the function of these words. It is not that the other language, e.g., French, is richer in resources for talking about such matters. More generally, the presence or absence of an equivalent for a word in any given language seems to be an accident *vis-à-vis* the semantic status of that word, so that it should be possible to get at that semantic status without depending on such factors. This impression can be reinforced by considering the possibility of *inventing* an equivalent and, with luck, of getting it accepted into current use. In that case a meaning-statement, and a sameness of use statement, would then become possible without any significant change having occurred in the semantic status of the word in question.

Speaking of going outside the language to find an equivalent brings to mind an important defect of our analysis of 'same use' for words, viz., that it works only for intra-lingual equivalents. Remember that our analysis is in terms of substituting the two words for each other in a variety of sentences. This operation can be carried out only when the two words belong to the same language. If we try substituting 'eau' for 'water' in 'Give me some water', nothing happens; we draw a blank.

Both of these deficiencies would be remedied by developing a way of *specifying* the use which a given word has. That would free us from any dependence on the fact that there happens to exist an approximate synonym. Presumably it would be possible to specify (in English) the use(s) of 'and' or 'is', or any other expression which we would be inclined to call meaningful. And we can bring in inter-lingual judgments of sameness of use by first separately specifying the use of each word and then basing assertions of (degrees of) equivalence of use on that. This indicates that for these reasons, as well as for many others, the next major step in the direction pointed out by this essay (after a thorough analysis of the notion of an illocutionary act) will be the development of a satisfactory way of identifying and describing the use(s) of a particular word. This is almost virgin territory. There are various terms in current use which might be thought to mark out large categories of such uses – 'denote', 'connote', 'refer', 'qualify', 'conjoin', etc.; but although some, especially 'refer', have received a great deal of discussion, some of it quite subtle, virtually nothing has been done in the direction of developing a general method for identifying, classifying and interrelating uses as a basis for semantic theory. At this point it can only be said that the difficulty of the enterprise is matched by its importance.

Commentary on Alston

In this Commentary, we shall look at how Alston thinks the idea of 'use' is best understood. And we shall reflect on some of the problems that he encounters in analysing 'meaning-statements'. But let us first place Alston's thoughts about meaning in a wider context by saying something quite general about the connection between *meaning* and *use*.

Meaning and use

Between [a]→ and [b]→ Alston considers three arguments which have led philosophers to link use with meaning. Think about these.

Alston's own project is to pin down a sense of 'use' that can be employed in the explication of *meaning*; and he finds the first two arguments unhelpful for his project. Nevertheless arguments such as these have been extremely influential in recent philosophical thinking about meaning. Argument (1) makes a metaphysical point: that the facts about what speakers do with words must in some sense settle the facts about what words mean. Argument (2) makes an epistemological point: that talk about meaning stems from the need sometimes to teach someone how to use a word (to get someone to *know* how to use it). A slightly different, and perhaps more telling, epistemological point is often made: human children learn a language (they come to *know* one), and all they have to go on, as the basis for their learning, is the use of the language among those around them. Such points at these have been summarized sometimes in the slogan 'Meaning is use'.

The slogan 'Meaning is use' serves as a reminder that language is a public, learned phenomenon; and it can help to stop us from thinking of 'meanings' as items hidden in individual speakers' minds, or as things that exist in some abstract realm set apart from human activity. Alston for his part makes it clear that he has no truck with the idea of an abstract realm of meanings. He says that he does not presuppose that there are things called 'meanings': see his footnote 3.

The last of the three arguments Alston considers is the one that he finds helpful for his project; and it is touched on below.

What notion of 'use'? More on illocution

Philosophers have sometimes raised the question, 'What are the units of significance – individual words or whole sentences?'. Alston would answer 'Both'; and this is surely the right answer. *Individual words* are the subjects of the meaning-statements that Alston starts off from; and he makes a point of saying that it is OK to think of *whole sentences* as having meaning (see [d]→). Sentence-sized units, Alston says, are what we must deal with when it comes to the question of the sort of thing that speakers do with words which fits into an account of use suited for the explication of meaning. See [c]→. This is important. It is generally accepted that in accounting for words' meaningfulness, one needs to think of individual words as combining one with another to make up meaningful sentences. The reason is that to perform a linguistic act – to do something significant with language – a speaker makes use of a whole sentence (except in cases where the context provides a way of supplementing the words she speaks).

Having established that linguistic acts performed with whole sentences are needed in his account of use, Alston recognizes that there are acts that speakers perform using sentences which don't have any bearing on questions about meaning. He gives the example of the act of impressing one's hearer at $\boxed{f} \rightarrow$. There would be a difficulty, then, if it were supposed that any old act performed by uttering a sentence belonged in the account. Alston responds by distinguishing *illocutionary* acts, which do belong, from *perlocutionary* ones, which don't. ('Illocutionary' is an Austinian term: see end of Commentary on Austin above.)

> Why and how does Alston distinguish illocutionary acts (in his list I) from perlocutionary acts (in his list II)? See passage from $\boxed{g} \rightarrow$ to $\boxed{h} \rightarrow$.

The question of what makes an act an *illocutionary* act assumes great importance if illocutionary acts are precisely the ones that provide Alston with the notion of use that he needs. Illocutionary acts are distinguished from perlocutionary acts in that (roughly!): (i) for an illocutionary act to have been performed, no result is required, except perhaps for the result which is the hearer's understanding the speaker; (ii) illocutionary acts cannot be performed except by using language; (iii) illocutionary acts may be done in order to do perlocutionary ones (whereas perlocutionary acts are not done in order to do illocutionary ones); and (iv) (though this is a 'rule of thumb' only) illocutionary acts can be performed using 'a sentence which includes a specification of the action performed' – or, to put it in Austinian terminology, they can be done using explicit performatives. Alston gives examples under all these heads; and you need to think about further examples in order to become *au fait* with the illocutionary/perlocutionary distinction.

Illocutionary acts have an importance in philosophy of language that is independent of Alston's particular project. The underlying idea is that where an act is illocutionary, performing it is *communicating* in a sense of 'communicate' which is central to language use. We return to this following the extract from Searle. (Alston's recent classification of illocutionary acts [see end of Commentary on Austin] obviously relies upon a prior conception of what the illocutionary acts are. Alston has worked out such a conception which supersedes the 'rough' one he presents here.)

From meaning-statements to use

Alston's project of analysing meaning requires a technical sense of 'use'. In attempting to capture this sense, we can now make a connection between Austin and Alston – specifically between Austin's notion of force and Alston's notion of use. Austin evidently thinks of the force of an utterance as a matter of the illocutionary act that the utterer went in for, where this is to be distinguished from what the sentence she uttered meant. So perhaps we can think of the *use* of a sentence, in Alston's sense, as something that would be specified when both the meanings of the words produced were specified *and* the force attaching to those words were specified.

Consider Alston's 'Can you reach the salt?' example at $\boxed{i}\mapsto$. How would you describe it, using Austin's notions of meaning and force?

Alston speaks of 'Can you reach the salt?' as sometimes meaning one thing, sometimes another, and sometimes a third thing. But if we think of the sentence as having a constant meaning, then we might describe it as uttered on different occasions with three different forces. Alston's explication of meaning in terms of use, then, would treat meaning as a matter of potential force. (Alston himself speaks of 'linguistic act potentials'.) This perhaps takes us to the nub of the disagreement that there is likely to be between Alston and his opponents. Alston thinks that a sentence means what it does because it potentially has the various forces that it does. Alston's opponents think that a sentence potentially has the various forces that it does because of what it means.

Even though Alston uses the word 'use' technically, the sense of 'meaning' that he hopes to analyse is not a technical one. We find the word 'means', in the relevant sense, in such everyday statements as Alston calls meaning-statements. An example is:

[MS] 'Procrastinate' means *put things off*.

Meanwhile the notion of use that requires a technical explication is found in [US].

[US] 'Procrastinate' has the same use as 'put things off'.

The italics in [MS], '*put things off*', signal that the words on the right-hand side are deployed in a special way – namely so as to exhibit an expression which has some sort of equivalence with the word on the left-hand side. The lesson of the third of the three arguments linking meaning with use (see above) is that the relevant sort of equivalence is equivalence of use.

Now, the first objection that Alston imagines to formulations on the pattern of [US] at the start of his §III is, in effect, this: [US] cannot really be equivalent to [MS], because someone could come to know that [US] was correct without gaining the faintest idea of what the word 'procrastinate' means, whereas someone who came to know that [MS] was correct *would* come to know what the word 'procrastinate' means. (This contrast can be hard to grasp if you know what these words mean, because it is hard to forget that you know. That is why Alston imagines the case where one is told that two Japanese words have the same use. See $\boxed{e}\mapsto$. Another way to see the point is to consider a meaning-statement that you actually find informative. If you don't know what 'navicular' means, then you will find ' "navicular" means *boat-shaped*' informative.)

Alston's response to the difficulty is to acknowledge that [US] is unlike [MS] insofar as understanding 'put things off' is presupposed to understanding [MS] but not to understanding [US]. This is a complication that we have to live with, Alston thinks. We may be sympathetic to Alston's response here if we consider that whenever we give any account of anything, we presuppose that we understand the words we use. Just because the account we want to give is an account of meaning, we cannot suddenly stop presupposing that we understand words.

But underlying the difficulty to which Alston responds, there is another point, which shows up at the end of his paper.

> What are the deficiencies of the sameness of use idiom that Alston recognizes from $\boxed{j}\mapsto$ on?

One deficiency of statements on the [US] pattern is that they rely on pairs of synonymous expressions; and many words simply do not have synonyms. Another deficiency is that, given the way Alston's account is developed, it depends upon sticking to a single language. The second deficiency can seem serious: it is surely possible to say something in English about what (for example) Japanese words mean. In order to do so, of course we should have to presuppose that we understand English, but we would not have to presuppose that we understand Japanese. Should not an account of meaning allow for this possibility – of saying what words mean without presupposing that we understand those very words?

Alston thinks that one could get round the deficiencies if one could find a way to *specify* the use that a word has. Here he casts a new light on the problem with [US] that we looked at. The problem was that someone could come to know that [US] was correct without coming to know what the word 'procrastinate' means. Put in another way, the problem is that [US] does not specify what 'procrastinate' means.

In the next chapter, we shall see that philosophers have attempted to develop a sort of theory for a language which can be thought of as providing specifications of meanings of its words and sentences. One of the ideas behind such a theory is that in specifying meanings, one can make use of words without having to find equivalents of them.[1] It seems that there cannot be any

---

[1] The difference between Alston's [MS] and [US] might be thought of as corresponding to a general difference between (on the one hand) statements in which words are used in order to specify words' meanings and (on the other hand) statements in which words are mentioned in order to say which words translate which other words. In distinguishing between a theory of interpretation and a translation manual, Davidson makes much of this difference: see the next chapter.

objection to using words in specifications of meanings, because, as we saw, when we give answers to questions about meaning we cannot suddenly stop presupposing that we understand words.

Introduction to Searle

John R. Searle is Mills Professor of the Philosophy of Mind and Language at the University of California, Berkeley, where he has taught since 1959. His many books include *Intentionality: An Essay in the Philosophy of Mind* (1983), *Minds, Brains and Science* (1984), *The Rediscovery of the Mind* (1992), *The Construction of Social Reality* (1995), *The Mystery of Consciousness* (1997), and *Rationality in Action* (2001). Searle calls his philosophy of mind 'biological naturalism', and he sets it against both Cartesian dualism and reductionism.

Searle's first book was *Speech Acts: An Essay in the Philosophy of Language* (1969). Here Searle builds on an Austinian notion of an illocutionary act to offer analyses of what it is to make statements, ask questions, make promises, etc. His analyses are given in terms of rules and intentional actions performed according to rules. In the very short extract from the book that we reprint here, Searle addresses the question of what it is to mean something by what one says. He takes the example of the act of telling someone something, and calls attention to what is involved in a performance of that act.

John R. Searle, 'Meaning' (extracts from Ch. 2 of *Speech Acts*)

Illocutionary acts are characteristically performed in the utterance of sounds or the making of marks. What is the difference between just uttering sounds or making marks and performing an illocutionary act? One difference is that the sounds or marks one makes in the performance of an illocutionary act are characteristically said to *have meaning*, and a second related difference is that one is characteristically said to *mean something* by the utterance of those sounds or marks. Characteristically, when one speaks one means something by what one says; and what one says, the string of sounds that one emits, is characteristically said to have a meaning. [...]

a→   But what is it for one to mean something by what one says, and what is it for something to have a meaning? To answer the first of these questions, I propose to borrow and revise some ideas of Paul

Grice. In an article entitled 'Meaning',[1] Grice gives the following analysis of the notion of 'non-natural meaning'.[2] To say that speaker S meant something by X is to say that S intended the utterance of X to produce some effect in a hearer H by means of the recognition of this intention. Though I do not think this is an adequate account [...], I think it is a very useful beginning of an account of meaning, first because it makes a connection between meaning and intention, and secondly because it captures the following essential feature of linguistic communication. In speaking I attempt to communicate certain things to my hearer by getting him to recognize my intention to communicate just those things. [...] He understands what I am saying as soon as he recognizes my intention in uttering what I utter as an intention to say that thing.

[...] Let us remind ourselves of a few of the facts we are seeking to explain. Human communication has some extraordinary properties, not shared by most other kinds of human behaviour. One of the most extraordinary is this: If I am trying to tell someone something, then (assuming certain conditions are satisfied) as soon as he recognizes that I am trying to tell him something and exactly what it is I am trying to tell him, I have succeeded in telling it to him. Furthermore, unless he recognizes that I am trying to tell him something and what I am trying to tell him, I do not fully succeed in telling it to him. In the case of illocutionary acts we succeed in doing what we are trying to do by getting our audience to recognize what we are trying to do. But the 'effect' on the hearer is not a belief or response, it consists simply in the hearer understanding the utterance of the speaker. It is this effect that I have been calling the illocutionary effect. The way the reflexive intention works then, as a preliminary formulation, is: the speaker *S* intends to produce an illocutionary effect *IE* in the hearer *H* by means of getting *H* to recognize *S*'s intention to produce *IE*.

Commentary on Searle

From Grice[1] Searle borrows the idea that speakers' meaning things is a matter of their having intentions of a particular sort. Grice's work on

---

[1]   *Philosophical Review* (July 1957), pp. 377–88.
[2]   He distinguishes 'meaning *nn*' (i.e. 'non-natural meaning') from such senses of 'mean' as occur in 'Clouds mean rain' and 'Those spots mean measles'.
[1]   H. P. (or Paul) Grice (1913–88) is famous not only for his work on the analysis of speaker meaning but also for his notions of implicature. On conversational implicature, there is more in Chapter 6.

speaker meaning has been very influential, and we shall say a little about it here before turning to the passage from Searle. Then we can focus on the kind of intention that Searle invokes in his account of telling someone something.

Grice and speaker meaning

In the Introduction to this chapter, we mentioned that some philosophers claim that an account of linguistic meaning should be *founded* in speech act theoretic notions. We have seen Alston embarking on a project pursuant to making out that claim. Another such project, and one of a more radical kind, is associated with the name of Grice. In Grice, the relevant thing that speakers do is *mean* things; and words' meanings are to be explained as what speakers *generally* mean when they use the words. If this could be made to work, then linguistic meaning would be reduced to speaker meaning: the semantic facts would be shown to boil down to facts about speakers' psychology.

This reductionist project has been called *intention-based semantics*. It is so called because *speaker meaning*, to which semantic notions are to be reduced, is itself to be analysed as a matter of speakers having intentions of a certain sort, intentions directed towards a hearer – for instance, that the hearer should form a certain belief. Now, in order for a person to have such intentions, they would need to think the sort of thought that language is used to communicate. In this project, then, thoughts of the kind that human beings express using language are supposed to exist prior to language. This is what makes the project radical. It is also what makes it objectionable to many. (It is found objectionable by those who think that human beings are the sort of thinking creatures they are *because* they are language users.)

Intention-based semantics no longer finds much favour with philosophers. Nevertheless, one idea that Grice had when first developing his thoughts about meaning continues to seem important. This idea is the one Searle refers to, which comes in a passage in Grice's first paper on meaning. It is the idea that speakers have so-called *reflexive* intentions: a speaker who means something intends her hearer to recognize the very intention that she has. Now some people have found the whole idea of reflexive intentions problematic; and certainly they may have seemed problematic to those who hoped to carry out the project of intention-based semantics. Grice himself sometimes made use of a different idea of what it is for a speaker to mean something, which can seem better suited to intention-based semantics. This different idea was that a speaker who means something has so-called *iterated* intentions. In the 1960s and 1970s, philosophers concentrated on these iterated intentions, and they suggested analyses of speaker meaning of tremendous complexity.[2] Many have objected to the complexity as artificial, and as psychologically implausible. Still, if Searle is right, then what we ought to have taken over from Grice are not iterated intentions at all. We need to go back to his reflexive intentions.

When Searle makes an objection to Grice in a passage we have cut from the extract above, he makes the point that what a speaker means when he utters a sentence is 'more than just randomly related to what the sentence he produces means in the language' he is speaking. And at [a]$\mapsto$, Searle distinguishes the question of what it is for a speaker to mean something by what they say from the question of what it is for something to have a meaning. Searle evidently wants a notion of speaker meaning that can work hand in hand with a notion of meaning that applies to the words and sentences of the speaker's language. It is such a notion of speaker meaning that he hopes to clarify here. Rather than trying to derive semantic notions from an idea of speaker meaning (as intention-based semanticists hoped to do), Searle is interested in a kind of intention which is typical of a speaker who uses words to communicate something to a hearer.

Illocutionary acts

Searle thinks of the intention of a person who performs an illocutionary act as an intention which is fulfilled when the hearer recognizes it. The intentions characteristic of illocutionary acts are ones whose recognition constitutes their fulfilment. (This is what makes them 'reflexive'.) Searle spells out the account for the particular case of telling someone something.

Notice that Searle actually speaks of *fully* succeeding in telling someone something at [b]$\mapsto$.

What might a case of telling someone something but not fully successfully be? Why do you think Searle focuses on 'fully successful' cases?

Cases in which S was less than fully successful in telling H something might be ones in which H was inattentive or was sceptical about what S had to say. We may vacillate over how to describe such cases, sometimes saying 'I *tried* to tell him, but he wasn't listening', and sometimes saying 'I told him, but he didn't take me seriously'. But even when we allow that the hearer *has* been told something by the speaker, we may think that the case falls short of a paradigm

---

[2] In a relatively simple version of the iterated intention account, a speaker who means something must intend: (i) that his utterance produce a certain response in an audience A; (ii) that A recognize intention (i); and (iii) that this recognition function as part of A's reason for the response. Much more complex versions are found in the literature, because the relatively simply account was supplemented in an attempt to avoid counterexamples. We supply a reading list on Intention-based Semantics.

piece of communication. For we may think that in a paradigm piece of communication the hearer's response is matched to the speaker's intention. Presumably Searle is concerned with what full success requires because he wants to uncover what is essential to linguistic communication. What we can take from Searle, then, is an idea of what it is to communicate. Communication between people requires understanding on the part of hearers that is attuned to speakers' attempted performances of acts like telling.

We can make a connection now with Alston on the subject of the illocutionary/perlocutionary distinction. Alston said that illocutionary acts, unlike perlocutionary ones, are not required to have results to have been performed, but he made an exception of the result that is being understood by a hearer. What Searle's account makes clear is that this is a very special result (and thus quite different from the results of perlocutionary acts). If Searle is right, then the result of an act which makes it illocutionary is this: the hearer's taking the act to be the act that it is (to be S's telling her something, or whatever). Thinking about acts that have such results can bring out the peculiar overtness of linguistic communication.

Conclusion

We can extract a general point from the readings here: any adequate philosophy of language must address questions about what speakers do with words as well as questions about how words behave. To appreciate the significance of a speaker's utterance, one needs to know not only the linguistic meaning of the sentence they utter but also the force with which they produce the utterance. It seems that a complete account of the use of a language might have as ingredients both a theory of meaning for the language and an account of those things that speakers do using language which speech act theorists are concerned with.

A two-ingredient account of language use appears to be implicit in Searle, and probably in Austin too. When Searle distinguishes between 'what a speaker means when he utters a sentence' and 'what the sentence he produces means in the language', he takes it for granted that there is a notion of linguistic meaning an account of which is separable from an account of things that speakers do using sentences of their language. When Austin distinguishes between force and meaning, he does not seem to think of speech act theory as in competition with the kind of account of meaning – of the words and sentences of a language – that Frege and his followers offer. Alston evidently wants to explain linguistic meaning in terms of things that speakers do, so that in his view, presumably, we should not look for a two-ingredient account of language use. However, as we shall see in the next three chapters, most philosophers think that we haven't accounted for linguistic meaning unless we have shown how the meanings of sentences depend upon the meanings of the words that make them up. And it is a question for Alston what account he would give of individual words as contributing to the meanings of whole sentences. (Alston characterized the use of *sentences* by employing the notion of an illocutionary act to, and he sought a way of specifying the use of individual *words*. The question for Alston concerns how specifications of word use might be brought into line with his characterizations of sentence use.)

There is a great deal more to be said about force and other speech act notions than is covered in the readings in this chapter. Searle is surely right that what a speaker means when he utters a sentence is 'more than just randomly related to what the sentence he produces means in the language'. But although the relation between speaker meaning and sentence meaning is not a random one, it would be quite wrong to think that in general what a speaker means when he utters a sentence is simply what the sentence he produces means. For speakers very often mean something different from what one could, as it were, read off from their words. We have one sort of example in which speakers do not mean what their sentences mean when speakers don't use their words literally. We shall come to non-literal language in the final chapter. But in concluding this one, we can look again at a different sort of example, by returning to one that Alston provides.

In Alston's example, the speaker uses language perfectly literally, but a hearer who took account only of what the speaker's words mean would not know what the speaker intended to communicate. The example is 'Can you reach the salt?' Alston himself said that this had a number of different meanings, depending upon the context. But intuitively 'Can you reach the salt?' is not an ambiguous sentence. In Searle's treatment of this, the sentence on an occasion can be used *both* as a question *and* as a request.[3] When it is so used, an illocutionary act of requesting the salt is performed indirectly – by way of performing an illocutionary act of questioning. This works, according to Searle, because the hearer is in a position to infer that the speaker has some purpose beyond discovering whether the salt is in the hearer's reach. The hearer can easily fathom the speaker's meaning, even though it is not simply conveyed in her words themselves. What depends upon the context, then, is not what the sentence means, but what the speaker means in using it, which the hearer is able to know.

---

[3] See *Expression and Meaning: Studies in the Theory of Speech Acts* (Cambridge University Press, 1979), p. 30. Notice that if Searle were right, then we should have an example in which two different illocutionary acts (questioning and requesting) were done by the speaker, whereas Austin and Alston both write as if a speaker does just one illocutionary thing in the case of any particular utterance. Against Searle, it might be said that the speaker who intends to request the salt doesn't go in for an *illocutionary* act of questioning (although of course the sentence she uses is a question). But whether we have two illocutionary acts here or only one doesn't affect Searle's main point, which is that the speaker makes a request using words whose meaning doesn't fit them for making a request directly.

We introduced the notion of speaker meaning above in connection with the different accounts that philosophers have given of the intentions of someone who means something. Whatever the right account of speakers' intentions may be, speaker meaning is actually an everyday notion. (Consider: 'What do you mean?') The notion assumes importance in explaining how people are able to communicate so much more than would be predictable if one considered just the words they use. And we shall come back to it in Chapter 6.

3

Meaning and Truth

Introduction

In this chapter, we return to the question: what is it for words to mean what they do? We look at an extremely influential approach to answering it associated with the slogan 'Meaning is truth-conditions', and with the name Donald Davidson.[1] We shall use this introduction to provide an initial sense of what the slogan means.

Consider Kim's utterance of the words 'George drinks'. We take her words to have a particular meaning. How might we go about saying what their meaning is? And how does the correctness of what we say depend on facts about Kim and other speakers of her language? In Chapter 1, we came across the idea that we might state the meaning of a proper name by saying whom (or what) it is that the name refers to. We also saw how Frege made allowance for the fact that two proper names that refer to the same person (or thing) might differ in meaning – as, for example, 'George Orwell' and 'Eric Blair' do. Frege called the dimension along which names with the same reference might differ in meaning *sense*; and he held that the reference of each proper name could be stated in a way guaranteed to reflect its sense. We can state the meanings of 'George Orwell' and 'Eric Blair' like this: 'George Orwell' refers to George Orwell, and 'Eric Blair' refers to Eric Blair. So we have come across a way of stating the meaning of one of the words that Kim used. This is a beginning. But it doesn't get us very far. What about the other word, 'drinks'?

---

[1] The idea that meaning might be explained by appeal to truth-conditions has figured widely in philosophy, although not all exponents of this idea pursue it in exactly the same way as Davidson.

As Mill recognized, it would be a mistake to treat predicates like 'drinks' in precisely the same way as names. And what about the meaning of the whole sentence that Kim used?

The idea encapsulated in the slogan 'Meaning is truth-conditions' is supposed to help us answer these questions. Obviously a sentence does not refer to some item in the world, as a proper name does. But a sentence can serve to provide us with information about the world. A sentence can do this because, when we understand it, we are in a position to know how the world must be if it is to be the way the sentence says it is. Suppose that you are lost in Paris, with a mastery of French just sufficient to ask where the nearest Metro stop is. You want to find out something about the world, specifically about the location of the Metro stop. If you manage to understand your French interlocutor, then that is exactly what you do find out. And we can say what it is that you come to know without using French – by saying, as it might be: the Metro is just around the next corner. When you understand a sentence, you know how things are if the sentence is true.

Returning to our original example, when you understand the sentence 'George drinks', you know that, if the world is as the sentence says it is, then George drinks. One way of putting this is to say that when one understands a sentence, one knows its *truth-conditions*. The idea that meaning is truth-conditions is the idea that one can state the meaning of a sentence by giving its truth-conditions – by saying how the world must be if the sentence is true. So we can state the meaning of 'George drinks' like this: 'George drinks' is true if and only if George drinks. Learning the truth-conditions of a sentence can put someone in a position to understand: consider that you might come to know that 'Bill marchait au tabac' is true as used by speakers of French if and only if Bill was walking to the tobacconist.

An advantage of thinking of sentence meaning as given by truth-conditions is that the notion of truth has obvious connections with the notion of reference. Much as a proper name is connected with the world through referring to an item in the world, a sentence is connected with the world through its possession of truth-conditions. And, of course, if a sentence involves a proper name – and, so, reference to an item – then whether the sentence is true will depend on whether the item the name refers to is as the sentence says it is. 'George drinks' is true if and only if the predicate 'drinks' applies to – is true of – what 'George' refers to – namely, George. That is, 'George drinks' is true if and only if George drinks. In making explicit this connection between reference and truth-conditions, we provide an answer to our earlier question about the other word used by Kim. The meaning of 'drinks' might be stated by saying that it is true of something if and only if the thing drinks. Here we see a connection between the meanings of individual words and what we said about the meanings of sentences: the meaning of an individual word is the contribution it makes to the meaning of sentences in which it occurs.

Suppose that giving sentences' truth-conditions is an adequate way of stating their meanings. Suppose, in other words, that giving sentences' truth-conditions is a way of stating the facts about what they mean. We would then have made some headway with our initial question, 'What is it for words to mean what they do?' But we would still want to know what it is that enables words to have the particular meanings we are now able to say they have. What makes a statement of truth-conditions correct?

Consider the sentence 'George sells gas'. We might say what this sentence means by saying that it is true if and only if George sells butane. For many users of the sentence this would be incorrect, however. For, as American English speakers use it, 'George sells gas' is true if and only if George sells *petrol*. It seems, then, that if we are to state correctly what words mean, we need to advert, not only to the words, but also to a language or a population of speakers. So should we simply say that (a) 'George sells gas' is true in British English if and only if (as British English speakers would say) George sells gas; (b) 'George sells gas' is true in American English if and only if (again, as British English speakers would say) George sells petrol? This is right as a description of what the words mean in the two versions of English, but we now want to know *why* the description is correct. Surely the difference in truth-conditions is a corollary of some further differences between British English speakers and American English speakers – differences in how they make use of the words in question. A statement of truth-conditions will only be correct if it reflects the facts about how speakers use words.

Of course, we are not interested only in how this particular difference in meaning depends on facts about speakers. A satisfying answer to our initial question about the nature of meaning should explain how truth-conditions depend *in general* on speakers' use of language. Generalizing in one direction, we would like to know what it is about speakers of American English that furnishes *all of their words* with the particular meanings they have. And generalizing in another direction, we seek an account applicable, in principle, to speakers of *any language*. As we shall see, philosophers have sometimes looked for a general account by considering how someone might go about figuring out what unfamiliar words mean with only speakers' uses of those words to go on. Their idea is that the way in which the truth-conditions of sentences in particular languages depends on their use is the upshot of more general connections between use and meaning – connections of a sort that might be exploited by someone trying to learn an alien language.

In this chapter, we shall see in more detail how Davidson attempts to provide an answer to our initial question about the nature of meaning by providing a truth-conditional account of statements of meaning and an account of how the correctness of such statements is responsive to speakers' linguistic behaviour. And we shall see Soames and Wright questioning aspects of Davidson's answers. In particular, we shall find them arguing that the connection between statements of meaning for a particular language and facts about speakers of the language may be less straightforward than Davidson makes it seem.

Introduction to Davidson

Donald Davidson (1917–2003) was one of the most important philosophers of the second half of the twentieth century. His ideas, presented in a series of essays from the 1960s onwards, have been influential across a range of areas from philosophy of language and mind through to metaphysics and epistemology. Many of Davidson's papers are collected in *Essays on Actions and Events* (1980, 2nd edn 2001), *Inquiries into Truth and Interpretation* (1984, 2nd edn 2001), and *Subjective, Intersubjective and Objective* (2001). His most important work in the philosophy of language can be found in *Inquiries into Truth and Interpretation*.

In 'Radical Interpretation', Davidson provides answers to two of the main questions raised in the Introduction. He does so through an investigation of what he calls *interpretation* – the activity of figuring out what a speaker's words mean. He seeks an account of what an *interpreter* – someone engaged in interpretation – might know that would enable such figuring out. Davidson also seeks an account of the basis for the interpreter's knowledge in the non-linguistic activities of speakers. He seeks one by exploring the scenario of *radical interpretation*, which is interpretation that makes use only of evidence available to someone who initially knows nothing of the speaker's language.

Davidson doesn't provide much by way of direct arguments for his view. He offers objections to alternative views, so that his positive argument is indirect. Davidson argues for certain *desiderata* (adequacy conditions) that an account should meet; some of these desiderata are derived from his objections to other positions. Then he argues that his own account meets those desiderata. In the absence of an account better able to meet them – or arguments for more demanding desiderata – we should endorse his account. This form of argument is known as *inference to best explanation*, and it is widely employed and accepted in empirical inquiry.

The central questions to consider as you read are the following. (a) Why does Davidson think that the best way of stating the meaning of the words in a language will be by stating their truth-conditions? What desiderata does Davidson think an adequate statement of meaning should meet? And why does he think that a truth-conditional statement is best able to meet those desiderata? (b) How exactly does Davidson think that the correctness of a statement of what the words in a language mean depends upon speakers of the language?

Donald Davidson, 'Radical Interpretation'[1]

Kurt utters the words 'Es regnet' and under the right conditions we know that he has said that it is raining. Having identified his utterance as intentional and linguistic, we are able to go on to interpret his words: we can say what his words, on that occasion, meant. What could we know that would enable us to do this? How could we come to know it? The first of these questions is not the same as the question what we *do* know that enables us to interpret the words of others. For there may easily be something we could know and don't, knowledge of which would suffice for interpretation, while on the other hand it is not altogether obvious that there is anything we actually know which plays an essential role in interpretation. The second question, how we could come to have knowledge that would serve to yield interpretations, does not, of course, concern the actual history of language acquisition. It is thus a doubly hypothetical question: given a theory that would make interpretation possible, what evidence plausibly available to a potential interpreter would support the theory to a reasonable degree? In what follows I shall try to sharpen these questions and suggest answers.

The problem of interpretation is domestic as well as foreign: it surfaces for speakers of the same language in the form of the question, how can it be determined that the language is the same? Speakers of the same language can go on the assumption that for them the same expressions are to be interpreted in the same way, but this does not indicate what justifies the assumption. All understanding of the speech of another involves radical interpretation. But it will help keep assumptions from going unnoticed to focus on cases where interpretation is most clearly called for: interpretation in one idiom of talk in another.[*]

What knowledge would serve for interpretation? A short answer would be, knowledge of what each meaningful expression means. In German, those words Kurt spoke mean that it is raining and Kurt was speaking German. So in uttering the words 'Es regnet', Kurt said that it was raining. This reply does not, as might first be thought, merely restate the problem. For it suggests that in passing from a description

---

[1] The term 'radical interpretation' is meant to suggest strong kinship with Quine's 'radical translation'. Kinship is not identity, however, and 'interpretation' in place of 'translation' marks one of the differences: a greater emphasis on the explicitly semantical in the former.

[*] **Editors' note:** see Quine 1960.

that does not interpret (his uttering of the words 'Es regnet') to interpreting description (his saying that it is raining) we must introduce a machinery of words and expressions (which may or may not be exemplified in actual utterances), and this suggestion is important. But the reply is no further help, for it does not say what it is to know what an expression means.

There is indeed also the hint that corresponding to each meaningful expression that is an entity, its meaning. This idea, even if not wrong, has proven to be very little help: at best it hypostasizes the problem.

Disenchantment with meanings as implementing a viable account of communication or interpretation helps explain why some philosophers have tried to get along without, not only meanings, but any serious theory at all. It is tempting, when the concepts we summon up to try to explain interpretation turn out to be more baffling than the explanandum, to reflect that after all verbal communication consists in nothing more than elaborate disturbances in the air which form a causal link between the non-linguistic activities of human agents. But although interpretable speeches are nothing but (that is, identical with) actions performed with assorted non-linguistic intentions (to warn, control, amuse, distract, insult), and these actions are in turn nothing but (identical with) intentional movements of the lips and larynx, this observation takes us no distance towards an intelligible general account of what we might know that would allow us to redescribe uninterpreted utterances as the right interpreted ones.

Appeal to meanings leaves us stranded further than we started from the non-linguistic goings-on that must supply the evidential base for interpretation; the 'nothing but' attitude provides no clue as to how the evidence is related to what it surely is evidence for.

Other proposals for bridging the gap fall short in various ways. The 'causal' theories of Ogden and Richards and of Charles Morris attempted to analyse the meaning of sentences, taken one at a time, on the basis of behaviouristic data. Even if these theories had worked for the simplest sentences (which they clearly did not), they did not touch the problem of extending the method to sentences of greater complexity and abstractness. Theories of another kind start by trying to connect words rather than sentences with non-linguistic facts. This is promising because words are finite in number while sentences are not, and yet each sentence is no more than a concatenation of words: this offers the chance of a theory that interprets each of an infinity of sentences using only finite resources. But such theories fail to reach the evidence, for it seems clear that the semantic features of words cannot be explained directly on the basis of non-linguistic phenomena. The reason is simple. The phenomena to which we must turn are the extra-linguistic interests and activities that language serves, and these are served by words only in so far as the words are incorporated in (or on occasion happen to be) sentences. But then there is no chance of giving a foundational account of words before giving one of sentences.

For quite different reasons, radical interpretation cannot hope to take as evidence for the meaning of a sentence an account of the complex and delicately discriminated intentions with which the sentence is typically uttered. It is not easy to see how such an approach can deal with the structural, recursive feature of language that is essential to explaining how new sentences can be understood. But the central difficulty is that we cannot hope to attach a sense to the attribution of finely discriminated intentions independently of interpreting speech. The reason is not that we cannot ask necessary questions, but that interpreting an agent's intentions, his beliefs and his words are parts of a single project, no part of which can be assumed to be complete before the rest is. If this is right, we cannot make the full panoply of intentions and beliefs the evidential base for a theory of radical interpretation.

$\boxed{d}\mapsto$ We are now in a position to say something more about what would serve to make interpretation possible. The interpreter must be able to understand any of the infinity of sentences the speaker might utter. If we are to state explicitly what the interpreter might know that would enable him to do this, we must put it in finite form.[2] If this requirement is to be met, any hope of a universal method of interpretation must be abandoned. The most that can be expected is to explain how an interpreter could interpret the utterances of speakers of a single language (or a finite number of languages): it makes no sense to ask for a theory that would yield an explicit interpretation for any utterance in any (possible) language.

It is still not clear, of course, what it is for a theory to yield an explicit interpretation of an utterance. The formulation of the problem seems to invite us to think of the theory as the specification of a function taking utterances as arguments and having interpretations as values. But then interpretations would be no better than meanings and just as surely entities of some mysterious kind. So it seems wise to describe what is wanted of the theory without apparent reference to meanings or interpretations: someone who knows the theory can interpret the utterances to which the theory applies.

$\boxed{e}\mapsto$ The second general requirement on a theory of interpretation is that it can be supported or verified by evidence plausibly available to an

---

[2]   See Davidson (1984), Essay 1.

interpreter. Since the theory is general – it must apply to a potential infinity of utterances – it would be natural to think of evidence in its behalf as instances of particular interpretations recognized as correct. And this case does, of course, arise for the interpreter dealing with a language he already knows. The speaker of a language normally cannot produce an explicit finite theory for his own language, but he can test a proposed theory since he can tell whether it yields correct interpretations when applied to particular utterances.

In radical interpretation, however, the theory is supposed to supply an understanding of particular utterances that is not given in advance, so the ultimate evidence for the theory cannot be correct sample interpretations. To deal with the general case, the evidence must be of a sort that would be available to someone who does not already know how to interpret utterances the theory is designed to cover: it must be evidence that can be stated without essential use of such linguistic concepts as meaning, interpretation, synonymy, and the like.

Before saying what kind of theory I think will do the trick, I want to discuss a last alternative suggestion, namely that a method of translation, from the language to be interpreted into the language of the interpreter, is all the theory that is needed. Such a theory would consist in the statement of an effective method for going from an arbitrary sentence of the alien tongue to a sentence of a familiar language; thus it would satisfy the demand for a finitely stated method applicable to any sentence. But I do not think a translation manual is the best form for a theory of interpretation to take.[3]

When interpretation is our aim, a method of translation deals with a wrong topic, a relation between two languages, where what is wanted is an interpretation of one (in another, of course, but that goes without saying since any theory is in some language). We cannot without confusion count the language used in stating the theory as part of the subject matter of the theory unless we explicitly make it so. In the general case, a theory of translation involves three languages: the object language, the subject language, and the metalanguage (the languages from and into which translation proceeds, and the language of the theory, which says what expressions of the subject language translate which expressions of the object language). And in this

---

[3] The idea of a translation manual with appropriate empirical constraints as a device for studying problems in the philosophy of language is, of course, Quine's. This idea inspired much of my thinking on the present subject, and my proposal is in important respects very close to Quine's. Since Quine did not intend to answer the questions I have set, the claim that the method of translation is not adequate as a solution to the problem of radical interpretation is not a criticism of any doctrine of Quine's.

general case, we can know which sentences of the subject language translate which sentences of the object language without knowing what any of the sentences of either language mean (in any sense, anyway, that would let someone who understood the theory interpret sentences of the object language). If the subject language happens to be identical with the language of the theory, then someone who understands the theory can no doubt use the translation manual to interpret alien utterances; but this is because he brings to bear two things he knows and that the theory does not state: the fact that the subject language is his own, and his knowledge of how to interpret utterances in his own language.

It is awkward to try to make explicit the assumption that a mentioned sentence belongs to one's own language. We could try, for example, '"Es regnet" in Kurt's language is translated as "It is raining" in mine', but the indexical self-reference is out of place in a theory that ought to work for any interpreter. If we decide to accept this difficulty, there remains the fact that the method of translation leaves tacit and beyond the reach of theory what we need to know that allows us to interpret our own language. A theory of translation must read some sort of structure into sentences, but there is no reason to expect that it will provide any insight into how the meanings of sentences depend on their structure.

A satisfactory theory for interpreting the utterances of a language, our own included, will reveal significant semantic structure: the interpretation of utterances of complex sentences will systematically depend on the interpretation of utterances of simpler sentences, for example. Suppose we were to add to a theory of translation a satisfactory theory of interpretation for our own language. Then we would have exactly what we want, but in an unnecessarily bulky form. The translation manual churns out, for each sentence of the language to be translated, a sentence of the translator's language; the theory of interpretation then gives the interpretation of these familiar sentences. Clearly the reference to the home language is superfluous; it is an unneeded intermediary between interpretation and alien idiom. The only expressions a theory of interpretation has to mention are those belonging to the language to be interpreted.

A theory of interpretation for an object language may then be viewed as the result of the merger of a structurally revealing theory of interpretation for a known language, and a system of translation from the unknown language into the known. The merger makes all reference to the known language otiose; when this reference is dropped, what is left is a structurally revealing theory of interpretation for the object language – couched, of course, in familiar words.

We have such theories, I suggest, in theories of truth of the kind Tarski first showed how to give.[4]

What characterizes a theory of truth in Tarski's style is that it entails, for every sentence s of the object language, a sentence of the form:

s is true (in the object language) if and only if *p*.

Instances of the form (which we shall call T-sentences) are obtained by replacing '*s*' by a canonical description of *s*, and '*p*' by a translation of *s*. The important undefined semantical notion in the theory is that of *satisfaction* which relates sentences, open or closed, to infinite sequences of objects, which may be taken to belong to the range of the variables of the object language. The axioms, which are finite in number, are of two kinds: some give the conditions under which a sequence satisfies a complex sentence on the basis of the conditions of satisfaction of simpler sentences, others give the conditions under which the simplest (open) sentences are satisfied. Truth is defined for closed sentences in terms of the notion of satisfaction. A recursive theory like this can be turned into an explicit definition along familiar lines, as Tarski shows, provided the language of the theory contains enough set theory; but we shall not be concerned with this extra step.

Further complexities enter if proper names and functional expressions are irreducible features of the object language. A trickier matter concerns indexical devices. Tarski was interested in formalized languages containing no indexical or demonstrative aspects. He could therefore treat sentences as vehicles of truth; the extension of the theory to utterances is in this case trivial. But natural languages are indispensably replete with indexical features, like tense, and so their sentences may vary in truth according to time and speaker. The remedy is to characterize truth for a language relative to a time and a speaker. The extension to utterances is again straightforward.[5]

What follows is a defence of the claim that a theory of truth, modified to apply to a natural language, can be used as a theory of interpretation. The defence will consist in attempts to answer three questions:

1. Is it reasonable to think that a theory of truth of the sort described can be given for a natural language?

----

[4]   A. Tarski (1956).
[5]   For a discussion of how a theory of truth can handle demonstratives and how Convention T must be modified, see S. Weinstein (1974).

2. Would it be possible to tell that such a theory was correct on the basis of evidence plausibly available to an interpreter with no prior knowledge of the language to be interpreted?
3. If the theory were known to be true, would it be possible to interpret utterances of speakers of the language?

The first question is addressed to the assumption that a theory of truth can be given for a natural language; the second and third questions ask whether such a theory would satisfy the further demands we have made on a theory of interpretation.

1. Can a theory of truth be given for a natural language?

It will help us to appreciate the problem to consider briefly the case where a significant fragment of a language (plus one or two semantical predicates) is used to state its own theory of truth. According to Tarski's Convention T, it is a test of the adequacy of a theory that it entails all the T-sentences. This test apparently cannot be met without assigning something very much like a standard quantificational form to the sentences of the language, and appealing, in the theory, to a relational notion of satisfaction.[6] But the striking thing about T-sentences is that whatever machinery must operate to produce them, and whatever ontological wheels must turn, in the end a T-sentence states the truth conditions of a sentence using resources no richer than, because the same as, those of the sentence itself. Unless the original sentence mentions possible worlds, intensional entities, properties, or propositions, the statement of its truth conditions does not.

There is no equally simple way to make the analogous point about an alien language without appealing, as Tarski does, to an unanalysed notion of translation. But what we can do for our own language we ought to be able to do for another; the problem, it will turn out, will be to know that we are doing it.

The restriction imposed by demanding a theory that satisfies Convention T seems to be considerable: there is no generally accepted method now known for dealing, within the restriction, with a host of problems, for example, sentences that attribute attitudes, modalities, general causal statements, counterfactuals, attributive adjectives, quantifiers like 'most', and so on. On the other hand, there is what seems to me to be fairly impressive progress. To mention some examples, there is the work of Tyler Burge on proper

---

[6] See J. Wallace (1970), and Davidson (1984), Essay 3.

names,[7a] Gilbert Harman on 'ought',[7b] John Wallace on mass terms and comparatives,[7c] and there is my own work on attributions of attitudes and performatives,[7d] on adverbs, events, and singular causal statements,[7e] and on quotation.[7f]

If we are inclined to be pessimistic about what remains to be done (or some of what has been done!), we should think of Frege's magnificent accomplishment in bringing what Dummett calls 'multiple generality' under control.[8] Frege did not have a theory of truth in Tarski's sense in mind, but it is obvious that he sought, and found, structures of a kind for which a theory of truth can be given.

The work of applying a theory of truth in detail to a natural language will in practice almost certainly divide into two stages. In the first stage, truth will be characterized, not for the whole language, but for a carefully gerrymandered part of the language. This part, though no doubt clumsy grammatically, will contain an infinity of sentences which exhaust the expressive power of the whole language. The second part will match each of the remaining sentences to one or (in the case of ambiguity) more than one of the sentences for which truth has been characterized. We may think of the sentences to which the first stage of the theory applies as giving the logical form, or deep structure, of all sentences.

2. Can a theory of truth be verified by appeal to evidence available before interpretation has begun?

Convention T says that a theory of truth is satisfactory if it generates a T-sentence for each sentence of the object language. It is enough to demonstrate that a theory of truth is empirically correct, then, to verify that the T-sentences are true (in practice, an adequate sample will confirm the theory to a reasonable degree). T-sentences mention only the closed sentences of the language, so the relevant evidence can consist entirely of facts about the behaviour and attitudes of speakers in relation to sentences (no doubt by way of utterances). A workable theory must, of course, treat sentences as concatenations of expressions of less than sentential length, it must introduce semantical notions like satisfaction and reference, and it must appeal to an ontology of sequences and the objects ordered by the sequences. All this apparatus is properly viewed as theoretical construction, beyond the reach of direct verification. It has done its work provided only it entails testable results in the form of T-sentences, and these make no mention of the

---

[7]   (a) T. Burge (1973). (b) G. Harman (1975). (c) Wallace (1972). (d) Davidson (1984), Essays 7 and 8. (e) Davidson (1980), Essays 6–10. (f) See Davidson (1984), Essay 6.
[8]   M. Dummett (1973).

machinery. A theory of truth thus reconciles the demand for a theory that articulates grammatical structure with the demand for a theory that can be tested only by what it says about sentences.

[k]→ In Tarski's work, T-sentences are taken to be true because the right branch of the biconditional is assumed to be a translation of the sentence truth conditions for which are being given. But we cannot assume in advance that correct translation can be recognized without pre-empting the point of radical interpretation; in empirical applications, we must abandon the assumption. What I propose is to reverse the direction of explanation: assuming translation, Tarski was able to define truth; the present idea is to take truth as basic and to extract an account of translation or interpretation. The advantages, from the point of view of radical interpretation, are obvious. Truth is a single property which attaches, or fails to attach, to utterances, while each utterance has its own interpretation; and truth is more apt to connect with fairly simple attitudes of speakers.

[l]→ There is no difficulty in rephrasing Convention T without appeal to the concept of translation: an acceptable theory of truth must entail, for every sentence s of the object language, a sentence of the form: s is true if and only if p, where 'p' is replaced by any sentence that is true if and only if s is. Given this formulation, the theory is tested by evidence that T-sentences are simply true; we have given up the idea that we must also tell whether what replaces 'p' translates s. It might seem that there is no chance that if we demand so little of T-sentences, a theory of interpretation will emerge. And of course this would be so if we took the T-sentences in isolation. But the hope is that by putting appropriate formal and empirical restrictions on the theory as a whole, individual T-sentences will in fact serve to yield interpretations.[9]

[m]→ We have still to say what evidence is available to an interpreter, evidence, we now see, that T-sentences are true. The evidence cannot consist in detailed descriptions of the speaker's beliefs and intentions, since attributions of attitudes, at least where subtlety is required, demand a theory that must rest on much the same evidence as interpretation. The interdependence of belief and meaning is evident in this way: a speaker holds a sentence to be true because of what the sentence (in his language) means, and because of what he believes. Knowing that he holds the sentence to be true, and knowing the meaning, we can infer his belief; given enough information about his beliefs, we could perhaps infer the meaning. But radical interpretation should rest on evidence that does not assume knowledge of meanings or detailed knowledge of beliefs.

[9] For essential qualifications see footnote 11 of Essay 2 in Davidson (1984).

A good place to begin is with the attitude of holding a sentence true, of accepting it as true. This is, of course, a belief, but it is a single attitude applicable to all sentences, and so does not ask us to be able to make finely discriminated distinctions among beliefs. It is an attitude an interpreter may plausibly be taken to be able to identify before he can interpret, since he may know that a person intends to express a truth in uttering a sentence without having any idea what truth. Not that sincere assertion is the only reason to suppose that a person holds a sentence to be true. Lies, commands, stories, irony, if they are detected as attitudes, can reveal whether a speaker holds his sentences to be true. There is no reason to rule out other attitudes towards sentences, such as wishing true, wanting to make true, believing one is going to make true, and so on, but I am inclined to think that all evidence of this kind may be summed up in terms of holding sentences to be true.

Suppose, then, that the evidence available is just that speakers of the language to be interpreted hold various sentences to be true at certain times and under specified circumstances. How can this evidence be used to support a theory of truth? On the one hand, we have T-sentences, in the form:

(T) 'Es regnet' is true-in-German when spoken by x at time t if and only if it is raining near x at t

On the other hand, we have the evidence, in the form:

(E) Kurt belongs to the German speech community and Kurt holds true 'Es regnet' on Saturday at noon and it is raining near Kurt on Saturday at noon.

We should, I think, consider (E) as evidence that (T) is true. Since (T) is a universally quantified conditional, the first step would be to gather more evidence to support the claim that:

(GE) $(x)(t)$ (if x belongs to the German speech community then (x holds true 'Es regnet' at t if and only if it is raining near x at t)).

The appeal to a speech community cuts a corner but begs no question: speakers belong to the same speech community if the same theories of interpretation work for them.

The obvious objection is that Kurt, or anyone else, may be wrong about whether it is raining near him. And this is of course a reason for not taking (E) as conclusive evidence for (GE) or for (T); and a reason not to expect generalizations like (GE) to be more than generally true. The method is rather one of getting a best fit. We want a theory that satisfies the formal constraints on a theory of truth, and that maximizes agreement, in the sense of making Kurt (and others) right, as far as we can tell, as often as possible. The concept of maximization cannot be taken literally here, since sentences are infinite in number, and anyway once the theory begins to take shape it makes sense to accept intelligible error and to make allowance for the relative likelihood of various kinds of mistake.[10]

The process of devising a theory of truth for an unknown native tongue might in crude outline go as follows. First we look for the best way to fit our logic, to the extent required to get a theory satisfying Convention T, on to the new language; this may mean reading the logical structure of first order quantification theory (plus identity) into the language, not taking the logical constants one by one, but treating this much of logic as a grid to be fitted on to the language in one fell swoop. The evidence here is classes of sentences always held true or always held false by almost everyone almost all of the time (potential logical truths) and patterns of inference. The first step identifies predicates, singular terms, quantifiers, connectives, and identity; in theory, it settles matters of logical form. The second step concentrates on sentences with indexicals; those sentences sometimes held true and sometimes false according to discoverable changes in the world. This step in conjunction with the first limits the possibilities for interpreting individual predicates. The last step deals with the remaining sentences, those on which there is not uniform agreement, or whose held truth value does not depend systematically on changes in the environment.[11]

This method is intended to solve the problem of the interdependence of belief and meaning by holding belief constant as far as possible while solving for meaning. This is accomplished by assigning truth conditions to alien sentences that make native speakers right when plausibly possible, according, of course, to our own view of

---

[10]   For more on getting a 'best fit', see Essays 10–12 in Davidson (1984).
[11]   Readers who appreciate the extent to which this account parallels Quine's account of radical translation in Chapter 2 of *Word and Object* will also notice the differences: the semantic constraint in my method forces quantificational structure on the language to be interpreted, which probably does not leave room for indeterminacy of logical form; the notion of stimulus meaning plays no role in my method, but its place is taken by reference to the objective features of the world which alter in conjunction with changes in attitude towards the truth of sentences; the principle of charity, which Quine emphasizes only in connection with the identification of the (pure) sentential connectives, I apply across the board.

what is right. What justifies the procedure is the fact that disagreement and agreement alike are intelligible only against a background
of massive agreement. Applied to language, this principle reads: the
more sentences we conspire to accept or reject (whether or not
through a medium of interpretation), the better we understand the
rest, whether or not we agree about them.

The methodological advice to interpret in a way that optimizes
agreement should not be conceived as resting on a charitable assumption about human intelligence that might turn out to be false. If we
cannot find a way to interpret the utterances and other behaviour of a
creature as revealing a set of beliefs largely consistent and true by our
own standards, we have no reason to count that creature as rational,
as having beliefs, or as saying anything.

Here I would like to insert a remark about the methodology of my
proposal. In philosophy we are used to definitions, analyses, reduc-
tions. Typically these are intended to carry us from concepts better
understood, or clear, or more basic epistemologically or ontologically,
to others we want to understand. The method I have suggested fits
none of these categories. I have proposed a looser relation between
concepts to be illuminated and the relatively more basic. At the centre
stands a formal theory, a theory of truth, which imposes a complex
structure on sentences containing the primitive notions of truth and
satisfaction. These notions are given application by the form of the
theory and the nature of the evidence. The result is a partially interpreted theory. The advantage of the method lies not in its free-style
appeal to the notion of evidential support but in the idea of a powerful theory interpreted at the most advantageous point. This allows us
to reconcile the need for a semantically articulated structure with a
theory testable only at the sentential level. The more subtle gain is
that very thin evidence in support of each of a potential infinity of
points can yield rich results, even with respect to the points. By
knowing only the conditions under which speakers hold sentences
true, we can come out, given a satisfactory theory, with an interpretation of each sentence. It remains to make good on this last claim. The
theory itself at best gives truth conditions. What we need to show is
that if such a theory satisfies the constraints we have specified, it may
be used to yield interpretations.

*3. If we know that a theory of truth satisfies the formal and empirical
criteria described, can we interpret utterances of the language for
which it is a theory?*
A theory of truth entails a T-sentence for each sentence of the object
language, and a T-sentence gives truth conditions. It is tempting,

therefore, simply to say that a T-sentence 'gives the meaning' of a sentence. Not, of course, by naming or describing an entity that is a meaning, but simply by saying under what conditions an utterance of the sentence is true.

But on reflection it is clear that a T-sentence does not give the meaning of the sentence it concerns: the T-sentence does fix the truth value relative to certain conditions, but it does not say the object language sentence is true because the conditions hold. Yet if truth values were all that mattered, the T-sentence for 'Snow is white' could as well say that it is true if and only if grass is green or $2 + 2 = 4$ as say that it is true if and only if snow is white. We may be confident, perhaps, that no satisfactory theory of truth will produce such anomalous T-sentences, but this confidence does not license us to make more of T-sentences.

A move that might seem helpful is to claim that it is not the T-sentence alone, but the canonical proof of a T-sentence, that permits us to interpret the alien sentence. A canonical proof, given a theory of truth, is easy to construct, moving as it does through a string of biconditionals, and requiring for uniqueness only occasional decisions to govern left and right precedence. The proof does reflect the logical form the theory assigns to the sentence, and so might be thought to reveal something about meaning. But in fact we would know no more than before about how to interpret if all we knew was that a certain sequence of sentences was the proof, from some true theory, of a particular T-sentence.

A final suggestion along these lines is that we can interpret a particular sentence provided we know a correct theory of truth that deals with the language of the sentence. For then we know not only the T-sentence for the sentence to be interpreted, but we also 'know' the T-sentences for all other sentences; and of course, all the proofs. Then we would see the place of the sentence in the language as a whole, we would know the role of each significant part of the sentence, and we would know about the logical connections between this sentence and others.

If we knew that a T-sentence satisfied Tarski's Convention T, we would know that it was true, and we could use it to interpret a sentence because we would know that the right branch of the biconditional translated the sentence to be interpreted. Our present trouble springs from the fact that in radical interpretation we cannot assume that a T-sentence satisfies the translation criterion. What we have been overlooking, however, is that we have supplied an alternative criterion: this criterion is that the totality of T-sentences should (in the sense described above) optimally fit evidence about sentences held true by native speakers. The present idea is that what Tarski assumed outright for each T-sentence can be indirectly elicited by a holistic constraint. If that constraint is adequate, each T-sentence will in fact yield an acceptable interpretation.

A T-sentence of an empirical theory of truth can be used to interpret a sentence, then, provided we also know the theory that entails it, and know that it is a theory that meets the formal and empirical criteria.[12] For if the constraints are adequate, the range of acceptable theories will be such that any of them yields some correct interpretation for each potential utterance. To see how it might work, accept for a moment the absurd hypothesis that the constraints narrow down the possible theories to one, and this one implies the T-sentence (T) discussed previously. Then we are justified in using this T-sentence to interpret Kurt's utterance of 'Es regnet' as his saying that it is raining. It is not likely, given the flexible nature of the constraints, that all acceptable theories will be identical. When all the evidence is in, there will remain, as Quine has emphasized, the trade-offs between the beliefs we attribute to a speaker and the interpretations we give his words. But the resulting indeterminacy cannot be so great but that any theory that passes the tests will serve to yield interpretations.

References

Burge, T. (1973). 'Reference and Proper Names', *Journal of Philosophy* 70: 425–39.

Davidson, D. (1980). *Essays on Actions and Events* (Oxford: Clarendon Press).

Davidson, D. (1984). *Inquiries into Truth and Interpretation* (Oxford: Clarendon Press).

Dummett, M. A. E. (1973). *Frege: Philosophy of Language* (London: Duckworth).

Harman, G. (1975). 'Moral Relativism Defended', *Philosophical Review* 84: 3–22.

Quine, W. V. (1960). *Word and Object* (Cambridge, Mass.: MIT Press).

Tarski, A. (1956). 'The Concept of Truth in Formalized Languages', in his *Logic, Semantics, Metamathematics* (Oxford: Clarendon Press).

Wallace, J. (1970). 'On the Frame of Reference', *Synthèse* 22: 61–94.

Wallace, J. (1972). 'Positive, Comparative, Superlative', *Journal of Philosophy* 69: 773–82.

Weinstein, S. (1974). 'Truth and Demonstratives', *Noûs* 8: 179–84.

---

[12]   See footnote 11 of Essay 2 and Essay 12 of Davidson (1984).

Commentary on Davidson

In the Introduction to Davidson, you were invited to think about two main questions. The first was the question why Davidson favours a truth-conditional approach to meaning. In order to take a broader perspective, let us think about a pair of related questions that are less narrowly focused than this one:

(QI) What form should a statement of the facts about what the words of a language mean take?

(QII) Under what conditions will a statement count as having captured the facts about word meaning?

An answer to (QI) needs to say, in general terms, how we should go about stating word meanings. One answer to this question would be that we should do so by giving truth-conditions. An answer to (QII) will tell us what conditions an adequate answer to (QI) should meet. Here one proposal would be that an answer to (QI) should explicitly state that which is known by ordinary speakers who know the language.

Our second question in the Introduction was about how Davidson thinks of the speakers of a language as relating to a statement of what the words of their language mean. Again, in order to broaden our perspective, we should turn to two more general questions:

(QIII) What sorts of fact are we entitled to appeal to in explaining the facts about word meaning?

(QIV) How are meaning-facts to be explained on the basis allowed by our answer to (QIII)?

An answer to (QIII) would specify a range of facts upon which meaning-facts depend. One proposal would be that meaning-facts depend upon speakers' use of language; another would be that meaning-facts depend upon what speakers know. An answer to (QIV) would say how meaning-facts depend on, say, facts about speakers' language use – how, for example, differences in the former are linked to differences in the latter.

We shall use this commentary as a way of eliciting Davidson's answers to (QI)–(QIV). That will provide a basis for attempting to evaluate Davidson's view. In the course of doing so, we shall try to highlight features of Davidson's view that our next two authors, Soames and Wright, pick up on.

Theories of meaning

Read [d]⇥ to [e]⇥ and [g]⇥ to [h]⇥. What is Davidson's answer to (QI)?

Davidson proposes that a statement of the facts about what words mean should take the form of a certain sort of *theory*, a *theory of interpretation* – i.e., a *theory of meaning* or *semantic theory*. These phrases are ambiguous. They can be understood as applying to a particular way of answering just (QI). But they can be understood as applying to an overall account of what it is for words to mean what they do, and Davidson himself sometimes uses them in that way.

Focusing on Davidson's answer to (QI), the basic idea here is quite simple. The way in which sentences are built from words means that a small supply of words can build an enormous (infinite) number of different sentences. To see this, consider

(1) Jen believes that Guy smokes
(2) Jen believes that Guy believes that Jen smokes
(3) Jen believes that Guy believes that Jen believes that Guy smokes

Just on the basis of elements in (1), we are able to construct novel sentences like (2) and (3), via principles that seem to know no limit. With sufficient time (and energy), we could keep going like this forever. If our aim is to state the meanings of all English sentences, we can't just provide a list, pairing sentences with their meanings. We'd never complete it. A *theory* is just a statement able to generate new statements in a systematic way (in some contexts, the new statements would be *predictions*). A finitely stated theory concerning words and ways of combining words into whole sentences might serve to generate meaning-statements about all English sentences.

Davidson holds that the best way to provide a theory of meaning for a language is to provide a theory that generates a statement about the circumstances in which each sentence of the language is true – its *truth-conditions*. This idea, first suggested by Frege, is plausible. If you know what a sentence means, and know that the sentence is true, then you know something about the circumstances. If you know what 'It's raining' means, and know that it is true, then you know that it's raining, so that you might think to carry an umbrella, for instance. Davidson's way of obtaining this result involves, roughly, *identifying* meaning with truth-conditions. In due course, we shall see that Soames objects to such an identification on the same sort of grounds as Frege objected to Mill's identification of a proper name's meaning with the object it refers to.

Desiderata

Davidson's aim is to support his answer to (QI) through an inference to best explanation. You should pay careful attention to the desiderata he places on an answer.

At ⌐a⌐→, Davidson raises two questions. Try to explain Davidson's answer to (QII). Can you think of reasons for endorsing Davidson's requirements rather than the stronger requirements he envisages but rejects?

Davidson requires that an adequate statement of meaning-facts be one such that *if it were known* it would suffice for interpretation, for 'saying what [a speaker's] words...meant'. Corresponding to the second component in an overall account, Davidson seeks an account of the facts that determine what a speaker in fact means. One might expect Davidson to require an account of the facts to which people actually appeal in trying to figure out what other speakers are saying. Davidson requires less. He seeks an account of facts such that, *if they were known*, they would enable a speaker to figure out the meaning-facts. We shall see that Soames and Wright have things to say about Davidson's answer to (QII).

At ⌐b⌐→, Davidson shows his hand on his answer to (QIII). The answer takes the form of a further requirement on the conditions to be imposed on finding a theory of meaning. Here, he says that the facts that determine what a speaker's words mean must be available to someone engaged in *radical interpretation*.

Davidson claims that interpretation among speakers of the same language is dependent on facts accessible to the radical interpreter. Is this claim plausible? What are Davidson's reasons for the claim: and are they compelling?

Other accounts

Between ⌐b⌐→ and ⌐c⌐→, Davidson considers and rejects two accounts. One of these takes the meanings of words as primitive; the other takes the relation between non-linguistic goings on and the meanings of words as primitive. Davidson's complaint is that neither account is illuminating. Indeed he seems to think they are worse than unilluminating: 'Appeal to meanings leaves us stranded further than we started from the non-linguistic goings-on that must supply the evidential basis for interpretation'. Davidson's suggestion is that it is difficult to see how to connect facts about what a speaker's words mean with the facts available to a radical interpreter. It is worth reflecting on this suggestion.

What sort of behaviour, available to a radical interpreter, might be cited in support of one or another claim about what a speaker means?

It is important to Davidson that this question is a difficult one to answer. This emerges at $\boxed{k}\mapsto$, where Davidson finds an analogous question about the *truth-conditions* of a speaker's words to be a much easier question to answer.

Between $\boxed{c}\mapsto$ and $\boxed{d}\mapsto$, Davidson considers and rejects three other accounts. The arguments against these views are used to generate additional desiderata on an adequate account.

State the three accounts found between $\boxed{c}\mapsto$ and $\boxed{d}\mapsto$ in your own words. What are Davidson's arguments against each of the three accounts? What desiderata do his arguments generate?

It is helpful here to reflect on Davidson's answers to (QI) and to (QIV). With that in mind, let us look at the three accounts in sequence.

1. A desideratum derived from consideration of the causal theories seems designed to support Davidson's idea that a theory of truth could supply a statement of the meaning-facts. It might seem, for example, that sentences like 'Bill smokes' and 'George drinks' connect fairly directly with speakers' behaviour. But the more complex 'Bill smokes or George drinks' seems not to. And what about 'Two plus two equals four', which is more *abstract*? Davidson's answer to (QI) is that a statement of the meaning-facts takes the form of a theory, generating statements about sentence meaning from statements about the meanings of words and the way they are combined. This answer allows for less direct connections between sentences and speakers' behaviour.

2. The second account seeks to tie individual words directly to bits of behaviour. Although Davidson thinks that an adequate account must explain how sentence meanings are determined by word meanings, he rejects this account too. His argument is that words only connect with behaviour via their roles within sentences. If that is right, it supports an element in Davidson's answer to (QIV) (see $\boxed{j}\mapsto$ and following $\boxed{n}\mapsto$), according to which the meanings of words are posited just in order to support the meanings of sentences in which those words occur.

3. The third account (which is one deriving from Grice[1]) seeks to account for sentence-meaning via appeal to the particular intentions with which the sentences are uttered. Davidson's main objection is extremely compressed, and amounts to the claim that one can't know speakers' intentions until one understands their words, and that an account of their words must be part of an overall account of the speaker's psychology. The import of Davidson's objection only emerges later in his answer to (QIV), from $\boxed{m}\mapsto$. There, Davidson presents an account of interpretation in

---

[1]   See the Commentary on Searle in the previous chapter. Davidson is here addressing a position like *intention-based semantics*.

which assignments of meaning to a speaker's words and assignments to the speaker of psychological attitudes – e.g., beliefs and intentions – are interdependent.

From $\boxed{d}\mapsto$ to $\boxed{f}\mapsto$, Davidson discusses the emerging desiderata on an adequate account in more detail. Use these passages to develop your account of Davidson's answers to (QI)–(QIII).

From $\boxed{f}\mapsto$ to $\boxed{g}\mapsto$, Davidson considers and rejects another answer to (QI), according to which a statement of meaning-facts involves a translation from the language to be interpreted into the interpreter's language.

Imagine trying to construct a translation of a language you don't speak into a language you do speak. (Something close is offered by, for example, French–English phrase books or dictionaries.) Recall Davidson's answer to (QII). Davidson thinks the account in terms of translation fails to meet his adequacy condition. Explain why he thinks this. Is he right?

For a translation manual to serve as an answer to (QI) – to provide an adequate statement of meaning-facts – Davidson requires that knowledge of what the translation manual states must suffice for understanding the language to be interpreted. Consider a sample statement derivable from a French–English phrase book:

(4) The French sentence 'Il pleut' translates the English sentence 'It's raining'

Suppose 'Il pleut' is the target of interpretation. Does (4) meet Davidson's condition? It appears so. But Davidson argues that the appearance is illusory. It is an artefact of the fact that the sentence doing the translating, 'It's raining', is in the language in which the translation manual is stated, so that being in a position to understand the manual enables one to understand the translating sentence. But the translation manual fails to make *explicit* what one would need to know in order to understand the French sentence.[2] In order to see this consider a sample statement from a possible (if somewhat unusual) translation manual, a French–German phrase book, also written in English:

(5) The French sentence 'Il pleut' translates the German sentence 'Es regnet'

---

[2] In Chapter 2, we saw Alston present a similar account. Alston agreed that such an account fails to make meaning-facts explicit. In his terms, the account fails to *specify* word meanings.

Someone who knows only English can know what (5) states. Does that knowledge suffice for understanding the French sentence? No. One would also need to know what 'Es regnet' means, something that is not stated in (5). The obvious solution would be to add to (5) a statement of what 'Es regnet' means. We could then put that statement together with (5) in order to specify the meaning of 'Il pleut'. Although that would suffice for understanding 'Il pleut', it is 'unnecessarily bulky'. If we had a statement of the meaning of 'Es regnet', we could have used it to directly state the meaning of 'Il pleut' without running the dogleg through translation.

Theories of truth as semantic theories

Between $\boxed{g}\mapsto$ and $\boxed{h}\mapsto$, Davidson presents his account of how interpretations are to be stated, his answer to (QI). Since his account is extremely compressed, let us pause to fill in some details.

What is wanted is a theory that states sentence-meanings in such a way that knowing what is stated suffices for understanding. We need to state the information that is conveyed to a speaker of English by a translation manual containing statements like (4). And we need to ensure that it is impossible to know this information without grasping the association of the target sentence with what is expressed by the translating sentence. To explain how we can do this, we need a distinction between *using* words, and *mentioning* them. One mentions words when one talks *about* them. One uses a sentence when one talks *with* it. Both (4) and (5) *mention* the French sentence 'Il pleut'. Both *use* the words 'The French sentence'. Mentioned words belong to the *object-language*, the language which one is talking *about*; used words belong to the *metalanguage*, in which the talking is done. To know what is stated when words are mentioned, one need only know which words are mentioned; one need not also grasp their content. But to know what is stated when words are used, one must grasp their content. So, we need something like a translation manual, except that it must associate mentioned target sentences with sentences *used* in the statement.

An account meeting this requirement can be provided by using the truth predicate, 'is true', as a device for moving from mentioned sentences to their used counterparts. For example, consider (6):

(6) 'Snow is white' is true in English if and only if (iff) snow is white

As in the translation account, the sentence mentioned on the left, 'snow is white', is matched with a sentence that has the same meaning on the right. But it is impossible to know what (6) states without grasping the content of the matching sentence. This is because the matching sentence – the right-hand side of the biconditional (iff) – is *used* and not simply mentioned.

This *disquotational* feature of the truth predicate is enshrined in the condition that theories of truth for particular languages must meet *Convention T*. For every sentence, *s*, in the object-language and every sentence, *p*, in the metalanguage such that *p* translates *s*, an adequate theory of truth must include an instance of (T):[3]

(T) *s* is true (in the object language) if and only if *p*

A theory meeting this condition includes, for every object-language sentence, an instance of (T), a so-called *T-sentence*. In a T-sentence, a target sentence is matched with a used sentence that means the same as the target.

Davidson's central claim – his answer to (QI) – is that a theory that includes a T-sentence for every sentence in a language can serve as an interpretation of the language. Knowing what the theory states can suffice for knowing what sentences in the language mean.

Davidson's claim, if acceptable, carries an important additional benefit. Alfred Tarski showed how to state theories of truth for languages containing indefinitely many sentences. Tarski presented a way of deriving T-sentences from truth-relevant properties of words and their modes of combination. Tarski's machinery might, then, be used to explain how the meanings of words and their modes of combination fix the meanings of sentences in which they occur.[4]

We now know Davidson's answer to (QI). If he is right, then we have the makings of an account of how the meanings of sentences depend on the meanings of their parts. In order to show that his account is acceptable, Davidson must supply affirmative answers to the three questions he raises at ⟨h⟩↦. His question 1 arises because Tarski's machinery only works for formally simple languages. So application of that machinery to natural languages is dependent on whether they can be treated by that machinery. Davidson lists some salient issues (⟨i⟩↦).[5] For present purposes, let's assume that Davidson's first question gets an affirmative answer and turn to the others. We can think about how Davidson's questions 2 and 3 relate to our (QII)–(QIV).

Radical interpretation

From ⟨k⟩↦ to ⟨l⟩↦, Davidson explains how his understanding of T-sentences differs from Tarski's. What is the key difference? What reason does Davidson give for the difference?

---

[3] Davidson, amongst others, sometimes writes that a truth-theory entails or implies, rather than includes, instances of (T). What he means is that part of a truth-theory, the axioms, entails the rest, the theorems.
[4] See the Apppendix to this chapter for an introduction to Tarski's truth-theoretic machinery.
[5] See the reading list on Semantic Theories for Natural Language.

Given Davidson's answer to (QI), his answer to (QIV) needs to explain how one can move from allowed evidence – allowed given his answer to (QIII) – to T-sentences. Since Davidson seeks a method of radical interpretation, he cannot assume knowledge of which sentences of the metalanguage translate target sentences. Davidson seeks to show how evidence can be gathered for the *truth* of T-sentences – where a T-sentence, like any other biconditional, is true when, and only when, the sentences flanking the biconditional have the same truth-value. This makes it easier to answer (QIV). However, Davidson notes, 'It might seem that there is no chance that if we demand so little of T-sentences, a theory of interpretation will emerge.' Davidson attempts to address this concern immediately, and from $\boxed{o}\rightarrow$. Notice how answers to the questions interact. The less one demands of an answer to (QI), the easier it becomes to answer (QIV). The less one demands of an answer to (QIV), the less compelling becomes one's answer to (QI).

From $\boxed{m}\rightarrow$, Davidson presents a difficulty. Explain his response to the difficulty in your own words.

The difficulty arises because the radical interpreter is not entitled to assume anything about the subject's language or the content of his beliefs prior to interpretation. So she can't appeal to detailed knowledge of the content of her subject's beliefs in determining what the subject's words mean. But without some knowledge of what the subject believes, it seems impossible to determine what his words mean, since meaning and belief are interdependent. Davidson's solution to this difficulty is to allow the interpreter access to the speaker's attitudes towards sentences – in particular, the fact that the speaker holds certain sentences true in certain circumstances. Since these attitudes do not make fine distinctions amongst sentences – they merely sort sentences into two piles, those held-true and those not held-true – Davidson is willing to allow the interpreter access to them prior to filling in a detailed scheme of interpretation. On the basis of matching sentences held-true with the circumstances in which they are held true, Davidson thinks that an interpreter will be able to work his way into a full interpretation, gradually assigning meanings and beliefs to his subject. Crudely, the idea is that the interpreter's task is to match sentences with the conditions in which they are true, thus matching the left-hand sides of T-sentences with their right-hand sides. The claim is, roughly, that evidence like (KE) can support T-sentences like (KT):

(KE) Kurt holds true 'Es regnet' when, and only when, it's raining near Kurt

(KT) 'Es regnet' is true in Kurt's language iff it's raining near Kurt

Following ⬚n→, Davidson raises another difficulty. What is the difficulty? How does Davidson respond?

The difficulty concerns the interdependence of meaning and belief. Kurt utters 'Es regnet' not simply because of what 'Es regnet' means and the present meteorological circumstances. Rather, Kurt utters 'Es regnet' in part because of what he *believes* about the weather. Suppose that whenever it rains, Kurt believes that it's snowing (perhaps he has got a defect of vision). In that case, (KE) would be evidence, not for (KT), but for (KS):

(KS) 'Es regnet' is true in Kurt's language iff it's snowing near Kurt

In the absence of an independent grip on the subject's beliefs, it is impossible to determine what the subject's words mean. We need a way of holding belief fixed so that we can begin to solve for meaning. Davidson's solution, which has become known as the *Principle of Charity*, is (very crudely) that an interpreter should assume, initially and then insofar as it is reasonable to do so, that his subject's beliefs are true (as far as the interpreter can tell). The Principle has been much discussed, and Davidson gives only a quick argument for it in the present paper.[6] Assuming Kurt's weather beliefs are true, we can reinstate the move from (KE) to (KT), as required.

From ⬚o→, Davidson raises an important objection to the proposal that knowing what is stated by a theory of truth for a speaker's language can suffice for understanding. This objection is re-presented by Soames and we shall consider it in the course of discussing his paper.[7]

Introduction to Soames

Scott Soames is Professor of Philosophy at the University of Southern California. Previously, he taught at Princeton University. He has written numerous books and articles, including *Understanding Truth* (1999), *Beyond Rigidity* (2002), and the two-volume *Philosophical Analysis in the Twentieth Century* (2003).

In the extract reprinted here, Soames argues against a common view of the relation between a statement of meaning-facts and speakers' ability to understand, or their 'semantic competence'. The common view is that speakers' semantic competence resides in their knowledge of the facts stated by a semantic theory. Soames raises two objections to the common view that

[6] See the reading list on Radical Interpretation and the Principle of Charity.
[7] For more discussion see the reading list on Davidson's Philosophy of Language.

may seem to strike against Davidson's view. Thus reflection on Soames's argument will help you to understand elements in Davidson's view and some of the difficulties it may be thought to face.

Some questions to ask in reading this extract are the following. (1) What is the precise content of the view Soames seeks to refute? (2) How does that view relate to Davidson's view? (3) What are Soames's arguments? (4) Are they compelling?

Scott Soames, 'Semantics and Semantic Competence' (extract)

a⟼ The central semantic fact about language is that it carries information about the world. The central psycho-semantic fact about speakers is that they understand the claims about the world made by sentences of their language. This parallel suggests an intimate connection between semantic theories and theories of semantic competence. A semantic theory should tell us what information is encoded by sentences relative to contexts. Since competent speakers seem to grasp this information, and since the ability to correctly pair sentences with their contents seems to be the essence of semantic competence, it might appear that a semantic theory is itself a theory of competence.

Such a view has, I think, been quite common. We are all familiar with syntacticians who tell us that their grammars are attempts to specify the grammatical knowledge in virtue of which speakers are syntactically competent. This knowledge is generally thought to include, though perhaps not be limited to, knowledge of which strings of words are genuine (or grammatical) sentences of the language. By extension, it would seem that a semantic theory ought to specify the semantic knowledge in virtue of which speakers are semantically competent. Presumably, this knowledge will include, though perhaps not be limited to, knowledge of the truth conditions of sentences.

The reason for focusing on truth conditions arises from the representational character of semantic information. A sentence that represents the world as being a certain way implicitly imposes conditions that must be satisfied if the world is to conform to the way it is represented to be. Thus, the semantic information encoded by a sentence determines the conditions under which it is true. There may be more to semantic information than truth conditions, but there is no information without them. Thus, if semantic competence consists in grasping the information semantically encoded by sentences, then it would seem that it must involve knowledge of truth conditions.

b→ The view that linguistic theories of syntax and semantics may double as psychological theories of competence comes in two main forms. The more modest form requires theories of syntax and semantics to provide theorems knowledge of which explains competence; however, it does not require these theories to specify the cognitive states and processes causally responsible for this knowledge. In particular, it does not require the theoretical machinery used in linguistic theories to derive theorems about grammaticality or truth conditions to be internally represented components of any psychologically real system. It simply leaves open the question of how the knowledge characterized by correct linguistic theories is psychologically realized.

The more robust form of the view that linguistic theories may double as psychological theories of linguistic competence tries to answer this question. According to this view, syntactic and semantic theories are required not only to characterize the linguistically significant properties of sentences, but also to do so on the basis of whatever internally represented cognitive apparatus is responsible for speakers' recognition of these properties. In short, linguistic theories are required to specify both the knowledge needed for linguistic competence, and the mechanisms from which that knowledge arises.

c→ Although the robust approach has been accepted by many syntacticians, it has also been highly controversial. I believe it should be rejected for syntax as well as semantics.[1] However, it is not my present target. What I would like to argue is that, at least in the case of semantics, the modest approach is also incorrect. Semantic theories do not state that which a speaker knows in virtue of which he or she is semantically competent. Semantic competence does not arise from knowledge of the semantic properties of expressions characterized by a correct semantic theory.

1. Knowledge of Truth Conditions

d→ Let us begin with the basics. The job of semantics is to specify the principles by which sentences represent the world. It is impossible to represent the world as being a certain way without implicitly imposing conditions that must be satisfied if the world is to conform to the representation. Thus, whatever else a semantic theory must do, it must at least characterize truth conditions. For certain languages, there are two standard ways of doing this. One involves the construction of a Davidson-style theory of truth for the language. The other

---

[1] See Soames (1984) and (1985).

involves the construction of a theory, or definition, of a relativized notion of truth for the language, truth-with-respect-to a world w. Both theories can be thought of as entailing statements that give the truth conditions of sentences. In one case, these statements are instances of schema T; in the other they are instances of schema T_W. (Instances are formed by replacing 'P' with a paraphrase of the sentence replacing 'S'.)

Schema T: 'S' is true (in L) iff P
Schema T_W: 'S' is true (in L) w.r.t. w iff in w, P

Now it might be thought that knowledge of truth conditions is the key to semantic competence, and hence that competence is the result of knowing that which is stated by each instance of one or the other of these schemas. But this is false. Knowledge of truth conditions (in this sense) is neither necessary nor sufficient for understanding a language.

It is not sufficient since it is possible for even the logically omniscient to know that

(1) 'Firenze è una bella città' is true in Italian (w.r.t. w) iff (in w) Florence is a beautiful city

while failing to believe that

(2) 'Firenze è una bella città' means in Italian that Florence is a beautiful city

and believing instead that

(3) 'Firenze è una bella città' means in Italian that Florence is a beautiful city and arithmetic is incomplete.

All that is necessary for this is for the agent to believe that (for any w) Florence is a beautiful city (in w) iff (in w) Florence is a beautiful city and arithmetic is incomplete. In short, true beliefs about truth conditions are compatible with false beliefs about meaning.

One sometimes sees it suggested that this problem can be avoided by requiring the agent's knowledge of truth conditions to encompass everything forthcoming from a finitely axiomatized theory of truth for the entire language. But this is not so. Given a first-order language, one can always construct extensionally correct, finitely axiomatizable truth theories each of whose theorems resembles (4) in correctly giving the truth conditions of an object language sentence, while failing to provide a basis for paraphrase or interpretation.

(4) 'Firenze è una bella città' is true in Italian (w.r.t. w) iff (in w) Florence is a beautiful city and arithmetic is incomplete.

Now imagine a person ignorant of the object language being given a finitely axiomatized theory of truth. Unless he is also given information about meaning, he will have no way of knowing whether it can be used to paraphrase and interpret object language sentences. In particular, he will have no way of knowing whether the result of substituting 'means that' for 'is true iff' in its theorems will produce truths, as in (2), or falsehoods, as in (3). Knowledge of truth conditions, even of this systematic sort, is simply not sufficient for knowledge of meaning, or semantic competence.[2]

It is also not necessary. Knowledge of truth conditions, as I have described it, presupposes possession of a metalinguistic concept of truth. Thus, the claim that such knowledge is necessary for understanding meaning entails that no one can learn or understand a language without first having such a concept. But this consequence seems false. Certainly, young children and unsophisticated adults can understand lots of sentences without understanding 'true', or any corresponding predicate.

Must they, nevertheless, possess a metalinguistic concept of truth, even though they have no word for it? I don't see why. Perhaps it will be suggested that a person who lacked such a concept couldn't be a language user, since to use language one must realize that assertive utterances aim at truth and seek to avoid falsity. But this suggestion is confused. The child will get along fine so long as he knows that 'Momma is working' is to be assertively uttered only if Momma is working; 'Daddy is asleep' is to be assertively uttered only if Daddy is asleep; and so on. The child doesn't have to say or think to himself, 'There is a general (but defeasible) expectation that for all x, if x is a sentence, then one is to assertively utter x only if x is true.' It is enough if he says or thinks to himself, 'There is a general (but defeasible) expectation that one should assertively utter "Mommy is working"

---

[2] For a more extended discussion of this point, as it applies to Davidsonian truth theories, see J. A. Foster (1976). Although Foster presses the point forcefully against Davidson, he exempts approaches based on theories of truth-with-respect-to a possible world from his criticism. This, in my opinion, is a mistake. In addition to extending to such theories, the basic argument can be made to apply to any attempt to found meaning, or knowledge of meaning, on theories of truth with respect to a circumstance – no matter how fine grained we make the circumstances (provided standard recursive clauses in the truth theory are maintained).

only if Mommy is working; assertively utter "Daddy is asleep" only if Daddy is asleep; and so on for every sentence.' For this, no notion of truth is needed.[3]

The point here is not that this truthless substitute says exactly the same thing as its truth-containing counterpart. In general, metalinguistic truth is not eliminable without loss of expressive power, and practical utility. The point is that it is not necessary to have such a concept in order to learn and understand a language. Thus, knowledge of that which is expressed by instances of schemas T and T_W is neither necessary nor sufficient for semantic competence.

[...]

References

Soames, S. (1984). 'Linguistics and Psychology', *Linguistics and Philosophy* 7/2: 155–79.

Soames, S. (1985). 'Semantics and Psychology', in *The Philosophy of Linguistics*, ed. J. J. Katz (Oxford: Oxford University Press), pp. 204–26.

Foster, J. A. (1976). 'Meaning and Truth Theory,' in *Truth and Meaning*, ed. G. Evans and J. McDowell (Oxford: Clarendon Press), pp. 1–32.

Commentary on Soames

Soames's target

As we have seen, some philosophers – e.g., Davidson – hope to illuminate linguistic meaning through reflection on the nature of semantic theories. Soames does not seek to undermine the project of those philosophers. However, he thinks that we should not expect that project to immediately answer every question about meaning. In particular, Soames denies that reflection on the nature of semantic theories will supply a straightforward account of speakers' semantic competence. Why does he issue that denial? Let's start

---

[3] I am not here suggesting that the child really must repeat or represent the latter (truthless) instruction to himself. Thus, I am not claiming that the child must have the notion assertive utterance in order to learn a language. My point is a negative one. If there is anything to the suggestion that language learners must realize that assertive utterances aim at truth, that realization need not involve possession of a concept of truth. It may be that the child ultimately must come to realize something like the following: One is to say that Mommy is working only if Mommy is working, that Daddy is asleep only if Daddy is asleep; and so on. A truth predicate comes in handy in stating such a rule, for it allows one to eliminate the 'and so on' in favor of quantification over assertions plus predications of truth. But handy or not, this logical technology is not necessary for learning.

trying to answer this question by trying to answer the first question raised in the Introduction to Soames: What is the view Soames seeks to refute?

> Read the paragraph starting at $\boxed{c}\mapsto$ and the paragraph starting at $\boxed{e}\mapsto$. How does Soames characterize his target?

Soames's central claim is put in two ways. First, at $\boxed{c}\mapsto$: 'Semantic theories do not state that which a speaker knows in virtue of which she is semantically competent'. Second, at $\boxed{e}\mapsto$: 'Knowledge of truth conditions...is neither necessary nor sufficient for understanding a language'. Soames takes his central claim to be enough to undermine something he calls *the modest approach* and, perhaps, something he calls *the robust approach*.

> What, in Soames's view, is 'the central semantic fact about language'? What, in Soames's view, is 'the central psycho-semantic fact about speakers'? Soames attempts to make plausible a certain view of the connection between the semantic fact and the psycho-semantic fact. What is this view? How does Soames attempt to make it plausible?

Soames seeks to make it initially plausible that semantic facts are intimately related to speakers' semantic competence. He begins by characterizing the semantic facts as information about the world carried by language. He is less forthcoming in his characterization of semantic competence. Here, he tells us 'competent speakers *seem to grasp* [semantic] information', and 'the ability to correctly pair sentences with their contents *seems to be* the essence of semantic competence' [emphasis added]. The only place that Soames offers an unguarded characterization of semantic competence is when he allows that competent speakers 'understand the claims about the world made by sentences of their language'. Notice that this characterization is neutral on the relation between semantic facts and what speakers know, since 'understanding claims made by sentences' need not be identified with 'knowing that sentences carry such-and-such information about the world'. Although Soames seeks to make plausible the common view about the relation between semantic theory and semantic competence, he is careful not to commit himself to the view.

> From $\boxed{b}\mapsto$ to $\boxed{c}\mapsto$ Soames distinguishes between two forms of the view that a theory of semantics may double as a theory of semantic competence, the *modest* and *robust approaches* mentioned above. What are these views?

The statements that comprise a semantic theory come in two sorts. *Axioms* are explicitly set out in the theory and used to generate theorems. *Theorems* are statements derivable from the axioms. Axioms deal with semantic properties of words – e.g., conditions on reference and satisfaction – and with modes of combination – e.g., the effect of combining singular terms and predicates.[1]

The *modest view* of the relation between semantic theory and semantic competence has it that a semantic theory will 'provide theorems knowledge of which explains competence'; but, it 'does not require these theories to specify the cognitive states and processes causally responsible for the knowledge'. So, the modest view has positive and negative components. The positive component asserts that semantic competence resides in speakers' knowledge of the *theorems* of a semantic theory. The negative component denies that (or is neutral whether) the *axioms* of the theory are 'internally represented components of any psychologically real system'.

The *robust view* agrees with the modest approach in its positive claim, but it disagrees with the negative claim. According to the robust view, each axiom of a semantic theory gives the content of a psychological state causally responsible for knowledge of the theory's theorems.

> Which of the two views do you think is closer to Davidson's view? Is either view equivalent to Davidson's?

On Davidson's view, an adequate semantic theory is such that, *if* someone knew the theory, they would (thereby) be semantically competent. So Davidson does not require that knowledge of any part of a semantic theory – axioms or theorems – plays a role in constituting semantic competence. It appears to be, as it were, even more modest than the modest view, to be *minimal*.

> At ⟦d⟧↦, Soames characterizes the job of a semantic theory. Put his characterization into your own words.

There are two central features. One feature, the importance of which is visible immediately, is that a semantic theory must 'specify the principles by which sentences represent the world'. Thus, a semantic theory must mention sentences in order to state the representational properties of those sentences. Crudely, a semantic theory will state relations between sentences and the circumstances they represent. The second feature is that, in order to perform the feat of specifying a relation between words and world, a semantic theory will be forced to employ the concept of truth (or a similar concept). The importance of this feature is revealed from ⟦g⟧↦, when it becomes clear that it is the role of the concept of truth in semantic theories that prevents them from serving as theories of what speakers know.

At ⟦e⟧↦, Soames makes his central claim: 'Knowledge of truth conditions [as stated by a semantic theory] is neither necessary nor sufficient for under-

---

[1]   For more detail, see the Appendix to this chapter.

standing a language.' The rest of this commentary looks at his arguments for this claim.

Is knowledge of a semantic theory sufficient for competence?

From $\boxed{e}{\mapsto}$ to $\boxed{g}{\mapsto}$, Soames argues against the sufficiency claim. He aims to show that one can know truth-conditions without being semantically competent.

> Explain Soames's argument between $\boxed{e}{\mapsto}$ and $\boxed{g}{\mapsto}$. Compare Davidson's argument (from $\boxed{o}{\mapsto}$ in Davidson).

Soames appears to state a problem for the sufficiency claim that Davidson recognized.[2] In fact, there would appear to be two closely related problems.

The first problem

The first problem arises as follows. First, assume that a proposed theory of what is known by semantically competent speakers can be tested by replacing occurrences of 'is true' in its theorems with 'means...that' and then judging the plausibility of the output. If the target theorem is

(1) 'Snow is white' is true in English iff snow is white,

replacement yields

(2) 'Snow is white' means in English that snow is white.

This seems plausible. Since T-sentences are biconditionals, they are true so long as left-and right-hand sides agree in truth-value. It follows that, since both 'Snow is white' and 'Grass is green' are true, (3) is true.

(3) 'Snow is white' is true in English iff grass is green

So, if the only constraint we place on the theorems outputted by a semantic theory is that the theorems be true, we must count T-sentences like (3) as theorems of our semantic theory. But the replacement test now yields

(4) 'Snow is white' means in English that grass is green

---

[2]   Arguments like Soames's became widely known through a paper by John Foster (cited by Soames). For additional discussion, see the reading list on Truth-theories and Understanding. Foster's views are also discussed in the extract from Wright.

which is obviously not something a semantic theory should say. The problem arises because 'iff' forms an *extensional* context, so that the truth-value of a sentence formed from it is dependent just on the truth-values of the sentences on its right-and left-hand sides. By contrast, 'means that' forms an *intensional* context, so that replacement by a sentence with the same truth-value can fail to preserve the truth-value of the whole. Hence, there is no guarantee that a theory that issues in true T-sentences issues in T-sentences able to sustain 'means...that' replacement. The name *interpretive* is sometimes given to T-sentences and truth-theories that do sustain 'means...that' replacement.

> Can you think of any responses that might be made to this difficulty? Once you have spent some time reflecting on this, you may find it helpful to look back at Davidson – from ⌈o⌉→ in Davidson.

Davidson attempted to respond to this difficulty by placing constraints on a semantic theory additional to the requirement that it deliver true T-sentences. His response appeals to the fact that a T-sentence in an adequate theory must be derived from axioms able to generate true T-sentences for each sentence in the target language. A theory which yielded the unwanted result in (3) might be one that included (5) among its axioms:

(5) 'Snow' refers in English to grass

But now the axioms will potentially allow *false* theorems like (6) to be derived:

(6) 'Snow is falling from the sky' is true iff grass is falling from the sky

Soames claims, however, that if it is possible to construct an interpretive truth-theory for a language, then it will be possible to construct a true but non-interpretive theory (see ⌈f⌉→). Another response is required.

A second response derives from reflection on the way assignments of meaning interact with assignments of psychological attitudes like beliefs. As we saw in Chapter 1, Frege held that 'Hesperus' and 'Phosphorus' differ from one another in sense. One way of understanding his view is as follows. We know that (Ax1) is a true reference axiom for 'Hesperus':

(Ax1) 'Hesperus' refers in English to Hesperus

But, since Hesperus *is* Phosphorus, (Ax2) is also true:

(Ax2) 'Hesperus' refers in English to Phosphorus

A theory containing (Ax1) allows the derivation of theorem (H1):

(H1) 'Hesperus is bright' is true in English iff Hesperus is bright

By contrast, a theory containing (Ax2) allows the derivation of theorem (H2):

(H2) 'Hesperus is bright' is true in English iff Phosphorus is bright

Only (H1) sustains 'means that' replacement. So, a theory containing (Ax1), unlike a theory containing (Ax2), is interpretive. But why should we prefer an interpretive theory?

Suppose we consider adding a reference axiom for 'Phosphorus' to each of the theories:

(Ax3) 'Phosphorus' refers in English to Phosphorus

Each theory now enables us to derive (P1):

(P1) 'Phosphorus is bright' is true in English iff Phosphorus is bright

Our subject utters 'Hesperus is bright'. According to (H1), this provides evidence that he believes that Hesperus is bright. According (H2), it provides evidence that he believes that Phosphorus is bright. Which assignment of belief is most plausible? Given (P1), our hypothesis is that the speaker believes that 'Phosphorus is bright' is true iff Phosphorus is bright. Hence, if we assign to the speaker the belief that Phosphorus is bright, we should predict that he holds true 'Phosphorus is bright'.

If we held that knowing a theory containing (Ax2) and (Ax3) would suffice for understanding English, then we should be committed to saying that a rational English speaker will hold true 'Hesperus is bright' when and only when he holds true 'Phosphorus is bright'. But if we hold that knowing a theory containing (Ax1) and (Ax3) would suffice for understanding English, we allow that a rational English speaker may hold true one of the sentences and not the other. And we do think that a rational English speaker can fail to believe that Hesperus is Phosphorus – i.e., knowing that Hesperus is Phosphorus is not part of understanding English. A rational speaker can hold true 'Hesperus is bright' without holding true 'Phosphorus is bright'. Since only an interpretive theory, like that containing (Ax1) and (Ax3), sustains this result, we prefer interpretive truth-theories. From Frege's perspective, we prefer theories that capture, not only reference, but also sense. Whereas a theory containing (Ax2) captures reference, it fails to capture sense.

The foregoing supports the idea that the ultimate source of our preference for interpretive truth-theories is the interaction of assignments of meaning with assignments of psychological attitudes. How does that help solve the first problem? It provides an additional constraint on acceptable truth-theories that can be stated without appeal to the notion of meaning: they must sustain plausible assignments of belief.

The second problem

The second problem emerges from the first. Suppose that one has found a way of ensuring that truth-theories are interpretive. The second problem arises because nothing in an interpretive truth-theory *states* that it is interpretive. All that is made explicit in its theorems is that certain biconditionals are *true*. But knowing that a biconditional is true does not suffice for knowing *that* it is interpretive.

Can you think of a response to the second problem? Once you have spent time reflecting on this, look at Davidson's response (see from $\boxed{o} \mapsto$ in Davidson again). His response has two components. Try to distinguish and then explain them.

The first component of Davidson's response concedes that knowledge of an interpretive truth-theory does not in itself suffice for understanding. In order to understand a language one also needs to know that the truth-theory is interpretive. This concession might seem to undermine the capacity of Davidson's account to illuminate meaning. If interpretiveness is characterized in terms of plausible replacement of 'is true' with 'means . . . that', knowing that a truth-theory is interpretive must be based on knowing what target sentences mean. Davidson avoids this difficulty by requiring, as sufficient for understanding, knowledge that a truth-theory meets constraints formulated without appeal to the notion of meaning – constraints supplied in response to the first difficulty.

The second component involves claiming that any theory able to meet the constraints – e.g., able to deliver T-sentences for every sentence in the language and to fit with plausible assignments of psychological attitudes, etc. – will serve all the purposes of interpretation. Crudely, Davidson thinks that differences that are not revealed through radical interpretation don't make a real difference.

Is knowledge of a semantic theory necessary for competence?

From $\boxed{g} \mapsto$ Soames argues that knowledge of the theorems of a truth-theory is not necessary for semantic competence. He aims to show that one can be semantically competent without knowing truth-conditions.

Consider Soames's argument from $\boxed{g} \rightarrow$. Is it plausible that children and unsophisticated adults lack a concept of truth? How might it be shown? Is it plausible that those who lack the concept of truth might be semantically competent? How might one determine whether they are?

Soames's claim that infants and the unsophisticated lack the concept of truth is, at least partly, an empirical claim. It is the sort of claim that psychologists might try to investigate and, as with other such investigations, the results might be surprising. However, the important question is whether it is *possible* that there be competent language users who lack the concept of truth.

One way of approaching this question would be to try to decide what range of abilities a creature would have to exhibit in order to count as semantically competent. Presumably, it is not enough that one is able to make some seemingly linguistic sounds. Otherwise, a CD player would count as semantically competent. A less minimal requirement would be that production of such sounds be keyed in an appropriate way to circumstances. The question now is whether a parrot able to perform some range of seemingly appropriate responses to circumstances – for example, making a 'cracker' sound when presented with a cracker – is to count as competent. Again, the answer is plausibly negative, so we might continue adding abilities and testing the result. The line where semantic competence emerges will be somewhere between the CD player and the obviously competent (such as sophisticated adults). But it is very difficult to locate that line. Although untutored judgements about cases will likely play a role in drawing it, development of a theory of competence is also crucial. In developing such theories, we need to think about the full range of capacities exhibited by competent speakers including, not only those exhibited by *speakers* – as in the cases mentioned here – but also those exhibited by *hearers*.

If successful, would Soames's argument serve to refute the modest view? Would it undermine Davidson's minimal view?

Davidson's minimal view has it that a semantic theory should be such that, if someone did know the theory, they would be competent. So Davidson is not committed to the claim that knowledge of T-sentences, or of any other statements involving a truth predicate, is necessary for understanding a language. But what is the relation between a semantic theory and what competent speakers *do* know?

One reason that knowing what is stated by an interpretive T-sentence might be taken to suffice for understanding is that it suffices for grasp of the content (or meaning) expressed by its right-hand side. Indeed, knowing an interpretive T-sentence suffices, not only for grasping the right content, but also for associating that content with a sentence of the object-language that expresses it. If recognition of such associations is all that is required for understanding, then it may be possible to explain the relation between theory and competence without running foul of Soames's objection. We might allow that competent speakers know the associations stated by a semantic theory without requiring that they know the theory. (Something like this may be what Soames had in mind at $\boxed{e} \!\mapsto$ in restricting his claims to a sense of knowledge of truth-conditions that involves knowing *in full* what is stated by T-sentences.)

Introduction to Wright

Crispin Wright is Leverhulme Research Professor and Bishop Wardlaw Professor at the University of St Andrews. He is also a regular visiting professor at Columbia University. His books include *Wittgenstein on the Foundations of Mathematics* (1980), *Frege's Conception of Numbers as Objects* (1983), *Truth and Objectivity* (1992), *Rails to Infinity* (2001), and *Saving the Differences* (2003). The extract reprinted here is from his collection of papers *Realism, Meaning, and Truth* (1987, 2nd edn 1993).

In the extract, Wright argues that Davidson's apparently insouciant attitude towards questions about speakers' knowledge is in tension with other elements in his view. Given Davidson's answer to (QII), Wright finds it difficult to understand the motivation for his requirement that semantic theories be *compositional* – that they show the meanings of whole sentences to be based on the meanings of their parts. Since Davidson's argument for using truth-theories in his semantic theory is based, to a large extent, on their capacity to sustain compositionality, it is crucial for the friend of Davidson's proposal to answer Wright's charge. Wright himself makes some suggestions about this. Ultimately, Wright's point is that the charge can be answered only by taking a firmer stand on the relation between speakers and semantic theories than Davidson seems willing to envisage.

Some questions to consider are the following. (1) What is Wright's argument for the claim that a justification for compositionality cannot be derived from Davidson's answer to (QII)? (2) Is the argument compelling? (3) If it is, should we give a more robust answer to (QII), or should we give up the compositionality requirement? (4) If we opt for a more robust answer to (QII), can we provide one compatibly with Soames's concerns?

Crispin Wright, 'Theories of Meaning and Speakers' Knowledge' (extract)

I

[...]
Davidson intends that a theory of truth is acceptable as a theory of meaning only if

(i) it is finitely axiomatizable and
(ii) it delivers a T-theorem for each declarative sentence of the object-language in a manner that reflects the semantic structure discerned in that sentence.[1]

Why should the theory be finitely axiomatizable? Different passages in Davidson's writings suggest slightly different answers. Sometimes the thought is that understanding a language involves the capacity to make sense of no end of distinct expressions, and that this (potential) infinity contrasts sharply with the finitude of our capacities in general (most relevantly, presumably, the finitude of our capacities for information storage). A finitely based theory of meaning of the sort he is recommending will, Davidson believes, give us an insight into

...how an infinite aptitude can be encompassed by finite accomplishments.[2]

A neighbouring but distinct point is that if a language admits of characterization by a finitely based Davidsonian theory, then we have an insight into how the language can be learnable.[3] The point is distinct because creatures with infinite capacities for information storage but no other infinitary abilities could only learn finitely much in a finite time. Finally, not quite the same thought as either of these is the idea that:

[1] See the indexed references under *finiteness requirement* in Davidson (1984) and pp.56–7 which the indexer missed. For those quite innocent of these matters, the 'T-theorems' take the form illustrated by

'Snow is white' is true if and only if snow is white,

whereby the quoted sentence is used to characterize its own truth-conditions and hence – controversially – its own meaning.
[2] Davidson (1984), p. 8.
[3] See, e.g., Davidson (1984), Essay 2, opening paragraph.

Speakers of a language can effectively determine the meaning or meanings of an arbitrary expression (if it has a meaning) and...it is the central task of a theory of meaning to show how this is possible.[4]

The theory of meaning is thus to contribute towards the explanation of how speakers can understand sentences which are novel to them. This thought is different because the question would arise – if it is a good question at all – for infinite creatures too, and for finite languages which, while semantically structured, possess no indefinitely iterable devices of the sort which generate a potential infinity of meaningful sentences.

a→ However, the marginal distinctions among the questions, 'How can finite minds have infinite abilities?', 'How can languages be learnable?', 'How can speakers determine the meanings of novel utterances?', are not important. What is important is that the capacity of Davidsonian theory to assist in the provision of answers to any of them requires that it be admissible to think of actual speakers as equipped with the information codified in the axioms of a successful Davidsonian theory, and as prone to deploy that information in ways reflected by the derivations of meaning delivering theorems afforded by the theory. Whether the theory aspires to cast light on *our* ability, finite as we are, to master a potentially infinite language, or *our* ability to complete the learning of the language, or on *our* ability to understand novel utterances, or on all three, success must depend, it seems, on its being permissible to suppose that it encodes information which *we* actually possess.

b→ If Davidson is somewhat inexplicit about this, Dummett is not. A very definite commitment to the idea that the explanatory ambitions of a theory of meaning depend upon recourse to some idea of speakers' *implicit knowledge* of its axiomatic contents is evinced in his writings on the topic. For instance:

> A theory of meaning will, then, represent the practical ability possessed by a speaker as consisting in his grasp of a set of propositions; since the speaker derives his understanding of a sentence from the meanings of its component words, these propositions will most naturally form a deductively connected system. The knowledge of these propositions that is attributed to a speaker can only be an implicit knowledge. In general, it cannot be demanded of someone who has any given practical ability that

---

[4] Davidson (1984), Essay 2, p. 35.

he have more than an implicit knowledge of those propositions by means of which we give a theoretical representation of that ability.[5]

In an earlier paper, Dummett refers to

...our intuitive conviction that a speaker derives his understanding of a sentence from his understanding of the words composing it and the way they are put together.[6]

and relates Davidsonian theory to this intuitive conviction by the remark that:

What plays the role, within a theory of meaning of Davidson's kind, of a grasp of the meanings of the words is a knowledge of the axioms governing these words.[7]

Further:

It is one of the merits of a theory of meaning which represents mastery of a language as the knowledge not of isolated, but of deductively interconnected propositions, that it makes due acknowledgement of the undoubted fact that a process of derivation of some kind is involved in the understanding of a sentence.[8]

For Dummett, the explanatory ambitions of a theory of meaning would seem to be entirely dependent upon the permissibility of thinking of speakers of its object-language as knowing the propositions which its axioms codify and of their deriving their understanding of (novel) sentences in a manner mirrored by the derivation, in the theory, of the appropriate theorems.

c→   There is accordingly a case for saying that, whatever their differences, Dummett and Davidson are in broad agreement about the interest of the project of a theory of meaning of this sort, and about the manner in which such a theory needs to be interpreted if it is to sustain that interest; and that they share a broad, underlying assumption about the nature of linguistic competence, viz, that it is fruitfully to be compared – at least in its basics – to any open-ended computational ability which – like, say, the ability to do simple arithmetical

---

[5] Dummett (1976), p. 70.   [6] Dummett (1975), p. 109.
[7] Ibid.   [8] Ibid., p. 112.

multiplications – deploys finite information in rule-prescribed ways. The difference is just that the knowledge which constitutes understanding of a language is gained, for the most part, not from an explicit statement – in contrast, e.g. with the multiplication tables, or the rules of chess – but by immersion in the practice of speaking the language in question.

d→ That we understand novel utterances because we understand the words in them and significance of the way in which they are put together is apt to strike one as a platitude. But it is no platitude that the sort of project which Dummett, explicitly, and Davidson, implicitly, seem to have in view makes philosophical sense. If the gap is not immediately apparent, it ought to suffice to reflect that the platitude need only be regarded as describing a feature of the 'grammar' of *misunderstanding*: nobody may properly be described as misunderstanding a sentence unless guilty of some more specific misunderstanding, either of words deployed within it or of its syntax. Contraposing, we have the incontestable claim that if someone understands the vocabulary and syntax of a significant sentence, then they understand the (type) sentence. Platitude is left behind when the antecedent of this conditional is taken to describe an ulterior state of information which *enables* a subject to understand the sentence.

Let us say that a theory is *compositional* just in case it meets the two Davidsonian constraints, (i) and (ii), noted above. Section II is concerned with the question whether there can be any good motive for insisting on compositionality in theories of meaning which avoids recourse to the idea of actual speakers' implicit knowledge. Baker and Hacker[9] have recently described Davidson's comparative inexplicitness on the topic as 'artful' – their thought being, I imagine, that, for the sort of reason outlined above, the questions on which Davidson hopes for illumination cannot be answered by Davidsonian theorizing unless implicit knowledge is invoked, but that Davidson has preferred not to elaborate on the issue, perceiving it for the Pandora's Box which they believe it to be. However that may be, it is important to be clear whether, besides the three mentioned, there is any different question, not directly concerned with the capacities of actual speakers, which devising a compositional theory of meaning might help to answer. Only if there is not is there any danger, should it emerge that there is absolutely nothing to be made of the notion of implicit knowledge, that Davidson's project will prove to have been a waste of time.

[...]

---

[9] Baker and Hacker (1984), p. 324.

II

e→   Doubts about the notion of implicit knowledge have surfaced frequently in the literature, even in the writings of those sympathetic
to the spirit of the Davidsonian project. John Foster, for instance,
writes

> ...having seen the generality of the theory required, we may
> wonder whether we should ascribe it to the speaker at all. The
> knowledge we would have to attribute to him is not, typically,
> what he would attribute to himself. His mastery of English
> equips him to interpret its expressions, but not to state the
> general principles to which these interpretations conform. Is it
> not unnatural, even incoherent, to ascribe states of knowledge to
> which the subject himself has no conscious access?[10]

But Foster believes that the issue can be side-stepped:

> ...we can capture all that matters to the philosophy of meaning
> by putting the original project the other way round. Rather than
> ask for a statement of the knowledge implicit in linguistic com-
> petence, let us ask for a statement of a theory whose knowledge
> would suffice for such competence. Instead of demanding a
> statement of those metalinguistic facts which the mastery of a
> language implicitly recognises, let us demand a statement of
> those facts explicit recognition of which gives mastery. What
> we are then demanding is still a theory of meaning, but without
> the questionable assumption that one who has mastered the
> language has, at some deep level, absorbed the information
> which it supplies. The theory reveals the semantic machinery
> which competence works, but leaves undetermined the psycho-
> logical form in which competence exists.[11]

There are two thoughts here. First, there is the idea that the quest for a
theory of meaning does not need to be motivated by the desire to
understand the capacities of actual speakers of a given language. It is
enough, in Foster's view, that we seek to describe knowledge which
would generate those capacities, whether or not it is the source of
actual speakers' possession of them. If it is wondered why we should
seek to do that, Foster's answer seems to be, second, that what the

---

[10]   From Foster (1976), pp. 1–2.
[11]   Ibid., p. 2.

theorist of meaning is interested in is primarily *the way the language works*. While we should not, perhaps, despair of the possibility that the theory might illuminate the 'psychological form' of actual speakers' linguistic competence, the primary object is to describe the 'semantic machinery' which drives the language.

f⟶ The trouble with this is that the demands which Foster is making of the notion of meaning – the demands implicit in the image of 'semantic machinery' – threaten no less conceptual strain than the demands on the notion of knowledge – those generated by its qualification as 'implicit' – which he is trying to avoid. The intuitive response to Foster's proposal would be that it generates an intolerable divide between the concepts of meaning and understanding: truths about meaning have to be, ultimately, constituted by facts about understanding, so to aspire to a theory which aims to describe 'semantic machinery' independently of any assumption about what speakers of the language know is to aspire to a theory with no proper subject matter.[12]

g⟶ This response may involve over-simplification – depending on how 'ultimately' is understood – but it has great force, it seems to me, at the level of semantic primitives: expressions whose meanings are independent of the meanings of all other expressions of the language except those of which they are constituents, and to which a Davidsonian theory would devote its proper axioms. I do not think we can attach any content to the supposition that such an expression has a meaning except in so far as meaning is thought of as constituted, at least in part, by *convention*; and I do not think we can attain an account of the distinction between a convention and a corresponding regularity except by invoking the idea of practitioners' *intention*, qualified in various ways, to uphold that regularity. If both these, admittedly very vague, thoughts are correct, then the proper standing of the axioms of a theory of meaning must, it would seem, be grounded in speakers' intentions; and Foster's apparent belief that the theory can have an autonomous subject matter is of doubtful coherence.

h⟶ There is another objection, perhaps less fundamental but more immediately clinically fatal. The fact is that there seems to be no necessary connection between Foster's recommendation that the theory should describe information which *would* suffice for mastery of a given, typical natural language and the constraints of compositionality. Or better: there seems to be no such connection in the case on which Davidsonians typically concentrate – the homophonic case. If

---

[12] Compare the 'metaphysical perspective' of Elizabeth Fricker's (1983), section I.

one is aiming at construction of a heterophonic theory – whether because the object-language is quite different from that in which the theory is to be couched, or because one is aiming at a high degree of *full-bloodedness* in Dummett's sense – it may very well be that there is no way of completing Foster's task unless one aims for compositionality; that no other approach can effectively provide meaning-delivering theorems for every declarative sentence in the object-language. In the homophonic case matters stand differently. Provided we have a recursive specification of the syntax of the (declarative part of the) language, and provided we are content with the disquotational form of meaning-delivering theorem for which theories of truth are famous, Foster's project is well enough served by a semantic 'theory' which merely stipulates as an axiom every instance of the schema:

A is T if and only if P,

where 'P' may be replaced by any declarative sentence of the object-language and 'A' by the quotational name of that sentence. This theory is not finitely axiomatized, but it is finitely *stated* and, in conjunction with the appropriate recursive syntax, it does yield the means for effectively arriving at a meaning-delivering theorem – assuming we have no independent reservations about truth theories on that score – for each declarative sentence in the object-language. It thus fits Foster's bill: it describes information whose possession would suffice for mastery of the (declarative part of the) object-language. At least, it does so provided a compositional Davidsonian theory whose T-theorematic output coincided with the axioms of this theory would do so. It is true, of course, that the non-compositional theory could not be used to *impart* this information to someone who did not already have it – but then no homophonic theory, whether compositional or not, fares better in that regard. The moral is simple: the ambition to describe information which would suffice for mastery of a particular language may impose certain constraints on the form taken by the theorems of a theory of meaning, but it imposes no interesting constraints on the mechanics of the theory.

We are looking for a project whose execution would call for a compositional theory of meaning but which would not demand that actual speakers be deemed to know the full contents of that theory. Foster's thought, in effect, was to idealize the language with a view to a theory of how *it*, autonomously, works. A quite different thought would aim to see compositionality as called for by the ambition to describe not some body of knowledge which speakers putatively have but what they are typically able *to do*. Suppose we essay to regard each of the T-theorems of a Davidsonian theory as descriptive of a sub-competence which someone who fully understands the object-language has: a sub-competence constituted by sensitivity, in using the relevant sentence, to the constraint which the appropriate T-theorem captures. Have we completely described the general competence in which mastery of the (declarative part of the) relevant language consists when we have a theory which correctly describes all these sub-competences? There is a prima facie persuasive reason why we should ask for more. No matter what ability we are concerned to describe, and however complete our characterization of its ingredient abilities, the description is incomplete if the ingredients have certain causal interrelations about which it keeps silence. Someone who has a strong tennis game may have a good drive, a good lob, and a good slice on his backhand wing; but a *full* description of his skills would not restrict itself to the statement that each of these strokes is dependable if, let us suppose, the lob and the drive – when, unusually, either is fragile – tend to break down together, although the slice tends to remain a strong shot even when the rest of his game is off-colour. So with the theory of meaning: a full description of the competence possessed by speakers should not merely characterize its ingredients but ought also to reflect their causal interrelations. This may inspire what Martin Davies[13] calls the *Mirror Constraint*. Suppose it is true of speakers (a) that once they know what $S_1, \ldots, S_n$ mean, they are able to know what the distinct sentence, S, means without any further exposure to the use of the language; and (b) that if induced to revise their belief about what S means, they would need no further inducement to revise their beliefs about what some of $S_1, \ldots, S_n$ mean. Then the Mirror Constraint says simply that if, and only if, speakers' sub-competences with $S, S_1, \ldots, S_n$ are so interrelated, an adequate theory of meaning for their language should ensure that those of its resources which suffice for the derivation of meaning-delivering theorems for each of $S_1, \ldots, S_n$ should also suffice for the derivation of such a theorem for S.[14] A theory which satisfies the Mirror Constraint will thus be one whose deductive structure reflects the (causal) interrelations among speakers' sub-competences. When speakers are able to move to understanding of a novel utterance without special explanation, the theory will mirror their ability by supplying the means for deriving an appropriate theorem utilizing only axioms adequate for the specification of the meanings of sentences which they previously

---

[13] Martin Davies (1981), chapter III, p. 53 and following.

[14] This does not coincide exactly with Davies' formulation, but differs, I believe, in no important respect.

understood; and when speakers change their beliefs about the meaning of some sentence, appropriate modifications to the meaning-delivering theorem for that sentence will enjoin revisions in its axiomatic parentage which in turn entail shifts of meaning in exactly those sentences of which they consequentially change their understanding.

Davies himself raises various objections to the Mirror Constraint.[15] But he does not raise what I think is the most serious: that it provides no real reason for putting structure into a *semantic* theory. Let it be granted that the interrelations of competence whose reflection the Mirror Constraint seeks to ensure are worth describing. Still, why not describe them directly – why run the dogleg of having them 'reflected' in the deductive articulation of a theory of meaning? There is nothing to prevent a critic of the Mirror Constraint from taking over the syntax and catalogue of semantic primitives incorporated in a theory of meaning which satisfies it. He may then advance a theory of meaning of the infinitary sort canvassed above, adding only a rider to the effect that speakers are generally able to understand novel sentences, provided they involve only familiar semantic primitives, and that changes in their semantic beliefs about a sentence tend to be associated with changes in their semantic beliefs about *all* sentences – or at least all about which they have any such belief – containing some one or more of the semantic primitives figuring in that sentence. Admittedly, such a rider would not be a detailed, or axiomatic, description of the interrelations which the Mirror Constraint would have a theory of meaning reflect. But there is every reason to think that the recursive *syntax* which the theorist adjoins to his infinitary semantic theory would supply the materials for the more specific descriptive task. He needs only to ensure that the syntax itself meets the Mirror Constraint: that when, and only when, speakers' understanding of $S_1, \ldots, S_n$ and S are interrelated as described, those ingredients in the axiomatic bases and set of recursions for the syntax which suffice to characterize each of $S_1, \ldots, S_n$ as well-formed suffice so to characterize S.

There is a different line of thought in Davies' discussion which seems more promising. It depends upon our being willing to entertain the idea that there is an admixture of rational inductive and deductive inference which can take a subject from knowledge of the meanings of a finite set of sentences to knowledge of the meaning of a sentence which is not in that set and is novel to him. It is, Davies writes,

---

[15] For instance, that the constraint provides no guidance to the semantic theorist if the studied language has no actual speakers; and leaves no space for the idea that speakers might fail to know the meanings of sentences which are nevertheless determinate, fixed by syntactic constructions and semantic features familiar to them.

...the possibility of self-conscious, reflective projection of meanings which encourages the attempt to provide a theory of meaning which not only delivers the correct meaning specifications but also reveals how the meanings of sentences depend upon the recurrence of particular syntactic constituents...[16]

Davies proceeds to propose what he calls the *Structural Constraint*: in effect, that if, but only if, it would be possible for someone who knew what $S_1, \ldots, S_n$ each mean to proceed, by rational inductive and deductive methods and without further empirical investigation, to knowledge of what S means, the smallest set of axiomatic resources which suffice, in a theory of meaning for the language in question, to furnish meaning-delivering theorems for each of $S_1, \ldots, S_n$ should also yield a meaning-delivering theorem for S. The effect of this constraint is that compositionality in a theory of meaning is demanded not by characteristics of actual speakers qua actual speakers but by the nature of an idealized epistemology of understanding. Whatever actual speakers do or do not know, it seems highly plausible that there is such a thing, in certain cases, as rational inference from knowledge of the meanings of the sentences in a particular set to knowledge of the meaning of a sentence outside that set: the cases in question are precisely those where, intuitively, the semantically contributive vocabulary and syntax of the new sentence are all variously on display among the sentences in the set. The effect of the Structural Constraint is that a satisfactory theory of meaning should mirror not the propensities for meaning-projection and revision of actual speakers but those of an ideal speaker, whose every semantic belief is informed by self-conscious rational inductive and deductive inference.

In fact it seems reasonable to demand more. A satisfactory theory of meaning should not merely 'reflect' the path that will be taken by the ideal speaker, by discerning structure whenever he discerns structure, but should represent the inferences which he would – or could, qua rational – actually draw. Thus whenever he is able to advance to knowledge of the meaning of S from knowledge of the meanings of $S_1, \ldots, S_n$, the latter knowledge should constitute good evidence for the truth of those axioms in the theory needed to derive the meaning-delivering theorem for S; and the movement up, as it were, to the axioms and then down to that theorem ought to be the very movement which knowledge of the meanings of $S_1, \ldots, S_n$ is deemed to put a rational speaker in position to make. It is not completely clear

[16] Davies (1981), p. 56.

whether Davies has this stronger interpretation of the Structural Constraint in mind. But it seems to be more satisfactory. The weaker interpretation is apt to make the constraint seem somewhat arbitrary: what question, exactly, would the theory of meaning have to be addressed to in order for it to be necessary that it discerns semantic structure in a group of sentences when and only when the ideal speaker would 'project' amongst them but not necessary that it represent inferential moves which he could, qua ideal, actually make? Under the stronger interpretation, however, the overriding question is clear. It is: granted that it is possible for a speaker to know, or at least to form rational beliefs, about the meanings of utterances whose use he has never witnessed, how in detail might this be possible?

□1→ This has to be a good question unless we are utterly sceptical about whether there is ever any rational route to an understanding of novel utterances. The project of trying to answer it has the interest that attaches to any programme of reconstructive analytic epistemology. Such projects have been a major current in the history of English-speaking philosophy: whether motivated by sceptical challenges or not, philosophers have repeatedly been drawn to the task of trying to explain how statements of some particular sort – about God, or the material world, or other minds, for instance – could be susceptible to rational cognition (even if our practice is to rely upon criteria of acceptability which fall far short of it). Admittedly, the sceptic about meaning is a somewhat recent entry on the philosophical scene; the project of constructing theories of meaning of the sort we are interested in did not originate as a response to sceptical pressure, and the various forms of scepticism about meaning which have comparatively recently come into prominence in any case concern more basic matters than knowledge of the meaning of novel utterances. Still, the possibility of such knowledge provides the material for a perfectly familiar species of analytical enquiry.

That is the principal recommendation of this section. There is a recognizably philosophical project – at least it ought to be recognizable to anyone educated in the twentieth-century Anglo-American philosophical tradition – to which constructing a formal theory of meaning would be a contribution. This project has no immediate connections with the quest to explain the capacities of actual speakers of natural languages; the task to which a completed, adequate theory of meaning would contribute would rather be that of explaining how a complete knowledge of a particular natural language could be a rational achievement. We have no conception of how that might be so unless the rational subject is permitted to discern sub-sentential semantic structure. It follows that such a theory would have to comply with the second ingredient condition of compositionality, as characterized above, that the meaning-delivering theorems for sentences be derived within the theory in a manner which reflects the semantic contribution made by those sentences' constituents. The need for the first ingredient, that the axiomatic basis be finite, is less immediate: it is not evident that a rational being could not be in possession of infinitely many logically independent items of information. But it may be anticipated that if we are concerned with the powers of an ideally rational *human* speaker – so that the finitude of our capacities remains a constraint on the form which the theory should take – the *learnability* of the language – the possibility of a finite but rational creature coming to know the meaning of any particular sentence of it by way of exposure to and projection from the use of finitely many other sentences – will require that only a finitely axiomatized theory will fit the bill.[17]

Whatever we conclude, then, about the capacity of a formal theory of meaning to be yoked to the task of explaining actual speakers' abilities, there is an interpretation of the Davidson/Dummett project which promises to allow it to stand independently as legitimate a priori philosophy. This interpretation may or may not accord with part of the intentions of the leading protagonists in the field. But it does contrive to supply, after all, some sense for Foster's notion that a natural language might have the sort of autonomy which would allow its theoretical description not to be directly a theory about actual speakers' semantic knowledge; and it suggests, in consequence, how the disinfection of the concept of implicit knowledge need not be a precondition for the philosophical health of the project of constructing theories of meaning.

[...]

References

Baker, G. P. and Hacker, P. M. S. (1984). *Language, Sense and Nonsense* (Oxford: Blackwell).

Davidson, D. (1984). *Inquiries into Truth and Interpretation* (Oxford: Clarendon Press).

Davies, M. (1981). *Meaning, Quantification, Necessity* (London: Routledge and Kegan Paul).

---

[17] Davies shows, in fact, that on natural assumptions about what is requisite for the learnability of a language, the Structural Constraint enjoins that a theory satisfying it will indeed be finitely axiomatized. See his (1981), chapter III, section 2.

Dummett, M. A. E. (1975). 'What is a Theory of Meaning?', in *Mind and Language*, ed. S. Guttenplan (Oxford: Oxford University Press), pp. 97–138; reprinted in Dummett, *Seas of Language* (Oxford: Clarendon Press, 1993).

Dummett, M. A. E. (1976). 'What is a Theory of Meaning? (II)', in *Truth and Meaning*, eds. G. Evans and J. McDowell (Oxford: Clarendon Press), pp. 67–137; reprinted in *Seas of Language*.

Dummett, M. A. E. (1979). 'What Does the Appeal to Use Do for the Theory of Meaning?', in *Meaning and Use*, ed. A. Margalit (Dordrecht: Reidel), pp. 123–35; reprinted in *Seas of Language*.

Foster, J. A. (1976). 'Meaning and Truth Theory', in *Truth and Meaning*, ed. G. Evans and J. McDowell (Oxford: Clarendon Press), pp. 1–32.

Fricker, E. (1983). 'Semantic Structure and Speakers' Understanding', *Proceedings of the Aristotelian Society* 83: 49–66.

Commentary on Wright

Compositionality and semantic competence

Wright begins by presenting Davidson's claim that a theory of meaning should be *compositional*. He explains some different ways in which Davidson has attempted to motivate this requirement. A language is *compositional* iff (i) the axioms of the theory are finite in number and (ii) each theorem is derived from axioms corresponding with words and modes of combination in the target sentence.

> Explain the three sorts of motivation that Wright takes Davidson to offer for compositionality up to $\boxed{a}\mapsto$. Does any of them seem most fundamental?

At $\boxed{a}\mapsto$ Wright claims that each of the three motivations relies for its efficacy on conceiving of a semantic theory as a theory of competence or the object of speakers' knowledge.

> Is Wright is correct in saying that considerations about competence motivate compositionality? Can you think of a way of understanding Davidson's motivations that does not rely on viewing a semantic theory as an object of speakers' knowledge?

Between $\boxed{b}\mapsto$ and $\boxed{c}\mapsto$ Wright explains some elements in Michael Dummett's views on the relation between semantic theory and semantic competence.

List what you take to be the main features of Dummett's view. Pay attention to (a) the way Dummett characterizes semantic competence and (b) his
view of the relation between semantic *axioms* and competence. Try to
locate Dummett's position in the taxonomy we derived from Soames: is
his view *robust, modest,* or *minimal* (i.e., Davidsonian)? If it is not obvious
how to position Dummett, explain why. If you think the taxonomy needs to
be revised, suggest a revision.

Dummett holds that speakers know the axioms of a semantic theory. So he
appears to be a robust theorist. However, the notion of knowledge he employs
is not ordinary, explicit knowledge. Rather, it is what he calls *implicit knowledge* – implicitly knowing that *p* amounts (roughly!) to possessing a practical
ability the theoretical representation of which makes appeal to the proposition that p. So implicit knowledge does not seem to be straightforwardly
psychological.[1]

Compositionality and language

From $\boxed{f}\mapsto$ to $\boxed{i}\mapsto$ Wright presents two arguments against Foster's view.

Read carefully from $\boxed{f}\mapsto$ to $\boxed{i}\mapsto$. Put the conclusions of each of Wright's
arguments into your own words. What are the respective targets of the two
arguments? How do the two targets differ? Which of the arguments is more
important for Wright's overall purposes?

The first objection (from $\boxed{f}\mapsto$ to $\boxed{h}\mapsto$) aims to show that Foster's view
involves an untenable gap between meaning and understanding. The second
objection (from $\boxed{h}\mapsto$ to $\boxed{i}\mapsto$) aims to show that views like Foster's are unable
to motivate compositionality. So the target of the second argument is any view
that attempts to combine a minimal view with compositionality. Since the
combined view is Wright's official target, the second argument is more important.

Put Wright's first argument (from $\boxed{f}\mapsto$ to $\boxed{h}\mapsto$) into your own words.
Notice that, although the argument has a single target, it consists of two
sub-arguments. Be sure to distinguish them.

Wright's argument aims to show that Foster's view distinguishes facts about
meaning from facts about understanding in a way that is problematic. So the

---

[1] For a more accurate view of Dummett's notion of implicit knowledge, see Dummett,
Chapter 4.

argument takes off from Wright's characterization of Foster's view, at $\boxed{e}\mapsto$. This is important, since Wright's argument may work against some views of the relation between semantic theory and competence even if it does not count against any view correctly attributable to Foster.

> Try to locate the sort of view Wright attributes to Foster in our taxonomy. Should the view be co-located with Foster's? It is important to think about the different ways Wright's use of 'know' can be understood.

If we understand Wright's use of 'know' as applying to explicit knowledge, Foster's view will count as aiming to describe semantic facts independently of what speakers know. But perhaps if we understand 'know' as applying to implicit knowledge, then Foster's view is that a semantic theory describes what speakers know. Since Wright wants to argue that Foster's view 'generates an intolerable divide between the concepts of meaning and understanding', he must show that an adequate account of semantic facts is an account of what is known in a richer sense than Foster allows.

Wright's second sub-argument assumes that we must view the meaning of 'semantic primitives' – elements, like individual words, that are treated by the axioms of a theory – as sustained by *convention*. What does this mean?

A convention is a particular sort of regularity. On Wright's view, it is a regularity that is adhered to intentionally by a population, though this element of his view is questionable. Typically, a convention arises where two (or more) courses of behaviour are possible, neither course of behaviour is intrinsically more valuable to members of the population, and yet there is intrinsic value in the population co-operating by following one or the other course. An example would be the practice amongst a population of driving on one side of the road rather than the other. Many philosophers have agreed that the notion of convention has a role to play in accounting for the semantic properties of language. (One notable dissenter is Davidson himself.[2]) One reason that is offered for appealing here to convention is that the relation between words and meanings seems to be largely arbitrary and yet speakers of a language typically agree in their word-meaning associations. For example, although 'cow' is used in English to refer to cows, the same word might have been used to refer to pigs; yet speakers of English agree in their usage. Notice that Davidson's account of how words come to mean what they do – his answer to question (IV) – does not employ the notion of convention.

> Check this by reading Davidson, from $\boxed{m}\mapsto$.

The next step in Wright's argument involves claiming that a conventional regularity is distinguished from other sorts of regularity by the fact that it is

---

[2] See the reading list on Language and Convention.

adhered to *intentionally*. On Wright's account, regularities are conventional just to the extent that a population intends to uphold them, so speakers of a language must intend to uphold the regular association of the word with its meaning. Hence, the semantic properties of words – and, so, statements of semantic theory designed to capture those facts – 'must be grounded in speakers' intentions'.

> Suppose that the semantic properties of words are grounded in speakers' intentions. Is this sufficient to refute Foster's view? If not, what must be added to secure a result in Wright's favour? It might be helpful to think here about the different views one might take about the relation between semantic theory and speakers' intentions – analogues for intention of robust, modest and minimal views.

One additional premise used by Wright is (A):

> (A) Intention plays a role in grounding semantic facts, not only at the level of sentences, but at the level of individual words

> See Davidson $\boxed{c}\mapsto$ and $\boxed{j}\mapsto$. Why does Davidson refuse a role for intention with respect to individual words?

Davidson denies a role for intention with respect to words because intention is only required to explain purposeful behaviour, or action. But, in Davidson's view, linguistic actions all involve sentences.

Another of Wright's premises is (B):

> (B) Since the semantic facts are grounded in intentions having as content propositions capturing those facts, an adequate semantic theory will involve axioms expressing those propositions. So, a semantic theory containing the axiom *an object satisfies 'red' in L iff the object is red* is adequate only if speakers of L intend that an object satisfies 'red' in L iff the object is red.

Assessment of (B) will involve issues like those in Soames (see $\boxed{g}\mapsto$ in Soames). Notice that theoretical characterizations of conventions need not be reflected directly in the intentions of those who follow the conventions. The best theory about the convention concerning the side of the road on which a population drives may have it that they drive on the left. But the intentions of members of the population might have the content: drive on the same side of the road as others.[3]

---

[3] See the reading lists for Language and Convention and for Intention-based Semantics.

From $\boxed{h}\!\!\rightarrow$ to $\boxed{i}\!\!\rightarrow$, Wright presents his second argument.

State Wright's second argument in your own words. Begin by stating his conclusion. Then reconstruct the steps he uses to reach it.

The conclusion of Wright's argument is that, if Foster's minimal view were true, there would be no motivation for compositionality. The argument has the following premises:

(P1) If we forgo interest in the details of speakers' knowledge, the strongest requirement on an adequate semantic theory would be that it state facts knowledge of which would suffice for understanding.

(P2) If an adequate semantic theory for a language need only state facts knowledge of which would suffice for understanding, it is possible to state such a theory in a way that is not compositional.

For immediate purposes, Wright assumes that (P1) is correct, and argues for (P2). (He returns to (P1) from $\boxed{i}\!\!\rightarrow$.) His argument for (P2) is as follows. On Davidson's view, knowledge of a theory that delivers theorems of form (T):

(T) 's' is true in L iff p

for every sentence, s, of the object-language and translation, p, of that sentence into the metalanguage, would suffice for understanding the language L. If that claim is correct, then any theory doing the same job would be adequate. But a non-compositional theory appears able to do the same job in cases where the object-language is the same as the metalanguage – where the theorems of the theory are *homophonic*. Wright presents a sketch of such a theory. Such a theory for English would have two parts. The first consists of a syntactic component able to generate every sentence of English. The second consists in the stipulation that every instance of (E) is to be an *axiom* of the theory, where an instance of (T) is derived by replacing 's' and 'p' with outputs of the syntax – i.e., sentences of English.

(E) 's' is true in English iff p

The axioms will include:

'Snow is white' is true in English iff snow is white
'Grass is green' is true in English iff grass is green
'Florence is beautiful' is true in English iff Florence is beautiful

together with an analogous instance for every other English sentence.

Wright's theory is not finitely axiomatized since it has an axiom for each of the indefinitely many sentences generated by the syntax. Hence it is not compositional. But the conjunction of a finitely axiomatized syntax with (E) is a statement of the theory. It seems that, if knowing what is stated by a compositional theory issuing in T-sentences would suffice for understanding, so would knowing what is stated in Wright's theory.

> Look back at your statement of Wright's argument. What would need to be shown in order to undermine each of the steps of Wright's argument? Is it plausible that those things can be shown?

To show that (P2) fails, it must be shown that Wright's theory differs from Davidson's theory in its capacity to describe the semantic facts. Specifically, it must be shown that, while knowing a theory of Davidson's sort might suffice for understanding, knowing Wright's theory would not. How might that be shown? Knowledge of a semantic theory would suffice for understanding just in case knowledge of the theory would suffice for possession of the range of abilities exhibited by competent speakers. What must be shown, then, is that knowing Wright's theory would not suffice for possession of the abilities of a semantically competent speaker. The central difference between compositional theories and Wright's theory concerns their inner articulation. What is wanted is reason to think that a speaker whose knowledge of meaning derived from knowledge of axioms for words and modes of combination would better approximate the ability of a normal speaker than would a speaker whose ability derived from knowing an independent axiom for each sentence.

From $\boxed{i}\!\mapsto$, Wright returns to (P1). His aim is to find a motivation for compositionality that does not depend on attributing knowledge of a semantic theory to ordinary speakers. Wright explains the *Mirror Constraint*. He begins by explaining how the aim of characterizing speakers' abilities might not be satisfied by a description just of those abilities.

> What analogy does Wright appeal to in explaining the Mirror Constraint? State the Mirror Constraint in your own words. Does Wright's analogy support imposition of the constraint? Does the Mirror Constraint involve the semantic theorist in studying speakers' knowledge?

From $\boxed{j}\!\mapsto$ to $\boxed{k}\!\mapsto$ Wright offers an objection to the Mirror Constraint. The objection is closely related to his argument for (P2).

> What is Wright's objection to the Mirror Constraint? How does it relate to his argument for (P2)?

In effect, the Mirror Constraint invites us to treat bits of the language as semantically related just in case speakers' abilities with those bits of language are themselves interdependent. Take a speaker who acquires competence with (1) and (2).

(1) Bill smokes
(2) George drinks

Suppose the speaker is brought thereby – without additional training – to be competent with (3) and (4).

(3) George smokes
(4) Bill drinks.

Then a semantic theory should account for the meanings of (3) and (4) in a way that shows how those meanings can be determined on the basis of the meanings of words and modes of combinations participating in (1) and (2). The axioms of the theory that determine theorems for (1) and (2) should suffice to determine theorems for (3) and (4).

Why should an adequate semantic theory track interdependencies among speakers' abilities? One answer to the question would be that an adequate semantic theory is a theory of the details of speakers' psychology – a theory concerning the specific organization of the systems responsible for competence. But that answer is not available from the standpoint of the minimal view. Wright argues that, even if we agree that some account is wanted of the interdependencies amongst speakers' abilities, no reason has been given for providing that account in a semantic theory. The account might, for example, be presented in the syntactic component of the theory, or elsewhere.

From $\boxed{k} \mapsto$ to $\boxed{l} \mapsto$ Wright presents the *Structural Constraint*. Explain this constraint in your own words. How does it differ from the Mirror Constraint? How might the differences motivate imposing the Structural Constraint on a semantic theory? How does employing the Structural Constraint avoid engagement with the details of actual speakers' knowledge?

The Structural Constraint imposes the following requirement. A semantic theory should treat the meanings of a sentence, S, as dependent on the meanings of sentences, $S_i \ldots S_n$, just in case it would be *possible* for someone who only knew the meanings of $S_i \ldots S_n$ to attain knowledge of the meaning of S in a rational way. Suppose that it is possible for someone who knows the meanings of (1) and (2) to determine, on the basis of rational inference, the meaning of (3). In that case, the axioms responsible for theorems governing (1) and (2) should suffice to generate a theorem governing (3).

The central difference between the Structural Constraint and the Mirror Constraint is that application of the former is dependent on *rational* relations between bits of knowledge. Hence, it supplies a justification, lacking in the Mirror Constraint, for imposing compositionality on semantic theory. The Structural Constraint achieves this by requiring that one's account record rational dependencies amongst bits of knowledge. It requires that the paths connecting interdependent sentences be knowledge-preserving paths – so that if one knows facts recorded at one end of the path, and traces only rational routes along the path, propositions at one's destination will also be known. Merely recording that there is *some* connection amongst speakers' abilities, as with the Mirror Constraint, will not suffice.

From $\boxed{I}\!\!\mapsto$ Wright explains his view of a project that would support the Structural Constraint. What is the aim of the project? Is the aim to characterize semantic facts? Or is it, rather, to supply an account – perhaps a special sort of account – of speakers' knowledge? How does Wright's account relate to the suggestion made above that the abilities of someone who knew a semantic theory of Davidson's sort might differ from one who knew a theory of Wright's sort? How does Wright's view bear on the question – thus far suppressed – of whether the minimal view involves a tacit concern with speakers' competence rather than with semantic facts?

We ordinarily take it that competent speakers are in a position to *know* what novel sentences mean. How could they know this? The account deriving from the Structural Constraint says that a speaker could know what a novel sentence means on three conditions: (i) the meaning of the novel sentences is derivable – along a route suitable for the preservation of knowledge – from the meanings of other sentences; (ii) the speaker knows the meaning of the other sentences; (iii) the speaker's derivation of the meaning of the novel sentence is (somehow) responsible to the knowledge-preserving route from familiar to novel sentences. At this point, it may seem that there is no need to appeal to ideally rational speakers. The crucial thing, apparently, is that the semantic facts be so related that the facts concerning familiar sentences entail the facts concerning novel sentences – crudely, that there is a knowledge-preserving route from propositions recording the former to propositions recording the latter. If that is right, a semantic theory can show how the semantic facts are so interrelated that it is possible for us to have the knowledge of meaning we ordinarily take ourselves to possess. And it can do so without seeking to record details of the actual means particular speakers – ideally rational or not – employ in attaining that knowledge.[4]

---

[4] For further discussion of the relations between compositionality and competence see the reading list on Tacit Knowledge and Compositionality.

Conclusion

We began this chapter by setting out a two-component approach to the question, What is it for words to mean what they do? The first component is a statement of the semantic facts of some language. The second component aims to relate those facts to speakers of the language, to say what it is about speakers that sustain the semantic facts. The first component of Davidson's account is an interpretive truth theory. In the second component, the semantic facts are seen as determined by speakers' behavioural abilities, viewed through the lens of the Principle of Charity.

Soames and Wright are both concerned with whether Davidson's account can fit with an adequate view of semantic competence – of what speakers know by virtue of understanding a language. We have seen that Davidson has a minimal view of the relation between semantic theory and competence.

Soames argues that the first component of Davidson's account is unable to sustain even a minimal link with competence. Wright, by contrast, argues that Davidson's minimal view is unable to underwrite a central plank in the first component of his account, the requirement that a statement of the semantic facts be compositional. Thus Soames suggests that the fit between semantic theory and competence can be looser than Davidson allows, while Wright suggests that it should be tighter. On either view, the ties between semantic theory, competence, and speakers' behaviour, on which the second component of Davidson's account depends, would be severed.

Soames and Wright suggest that there are questions about speakers' competence which Davidson does not face up to. If we are to resolve this dispute, we will need to attain a clearer view of the nature of semantic competence. Is competence best viewed as an ordinary form of knowledge, perhaps reflected only indirectly in behaviour? Or is competence mere practical ability? These are the topics of the next chapter.

Appendix: Tarski's Truth-theoretic Machinery

To see how Tarski's machinery might be employed to explain how sentence meanings are determined by word meanings, consider a toy language (TL). TL has very few words; but the words it does have are English words.

Let's begin with (TL)'s *syntax* – rules for the construction of sentences:

Singular terms: 'Bill', 'George'
Predicates: 'smokes', 'drinks'
Sentential connective: 'and'

We now define *sentence of TL* as follows:

(1) A predicate preceded by a singular term is a sentence of TL
(2) If *A* is a sentence of TL and *B* is a sentence of TL then *A* followed by a sentential connective followed by *B* is a sentence of TL
(3) Nothing else is a sentence of TL

Hence, the following are sentences of TL:

'Bill smokes'
'Bill drinks'
'George smokes'
'George drinks'

Since each of these is a sentence, interposing the sentential connective 'and' between any two of them creates a sentence. For example:

'Bill smokes and George drinks'
'Bill drinks and George smokes'

Since these are sentences, we can perform the same operation on them:

'Bill smokes and George drinks and Bill drinks and George smokes'

So, our toy syntax generates indefinitely many sentences.

Suppose we take it that each sentence translates its English counterpart, then an adequate truth-theory should generate – amongst many others – the following T-sentences:

(4) 'Bill smokes' is true in TL iff Bill smokes
(5) 'George drinks' is true in TL iff George drinks

To secure this result, we provide a *semantic theory* for TL, consisting of these *axioms*:

Singular terms:	(i)	'Bill' refers in TL to Bill
	(ii)	'George' refers in TL to George
Predicates:	(iii)	An object satisfies 'smokes' in TL iff the object smokes
	(iv)	An object satisfies 'drinks' in TL iff the object drinks
Sentences:	(v)	A sentence consisting of a singular term followed by a predicate is true in TL iff the object to which the singular term refers satisfies the predicate

(vi)   A sentence consisting of a sentence followed by
       'and' followed by a sentence is true in TL iff the
       first sentence is true in TL and the second sentence
       is true in TL

The unfamiliar notion here is *satisfaction*. In TL, satisfaction can be thought
of as the converse of the *true of* relation. So, an object *satisfies* 'smokes' iff
'smokes' is *true of* the object; and 'smokes' is true of an object just in case the
object smokes. We are now in a position to informally derive T-sentences from
the axioms of our semantic theory. These are the theory's *theorems*. Let's take
(6) as our target:

(6)   'Bill smokes'

From our syntax and (v) we can derive:

(7)   'Bill smokes' is true in TL iff the object to which 'Bill' refers in TL
      satisfies 'smokes' in TL

From (i) we can now derive:

(8)   'Bill smokes' is true in TL iff Bill satisfies 'smokes'

From (iii) we can derive:

(9)   'Bill smokes' is true in TL iff Bill smokes

the result we wanted, (4) above.

> Construct informal derivations of T-sentences for 'George drinks' and 'Bill
> smokes and George drinks'.

Real truth-theories involve additional technicalities, many of which arise in
the treatment of quantification.[5] But the basic principles are revealed in the
toy language. Derivation of T-theorems is a matter of applying fairly minimal
logical machinery to axioms stating the semantically relevant features of
words (stated in (i)–(iv)) and modes of combination (stated in (v) and (vi)).

---

[5]   For more rigorous treatments see the reading list on Tarski's Truth-theoretic Machinery.

4

Knowledge of Language

Introduction

Kurt utters the words 'Es regnet'. Some members of his audience seek cover; others are simply baffled. What distinguishes the two groups? A natural answer is that some members of Kurt's audience know something that others do not: namely, German (or, at least, enough German to know that 'Es regnet' can be used to say that it is raining). Although talk of knowledge comes naturally in this context, the proper understanding of such talk is not straightforward. Should we think of Kurt's knowledge of German as ordinary knowledge, akin to his knowledge that it is raining? Or is talk of knowledge of a language – German, say, or Icelandic – only a *façon de parler*, perhaps a means of referring to the complex of abilities possessed by competent speakers of the language?

This question is addressed by philosophers who seek an account of *linguistic competence* (a label chosen for its neutrality on the question whether knowledge of a language is ordinary knowledge). In the previous chapter, we considered a closely related question: what properties of words are exploited by those who know a language? And we saw how this question about semantic properties might be connected to our question about linguistic competence. We saw that, while Davidson seeks to remain neutral on the precise relation between competence and semantic theory, Soames and Wright suggest that a more committal view may be appropriate.

Questions about the nature of linguistic competence have come to assume great importance in the philosophy of language. One reason for this stems from inquiry in linguistics, especially from a programme of research instigated by Noam Chomsky. Chomsky's most important contributions here are twofold. First, he supplied the initial impetus for this programme by proposing that linguistic theorizing should aim to provide an explicit account of the range of linguistic judgements available to competent speakers. Secondly, he has been at the forefront of attempts to meet that aim through the development of increasingly sophisticated theories. As the programme has been pursued, it has become apparent that the judgements available to competent speakers reflect a system of enormous complexity, a system whose elements and interconnections are not immediately evident to ordinary speakers.

Although a proper grasp of the complexity of the system can be gleaned only by considering the details of linguistic theory, a simple example, chosen from hundreds of comparable ones, may serve to bring out the fact that its features are not immediately evident. Consider: 'Kim believes that London is pretty'. Since you know English, you know that the 'that' here is optional. 'Kim believes London is pretty' is perfectly acceptable. Is use of 'that' following 'believes' always optional in this way? Whether or not one is prepared to take a view on this question, it should be clear that the answer is not immediately available to us just because we know English. In order to find out whether 'that' is optional, we need to deploy our knowledge in response to a range of examples. We might consider examples like 'Kim believes that Bill smokes', 'Jo believes that snow is white', and 'George believes that linguistics is hard'. In all these cases, 'that' can be left out. Hence, we might arrive at the view that 'that' following 'believes' is optional. Well, this view is actually incorrect. 'That' is not an option – its absence is mandatory – in constructions like 'Kim believes Bill to be a smoker', 'Jo believes snow to be white', and 'George believes linguistics to be hard'. Even though we are English speakers, we may have been unable to say whether 'that' is optional following 'believes'.

Examples of this sort, and the enormously complicated accounts of language that have been developed on their basis, place pressure on the idea that our knowledge of language is *ordinary knowledge*. We are typically aware of what we know, and do not need to find out what we know through the sort of experiment that we just carried out with 'that'. (And even if we need to think a bit in order to discover what we know, we expect to get the answer right.) Some philosophers, including Chomsky, argue that our lack of awareness of many facts about our language shows that knowledge of language is a special sort of knowledge, sometimes called *tacit knowledge*. (We shall shortly see that it is controversial exactly what tacit knowledge is supposed to be.) Another sort of reason for doubting whether knowledge of language is ordinary knowledge is that there are many facts about our language which we recognize but which we appear never to have been taught. For example, if we had actually been taught how 'believes' and 'that' work together, then we might expect this to be something we could simply remember. And if it is suggested that we have forgotten what we were taught, then it is puzzling how our judgements can continue to reflect something that we no longer remember. Some philosophers, again including Chomsky, argue that our knowledge of language is largely unlearned or *innate*. Their arguments don't settle our question about the nature of semantic competence, however, because we may still want to know whether what is innate is itself like ordinary knowledge. And when we come to our other authors, we shall see a proliferation of responses to our question about the nature of linguistic competence and about its relation to semantic theories.

In order to gain a sense of what is in dispute between the authors of the pieces in this chapter, it will be helpful to outline a rough taxonomy of positions on the nature of linguistic competence. We've encountered two basic positions. The first has it that competence consists in a system of abilities, which may include abilities to attain, on occasion, knowledge of the meanings of uttered sentences. If speakers' abilities are best represented in a semantic theory, then competence may now be taken to reside in *implicit knowledge* of the theory.[1] According to the second position, competence consists in ordinary knowledge of a semantic theory. So, for instance, it might be said that speakers know that 'Bill smokes' is true if and only if Bill smokes, and that this perfectly ordinary piece of knowledge underwrites their understanding of 'Bill smokes'. Additions to the basic taxonomy are motivated by apparent weaknesses in these two positions. Against the first, it is alleged that competence underlies and explains linguistic ability, so cannot just be a matter of possessing those abilities. Against the second, it is claimed that a semantic theory is forced to deploy theoretical notions and statements beyond the ken of ordinary folk.[2] The objection to the first position may make one think that the idea of implicit knowledge is inadequate for capturing linguistic competence. The objection to the second position may make one think that it is simply an error to equate linguistic competence with ordinary knowledge. Thus we find the idea of *tacit knowledge*, which is taken to differ both from implicit knowledge and from ordinary knowledge.

But now we come to a further wrinkle. For there seems to be no single account of tacit knowledge that everyone who appeals to the notion would endorse. In fact, there are two main views about the nature of tacit knowledge.

On the first view, tacit knowledge is taken to differ from ordinary knowledge in that those who possess it are not conscious of possessing it and are unable to say what they tacitly know. But otherwise, tacit knowledge is thought to resemble ordinary knowledge: like states of ordinary knowledge, states of tacit knowledge are taken to play a role in ordinary psychological

---

[1] See Chapter 3, Wright (from $\boxed{b} \mapsto$ in Wright).

[2] Think here about the semantic theory for a toy language in the Appendix to Chapter 3. That theory is far simpler than a theory for a non-toy language would be; but it uses technology unfamiliar to most competent speakers. Cf., also, Soames in Chapter 3 (from $\boxed{g} \mapsto$ in Soames).

explanations. An explanation of how Kim knows that Bill smokes might appeal to the facts that Kim knows that Bill has an office in 12 Gower Street and that everyone with an office in 12 Gower Street smokes, and that Kim is able to put these two pieces of knowledge together. In a similar way one might seek to explain how Kim knows that 'Bill smokes' can be used to say that Bill smokes. Here, one might appeal to the facts that Kim tacitly knows what 'Bill' means and what 'smokes' means and that she tacitly knows the effect of combining words with those meanings. Notice that in order to say explicitly what Kim is supposed to tacitly know, theoretical resources like those to which Davidson appeals – e.g., notions of truth, reference, and satisfaction – have to be introduced. It is because these notions, and the semantic theories that they inhabit, are unfamiliar to ordinary speakers that their knowledge is said to be merely tacit. It has to be allowed, then, that, unlike ordinary states of knowledge, states of tacit knowledge in this sense are unconscious, and that their interactions with other psychological states are limited. Because of these differences between tacit knowledge and ordinary knowledge, some philosophers worry that this notion of tacit knowledge might not be coherent. There is, after all, no guarantee that one can always derive a coherent notion by suppressing features of a coherent one.[3]

On the second view of 'tacit knowledge', it is taken to apply to certain sorts of merely neurological states, without any commitment to those states being similar to states of ordinary knowledge.[4] To possess a piece of tacit knowledge on this second view is to have a brain which is a certain way. The use of 'knowledge' is now evidently something of a courtesy.[5]

Introduction to Chomsky

Noam Chomsky is Professor of the Institute of Philosophy and Linguistics at Massachusetts Institute of Technology. His work in linguistics has revolutionized the study of language. He has written numerous books and articles in philosophy and linguistics, as well as on politics. His non-political books include *Logical Structure of Syntax* (1955/1975), *Syntactic Structures* (1957), *Aspects of the Theory of Syntax* (1965), *Cartesian Linguistics* (1966), *Language and Mind* (1968, 2nd edn 1972), *Reflections on Language*

---

[3] For example, no coherent notion can be derived from the concept *red* by suppressing the feature that it applies to a colour.

[4] Note that such views often treat neurological systems as *computational systems* – as systems that operate over formal structures akin to sentences. So there is no immediate conflict between treating states of tacit knowledge as neurological states and treating them as having 'contents' given by the statements of a semantic theory. Strictly, computational characterizations should be distinguished from neurological ones. But in what follows, we use 'neurological' as if it covered both. For more detail see the reading list on Computational Psychology.

[5] See also the reading list for Tacit Knowledge: Its Nature.

(1975), *Rules and Representations* (1980), *Language and Problems of Knowledge* (1988), and *New Horizons in the Study of Language and Mind* (2000).

In the following extract from *Knowledge of Language* (1986), Chomsky sets out his view of the aims of an account of language. Chomsky holds that an account of language should be an account of what competent speakers know – an account of their competence. Chomsky does not think such an account can be given on the basis of what speakers would ordinarily be said to know. He is famous for holding that speakers' competence is constituted by *tacit knowledge*, although he does not use the phrase in the extract we reprint. But is tacit knowledge a species of *knowledge*? Chomsky seems to suggest an affirmative answer in the extract. In order to establish whether he is right, we need to determine what properties he requires tacit knowledge to have.

Some questions to ask in reading this extract are the following. (1) What does Chomsky think should be the aim of an account of language? (2) Is the aim appropriate? (3) What is Chomsky's view of the nature of linguistic competence? Specifically, in what sort of knowledge does Chomsky think competence consists?

Noam Chomsky, 'Knowledge of Language as a Focus of Inquiry' (extracts from Ch.1 of *Knowledge of Language*)

The generative grammar of a particular language (where 'generative' means nothing more than 'explicit') is a theory that is concerned with the form and meaning of expressions of this language. One can imagine many different kinds of approach to such questions, many points of view that might be adopted in dealing with them. Generative grammar limits itself to certain elements of this larger picture. Its standpoint is that of individual psychology. It is concerned with those aspects of form and meaning that are determined by the 'language faculty', which is understood to be a particular component of the human mind. The nature of this faculty is the subject matter of a general theory of linguistic structure that aims to discover the framework of principles and elements common to attainable human languages; this theory is now often called 'universal grammar' (UG), adapting a traditional term to a new context of inquiry. UG may be regarded as a characterization of the genetically determined language faculty. One may think of this faculty as a 'language acquisition device', an innate component of the human mind that yields a particular language through interaction with presented experience, a device that converts experience into a system of knowledge attained: knowledge of one or another language.

The study of generative grammar represented a significant shift of focus in the approach to problems of language. Put in the simplest terms, to be elaborated below, the shift of focus was from behaviour or the products of behaviour to states of the mind/brain that enter into behaviour. If one chooses to focus attention on this latter topic, the central concern becomes knowledge of language: its nature, origins, and use.

The three basic questions that arise, then, are these:

(1)   i. What constitutes knowledge of language?
      ii. How is knowledge of language acquired?
      iii. How is knowledge of language put to use?

The answer to the first question is given by a particular generative grammar, a theory concerned with the state of the mind/brain of the person who knows a particular language. The answer to the second is given by a specification of UG along with an account of the ways in which its principles interact with experience to yield a particular language; UG is a theory of the 'initial state' of the language faculty, prior to any linguistic experience. The answer to the third question would be a theory of how the knowledge of language attained enters into the expression of thought and the understanding of presented specimens of language, and derivatively, into communication and other special uses of language.

So far, this is nothing more than the outline of a research program that takes up classical questions that had been put aside for many years. As just described, it should not be particularly controversial, since it merely expresses an interest in certain problems and offers a preliminary analysis of how they might be confronted, although as is often the case, the initial formulation of a problem may prove to be far-reaching in its implications, and ultimately controversial as it is developed.

Some elements of this picture may appear to be more controversial than they really are. Consider, for example, the idea that there is a language faculty, a component of the mind/brain that yields knowledge of language given presented experience. It is not at issue that humans attain knowledge of English, Japanese, and so forth, while rocks, birds, or apes do not under the same (or indeed any) conditions. There is, then, some property of the mind/brain that differentiates humans from rocks, birds, or apes. Is this a distinct 'language faculty' with specific structure and properties, or, as some believe, is it the case that humans acquire language merely by applying generalized learning mechanisms of some sort, perhaps with greater efficiency or scope than other organisms? These are not topics for speculation or *a priori* reasoning but for empirical inquiry, and it is clear enough how to proceed: namely, by facing the questions of (1). We try to determine what is the system of knowledge that has been attained and what properties must be attributed to the initial state of the mind/brain to account for its attainment. Insofar as these properties are language-specific, either individually or in the way they are organized and composed, there is a distinct language faculty.

Generative grammar is sometimes referred to as a theory, advocated by this or that person. In fact, it is not a theory any more than chemistry is a theory. Generative grammar is a topic, which one may or may not choose to study. Of course, one can adopt a point of view from which chemistry disappears as a discipline (perhaps it is all done by angels with mirrors). In this sense, a decision to study chemistry does stake out a position on matters of fact. Similarly, one may argue that the topic of generative grammar does not exist, although it is hard to see how to make this position minimally plausible. Within the study of generative grammar there have been many changes and differences of opinion, often reversion to ideas that had been abandoned and were later reconstructed in a different light. Evidently, this is a healthy phenomenon indicating that the discipline is alive, although it is sometimes, oddly, regarded as a serious deficiency, a sign that something is wrong with the basic approach. I will review some of these changes as we proceed.

In the mid-1950s, certain proposals were advanced as to the form that answers to the questions of (1) might take, and a research program was inaugurated to investigate the adequacy of these proposals and to sharpen and apply them. This program was one of the strands that led to the development of the cognitive sciences in the contemporary sense, sharing with other approaches the belief that certain aspects of the mind/brain can be usefully construed on the model of computational systems of rules that form and modify representations, and that are put to use in interpretation and action. From its origins (or with a longer perspective, one might say 'its reincarnation') about 30 years ago, the study of generative grammar was undertaken with an eye to gaining some insight into the nature and origins of systems of knowledge, belief, and understanding more broadly, in the hope that these general questions could be illuminated by a detailed investigation of the special case of human language.

[...]
I want to consider [...] two major conceptual shifts, one that inaugurated the contemporary study of generative grammar, and a second, more theory-internal, that is now in process and that offers some new perspectives on traditional problems.
[...]
Traditional and structuralist grammar did not deal with the questions of (1), the former because of its implicit reliance on the unanalyzed intelligence of the reader, the latter because of its narrowness of scope. The concerns of traditional and generative grammar are, in a certain sense, complementary: a good traditional or pedagogical grammar provides a full list of exceptions (irregular verbs, etc.), paradigms and examples of regular constructions, and observations at various levels of detail and generality about the form and meaning of expressions. But it does not examine the question of how the reader of the grammar uses such information to attain the knowledge that is used to form and interpret new expressions, or the question of the nature and elements of this knowledge: essentially the questions of (1), above. Without too much exaggeration, one could describe such a grammar as a structured and organized version of the data presented to a child learning a language, with some general commentary and often insightful observations. Generative grammar, in contrast, is concerned primarily with the intelligence of the reader, the principles and procedures brought to bear to attain full knowledge of a language. Structuralist theories, both in the European and American traditions, did concern themselves with analytic procedures for deriving aspects of grammar from data, as in the procedural theories of Nikolay Trubetzkoy, Zellig Harris, Bernard Bloch, and others, but primarily in the areas of phonology and morphology. The procedures suggested were seriously inadequate and in any event could not possibly be understood (and were not intended) to provide an answer to question (1ii), even in the narrower domains where most work was concentrated. Nor was there an effort to determine what was involved in offering a comprehensive account of the knowledge of the speaker/ hearer.

$\boxed{c}$ As soon as these questions were squarely faced, a wide range of new phenomena were discovered, including quite simple ones that had passed unnoticed, and severe problems arose that had previously been ignored or seriously misunderstood. A standard belief 30 years ago was that language acquisition is a case of 'overlearning'. Language was regarded as a habit system, one that was assumed to be much overdetermined by available evidence. Production and interpretation of new forms was taken to be a straightforward matter of analogy, posing no problems of principle... Attention to the questions of (1) quickly reveals that exactly the opposite is the case: language poses in a sharp and clear form what has sometimes been called 'Plato's problem', the problem of 'poverty of stimulus', of accounting for the richness, complexity, and specificity of shared knowledge, given the limitations of the data available. This difference of perception concerning where the problem lies – overlearning or poverty of evidence – reflects very clearly the effect of the shift of focus that inaugurated the study of generative grammar.

d ↦   A great many examples have been given over the years to illustrate what clearly is the fundamental problem: the problem of poverty of evidence. A familiar example is the structure dependence of rules, the fact that without instruction or direct evidence, children unerringly use computationally complex structure-dependent rules rather than computationally simple rules that involve only the predicate 'leftmost' in a linear sequence of words. To take some other examples [...] consider sentences (2)–(7):

(2) I wonder who [the men expected to see them]
(3) [the men expected to see them]
(4) John ate an apple
(5) John ate
(6) John is too stubborn to talk to Bill
(7) John is too stubborn to talk to

Both (2) and (3) include the clause bounded by brackets, but only in (2) may the pronoun *them* be referentially dependent on the antecedent *the men*; in (3) the pronoun is understood as referring in some manner indicated in the situational or discourse context, but not to the men. Numerous facts of this sort, falling under what is now generally called 'binding theory,' are known without relevant experience to differentiate the cases. Such facts pose a serious problem that was not recognized in earlier work: How does every child know, unerringly, to interpret the clause differently in the two cases? And why does no pedagogic grammar have to draw the learner's attention to such facts (which were, in fact, noticed only quite recently, in the course of the study of explicit rule systems in generative grammar)?

Turning to examples (4)–(7), sentence (5) means that John ate something or other, a fact that one might explain on the basis of a simple inductive procedure: ate takes an object, as in (4), and if the object is missing, it is understood as arbitrary. Applying the same inductive procedure to (6) and (7), it should be that (7) means that John is so stubborn that he (John) will not talk to some arbitrary person, on the analogy of (6). But the meaning is, in fact, quite different: namely, that John is so stubborn that some arbitrary person won't talk to him (John). Again, this is known without training or relevant evidence.[1]

The situation is, in fact, more complex. Although plausible, the inductive procedure suggested for the relatively straightforward examples (4)–(5) does not seem correct. As noted by Howard Lasnik, the word *eat* has a somewhat different meaning in its intransitive usage, something like dine. One can say 'John ate his shoe', but 'John ate' cannot be understood to include this case. The observation is general for such cases. The intransitive forms differ from normal intransitives in other respects; for example, we can form 'the dancing bear' (corresponding to 'the bear that dances'), but not 'the eating man' (corresponding to 'the man who eats') [...] Such facts pose further problems of poverty of stimulus.

Children do not make errors about the interpretation of such sentences as (6)–(7) past a certain stage of development, and if they did, the errors would largely be uncorrectable. It is doubtful that even the most compendious traditional or teaching grammar notes such simple facts as those illustrated in (2)–(7), and such observations lie far beyond the domain of structural grammars. A wide variety of examples of this sort immediately come to attention when one faces the questions formulated in (1).

e ⟶ Knowledge of language is often characterized as a practical ability to speak and understand, so that questions (1i) and (1iii) are closely related, perhaps identified. Ordinary usage makes a much sharper distinction between the two questions, and is right to do so. Two people may share exactly the same knowledge of language but differ markedly in their ability to put this knowledge to use. Ability to use language may improve or decline without any change in knowledge. This ability may also be impaired, selectively or in general, with no loss of knowledge, a fact that would become clear if injury leading to impairment recedes and lost ability is recovered. Many such considerations support the commonsense assumption that knowledge cannot be properly described as a practical ability. Furthermore, even if this view could somehow be maintained, it would leave open all of the

---

[1] The reaction to such phenomena, also unnoticed until recently, again illustrates the difference of outlook of structuralist-descriptive and generative grammar. For some practitioners of the former, the statement of the facts, which is straightforward enough once they are observed, is the answer – nothing else is necessary; for the latter, the statement of the facts poses the problem to be solved. Cf. Ney (1983), particularly, his puzzlement about the 'peculiar view of grammar [that] unnecessarily complicates the whole matter' by seeking an explanation for the facts. Note that there is no question of right or wrong here, but rather of topic of inquiry.

serious questions. Thus, what is the nature of the 'practical ability' manifested in our interpretation of the sentences (2)–(7), how is it properly described, and how is it acquired?

f → Often it is not immediately obvious what our knowledge of language entails in particular cases, a fact illustrated even with short and simple sentences such as (8)–(10):

(8) His wife loves her husband
(9) John is too clever to expect us to catch Bill
(10) John is too clever to expect us to catch

In the case of (8), it takes some thought to determine whether *his* can be referentially dependent on *her husband* if *her* is dependent on *his wife* – that is, if the reference of either *he* or *she* is not somehow contextually indicated.[2] Examples (9) and (10) are, in fact, analogous to (6) and (7), respectively, but again, it takes some thought to discover that (10) means that John is so clever that an arbitrary person cannot expect us to catch him (John), although it is clear at once that it does not mean that John is so clever that he (John) cannot catch some arbitrary person, on the analogy of (9) (and (4), (5)). Our abilities seem limited somehow in such cases (and there are far more complex ones), but it would make little sense to speak of our knowledge of language as 'limited' in any comparable way.

Suppose we insist on speaking of knowledge of language as a practical ability to speak and understand. Then normal usage must be revised in numerous cases such as those just discussed. Suppose that Jones takes a public speaking course and improves his ability to speak and understand without any change in his knowledge of English, as we would describe the situation in normal usage. We must now revise this commonsense usage and say, rather, that Jones has improved his ability$_1$ to use his ability$_2$ to speak and understand; similar translations are required in the other cases. But the two occurrences of 'ability' in this description are hardly more than homonyms. Ability$_1$ is ability in the normal sense of the word: it can improve or decline, can be inadequate to determine consequences of knowledge, and so on. Ability$_2$, however, remains stable while our ability to use it changes, and we have this kind of 'ability' even when we are unable to detect what it entails in concrete cases. In short, the neologism 'ability$_2$' is invested with all the properties of knowledge. Note that there are cases when we do speak of abilities that we cannot

---

[2] On structures of this type, and problems of binding theory, more generally, see Higginbotham (1983), among much other work.

put to use: for example, the case of swimmers who cannot swim because their hands are tied, although they retain the ability to swim. The cases in question are not of this sort, however.

g⟶ The purpose of the attempt to reduce knowledge to ability is, presumably, to avoid problematic features that seem to inhere in the concept of knowledge, to show that these can be explained in dispositional or other terms more closely related to actual behaviour (whether this is possible even in the case of ability$_1$, the normal sense, is another question). But nothing of the sort is achieved by this departure from ordinary usage; the problems remain, exactly as before, now embedded in terminological confusion. The task of determining the nature of our knowledge (= ability$_2$), and accounting for its origins and use, remains exactly as challenging as before, despite the terminological innovations.

Other examples similar to (8)–(10) raise further questions. Consider the following sentences:

(11) John is too stubborn to expect anyone to talk to Bill
(12) John is too stubborn to visit anyone who talked to Bill

Suppose we delete *Bill* from (11) and (12), yielding (13) and (14), respectively:

(13) John is too stubborn to expect anyone to talk to
(14) John is too stubborn to visit anyone who talked to

Sentence (13) is structurally analogous to (10), and is understood in the same manner: it means that John is so stubborn that an arbitrary person would not expect anyone to talk to him (John). 'By analogy', then, we would expect sentence (14) to mean that John is so stubborn that an arbitrary person would not visit anyone who talked to him (John). But it does not have that meaning; in fact, it is gibberish. Here we have a double failure of analogy. Sentence (14) is not understood 'on the analogy' of (4), (5), (6), (9), and (12) (hence meaning that John is so stubborn that he (John) would not visit anyone who talked to some arbitrary person), nor is it understood 'on the analogy' of (7), (10), and (13); rather, it has no interpretation at all. And while the status of (11), (12), and (14) is immediately obvious, it takes some thought or preparation to see that (13) has the interpretation it does have, and thus to determine the consequences of our knowledge in this case.

h⟶ Again, these are facts that we know, however difficult it may be to determine that our system of knowledge has these consequences. We know these facts without instruction or even direct evidence, surely without correction of error by the speech community. It would be absurd to try to teach such facts as these to people learning English as a second language, just as no one taught them to us or even presented us with evidence that could yield this knowledge by any generally reliable procedure. This is knowledge without grounds, without good reasons or support by reliable procedures in any general or otherwise useful sense of these notions. Were we to insist that knowledge is a kind of ability, we would have to claim that we lack the ability to understand 'John is too stubborn to talk to' as meaning 'John is too stubborn to talk to someone or other' (on the analogy of 'John ate an apple' – 'John ate'), and that we lack the ability to understand (14) on the analogy of 'John ate an apple' – 'John ate' (so that it means that John is too stubborn to visit anyone who talked to someone or other) or on the analogy of 'John is too stubborn to talk to', with the 'inversion strategy' that we some-how use in this case (so that (14) means that John is too stubborn for someone or other to visit anyone who talked to him, John). But these would be odd claims, to say the least. These are not failures of ability. It is not that we are too weak, or lack some special skill that could be acquired. We are perfectly capable of associating the sentence, (14), for example, with either of the two meanings that would be provided 'by analogy' (or others), but we know that these are not the associations that our knowledge of the language provides; ability is one thing, knowledge something quite different. The system of knowledge that has somehow developed in our minds has certain consequences, not others; it relates sound and meaning and assigns structural properties to physical events in certain ways, not others.

It seems that there is little hope in accounting for our knowledge in terms of such ideas as analogy, induction, association, reliable pro-cedures, good reasons, and justification in any generally useful sense, or in terms of 'generalized learning mechanisms' (if such exist). And it seems that we should follow normal usage in distinguishing clearly between knowledge and ability to use that knowledge. We should, so it appears, think of knowledge of language as a certain state of the mind/brain, a relatively stable element in transitory mental states once it is attained; furthermore, as a state of some distinguishable faculty of the mind – the language faculty – with its specific properties, struc-ture, and organization, one 'module' of the mind.[3]

---

[3] See Fodor (1983). But it is too narrow to regard the 'language module' as an input system in Fodor's sense, if only because it is used in speaking and thought. We might consider supplement-ing this picture by adding an 'output system', but plainly this must be linked to the input system; we do not expect a person to speak only English and understand only Japanese. That is, the input and output systems must each access a fixed system of knowledge. The latter, however, is a central system which has essential problems of modularity, a fact that brings the entire picture into question. Furthermore, even regarded as an input system, the language module does not

References

Fodor, J. (1983). *The Modularity of Mind* (Cambridge, Mass.: MIT Press).

Higginbotham, J. (1983). 'Logical Form, Binding and Nominals', *Linguistic Inquiry*, 14.3.

Ney, J. (1983). 'Review of Chomsky's *Some Concepts and Consequences of the Theory of Government and Binding*', *Language Sciences*, 5.2.

Commentary on Chomsky

The aims of linguistic theory

Chomsky begins the extract (up to $\boxed{a} \mapsto$) with a statement of what he takes to be the aims of a *generative grammar* – an explicit theory of the workings of language. In setting out these aims, Chomsky draws two sets of distinctions.

> State the two sets of distinctions in your own words. What is the relation between the second set of distinctions and Chomsky's question (1)? Make a note of how the distinctions correspond with labels like 'UG'.

First, Chomsky distinguishes linguistic behaviour and 'states of the mind/brain that enter into behaviour' and takes the latter – the *language faculty* – as the focus of his inquiry. Second, he distinguishes three components from amongst the states of the mind/brain responsible for linguistic behaviour. The components are: (i) the knowledge of language possessed by competent speakers; (ii) the knowledge nascent speakers bring to bear on experience in order to acquire knowledge of language; (iii) the systems responsible for translating knowledge of language into linguistic behaviour.

Chomsky's use of 'mind/brain' suggests that he does not distinguish here between minds and brains. This might represent either that he identifies ordinary states of knowledge with neurological states of the brain or, rather, that he is interested in neurology, rather than in ordinary states of knowledge.[1] Notice that the former view, unlike the latter, expresses a controversial philosophical commitment.

---

appear to have the property of rapidity of access that Fodor discusses, as indicated by (8)–(14). Note also that even if Fodor is right in believing that there is a sharp distinction between modules in his sense and 'the rest', which is holistic in several respects, it does not follow that the residue is unstructured. In fact, this seems highly unlikely, if only because of the 'epistemic boundedness' that he notes. Many other questions arise concerning Fodor's very intriguing discussion of these issues, which I will not pursue here.

[1] Note that Chomsky wants to provide a computational characterization of neurology: see the Introduction to this chapter, fn. 4.

As you work through the rest of the commentary, try to decide which view Chomsky's use of 'mind/brain' represents.

Between $\boxed{a} \mapsto$ and $\boxed{b} \mapsto$ Chomsky suggests that it is not controversial to think that there is a *language faculty* which we may choose to investigate.

Can you think of ways in which choice of investigative focus might be criticized? How does Chomsky attempt to show that elements of his picture are less controversial than they appear? Does he succeed?

Chomsky argues that the language faculty exists by identifying it with whatever distinguishes things able to acquire competence – normal humans – from those that are not – rocks, birds, and apes. It seems reasonable to ask what distinguishes the two groups. That suffices for the existence of Chomsky's subject matter.

Notice that Chomsky's argument does not support the claim that the language faculty should be characterized in terms of *knowledge*, rather than in, say, neurological terms. Since Chomsky sometimes characterizes his subject as *knowledge* of language, that might seem a serious omission. Whether it is depends on what Chomsky expresses by using 'mind/brain'.

Innate knowledge and 'poverty of stimulus'

From $\boxed{c} \mapsto$ to $\boxed{e} \mapsto$ Chomsky states and illustrates the problem of 'poverty of stimulus'.

Chomsky briefly states the problem (see $\boxed{c} \mapsto$ to $\boxed{d} \mapsto$). Put the problem in your own words. Think about the sorts of evidence that might go towards filling out a statement of the problem (see $\boxed{d} \mapsto$ to $\boxed{e} \mapsto$).

Somehow children change from being linguistically incompetent to being competent. How do they make that transition? Because children typically acquire competence in the language(s) to which they are exposed, it is plausible that they do so on the basis of experience of the use of language made by speakers in their environment.[2] What is wanted, then, is an explanation of how children use their experience in building competence.

---

[2] Some philosophers assume that the most natural view of language acquisition is that it is wholly based on learning from evidence, so that argument is needed for the view that acquisition depends largely on innately specified neural or psychological structure. Chomsky thinks the most natural view is that linguistic competence is wholly innate, so that argument is required for invoking learning at all.

Given an account of the evidence available to children and an account of adult competence, we want to know how the former can supply a basis for the latter. Labelling the child's evidence *Primary Linguistic Data* (PLD) and the acquired, adult competence, *LC*, what is wanted is an account of the systems within the child responsible for taking the PLD as input and delivering LC as output, an account of UG (for *Universal Grammar*) in the following diagram:

$$PLD \rightarrow UG \rightarrow LC$$

As explicit accounts of LC were developed, it quickly became apparent that LC is enormously rich and complex and that it is also language-specific – i.e., not what would be expected if competence were designed on the basis of general canons of reason. Since the child's *stimulus* – PLD – is impoverished relative to LC, the problem about how to account for LC is one of 'poverty of stimulus'. The response proposed by Chomsky is that UG itself suffices, more or less, for LC. Crudely, the child is born with adult competence. Rather than serving as evidence for LC, the PLD, in Chomsky's view, plays a more limited role, tuning a universally shared initial endowment. Although different natural languages are apt to seem very different, Chomsky thinks that, on closer inspection, the differences are less striking than the similarities.

The justification for this view of UG is an inference to best explanation. The discrepancy between PLD and LC does not supply a deductive argument for Chomsky's view. Rather, detailed accounts of UG are compared as to their ability to explain the transition from PLD to LC. Thus far, in Chomsky's view, the best available accounts all involve viewing LC as largely innate – present in UG independently of the PLD.[3]

The force of an argument to best explanation depends on the absence of equally good explanations. In this case, that depends on the extent to which LC is rich, complex, and arbitrary. From $\boxed{d}\!\mapsto$ to $\boxed{e}\!\mapsto$ Chomsky outlines some of the respects in which it is. Although Chomsky does not go into details in the extract, the examples to which he appeals are supposed to be *explained* in a systematic way by a body of rules and principles taken to constitute LC.[4]

One unfamiliar notion here is *referential dependence*. Roughly, an expression *e* is referentially dependent on another expression *f*, when *e*'s reference is determined on the basis of *f*'s. In (1), the pronoun 'she' can be referentially dependent on 'Kim':

(1) Kim smoked because she liked to.

---

[3] See the reading list on Innate Knowledge and 'Poverty of Stimulus'.
[4] For more detail, see the reading list on Syntactic Theory.

Sometimes, referential dependency between expressions is prohibited, as with 'Mary' and 'her' in (2):

(2) Mary washed her.

Sometimes, referential dependency is mandatory, as with 'Mary' and the reflexive 'herself' in (3):

(3) Kim asked Mary to wash herself.

Try swapping 'her' and 'herself' in (2) and (3). What is the effect?

> Work through Chomsky's examples. Test your intuitions against Chomsky's descriptions. How do Chomsky's examples, and his discussion of them, support his view of the 'poverty of stimulus' problem?

Competent speakers' judgements about sentences are a major source of evidence for accounts of LC. That fact might be taken to bear on the question of Chomsky's view of the sort of knowledge implicated in LC.

There are three questions to consider about the 'poverty of stimulus' problem. First, does the best solution involve viewing LC as dictated by UG – as largely innate? Second, does the innate endowment amount to *knowledge*? Third, what sort of knowledge would this be? The first question is mainly empirical, but the second and third are primarily philosophical.

Competence and performance

From $\boxed{e} \mapsto$ to $\boxed{g} \mapsto$ Chomsky argues that knowledge of language should not be viewed as a form of ability. His arguments are designed to support his initial distinction between linguistic competence – a system of knowledge – and the systems responsible for the use of that knowledge, a distinction corresponding to the difference between his questions (1i) and (1iii). In other work, Chomsky calls this the distinction between competence and *performance*.

> Chomsky offers two related arguments against the ability view, one beginning at $\boxed{e} \mapsto$, one at $\boxed{f} \mapsto$. What are they? How might a defender of the ability view respond?

Chomsky's arguments both aim to show that competence and ability vary independently of one another. The first argument appeals to cases like loss of ability due to injury. If someone lost their ability to speak, we might claim they had ceased to know their language. But if they recovered ability, without relearning the language, it would seem that they had retained competence.

Hence, competence is possible in the absence of ability. The second argument is based on the observation that judgements about meaning sometimes take time to emerge. Perhaps the most famous case of this sort is given in (4):

(4) The horse raced past the barn fell.

In such cases, we seem, for a time, unable to judge correctly; but it would make little sense to suppose we lacked competence. For a time, what we are able to *do* – our performance – is out of alignment with what we *know* – our competence.

At [g]→ Chomsky notes a feature of competence that follows from his arguments: competence need not be perfectly reflected in behaviour. At [h]→ he presents an additional argument against the view that competence resides in ability, based on the meanings we do, and the meanings we do not, assign to sentences.

> What is Chomsky's argument at [h]→? Is it compelling?

Chomsky's argument begins from the fact that we judge that some strings of words do not bear particular meanings. So, for example, we judge that (5) (Chomsky's (14)), has no meaning.

(5) John is too stubborn to visit anyone who talked to

Chomsky argues that, if the source of our judgement were an ability, then we should have to say that we lacked the ability to understand (5) as having a particular meaning, say that of (6).

(6) John is so stubborn that an arbitrary person would not visit anyone who talked to him (John)

But Chomsky thinks that it is implausible to describe the case in that way. According to Chomsky, the fact that we don't take (5) to mean the same as (6) is not due to our lack of ability. He thinks that we *are* able to associate (5) with the meaning indicated in (6). What prevents us from making this association is that we know that (5) doesn't mean the same as (6).

Tacit knowledge

Suppose that competence resides in knowledge. What type of knowledge is this? Could it be ordinary knowledge? If we claim it is, we need to explain how we might fail to draw consequences of this knowledge. Moreover, we need to explain speakers' inability to put what they know into words, to state the rules guiding their judgements. The remaining option is that competence consists in tacit knowledge. The question now is: Is tacit knowledge a special form of knowledge? This question is not to be answered by appeal to the fact that we ordinarily describe the linguistically competent as knowing a language. Rather, we need to describe features of competence and of ordinary knowledge and judge the extent to which those features agree.

Look again at $\boxed{e}\mapsto$ to $\boxed{h}\mapsto$ and compile lists of features appearing in Chomsky's characterizations of competence that are, and are not, features of ordinary knowledge.

In attempting to determine Chomsky's view of linguistic knowledge, we should make the usual distinction between knowledge of sentence-meaning and knowledge from which that knowledge may be derived.

It is initially plausible that knowledge of sentence-meaning is ordinary. It might be suggested that reflection on (7) (Chomsky's (10)) suggests otherwise.

(7) John is too clever to expect us to catch

The suggestion is that even while we are unable to attain conscious knowledge of the meaning of (7), we possess tacit knowledge of that meaning. But given the distinction between ordinary knowledge and its basis, the suggestion is unmotivated. More plausible is that we have knowledge from which knowledge of the meaning of (7) may be derived, but we have not yet derived it. Compare knowing arithmetic and knowing the solution to a particular equation.

Potentially more problematic for the ordinary knowledge view is that we seem unable to report on what we are consciously aware of in being aware of meanings. Typically, the best we can do is offer more or less satisfactory paraphrases. But the ability to paraphrase only demonstrates that we have ordinary knowledge *about* the meanings of sentences, not that our knowledge of their meanings is itself ordinary. It is worth reflecting here on the difference between the ordinary knowledge you acquire by being *told* what (7) means with your state of mind on coming to *understand* (7) as having that meaning. Moreover, even if we have ordinary knowledge of sentence meaning, it does not follow that we have ordinary knowledge of what linguistic theory states about sentence meaning. (This was a point made by Soames in the previous chapter.)

What about the bases of knowledge of sentence-meaning? We are typically unconscious of the bases and unable to report on them. At best, then, we have tacit knowledge of those bases. How much like ordinary, conscious knowledge is tacit knowledge?

The question is difficult to answer. In favour of likeness, Chomsky refers to what we know about sentence meanings as being *entailed* by, *derived* from, or as *consequences* of, what we know of the bases. That makes tacit knowledge seem like an attitude towards things that can stand in relations of entailment, derivation, and consequence – i.e., an attitude towards propositions. Against likeness, not only is tacit knowledge taken to be unconscious, Chomsky argues at ⟦h⟧→ that linguistic knowledge is 'without grounds, without good reasons or support by reliable procedures'. In fact, it is not entirely clear to which aspect of competence Chomsky is here referring. If he is referring to knowledge of the bases, lack of grounds is just another respect in which tacit knowledge differs from typical cases of ordinary knowledge. But if he is referring to knowledge of sentence meaning – as the context and opening sentence of ⟦h⟧→ suggests – then he appears to hold that the bases from which knowledge of sentence meaning derives need not justify the knowledge. If that is right, then it is unclear what motivation remains for insisting that the bases underwriting competence are states of *knowledge*. An important unresolved question is whether tacit knowledge should be viewed as another sort of propositional attitude.

Chomsky sometimes appears to think that the states of knowledge that he thinks are implicated in explaining linguistic competence are not propositional attitudes. However, the question is not to be settled by fiat. Rather, it is a question of the best interpretation of the explanatory strategy of successful linguistic theory. Since we know that ordinary knowledge is (or, at least, involves) a propositional attitude, one question here concerns the relation between the systems characterized in the theory and the ordinary knowledge we attain on their basis – for instance, knowledge of the meaning of particular utterances. If we find that the relation is analogous to the relation between bits of ordinary knowledge, then we have evidence in favour of a propositional attitude interpretation. But not all relations between bits of knowledge and their bases are like that. For example, the knowledge we acquire from perception may be thought to be different.[5]

Introduction to Dummett

Sir Michael Dummett was, from 1979 until his retirement in 1992, Wykeham Professor of Logic at the University of Oxford. His books include *Frege: Philosophy of Language* (1973, 2nd edn 1981), *Truth and Other Enigmas* (1978), *The Logical Basis of Metaphysics* (1991), *Frege: Philosophy of Mathematics* (1991), *The Seas of Language* (1993), and *Origins of Analytical Philosophy* (1993). Dummett is perhaps most famous for proposing that the study of linguistic meaning might reveal that claims in some areas are unfit either to be true or to be false. That is, it might sustain what Dummett calls

---

[5] For further discussion see the reading lists on Chomsky's Philosophy of Language and on Tacit Knowledge: Its Nature.

'anti-realism' about those areas. Dummett argues that anti-realism is the core of more traditional rejections of realism – for example, views that hold reality (or, at least, aspects of reality) to be constituted by human ideas or experiences. In Dummett's view, the disagreement between realist and anti-realist is best pursued by examining the nature of meaning, and hence the nature of linguistic competence.[1]

Dummett thinks that linguistic competence – which he calls *mastery* of a language – resides in a form of knowledge intermediate between ordinary knowledge and mere ability. The intermediate form is *implicit* knowledge. Dummett uses this notion to underpin his view of the relation between competence and semantic theory. According to Dummett, ordinary speakers have implicit knowledge of a semantic theory. He explains how this view arises from reflection on the relation between thought and its linguistic expression.

Some questions to consider in reading 'What do I Know when I Know a Language?' are the following. (1) How does Dummett characterize the notion of implicit knowledge? (2) What requirements must the notion meet in order to play its role in his account? (3) Does it meet those requirements? (4) What argument does Dummett provide for his view of the relation between competence and semantic theory? (5) Is the argument compelling?

Michael Dummett, 'What Do I Know When I Know a Language?'

Our usual ways of thinking about the mastery of a language, or of this and that element of it, are permeated by the conception that this mastery consists in *knowledge*. To understand an expression is to know its meaning; we speak of knowing what an ostrich is, of knowing what 'credulous' means, and, above all, of knowing Swedish or Spanish. Are we to take seriously the use of the verb 'to know' in this connection? Is an ability to speak a language really a case of knowledge?

The verb 'to know' is used in connection with many practical abilities: in English we speak of '*knowing* how to swim/ride a bicycle' and in French, for example, one says 'Il sait nager' rather than 'il peut nager'. But does the knowledge – the practical knowledge – involved in these cases *explain* the practical ability, or is it, rather, that the practical ability is all there is to the practical knowledge, that our appeal in these cases to the concept of knowledge is a mere manner of

[1]   There is a reading list on Dummett's Philosophy of Language.

speaking, not to be taken seriously? And, if the latter view is correct, does not the same hold of the mastery of the language, which is also a practical ability?

[b]→ A character in one of the novels of the English humourist P. G. Wodehouse, asked whether she can speak Spanish, replies, 'I don't know: I've never tried'. Where does the absurdity of this lie? Would there be the same absurdity in giving that answer to the question, 'Can you swim?' The suggestion that the absurdity would be the same in both cases amounts to the proposal that our use of the verb 'to know' in these two connections – 'knowing Spanish', 'knowing how to swim' – is due to the empirical fact that speaking Spanish and swimming are things no one can do unless he has been taught, that is, has been subjected to a certain training; 'to know', in these cases, means 'to have learned'. But is this right? It is only an empirical fact that we cannot swim unless we have been taught. It would not be magic if someone were, instinctively as we should say, to make the right movements the first time he found himself in water, and, indeed, I have heard it said that this is just what happens when very small infants are put in water. But it seems natural to think that it would be magic if someone who had not been brought up to speak Spanish and had never learned it since were suddenly to start speaking it. If asked for an explanation of the difference, we should be inclined to say that, if you are to speak Spanish, there are a great many things that you have to know, just as there are many things that you have to know if you are to play chess.

The difference lies in the fact that speaking a language is a conscious process. We can conceive that someone, put in the water for the first time, might simply find himself swimming. He need not, in any sense, know what he is doing; he need not even know that he is swimming. But what are we imagining when we imagine that someone, arriving for the first time in his life in a Spanish speaking country, should find himself speaking Spanish? There are two different cases, according as we suppose that he knows what he is saying or that he just hears the words coming out of his mouth without knowing what they mean. In either case, it is magic, but, in the latter case, although, miraculously, he *can* speak Spanish, he still does not *know* Spanish. Knowing Spanish, or knowing how to speak Spanish, is not, after all, to be compared with knowing how to swim. Both may be called practical capacities: but practical capacities are not all of one kind.

What do you not know if you have not learned to swim? You know what swimming is; you just do not know how to do it. And, if you found yourself in water, you might do it all the same, without knowing how you did it. You know what it is to swim; you can, for example, tell whether or not someone else is swimming: that is why, if you had to, you might try to swim, and you might find out that you could. But, if you have not learned Spanish, you do not even know what it is to speak Spanish; you could not tell (at least for sure) whether someone else was speaking it or not: and that is why you could not even try to speak Spanish. Indeed, when you learn Spanish, you do not learn a technique for accomplishing the already known end of speaking Spanish. There is no gap between knowing what it is to speak Spanish and knowing how to do so (save in special cases of a psychological inhibition or the like): you do not first learn what speaking Spanish is and then learn a means by which this feat can be executed.

There are degrees of consciousness with which a person may perform a skilled operation. At one extreme, he will formulate to himself the action to be carried out at each step and the manner in which it is to be done, as when someone unaccustomed to such tasks has memorized instructions how to cook a certain dish, or how to assemble a machine. This is the case in which a person has explicit knowledge how to perform the operation, and appeals to that knowledge in the course of performing it. At the other extreme, someone may simply be unable to say what it is that he does, even on reflection or when he tries to observe himself very closely; notoriously, those who have acquired physical skills may be quite unable to explain to others how to perform those feats. This is the case in which, if we speak of him as knowing how to perform the operation (say swimming or riding a bicycle), the expression 'knows how to do it' has only the force of 'can do it as the result of having learned to do it'. But there are also intermediate cases. In these, someone may be unable to formulate for himself the principles according to which he acts, but may nevertheless be capable of acknowledging, and willing to acknowledge, the correctness of a statement of those principles when it is offered to him.

In cases of this intermediate kind, it seems to me, we have to take more seriously the ascription of knowledge to someone who possesses the practical ability in question: 'knows how to do it' is not here a mere idiomatic equivalent of 'can do it'. Rather, we may say of the agent that he knows *that* certain things are the case, that he knows certain propositions about how the operation is to be performed; but we need to qualify this by conceding that his knowledge is not *explicit* knowledge, that is, knowledge which may be immediately elicited on request. It is, rather, *implicit* knowledge: knowledge which shows itself partly by manifestation of the practical ability, and partly by a readiness to acknowledge as correct a formulation of that which is known when it is presented. Consider, as an example, the knowledge of how to play chess. As a matter of fact, no one ever learns chess without being given some explicit information, such as that no piece except the knight may leap over another. Nevertheless, I can see no reason why it should be in principle unthinkable that someone should learn the game without ever being *told* anything, and without even framing rules to himself, simply by being corrected whenever he made an illegal move. Now, if we said, of such a person, that he knew how to play chess, should we be using the verb 'to know' solely in that sense which is involved in saying that someone knows how to swim? It appears to me that we should not. The reason is that it *would* be unthinkable that, having learned to obey the rules of chess, he should not then be able and willing to acknowledge those rules as correct when they were put to him, for example, to agree, perhaps after a little reflection, that only the knight could leap over another piece. Someone who had learned the game in this way could properly be said to know the rules *implicitly*. We might put the point by saying that he does not merely follow the rules, without knowing what he is doing: he is *guided* by them.

[d]→ There now arises a further question, not so easy to answer or even to state. The central task of the philosopher of language is to explain what *meaning* is, that is, what makes a language *language*. Consider two speakers engaged in conversation. To immediate inspection, all that is happening is that sounds of a certain kind issue from the mouths of each alternately. But we know that there is a deeper significance: they are expressing thoughts, putting forward arguments, stating conjectures, asking questions, etc. What the philosophy of language has to explain is what gives this character to the sounds they utter: what makes their utterances expressions of thought and all these other things?

The natural answer is that what makes the difference is the fact that both speakers *understand* or *know* the language. Each has, so to speak, the same piece of internal (mental) equipment, which enables each to interpret the utterances of the other as an expression of thought, and to convert his own thoughts into sentences that the other can likewise understand. It thus seems as though the key to the explanation of the expressive power which makes a language a language is an individual speaker's mastery of the language; and this mastery, as we saw, requires the notion of knowledge for its explication.

[e]→ This, then, becomes our second question: Is the significance of language to be explained in terms of a speaker's knowledge of his language? Philosophers before Frege assumed that it is; and they

assumed, further, that what a speaker knows is a kind of code. Concepts are coded into words and thoughts, which are compounded out of concepts, into sentences, whose structure mirrors, by and large, the complexity of the thoughts. We need language, on this view, only because we happen to lack the faculty of telepathy, that is, of the direct transmission of thoughts. Communication is thus essentially like the use of a telephone: the speaker codes his thought in a transmissible medium, which is then decoded by the hearer.

f→   The whole analytical school of philosophy is founded on the rejection of this conception, first clearly repudiated by Frege. The conception of language as a code requires that we may ascribe concepts and thoughts to people independently of their knowledge of language; and one strand of objection is that, for any but the simplest concepts, we cannot explain what it is to grasp them independently of the ability to express them in language. As Frege said, a dog will no doubt notice a difference between being set on by several dogs and being set on by only one, but he is unlikely to have even the dimmest consciousness of anything in common between being bitten by one larger dog and chasing one cat, which he would have to do were we to be able to ascribe to him a grasp of the concept we express by the word 'one'. Or, again, as Wittgenstein remarked, a dog can expect his master to come home, but he cannot expect him to come home next week; and the reason is that there is nothing the dog could do to *manifest* an expectation that his master will come home next week. It makes no sense to attribute to a creature without language a grasp of the concept expressed by the words 'next week'.

g→   It is, however, a serious mistake to suppose this to be the principal objection to the conception of language as a code. That conception involves comparing someone's mastery of his mother tongue with his mastery of a second language. His mastery of a second language may be represented as a grasp of a scheme of translation between it and his mother tongue: by appeal to this, he can associate expressions of the second language with expressions of his mother tongue. In a similar way, his mastery of his mother tongue is viewed, on this conception, as an ability to associate with each of its words the corresponding concept, and thus with each sentence of the language a thought compounded of such concepts.

The fundamental objection to this conception of language is that the analogy it uses breaks down. If we explain someone's knowledge of a second language as consisting in his grasp of a scheme of translation between it and his mother tongue, we tacitly presuppose that he understands his mother tongue; it then remains to be explained in what his understanding of his mother tongue consists. We can, in this way, proceed to explain his understanding of the second language in two stages – first, his ability to translate it into his mother tongue, and, secondly, his understanding of his mother tongue – precisely because, in principle, the ability to translate does not involve the ability to understand. In principle, we can imagine a person – or a very skilfully programmed computer – able to translate between two languages without understanding either. That is why, when we explain someone's knowledge of a second language as an ability to translate it into his mother tongue, we are not giving a circular account: the ability to translate does not, in itself, presuppose an understanding of the second language like the understanding someone has of his mother tongue. It is quite otherwise when we try to explain someone's understanding of his mother tongue after the same model, namely as consisting in his associating certain concepts with the words. For the question arises what it *is* to 'associate a concept with a word'. We know what it is to associate a word of one language with a word of another: asked to translate the one word, he utters, or writes down, the other. But the concept has no representation intermediate between it and its verbal expression. Or, if it does, we still have the question what makes it a representation of *that* concept. We cannot say that someone's association of a particular concept with a given word consists in the fact that, when he hears that word, that concept comes into his mind, for there is really no sense to speaking of a concept's coming into someone's mind. All that we can think of is some image's coming to mind which we take as in some way representing the concept, and this gets us no further forward, since we still have to ask in what his associating that concept with that image consists.

Rather, any account of what it is to associate a concept with a word would have to provide an explanation of one thing which might constitute a grasp of the concept. What is it to grasp the concept *square*, say? At the very least, it is to be able to discriminate between things that are square and those that are not. Such an ability can be ascribed only to one who will, on occasion, treat square things differently from things that are not square; one way, among many other possible ways, of doing this is to apply the word 'square' to square things and not to others. And it can only be by reference to some such use of the word 'square', or at least of some knowledge *about* the word 'square' which would warrant such a use of it, that we can explain what it is to associate the concept *square* with that word. An ability to use the word in such a way, or a suitable piece of knowledge about the word, would, by itself, *suffice* as a manifestation of a grasp of the concept. Even if we grant that there is no difficulty in supposing someone to have, and to manifest, a grasp of the concept antecedently to an understanding of the word, we can make no *use* of this assumption in explaining what it is to understand the word: we cannot appeal to the speaker's prior grasp of the concept in explaining what it is for him to associate that concept with that word. The question whether a grasp of the concepts expressible in language could precede a knowledge of any language thus falls away as irrelevant.

h ⊢→ We have, therefore, to replace the conception of language as a code for thought by some account of the understanding of a language that makes no appeal to the prior grasp of the concepts that can be expressed in it. Such an account presents language, not just as a means of expressing thought, but as a vehicle for thought. The idea of a language as a code became untenable because a concept's coming to mind was not, by itself, an intelligible description of a mental event: thought *requires* a vehicle. And for this reason, the philosophical study of language assumes a far greater importance as being, not just a branch of philosophy, but the foundation of the entire subject, since it has to be, simultaneously, a study of *thought*. Only if we take language to be a code can we hope to strip off the linguistic clothing and penetrate to the pure naked thought beneath: the only effective means of studying thought is by the study of language, which is its vehicle.

The observation that there is no such mental event as a concept's coming to mind is paralleled by Wittgenstein's remark that understanding is not a mental process. One of the advantages of the approach to language as a vehicle of thought is that we do not need to look for any *occurrence* save the expression of the thought. Suppose that I am walking along the street with my wife, and suddenly stop dead and say (in English), 'I have left the address behind'. What constitutes my having at that moment had the thought I expressed need be no more than just the fact that I know English and said those words; there does not have to have been anything else that went on within me simultaneously with my utterance of the sentence. Wittgenstein said, 'To understand the sentence is to understand the language'. He did not mean that (as some American philosophers believe) you would not understand the sentence in the same way if you knew only a fragment of the language to which it belonged. He meant, rather, that, given you understand the *language*, that you are, as it were, in that *state* of understanding, nothing need happen, in which your understanding of the sentence consists, no *act* of understanding, other than your hearing that sentence.

[i]→   This consideration only reinforces our initial idea, that the key to an account of language – and now, it seems, of thought itself – is the explanation of an individual speaker's mastery of his language. According to the conception of language as a vehicle of thought, this explanation must embody an account of what it is to have the concepts expressible in the language; and Frege, who originated this new approach, gave the outlines of an explanation of this kind. Naturally, I cannot here do more than gesture towards his theory: it involves distinguishing three different types of ingredient in meaning, sense (*Sinn*), force (*Kraft*) and colour (*Färbung*). The fundamental conception is that of the primacy of sentences. To a fair degree of approximation, we may say that what a speaker does by uttering a sequence of sentences is the sum of what he could do by uttering each sentence on its own. Nothing of the kind, however, holds good of the words that make up a single sentence: save in special contexts, nothing at all is conveyed by uttering a single word. The words do not make up the sentence in the same way that the sentences make up the paragraph. We indeed understand new sentences that we have never heard before because we already understand the words that compose them and the principles of sentence-construction in accordance with which they are combined. But we cannot explain the meanings of words independently of their occurrence in sentences, and then explain the understanding of a sentence as the successive apprehension of the meanings of the words. Rather, we have to have first a conception of what, in general, constitutes the meaning of a sentence, and then to explain the meaning of each particular word as the contribution it makes to determining the meaning of any sentence in which it may occur. As regards that ingredient of meaning which Frege called *sense*, which is that which determines the specific content of a sentence, Frege proposed that to grasp the sense of a sentence is to know the condition for it to be true; the sense of a word consists in the contribution it makes to determining the truth-condition of any sentence of which it forms part; and he went on to give a detailed theory concerning the manner in which the senses of words of different categories are given, so as jointly to determine the truth condition of any given sentence, the whole theory thus displaying the way in which the sense of a sentence is determined in accordance with its composition out of its component words.

[j]→   I am not here concerned with the particular features of Frege's theory, but only with the general line of approach to the philosophy of language of which it was the earliest example. Frege's theory was the first instance of a conception that continues to dominate the philosophy of language, that of a *theory of meaning* for a specific

language. Such a theory of meaning displays all that is involved in the investment of the words and sentences of the language with the meanings that they bear. The expression 'a theory of meaning' may be used in a quite general way to apply to any theory which purports to do this for a particular language: but I shall here use the phrase in a more specific sense. As I have here presented Frege's ideas, and as, I think, it is natural to conceive the matter from what he said about it, a theory of meaning is not a description from the outside of the practice of using the language, but is thought of as an object of *knowledge* on the part of the speakers. A speaker's mastery of his language consists, on this view, in his knowing a theory of meaning for it: it is this that confers on his utterances the senses that they bear, and it is because two speakers take the language as governed by the same, or nearly the same, theory of meaning that they can communicate with one another by means of that language. I shall reserve the phrase 'a theory of meaning' for a theory thus conceived as something known by the speakers. Such knowledge cannot be taken as explicit knowledge, for two reasons. First, it is obvious that the speakers do not in general have explicit knowledge of a theory of meaning for their language; if they did, there would be no problem about how to construct such a theory. Secondly, even if we could attribute to a speaker an explicit knowledge of a theory of meaning for a language, we should not have completed the philosophical task of explaining in what his mastery of the language consisted by stating the theory of meaning and ascribing an explicit knowledge of it to him. Explicit knowledge is manifested by the ability to state the content of the knowledge. This is a sufficient condition for someone's being said to have that knowledge only if it is assumed that he fully understands the statement that he is making; and, even if we make this assumption, his ability to say what he knows can be invoked as an adequate explanation of what it is for him to have that knowledge only when we can take his understanding of the statement of its content as unproblematic. In many philosophical contexts, we are entitled to do this: but when our task is precisely to explain in what, in general, an understanding of a language consists, it is obviously circular. If we say that it consists in the knowledge of a theory of meaning for the language, we cannot then explain the possession of such knowledge in terms of an ability to state it, presupposing an understanding of the language in which the theory is stated. For this reason, the philosophical task of explaining in what a mastery of a language consists is not completed when we have set out the theory of meaning for the language. Whether the speaker's knowledge of that theory is taken to be explicit or merely implicit, we have to go on to give an account of what it is to have such knowledge. This account can only be given in terms of the practical ability which the speaker displays in using sentences of the language; and, in general, the knowledge of which that practical ability is taken as a manifestation may be, and should be, regarded as only implicit knowledge. I have already defended the conception of implicit knowledge, and argued that we need to invoke it in explaining certain, but not all, types of practical ability.

1⟶ The conception of mastery of a language as consisting in the implicit knowledge of a theory of meaning is just as much in accordance with our original notion that what makes the utterances of a speaker to be expressions of thought is a piece of internal equipment that he has, namely his general understanding of the language, as was the conception of language as a code. Anyone who knows the writings of Frege will object that I have either misrepresented him or, at best, have expounded only half his thought on this subject: for when Frege writes, not in detail, but on the general principles governing the notion of sense, he strenuously combats what he calls 'psychologism', that is, the explanation of sense in terms of some inner psychological mechanism possessed by the speakers; and this seems in flat contradiction to the conception of a theory of meaning as I have expounded it.

The principle which Frege opposes to psychologism is that of the communicability of sense. Of some inner experience of mine, a sensation or a mental image, I can tell you what it is like. But, in the case of thought, I do not have to confine myself to telling you what it is like to have a thought that I have had: I can communicate to you that very thought. I do this by uttering a sentence which expresses that thought, whose sense is that thought, without any auxiliary contact between mind and mind by any non-linguistic medium.

Moreover, what enables me to express my thought by means of that sentence, and you to grasp the thought so expressed, lies open to view, as much so as the utterance of the sentence itself. The objection to the idea that our understanding of each other depends upon the occurrence in me of certain inner processes which prompted my utterance, the hearing of which then evokes corresponding inner processes within you, is that, if this were so, it would be no more than a *hypothesis* that the sense you attached to my utterance was the sense I intended it to bear, the hypothesis, namely, that the same inner processes went on within both of us. If such a hypothesis could not be established conclusively, if it were in the end an act of faith, then thought would not be in principle communicable: it would remain a possibility, which you could never rule out, save by faith, that I systematically attached different senses to my words from those you associated with them, and hence that the thoughts you took me to be expressing were not those I understood myself to be expressing. If, on the other hand, the hypothesis were one that could be conclusively established, either by asking me to elucidate my words or by attending to the uses I made of them on other occasions, then the hypothesis would not be needed. It would, in that case, amount to no more than the assumption, which is, indeed, required if we are to be able to communicate by means of our utterances, that we are talking the same language, a language that we both understand: but that in which our understanding of the language consisted would lie open to view, as Frege maintained that it does, in our use of the language, in our participation in a common practice.

[m]→ This argument can be directed against the idea of a theory of meaning, conceived as the object of implicit knowledge by the speakers, as much as against an account in terms of psychological processes of the kind that was the immediate target of Frege's criticism. However, I have already answered such an argument: for I said earlier that implicit knowledge ascribed to the speakers must be manifested in their use of the language, and that it is part of the business of a philosopher of language to explain in what specific feature of this use a speaker's knowledge of each particular part of the theory of meaning is so manifested. There is no need for any act of faith.

[n]→ But now it seems that the objection can be put in another way. If the speaker's implicit knowledge must be manifested by his actual use of the language, why not describe that use directly? Let us here make the well-known and often fruitful comparison of a language with a board-game. To immediate inspection, all that happens when two people play chess is that they alternately move pieces around the board, and sometimes remove them. Nevertheless, a move in chess has a significance not apparent to immediate inspection, a significance grasped by the players in virtue of their knowledge of the rules. It is a legitimate philosophical enquiry in what an individual player's mastery of the rule consists. Can it be a mere practical ability, or must it rest on knowledge, and, if on knowledge, must that knowledge be explicit or can it be only implicit? For all that, we do not attempt to explain the significance of a move, that is, the character of the game as a game, by reference to the individual player's mastery of the rules: rather, we simply state the rules, that is, we describe the *practice* of playing the game. And, according to this objection, this is what we should do in the case of language. What an individual speaker's understanding of his language consists in is a legitimate philosophical enquiry; and it may be that, to explain this, we must invoke the notion of implicit knowledge. But to answer the central question of the

philosophy of language, we do not need, on this view, to appeal to the notion of an individual speaker's mastery of the language: we simply describe the social practice in which that mastery enables him to participate, and so need not invoke the notion of knowledge at all.

We could express this argument in the following way. Suppose that someone wishes to represent a practical ability, say that of riding a bicycle, as consisting in practical knowledge: so he says, for example, that the bicycle-rider knows that, when he goes round a bend, he must incline at an angle that is such-and-such a function of his speed and of the radius of curvature. This is, of course, one of the cases about which I said that we do *not* need to invoke the idea of implicit knowledge. But at least the representation of the ability as a piece of knowledge is unperplexing, because we can so easily convert the account of what the bicycle-rider is supposed to know into a description of what he *does*; for example, when he goes round a bend, he does incline at such-and-such an angle. Now we can represent the objection to the conception of a theory of meaning by means of the following dilemma. If the theory of meaning can be converted into a direct description of actual linguistic practice, then it is better so converted; and we have then eliminated any appeal to the notion of knowledge. If, on the other hand, it cannot be converted into such a description, it ceases to be plausible that, by ascribing an implicit knowledge of that theory to a speaker, we have given an adequate representation of his practical ability in speaking the language. The appeal to the notion of knowledge is therefore either redundant or positively incorrect.

I believe this objection, though very powerful, to be mistaken. We can best see this by considering again the analogy with a game. The mistake in our discussion of this analogy lay in taking for granted the notion of the rules of the game. What these rules are is also not given to immediate inspection: they do not, for instance, exhaust the observable regularities in play. Suppose that a Martian observes human beings playing a particular board-game, chess or some other. And suppose that he does not recognize the game to be a rational activity, nor the players to be rational creatures: he may perhaps lack the concept of a game. He may develop a powerful scientific theory of the game as a particular aspect of human behaviour: perhaps, after carrying out certain tests on the players, he is able to predict in detail the moves which each will make. He now knows a great deal more than anyone needs to know in order to be able to play the game. But he also knows *less*, because he cannot say what are the rules of the game or what is its object; he does not so much as have the conception of a lawful move or of winning and losing. He could simulate the play of a human player, but, for all the superior intelligence I am attributing to him, he could not play the game better than a human player, because he knows neither what is a lawful move nor what is a good move.

Any adequate philosophical account of language must describe it as a rational activity on the part of creatures to whom can be ascribed *intention* and *purpose*. The use of language is, indeed, the primary manifestation of our rationality: it is *the* rational activity *par excellence*. In asking for an explanation of what gives to a particular activity the character of a game, we are putting ourselves in the position of one who is trying to understand an unfamiliar game, and for some reason, cannot communicate with the players: he does not demand a theory that will enable him to predict the move that each player will make, even if there is such a theory to be had; he needs only so much as to comprehend the playing of the game as a rational activity. He wants, that is, to know just so much as anyone needs to know if he is to know how to play the game, and so to know what playing the game consists in. An account of language by means of a causal theory such as Quine appears to envisage, representing it as a complex of conditioned responses, is not the sort of theory that we need or should be seeking, even if we knew how to construct such a theory. To represent speech as a rational activity, we must describe it as something on to which the ordinary procedures of estimating overt motive and intention are brought to bear. This requires a place, for which a purely causal theory allows no room, for the distinction, essential to the comprehension of an utterance, between why a speaker says what he does and what it is that he says, that is, what his words mean, as determined by the linguistic conventions that have to be specially learned. The concept of intention can in turn be applied only against the background of a distinction between those regularities of which a language speaker, acting as a rational agent engaged in conscious, voluntary action, *makes use* from those that may be hidden from him and might be uncovered by a psychologist or neurologist; only those regularities of which, in speaking, he makes use characterize the language as a language. He can make use only of those regularities of which he may be said to be in some degree aware; those, namely, of which he has at least implicit knowledge.

If this is right, it follows that the notion of knowledge cannot, after all, be extruded from the philosophy of language. It has also a further consequence for the criterion of success in constructing a theory of meaning for a language. For it follows that such a theory is not open to assessment in the same way as an ordinary empirical theory; it is not to be judged correct merely on the ground that it tallies satisfactorily with observed linguistic behaviour. Rather, the only conclusive criterion for its correctness is that the speakers of the language are, upon reflection, prepared to acknowledge it as correct, that is, as embodying those principles by which they are in fact guided. Such a theory cannot be arrived at by observation alone, but requires reflection; and it is by reflection that it must be decided whether it succeeds or fails.

Commentary on Dummett

Let's begin by assembling some signposts. Dummett seeks answers to two questions: (I) Does mastery of a language reside in knowledge or in mere practical ability? (II) Is meaning to be explained by appeal to speakers' implicit knowledge of their language?

Question (I) is raised at $\boxed{a} \mapsto$ and answered at $\boxed{d} \mapsto$. Dummett's answer is given in his claim that mastery of a language resides in a special form of knowledge: *implicit knowledge*. That claim is then at the service of the second question (II), which Dummett answers affirmatively.

Question (II) is raised at $\boxed{e} \mapsto$ and not answered until the final paragraph. The argument is not so straightforward. Between $\boxed{e} \mapsto$ and $\boxed{f} \mapsto$, Dummett describes a conception of the relation between thought and language – the *code conception* – which would support his own view that meaning can be explained in terms of speakers' implicit knowledge. Nevertheless Dummett rejects the code conception: he spends $\boxed{f} \mapsto$ to $\boxed{i} \mapsto$ demolishing it. His conclusion is not simply that the conception fails, but that it should be replaced with a conception of language as 'a vehicle for thought'. From $\boxed{i} \mapsto$ to $\boxed{l} \mapsto$ this conception is developed through the idea that an account of language should involve construction of a *theory of meaning* for a language.

Implicit knowledge and competence

From $\boxed{b} \mapsto$ to $\boxed{c} \mapsto$, Dummett argues that, although knowledge of language involves practical abilities, it is not to be identified with those abilities. Dummett suggests some differences between knowing a language and merely practical abilities.

List the differences. How are they related? Are Dummett's characterizations of them convincing? Are the differences a matter of principle or degree? Do they support the view that linguistic ability involves knowledge?

There are three differences. Merely practical abilities and linguistic abilities are alike in being acquired on the basis of learning. The first difference is that, while this is conceivably a contingent feature of practical abilities, it is necessarily true of knowing a language.

> Do you agree? Compare Chomsky's claim that linguistic competence has a large *innate* component. How might Dummett's claim be supported? Does it follow from the nature of ordinary knowledge that it must be acquired through learning? Does it, for example, derive from a requirement that knowledge be justified? Does it follow from the nature of linguistic facts that they must be learnt?

The second difference – Dummett's explanation of the first – is that speaking a language, unlike exercising a practical ability, is a *conscious* process. Here Dummett asks us to reflect on the difference between someone who merely utters what are in fact Spanish words, and someone who knows what he is thereby saying. This difference between someone who has an ability to speak Spanish and someone who *knows* Spanish resides in the fact that the person who knows Spanish is conscious of what he is doing.

> Could the person who merely utters Spanish sentences be in some sense conscious of what he is doing? Explain in more detail the difference between Dummett's two speakers. Does your explanation support Dummett?

Dummett states the third difference in the claim that there 'is no gap between knowing what it is to speak Spanish and knowing how to do so'.

> Explain this claim. How does it support Dummett's view? Compare Dummett's distinction between knowledge and ability with Chomsky's. Are the distinctions identical? If not, how do they differ?

Between $\boxed{c}\!\!\rightarrow$ and $\boxed{d}\!\!\rightarrow$, Dummett uses the differences between linguistic competence and mere practical ability to explain a species of knowledge intermediate between ordinary knowledge and mere ability. The intermediate species is *implicit* knowledge.

> How does Dummett characterize each of these species? Pay particular attention to implicit knowledge. How does implicit knowledge differ from explicit knowledge? What is the fundamental difference between implicit knowledge and mere ability? How does the notion of implicit knowledge differ from the notion employed in Chapter 3 as part of the *minimal* view?

The fundamental difference between implicit knowledge and mere ability is that possessing the former requires 'a readiness to acknowledge as correct a formulation of that which is known when it is presented'.

> Why does Dummett impose this requirement on possession of implicit knowledge? Is it motivated by the differences between mere ability and linguistic competence? Does the requirement deliver a sharp distinction between implicit knowledge and practical ability? If not, is this problematic? Are there other problems with the requirement?

One worry about the requirement on implicit knowledge is that one's ability to meet it may simply reflect the amount of attention one pays to what one is doing. For example, I may attend closely to the movements of my arms involved in swimming the crawl. Having done so, I may be willing to acknowledge as correct a presentation – verbal or otherwise – of the movements involved in the crawl. Accordingly, my ability to swim the crawl seems to involve implicit knowledge. Of more concern is that my implicit knowledge of how to swim seems not to *explain* exercises of my ability; rather, it seems to be explained by my attention to those exercises. If that is right, then even if it were shown that speakers possess implicit knowledge of language, it would not follow that their ability is explained by that knowledge. Finally, one sometimes comes to know things through being asked. Are there more than 60 taxis in London? You may never have considered the question before, but may be willing to acknowledge the correctness of a presented answer. It seems that we should say that you implicitly knew the answer all along. But is it plausible that you already *knew* the answer, rather than, say, knowing some things from which the answer can be derived?

> How might Dummett respond to these worries? Can he respond on the basis of his characterization of implicit knowledge, or should that characterization be revised? If the latter, what revisions would you propose?

Dummett's answer to question (I), then, is that mastery of a language resides in implicit knowledge, a form of knowledge intermediate between mere practical ability and ordinary knowledge of facts. Like the former, one's implicit knowledge is intimately connected with what one is able to do; like the latter, one is in some sense conscious of what one implicitly knows.

We turn now to Dummett's second main argument, addressed to question (II).

> State Dummett's second question and its 'natural answer' in your own words. See between $\boxed{d}\mapsto$ and $\boxed{e}\mapsto$

The code conception of language

Dummett describes a *code* conception of the relation of language and thought.

> Explain in your own words the code conception of language that Dummett describes from $\boxed{e}\mapsto$ to $\boxed{f}\mapsto$. You may recognize it from Locke in Chapter 1. How does the code conception support the 'natural answer'?

From $\boxed{f}\mapsto$ to $\boxed{h}\mapsto$, Dummett presents two objections to the code conception.

> Explain the first objection ($\boxed{f}\mapsto$ to $\boxed{g}\mapsto$) in your own words. Is it convincing? Since it is not the 'principal objection', what purpose does it serve?

The second objection is made between $\boxed{g}\mapsto$ and $\boxed{h}\mapsto$. The objection is best approached by breaking it into three steps, corresponding to Dummett's three paragraphs here.

> State the central claim in each of the paragraphs between $\boxed{g}\mapsto$ and $\boxed{h}\mapsto$. How do the claims fit together to support Dummett's conclusion? What are the arguments for each of the three claims?

The principal objection aims to show that the code conception is unable to underwrite an adequate explanation of linguistic competence. The first step explains that, on the code conception, mastery of a language is treated as an ability to translate the language, not into a second language, but into *thoughts* expressible in the language.

The second step explains the 'fundamental objection' to this treatment of the relation between spoken language and the thoughts expressible therein. The objection is that explaining language mastery as translation ability fails to explain what it is to associate elements of spoken language with the concepts they express. Two options are explored. According to one, concepts are already associated with *vehicles*, say words in a *lingua mentis* (language of thought) or mental images. The idea of translating spoken language into inner media – linguistic or imagistic – makes sense. However, it provides no account of the association of inner vehicle and concept, so simply assumes what we want explained. According to the second option, concepts lack vehicles. Dummett argues that this view of concepts is nonsensical.[1]

The third step begins by imposing the requirement that an account of the association between word and concept must explain what it is to possess a concept – to have the ability to think thoughts involving the concept. What is

---

[1] See Davidson $\boxed{f}\mapsto$ to $\boxed{g}\mapsto$ on the incapacity of translation manuals to serve as semantic theories.

required is an account of what distinguishes those who can think thoughts involving a concept from those who cannot. For example, with respect to the concepts *one* and *next week*, we need an account of the difference between those who can think that next week is one day away and those who cannot. Compare ⸢f⸥↦. As Dummett puts it, an account is required of how conceptual abilities are *manifested* in behaviour.

Language as a vehicle for thought

From ⸢h⸥↦ to ⸢i⸥↦ Dummett explains how the argument against the code conception gives rise to an alternative, according to which language is a *vehicle* for thought. He illustrates the alternative through a claim of Wittgenstein's.

> Explain the view that language is a vehicle for thought. How is it supported by the objections to the code conception? How does it relate to Wittgenstein's claim? Is Wittgenstein's claim plausible? Could a generally competent English speaker who utters the words 'I've left the address behind' fail to have the thought ordinarily expressed by those words? If so, what must be added to competence and utterance to ensure the utterance constitutes having the thought expressed?

Dummett's argument against the code conception – and in favour of the vehicle of thought conception – ends at ⸢i⸥↦. From ⸢i⸥↦, Dummett explains how an account of the linguistic manifestation of thought may be developed through construction of a theory of meaning. The crucial idea here is one we have come across before. What we seek is an account of the manifestation of conceptual abilities through the use of individual words. But words are not used individually. They are used only within sentences. The solution involves providing an account of the ability to express thoughts through sentences together with an account of the contribution made by constituent words to the thoughts so expressed.

Between ⸢j⸥↦ and ⸢k⸥↦, Dummett explains that he takes a theory of meaning to be 'an object of *knowledge* on the part of speakers'. From ⸢k⸥↦ to ⸢l⸥↦ he argues that it is an object of implicit knowledge.

> What are Dummett's reasons for claiming that knowledge of a theory of meaning cannot be explicit? Does it follow that linguistic knowledge is implicit?

First, speakers are able to say what they explicitly know. Indeed, Dummett thinks exercises of that ability are *manifestations* of explicit knowledge. But speakers are not able to state theories of meaning. Second, since the manifestation of explicit knowledge involves the use of language, explicit knowledge involves linguistic mastery. Hence, explicit knowledge cannot participate in (non-circular) explanations of linguistic competence. This second step relies on two claims made earlier. First, manifestations of psychological states, like knowledge, are partly *constitutive* of occupancy of those states and do not merely provide *evidence* of occupancy. Second, explicit knowledge is – in the constitutive sense – 'manifested by the ability to state the content of the knowledge'. If those claims are true, possession of explicit knowledge is partly constituted by competence with the words used to express its content. Hence, explicit knowledge can no more explain linguistic competence than having two hands can explain having at least one hand.[2]

If knowledge of semantic theory is not explicit, is it implicit? Before an affirmative answer can be given, a response is needed to the following difficulty. Recall that possession of implicit knowledge of a rule requires readiness to acknowledge as correct formulations of the rule. But being in a position to acknowledge a formulation would appear to require understanding it. So the worry about circularity is reinstated.

> How should Dummett respond? Where does Dummett's view fit on the taxonomy developed in Chapter 3? Is it robust, modest, or minimal?

Two objections: anti-psychologism and behaviourism

From $\boxed{1}{\mapsto}$ to $\boxed{m}{\mapsto}$ Dummett presents an objection to the view that language mastery resides in implicit knowledge of a semantic theory.

> What is the objection? Begin by stating the requirement Dummett calls 'the communicability of sense'. Then state the model of communication Dummett thinks is unable to meet the requirement. Finally, explain why the model fails to meet the requirement.

Between $\boxed{m}{\mapsto}$ and $\boxed{n}{\mapsto}$ Dummett responds to the objection.

> What is Dummett's response? Is it convincing? Does it change your view of where Dummett should be located on our taxonomy? Compare Dummett's response with Chomsky's view (at $\boxed{g}{\mapsto}$ in Chomsky) of the relation between competence and its expression in behaviour. How might Chomsky respond to Dummett here?

---

[2] Campbell discusses Dummett's second reason (from $\boxed{p}{\mapsto}$ in Campbell).

The objection stems from the fact that it is possible for us to figure out what other speakers' words mean. Suppose that what a speaker's words mean is dependent on their knowledge of meaning. Combined with a view of knowledge of language that sees it as the causal-explanatory source of ability – a view like Chomsky's – that supposition threatens to make our beliefs about the meanings of other speakers' words mere *hypotheses* about the source of their use. On such a view, we could never conclusively establish what others meant; communication would rest on faith. Dummett responds that the determinants of word meaning – for Dummett, speakers' linguistic knowledge – must be fully *manifested* – i.e. fully constituted by speakers' behaviour. This requirement appears to apply, not only to knowledge of sentence meaning, but also to knowledge of word meaning, as dictated by semantic axioms. If so, Dummett's view is robust. Dummett holds that the manifestation requirement is met if competence consists in implicit knowledge.[3]

From $\boxed{n}\rightarrow$ to $\boxed{o}\rightarrow$ Dummett makes his account of the manifestation of linguistic knowledge the basis of a second objection. In the remainder, from $\boxed{o}\rightarrow$, Dummett responds to the objection.

What is the objection? What is Dummett's response? To what extent does it rely on the requirement that possessors of implicit knowledge be in a position to acknowledge formulations of what they know?

Introduction to Campbell

John Campbell is Professor of Philosophy at the University of California, Berkeley. He was previously Wilde Professor of Mental Philosophy at the University of Oxford. His many publications on the philosophies of mind and language include the books *Past, Space and Self* (1994) and *Reference and Consciousness* (2002).

In the extract reprinted here, Campbell defends a third view of linguistic competence and its relation to semantic theory: mastery resides in (something like) ordinary knowledge of semantic theory. He is a *robust* theorist, apparently of the ordinary knowledge variety. Campbell calls his view *cognitivism*. He argues for cognitivism by eliminating rivals. Assessment of his argument should be based, then, on two factors. (1) Is he successful in eliminating the rivals he explicitly considers? (2) Does he consider *all* rivals and, if not, can the considerations he presents be turned against those he ignores? In thinking about Campbell's positive view it is helpful to contrast it with views he rejects. The main question to consider about Campbell's view is, (3) Does Campbell's robust view involve ordinary knowledge or tacit knowledge (in the first of the two senses of 'tacit knowledge' distinguished in the chapter's Introduction)?

---

[3]   See the reading list on Dummett's Philosophy of Language.

John Campbell, 'Knowledge and Understanding'

I

a→ Is linguistic understanding a form of knowledge? Should a theory of understanding specify the content of *knowledge* constitutive of language-mastery? An affirmative reply to these questions obviously constitutes an attractive basis for semantics and linguistic theory. My aim in this paper is to supply a foundation for that basis, in the face of recent attempts to undermine it.

b→ In comprehending speech-acts couched in one's mother tongue, there is typically no need for conscious deliberation over their construal. One simply perceives them as having the meaning and grammatical structure that they do. In itself this raises no difficulty for the view that understanding is cognitive. Just as I may perceive a piece of music differently when I know its place in musical history, so linguistic perception may be viewed as a result of mastery's being a kind of knowledge. It has, however, recently been given central place by cognitivism's opponents.

According to John McDowell, possession of such a perceptual capacity is constitutive of mastery of a language. The aim of a theory of understanding, on this view, is to specify, for every possible speech-act of the language, the meaning which one who understands the language will thereby perceive it as having. And the theory must not attempt to explain that capacity in terms of underlying knowledge (McDowell 1977, pp.165–9). However, McDowell does not say whether, on his account, possession of the capacity is wholly, or partially, constitutive of understanding. And I believe that problems arise no matter which line is taken. Mastery of a language typically enables one not only to comprehend its speech-acts, but also to perform them. Any view which maintains that perfectly normal individuals may have mastery of a language yet be simply incapable (and not because of any deficiency in their physical productive powers) of free unreflective speech in that language, is surely not credible. And so, it would appear that the perceptual capacity on which McDowell concentrates cannot plausibly be regarded as *wholly* constitutive of speaker competence.

What, then, would a completed McDowellian theory of understanding look like? It would have to characterise at least two capacities: to *comprehend* perceived speech-acts, and to *perform* them. And it seems that these capacities would be thought of as intrinsically unrelated, with no explanatory structure typically underlying possession of both.

Yet we simply do not find people who, though not deficient in rationality or perception, are quite able to express their thoughts in their native tongue but are simply incapable of comprehending speech-acts couched in that language; or vice versa. Moreover, it seems that, by and large, the operation of some *one* process is all that is required for people to acquire these two capacities. The reason seems obvious. Some one thing – some one structural property of a person – typically grounds his possession of *either* capacity. For McDowell, however, the facts for which this explanation accounts seem destined to remain opaque.

There appears, then, to be good reason to try to delineate a structure constitutive of understanding, which would reveal both capacities to be *consequences* of language-mastery. But why should we think that the structure in question has to be described specifically in terms of *knowledge*? The important point seems to be that those who understand a language are thereby capable of learning, on occasion, by dint of their own sensory experience and reasoning, that its sentences are true; they are able to know their truth. If the intensional basis of one's interpretation of a sentence were epistemically unsound, if it comprised merely wishful thinking, or accidentally true beliefs, or indeed anything other than knowledge as to how the language is to be understood, then it would be simply incomprehensible how, on such a basis, one could *know* the truth of a sentence, or its falsity; we could not explain our own epistemic abilities.

Once we admit the legitimacy of seeking a unified explanation of the intensional phenomenon of the concomitance of speech-productive and perceptual linguistic capacities, we are driven to look for an intensional explanation of them; for neural explanations seem to serve only to account for physically described effects. And then, if we are not immediately to be forced to radical scepticism about knowledge of the truth of sentences, we appear to be compelled to characterise language-mastery as a form of knowledge: for no other intensional state seems capable of supplying a sufficiently firm epistemic base for our manifest cognitive powers here.

Furthermore, comprehension of our language serves as an epistemic basis for the acquisition of knowledge of other types. Those with a certain minimum of rational creative ingenuity are capable of exploiting their language-mastery to develop an open-ended variety of sophisticated indirect tests for finding the truth-values of various sentences. The same points may also clearly be made about knowledge acquired through hearsay or testimony. Now of course, it may emerge that there just is no explanatory structure of the type which we seek; that McDowell is right and that all there is in common between most of those who have mastered a language is the perceptual capacity he describes. Our conclusion is only that there is, at the moment, reason to look for a deeper account.

II

d⇥ According to Michael Dummett, a theory of understanding should proceed by characterising that knowledge whose possession is constitutive of mastery of the language in question. Moreover, understanding is held to be a behavioural matter. Dummett connects these theses by this demand: for every statement (in a theory of meaning) which specifies the interpretation of a sentence, a theory of understanding must provide a behavioural account of what it is to have implicit knowledge of that statement (Dummett 1976, pp. 67–76; cf. his 1979, p. 134). It may be wondered, however, whether we could not accept both that understanding is cognitive, and that mastery is behavioural, without imposing this reductionist requirement. But the upshot of this would be that the theory, while purporting to describe a form of behaviour, is in fact employing concepts which do not effect any systematic classification of behaviour at all. Such a theory would appear to be an exercise in futility. (Dummett suggests that a theory of this type would be holistic, and the above is the core of his objection to it. Cf. Dummett 1975, p. 116; 1976, pp. 70–2.) But if it must be reductionist, the theory faces a formidable task; and it is not clear that it can be performed.

The theory has to distil an account of what understanding *alone* is. So it has to filter out all except those aspects of behaviour which manifest only a person's grasp of the language. Yet surely, it is only in conjunction with the causal operation of propositional attitudes that mastery manifests itself behaviourally. To take a simple example, an assent to a question may depend not only on the subject's comprehending the query, but on his desires to be sincere and forthcoming, and his beliefs about the world. So at the level of behaviour there appears, at first sight at any rate, to be nothing salient for the theory to distil. Every aspect of behaviour which looks as if it might be relevant is coloured by the subject's beliefs and desires, which are extraneous to his understanding.

e⇥ In the face of this fact, there are two general ways in which one might try to supply a behaviourist description of understanding. But I cannot see how to make either of them work. One would be to give a general formula which yields, for any set of propositional attitudes, a behavioural description of what it is for someone with those attitudes to have a grasp of the language. Now, the only way I can see of doing this is by redefining the role of the concept of knowledge in the account. Thus, the theory will characterise knowledge whose possession is not constitutive of, but merely sufficient for, mastery. Possession of that knowledge will be seen not as a behavioural matter, but as a causal factor underlying behaviour. And the formula will be this: someone with a particular set of propositional attitudes understands the language just in case his behaviour is the same as that of someone with those attitudes plus the knowledge characterised by the theory.

It is clearly crucial to this approach that the knowledge in question is not seen as part of the common property of masters of the language. For the theory aims to sustain behaviourism; but possession of that knowledge must be seen as a causal factor underlying behaviour, and not itself a behavioural matter. It is after all only in virtue of its causal role that the knowledge serves to provide an adequately relativized description of behaviour-patterns. So typically, although a master of the language will behave as if he has that knowledge, it will not be possession of it which explains his behaviour, but merely some internal neural structure. The problem here becomes apparent, however, when we consider that propositional attitudes ordinarily vary over time. For the neural structure then turns out to have a certain amazing property: it *interlocks* and *combines* with the agent's beliefs and desires to produce his behaviour *exactly* as would a certain propositional-attitude complex: namely, the knowledge specified by the theory of understanding. There is surely but one explanation of this phenomenon: but the abandonment of behaviourism appears to be the price of accepting it.

The other approach to providing a behaviourist description of understanding is to employ the way of brute force. The theory will supply an exhaustive statement of the sets of propositional attitudes a subject may hold, perhaps allowing also for variations in subjective probability and utility assignments. And for each such set, it will characterise behaviourally what it is for someone with that combination of propositional attitudes to understand the language. However, while such an account purports to tell us what understanding is, it can offer no explanation of the fact that mastery of a language is something which once acquired is typically *retained* through alterations in the subject's beliefs and desires; for it postulates no continuous underlying structure constitutive of understanding. One might reply that fortunately, those who at some point acquire understanding do also acquire a neural structure which not only interacts with their current propositional attitudes to yield the appropriate behaviour-pattern, but can also be relied upon to interact appropriately with updated stocks of beliefs and desires as they develop over time. This neural structure, too, however, clearly has to be capable of interlocking and combining with a subject's beliefs and desires to produce his linguistic behaviour exactly as would a propositional-attitude complex. And in that case we would do better to forget the behaviour and concentrate on characterising the complex. There is, so far as I can see, no way round the difficulties for the project of supplying a behaviourist account of mastery; I propose, therefore, that we consider the prospects for a cognitivism which employs a non-behaviourist conception of knowledge.

III

Many philosophers have insisted that a description of understanding must be compositional; that it must display the meanings of sentences as systematically dependent upon the meanings of their parts. And the philosophical interest of a description of language-mastery is to a great extent dependent upon its being, in this sense, structure-discerning. For languages do not have semantic features which are somehow independent of the way in which they are understood by their speakers. Now, one aim of (nonbehaviourist) cognitivism is to expand the range of propositional-attitude explanation; to enlarge (*inter alia*) the sphere of recognisably intentional (which is not to say, reflective) action. For it is by giving such an explanation of an action that we show it to be intentional. And the aim is to do this for various aspects of linguistic behaviour, such as the speaker's choice of words in speech, or his reactions to heard utterances. Yet at the level of action-explanations, we shall often be concerned with the speaker's knowledge of the meaning of this or that *sentence*. So one way for the theory to proceed would be by specifying the content of knowledge held to constitute understanding of each sentence of the language. Some urgency thus attaches to the question raised by Crispin Wright (1981): under what circumstances should an account of language-mastery be compositional? What would force compositionality upon us?

We have seen, however, that one aim of a cognitivist description of understanding ought to be to explain the capacities of speakers to perceive the meanings of heard sentences. Now, it seems plausible to suppose that we perceive heard sentences as fragmented into words in a certain way; and this seems essential for unreflective comprehension of them. Think, for example, of the familiar experience of hearing someone talking heavily accented English which is simply unintelligible until one starts to pick out the clauses and words, to hear the structure in what he says. To perceive a speech-act as having a certain meaning, one must surely perceive it as having a certain structure; as being organised out of constituent words in some one way. Such a hypothesis clearly favours a compositional account of mastery. For if understanding were explained solely on a sentence-by-sentence basis, then we could not say why perception of structure should be at all relevant to perception of meaning.

[i] → We find a rich and satisfying explanation of the phenomenon, however, if we suppose that the knowledge constitutive of understanding relates primarily to words and their composition into sentences. For then, it will not be enough for comprehension of a heard sentence that one be master of the language in which it is couched. For, it is not enough that one know what sentence one has heard, and know the significance of its words, and the significance of the manner in which they are in fact organised in the sentence. For comprehension, one will need also to know that that heard sentence *is* compounded from those words in just that manner. And that latter knowledge is exactly what one unreflectively obtains only by trusting one's perception of the structure of the sentence. We sought an explanation of why perception of meaning should depend upon perception of structure, and now we have one. I shall argue that in fact, such an explanation can only be supplied by a knowledge-based approach to understanding.

[j] → There is further motivation for compositionality in a cognitive account of understanding. Thus consider that one central practical test for the intelligent use of language is the ability to explain the meanings of the words used. This is the criterion we employ whenever – as for example in examinations – we want to know whether someone is merely repeating heard noises. Of course some people are more articulate than others; we are not always capable of delivering polished paraphrases of our words. Whether they use ostension, metaphor or paraphrase, however, the general run of speakers are quite capable of supplying explanations of the meanings of words which they employ. The point is not confined to terms learnt by verbal definition: there is, for example, a good deal to be said about the meanings of colour terms, drawing out the intricate relations between them, and any competent speaker can at least begin to articulate some of the relevant information here. And surely only an account of mastery which takes it to consist in knowledge of the meanings of terms, rather than as relating directly to sentences, can concede the possibility of this phenomenon.

We should remark also that those who understand a language are often capable of comprehending words outwith the context of sentences; for we often use individual words as *elliptical* for full sentences. This imposes on our audience the burden of recognising *which* sentence the solitary word is elliptical for. Suppose that, as the nervous guest stands petrified by the appearance of a snake at a party, the host murmurs 'Stuffed'. One's grasp of the meaning of the individual word used is *immediate*: we recognise immediately that it is being said of something that it is stuffed and, in the total context, look around for something that may reasonably be being said to be stuffed, alighting on the snake. The moral is that our language-mastery does not relate purely to grasping the meanings of sentences. For even if speech-acts involving solitary words must invariably be elliptical for sentential speech-acts, still a direct grasp of the meaning of the solitary word may be an essential datum in realising what the relevant sentence is. The point is, I think, too easily obscured by reliance on the dictum that it is only in the context of a sentence that words have any meaning.

$\boxed{k} \rightarrow$ Gareth Evans (1981) supplies further motivation for compositionality. If one who has had explained to him certain sentences containing a new word is thereby capable of comprehending other (new) sentences containing the word, then his understanding must surely be word-oriented. Or again, if someone who *loses* competence with certain sentences containing some word loses competence with *all* sentences containing that word, then a compositional account offers the obvious explanation of the situation. (As we shall see, Evans does not give a cognitivist reading of the upshot of these remarks; yet plainly the cognitivist may take them to show a need for discernment of structure.)

$\boxed{l} \rightarrow$ It seems, then, that compositionality has a powerful explanatory role to play within the context of a knowledge-based approach to understanding. It is an open question whether any point can be assigned, on any other approach, to the idea of displaying the composition of a sentence (cf. Wright 1981). It seems also to be an open question whether any alternative to cognitivism can explain the data for which compositionality accounts within the context of a knowledge-based approach. To bring out some of the difficulties here, I shall deal with two recent accounts of structure-discernment.

The natural way to state the knowledge described by a cognitivist view of understanding is by an axiom-system: the axioms specifying the meanings of words of the language, the theorems (*inter alia*) specifying the meanings of sentences. Now many who shun cognitivism would favour the axiomatic approach; but it is really not clear why. According to McDowell (1980), the axioms are merely convenient computational devices for entailing the theorems; the account makes contact with reality, in particular with language-mastery, not at the level of the axioms, but of the theorems. McDowell insists on the axioms; it is an *a priori* constraint on his account that it discern structure. But why? All the theory has to do, on McDowell's view, is to specify the perceptual capacity he takes to be (at least partly) constitutive of competence. And, complications about indexicals and force aside, it will have done this, for indicative sentences at least, when it delivers the result that, for every sentence, 'φ', competent speakers perceive utterances of 'φ' as assertions that φ. So on the face of it, it would seem that a great deal of pointless labour would be saved if, in specifying his perceptual capacity, McDowell contented himself with the infinitary schema: 'φ' is T iff φ. The demand for axiom/theorem presentation seems, on this approach, to have nothing whatsoever to do with the description of mastery. It might be replied that McDowell wishes to take into account the fact that we typically perceive heard sentences as having a certain structure. Yet it is not at all clear *why* he should want to do so. For there appears on this account to be no reason whatsoever why perception of structure should be essential for perception of meaning. And if perception of structure is really a peripheral epiphenomenon in our use of language, then it is totally gratuitous to demand that a description of understanding should deal with it. Thus we have yet to see what objection there could be to the use of the infinitary schema, on this approach to language-mastery.

Suppose that the demand that a description of mastery characterise the structures perceived by speakers were, for whatever reason, legitimate. Even this would not in itself yield the result which McDowell desires. For there is as yet no motivation for insistence on the *derivability* from axioms of theorems which deal with the meanings of sentences. For we have no reason yet to think that the structure in question is *semantic*. To see this, remember that for McDowell there appears to be no reason whatsoever why there should be any essential connection between perception of structure and perception of meaning. His position, therefore, seems to offer no objection to an account which describes the structures speakers typically perceive in sentences quite independently of a description of perception of meaning. For this latter task, we might employ the infinitary schema. On this view, any connection between the two descriptions would be purely fortuitous. Of course, this view is not McDowell's; but it is not obvious that he can say why not without appealing to a compositional knowledge-based conception of understanding.

m→   In reply to Wright's challenge to motivate compositionality, Evans (1981) makes the following suggestion: the discernment of structure by a description of understanding is in effect a discernment of non-psychic, purely neural structure. The leading idea can be put crudely as follows. Suppose the theory identifies w as a word. That identification is correct just in case for any speaker of the language, there is a partial neural cause common to all of his perceptions of the meanings of heard sentences containing w. Thus the total fragmentation of the language into words and their modes of organisation into sentences constitutes a complex hypothesis about the structure of a network of states which are partial causes of sentence comprehension.

Now the resultant view of semantic structure may seem to provide a vindication of McDowell's views; it fits in beautifully with his opposition to the insistence that cognitive structure be discerned. For it seems to offer structure without making any essential use of the notion of knowledge. It is true that Evans employs the notion of 'tacit knowledge' in stating his view, but its use is dispensable. The theory could be stated as above and elaborated as a purely neural hypothesis which makes no essential use of any psychological concepts other than that of comprehension, or perception of the meaning, of a sentence. Indeed, it may serve to explain the word-by-word acquisition of language, and the point that loss of linguistic competence may be expected to be a word-by-word matter too. For on this account, the neural structure which realises language-mastery is composed of a battery of states, each of which is a partial cause of the comprehension of a wide range of sentences. So the instillation of a new state of this type will, in co-operation with other, already present states, typically result in a capacity for comprehension of a wide range of new sentences. Destruction of any one such state will, since all the rest are merely partial causes of sentence-comprehension, result in loss of competence with all those sentences in the causation of whose comprehension that state was a necessary factor.

n→   We should, however, have considerable reservations about this apparently attractive view. For it denies much that we should expect the compositionality of a description of understanding to explain. Can it explain why perception of structure should be essential for perception of meaning? Evans insists that his theory can give an explanation here; but in this he is surely wrong. The key point is that on this view, episodes of perception of meaning have no explanation, though they are caused. That sounds paradoxical, but in fact the point is familiar.

There is, on this view, no *psychological* machinery which typically explains a speaker's perception of the meaning of a heard sentence.

Now a perception of meaning may well be identical with a physical event. And that physical event doubtless has a neural explanation; that is what is meant by saying that the perception has a physical cause. It is, however, fallacious to infer from this that qua perception of meaning, it has an explanation. For the neural event might explain the right event, but under the wrong description. As Evans stresses, and this is exactly what opposition to cognitivism amounts to, the perception of meaning is held to have no explanation in psychological terms. But surely qua perception it could only be given an explanation in those terms. It thus transpires that on Evans' approach, perceptions of meaning have no psychological explanation whatsoever.

So perception of structure has no role to play either in the explanation of perceptions of meaning physically described – for here it is the purely neural account that is relevant – or in the explanation of such episodes described as perceptions – for in that guise they have no explanation at all. Perception of structure thus turns out, on this view, to be essentially irrelevant to perception of meaning; it is at best an epiphenomenon in the use of language. And so with Evans we are no closer than we were with McDowell to an explanation of why perception of structure is essential to perception of meaning. As noted earlier, it is true that Evans introduces his theory by using the words 'tacit knowledge'; but this cannot help here. For all that distinguishes Evans' view from a knowledge-based explanation of understanding is his insistence that such talk is merely a convenient *façon de parler* in discussing neural states; it is to be taken with a pinch of salt.

There are, indeed, further problems here. Evans' account cannot explain – and, it seems, must rather deny – two phenomena alluded to earlier: our capacity to explain the meanings of the individual words we use, and our capacity to recognise for which sentence an utterance of a solitary word is elliptical. Again, it is natural to suspect that justice to the phenomena can only be done by a knowledge-based explanation of mastery.

There is one type of response which may save an Evans-type account here; but it is important to beware of its pitfalls. The idea would be to enrich the characterisation of the components of the neural structure realising mastery. Evans was content to assign to these states the causal role alone of producing comprehension of sentences. But we might try to go further, and insist that these states invariably also either realise or cause perception of structure in producing perception of meaning, in the hope of explaining away the fact that the former appears to be essential for the latter. We might insist also that these states produce in the subject the capacity to explain the meanings of the words he uses, and the ability to understand solitary words used as elliptical for sentences. The problem with such *ad lib* enrichment is that the neural states described grow progressively harder to distinguish from intensional states. It becomes more and more difficult to see how they could have the properties ascribed to them unless they were intensional. And so we may end by being committed to cognitivism.

To this Evans points out that linguistic knowledge is ordinarily of use to its possessor only in speaking and understanding. This merely displays, however, the oblique relation of the content of such knowledge to many characteristic human interests: knowledge of the plot structure of *Bleak House*, for example, is still knowledge though its use is limited.

Again, Evans holds that linguistic knowledge cannot combine with the subject's thought in general to yield new beliefs. Yet the pervasiveness of context dependence means that linguistic knowledge is often not sufficient for speech comprehension. Understanding of a speech-act is typically derived jointly from linguistic and non-linguistic knowledge. As Bar-Hillel stressed, there is no demarcating the salient information in advance. Something as unexpected as knowledge of the sizes and shapes of play pens and writing pens may be needed to construe 'The box was in the pen'. The alleged inferential insulation of semantic knowledge is, then, a myth.

IV

$\boxed{\text{p}}\!\!\rightarrow$ It thus appears that a knowledge-based approach offers our best hope of achieving insight into language-mastery. What are the problems for such an approach? Potentially the most decisive criticism, it seems to me, is that such an explanation must inevitably be circular. So we now ask where, exactly, the circularity is held to enter. It seems that the very same issues will arise if we view cognitivism as aiming to explain understanding as a type of belief. By doing so we may hope to avoid irrelevant complications about the evidential ancestry and truth of what one knows; so in this section I shall take that view. We cannot begin better than by distinguishing very roughly between three possible responses to the question: what is it to believe that φ?

One view proceeds by drawing a sharp distinction between sentential and other beliefs. For present purposes a sentential belief is of the form: the belief that 'φ' is true. The view is that belief generally is to be explained in terms of sentential belief. With this view we may contrast two others. First, it might be held that to believe that φ is to possess a neural state having a certain causal role. Functionalism might be seen as one version of this. Secondly, it might be held that it is simply wrong to seek any type of reduction or explanation of what it is to believe that φ. Now some important distinctions are being fudged here; but my aim is not to present three views which are necessarily exclusive; rather, they are to be *independent*, in that one could hold any one without subscribing to the others.

The thought behind the charge that cognitivism is circular must surely be that belief (or knowledge) is ultimately to be explained in terms of understanding. So the objection presupposes that a substantive answer can be given to the question: 'What is it to believe that φ?', an answer which ascribes understanding of something (linguistic) to the believer. But understanding of what, precisely? The only remotely plausible candidate as a reply is surely: understanding of 'φ' or some synonymous sentence. No other linguistic expression seems to be relevant. Yet clearly, such understanding is not sufficient for the belief that φ. And it would seem that the only plausible condition we can add to ensure sufficiency, while retaining the necessity of the clause that the believer must understand 'φ' or some synonym, is this: the subject must believe that 'φ' (or the synonym) is true. It thus transpires that the criticism of cognitivism as circular depends on the view that belief is to be explained in terms of sentential belief, that is, the first of the theses stated above.

Michael Dummett (1975) has presented a version of the 'circularity' charge which may at first sight seem to be free from such theoretical commitments. The cognitivist, Dummett points out, must distinguish between knowledge that the sentences of his semantic theory are true, and knowledge of what the theory states; that is, between knowing merely that 'φ' is true, and knowing that φ. Yet how is this distinction to be explained, except by noting that in the latter case, but not in the former, the speaker must understand 'φ' or some synonym? (Dummett 1975, pp. 110ff.) At first, then, this argument appears not to depend on any contentious doctrine about the nature of belief or knowledge, but only on the demand that a distinction be explained. But what kind of explanation is required? Surely one could *communicate* to someone the gist of the distinction by, for example, pointing to the difference in explanatory role of belief and sentential belief. Thus a hungry monolingual Frenchman who knows only that 'Supper is on the table' is true is in a very different position from one who knows (by looking) that supper is on the table. Once we explain that one is, while the other is not, in a position to sate his hunger, surely anyone would catch on? Yet here there is nothing which only one of the two grasps. Dummett's reason for insisting that an explanation of the distinction must appeal to the notion of language-mastery must, so far as I can see, be that he requires a *deep* explanation of the distinction, rather than a cursory guide to its application. And a deep explanation will be one which tells us what it is to believe that φ, tells us what it is to believe that 'φ' is true and thereby makes manifest the difference between them. The thought is then that in giving such a deep explanation we shall have to employ the notion of understanding. But it is hard to see anything inevitable about this. It is certainly not obviously wrong to suppose that one might give an explanation, in terms of causal role, of what it is to believe that φ and of what it is to believe that 'φ' is true, without using 'understands'. The cognitivist who gave such an explanation would have shown his account to be free of circularity. Or again, it may be correct to insist that *no* deep explanation can be given of the distinction to which Dummett alludes. And then again there is no circularity in cognitivism. It is only when we assume that in explaining what it is to believe that φ, as part of giving a deep explanation of that distinction, one must ultimately appeal to the idea that the subject understands 'φ' or some synonym, that we see where the circularity in cognitivism is supposed to enter. But now we are back with the idea that belief is to be explained in terms of sentential belief. Of course, none of this denies something to which Dummett is obviously appealing: namely, that to acquire belief or knowledge by testimony, one must understand the expressions used. We need not deny either that a necessary condition of believing that φ is understanding 'φ' or some synonym. What is at issue is rather the question of what role, if any, these conditions are to play in *explaining* what it is to believe that φ.

It thus seems plausible that all versions of the criticism of cognitivism as circular or regressive depend on supposing that belief is to be explained in terms of sentential belief. Those who view the proponent of a knowledge-based approach to comprehension as committed to an infinite chain of homunculi within the speaker (the homunculi being those who understand the semantic sentences and believe them to be true), and those who view him as explaining understanding of one language in terms of understanding another, obviously fall into this camp; together, of course, with those who do not envisage the cognitivist as making these regressive moves but simply take his account to be circular. Let us, then, assess this worry. I shall not here essay a definite answer; the objection, however, seems to me to be at the moment less than decisive.

The most cautious reply to the criticism would be that it sets too high standards for a description of understanding. A cognitivist description of language-mastery, even if it were circular, would not leave us exactly where we began. Rather, we would have fragmented mastery into comprehension of individual words and their modes of composition, and *a fortiori*, analysed the structure of the language to some degree. What we would have done also would have been to *relate* understanding to other psychological states, rather than in some strict sense explained the former in terms of the latter. It should be obvious that as a response to the charge of circularity this has much polemical strength; for anyone who presses that criticism appears to be committed to the enterprise of explaining belief in terms of sentential belief. And that seems doomed to either circularity or regression.

Nevertheless, I suspect that we ought to pursue the path of considering whether language-mastery can be given a genuinely reductive explanation in terms of knowledge; such an explanation would clearly be highly satisfying. We could then both articulate in detail how understanding relates to the propositional attitudes in, e.g., action-explanation, and we could see the explanatory role of various components of understanding. We might thus gain greater insight into the structure not only of our mental states but of our language.

It is in any case not obvious that the theoretical presuppositions of the 'circularity' criticism are correct. We should certainly feel sceptical about the play that is made with the notion of synonymy. Such play is essential, of course, if we are to acknowledge that monolingual speakers of different languages may share beliefs. Yet in using the notion of synonymy to explain what it is to believe that φ, we apparently commit ourselves to employing it to explain when two propositional-attitude states are the same. And now it would seem that any explanation of synonymy must eschew the intensional. So we seem likely to end by giving behavioural or neural criteria of identity for beliefs, if we are not willing to take the notion of synonymy as primitive. We have yet to see a plausible set of such criteria, however.

Moreover, it is not clear that the proposed explanation of belief in terms of sentential belief is even extensionally correct. It is not clear that believing that φ is not a characteristic consequence of understanding 'φ' or some synonym, and believing that it is true; rather than having to be explained as actually consisting of such understanding and belief. The point is that one has to connect the understanding and sentential belief and – as it were – draw a conclusion from them if one is to believe that φ. Thus, consider someone who hears catastrophically bad news – say, a mother who hears that her son has almost certainly been killed. Perhaps the statement derives from an authoritative source, so that whenever she considers the sentence 'N.N. has been reported missing in action', she is ready to admit its truth; it is just that whenever she does so, her mind goes blank as to its meaning. But when she considers the sentence without considering its truth, she is perfectly capable of comprehending it. It would be wrong to ascribe to her

the belief that N.N. has been reported missing in action, if that belief is the basis of none of her actions. But if this description of the case is correct, then understanding and sentential belief are typically causes of the belief that φ, rather than being constitutive of it.

We have, I submit, found clear motivation for a knowledge-based approach to speaker competence; whether or not such an approach is in the end correct, it is surely worth serious investigation.[1]

[...]

References

Chomsky, N. (1980). *Rules and Representations* (Oxford: Blackwell).

Dummett, M. A. E. (1975). 'What is a Theory of Meaning?', in *Mind and Language*, ed. S. Guttenplan (Oxford: Oxford University Press), pp. 97–138. Reprinted in his *Seas of Language* (Oxford: Oxford University Press, 1993).

Dummett, M. A. E. (1976). 'What is a Theory of Meaning? (II)', in *Truth and Meaning*, ed. G. Evans and J. McDowell (Oxford, 1976), pp. 67–137. Reprinted in *Seas of Language*.

Dummett, M. A. E. (1979). 'What Does the Appeal to Use Do for the Theory of Meaning?', in *Meaning and Use*, ed. A. Margalit (Dordrecht: Reidel), pp. 123–35. Reprinted in *Seas of Language*.

Evans, G. (1981). 'Semantic Theory and Tacit Knowledge', in *Wittgenstein: To Follow a Rule*, ed. S. Holtzman and C. H. Leich (London: Routledge and Kegan Paul), pp. 118–37. Reprinted in Evans, *Collected Papers* (Oxford: Clarendon Press, 1985).

McDowell, J. (1977). 'On the Sense and Reference of a Proper Name', *Mind*, 86: 159–68. Reprinted in his *Meaning, Knowledge, and Reality* (Cambridge, Mass.: Harvard University Press, 1998).

McDowell, J. (1980). 'Physicalism and Primitive Denotation: Field on Tarski', in *Reference, Truth and Reality*, ed. M. Platts (London: Routledge and Kegan Paul), pp. 111–30. Reprinted in *Meaning, Knowledge, and Reality*.

Wright, C. (1981). 'Rule-Following, Objectivity and the Theory of Meaning', in *Wittgenstein: To Follow a Rule*, pp. 99–117.

---

[1] For criticism of earlier drafts, I am much indebted to Michael Dummett, John McDowell and Robert X. Ware.

Commentary on Campbell

Since Campbell seeks to eliminate rivals to his view, we need a perspective on the space of options he needs to close. As we have seen, the first dimension along which accounts of competence vary concerns the relation between speakers and semantic theories. We have distinguished the claims that the relation involves ordinary, implicit, or tacit knowledge. We have also distinguished between two notions of tacit knowledge. The first is similar to the notion of ordinary knowledge except that it is taken to be unconscious. Let's confine 'tacit knowledge' to that notion. The second is (roughly) neurological. Since we need a label for views involving that notion, as well as for other views that involve denying that speakers must *know* a semantic theory, let's call them all *innocent* views. The second dimension along which accounts of competence vary concerns whether competent speakers are viewed as related to the axioms, or only the theorems, of semantic theory. This is the question of robustness versus modesty that we considered in Chapter 3. So, in order of decreasing strength, views might involve ordinary, implicit or tacit knowledge, or innocence, of theorems or of axioms.

> Suppose, first, that speakers are related to a semantic theory for their language. Suppose, second, that any plausible view will view speakers as related to *theorems* in a way that is stronger than, or equal in strength, to the way they are related to axioms. Construct a table detailing the ten views available on those suppositions. Remind yourself of their key features. Locate Campbell's view, initially stated at $\boxed{a}$→, on the table. As you work through the reading, locate the views Campbell seeks to eliminate.

A perception-based account

From $\boxed{b}$→ to $\boxed{c}$→, Campbell sketches a view we have not yet come across, John McDowell's *perceptual* view. Campbell thinks that, as it stands, the view is unsatisfactory.

> What are the central features of the perceptual view? How does it characterize the relation between speakers' capacities and semantic theory? Where does it appear on our taxonomy? What is Campbell's objection to the view? Does the objection support a knowledge-involving view?

According to the perceptual view, the job of a semantic theory is to characterize the semantic facts made available to speakers' perceptual capacities: their capacity to hear words as meaning what they do. Semantic competence is constituted, on this view, by possession of perceptual capacities able to retrieve those facts. The view denies that the perceptual capacities involved draw on knowledge of the axioms of semantic theory. But it is important to bear in mind that exercises of perceptual capacities typically put people in a position to know things. Seeing a book in front of you puts you in a position to know that there is a book there. Similarly, perceiving words as meaning what they do might put one in a position to know what they mean. So the perceptual view is not incompatible with a view that says speakers have knowledge of semantic theorems.

Campbell's objection to the view that possession of a perceptual capacity constitutes competence is that competence also involves the capacity to *produce* significant words. Since the two capacities – perceptual and productive – typically appear together directed, crucially, onto the same linguistic objects – the same language – we should seek a unifying account of their basis. It is not obvious that the unified basis, rather than the perceptual and productive abilities it sustains, should be taken to be *constitutive* of competence. But perhaps Chomsky's suggestion (see $\boxed{e}\mapsto$ in Chomsky) that competence might be retained through transient loss of those abilities might sponsor an argument for that claim.[1]

Suppose the claim supported. It does not follow that the basis of linguistic abilities resides in knowledge. From $\boxed{c}\mapsto$ to $\boxed{d}\mapsto$, Campbell seeks to make plausible that it does.

Campbell's argument spreads across the three paragraphs following $\boxed{c}\mapsto$. The central argument is to be found in the second paragraph. The first and third paragraphs contain argument for the final steps in the argument. (One unfamiliar notion is *intensional*. Campbell uses this notion to cover psychological attitudes with propositional contents, like belief and knowledge.)

> State the central argument in your own words and explain how the considerations in the first and third paragraphs support the final steps. Is Campbell's argument persuasive?

Campbell's argument can be reconstructed as follows:

(P1)   We should seek a unified explanation of speech perception and production – an account of linguistic competence;

(P2)   Speech perception and production involve psychological attitudes with propositional contents – i.e., are *intensional* phenomena;

(P3)   The explanation of attitudes with contents must proceed on the basis of other attitudes with content; neural explanations can only explain physical effects, not attitudes with content;

(P4)   Since linguistic abilities sustain the acquisition of knowledge, their explanation should be compatible with this;

---

[1]   For further discussion see the reading list on Perceptual Views of Linguistic Competence.

(P5) A state amounts to knowledge only if all attitudes with content involved in explaining the state are themselves states of knowledge;

(C) Therefore, the unified account of perception and production must involve knowledge.

The first and third paragraphs argue for (P4). The first observes that if one understands a sentence – say, 'It's raining' – and one knows about the circumstances – knows, e.g., that it's raining – one is in a position to know the truth of the sentence. The third observes that if one understands a sentence – say 'It's snowing' – and one knows that it is true – say, through trusting an informant – one is in a position to know that it's snowing. These are important considerations, and make plausible the view that understanding either involves – or sustains – knowledge of what sentences mean.

> How might those facts about understanding play a role in explaining the communication of knowledge from one speaker to another (*testimony*)?

We noted earlier that the perceptual view is compatible with speakers' knowing sentence meanings. What is required, and what Campbell's argument is intended to supply, is reason for thinking the explanation of the perceptual capacities that put one in a position to know what sentences mean must invoke knowledge of semantic axioms.

Although (P2) and (P5) are controversial, the key premise is (P3). ((P3) also figures in a later argument ([n]→).) Very often, we explain someone's attitudes by appeal to their other attitudes. So, for example, we might explain Bill's belief that there is a book on the table by appeal to his belief that he left it there earlier. Might there be alternative explanations of Bill's belief, not based on his other attitudes? One alternative explanation is that Bill saw the book there. Does that explanation appeal to other of Bill's attitudes? That depends on the status of (P2). What Campbell really wants to rule out is the possibility of *neural* explanations of contentful attitudes. Campbell claims that neurally based accounts are bound to explain the wrong thing – other neural states and occurrences rather than states like knowledge and belief.

A reason sometimes given for (P3) is that psychological states are *variably* (or *multiply*) *realized* by neural states: the same psychological states might correspond to a variety of neural states. Hence, descending to a neural level would involve sacrificing some of the generality of psychological explanation, since the psychological explanation applies more widely than the particular neural account. Another motivation for (P3) is the converse: the same neural states might correspond with a variety of psychological states. This might be because the neural states to which appeal is made are localized in the brain, while the facts responsible for the psychological states are distributed more widely, either in the brain or in the thinker's environment. Here, descending to a neural level would involve sacrificing specificity: the neural explanation would be compatible with a variety of psychological explananda.[2]

In assessing (P3), it is important to distinguish two things we might want explained. On one hand, we might seek an explanation of how Bill came to hold the beliefs he does. Here it might seem plausible that what is required is explanation in terms of other attitudes or perceptions. On the other hand, we might seek an explanation of Bill's *capacities* to believe, know, or perceive certain things. Here it is less plausible that any account must be framed in terms of the sorts of attitudes or episodes sustained by the capacities.

> Do you think an account of psychological capacities – e.g., perceptual capacities – must appeal to psychological states and capacities? Is the unified explanation Campbell seeks supposed to explain episodes or capacities?

Campbell does not take the foregoing to refute the perceptual view. Further objections are offered from $\boxed{h}\mapsto$.

An implicit knowledge-based account

From $\boxed{d}\mapsto$ to $\boxed{g}\mapsto$ Campbell seeks to eliminate Dummett's view, that competence consists in *implicit* knowledge. The focus of Campbell's attack is on a *reductionist* requirement he finds in Dummett. The requirement is that 'every statement (in a theory of meaning) which specifies the interpretation of a sentence' must be connected with an account of the behaviour taken to manifest implicit knowledge of it.

> Campbell's statement of the reductionist requirement is neutral between robust and modest views. Which version of the requirement best fits Dummett?

Campbell argues that the reductionist requirement is incompatible with the fact that speakers' behaviour is a function, not only of their linguistic competence, but also of their other attitudes – beliefs, desires, etc. In order to characterize the behavioural manifestations of elements of *competence* some means is required of filtering out noise, aspects of behaviour that flow from the interaction of competence with other elements of speakers' psychology. Campbell considers two filters, one from $\boxed{e}\mapsto$, the other from $\boxed{f}\mapsto$, and argues neither is viable.

Campbell's arguments are difficult to reconstruct. You may find it helpful to draw a diagram. The aim of a filter is to characterize the behaviour that would be exhibited by any speaker, regardless of their other attitudes, if they

---

[2] See also the reading list on Computational Psychology.

had those attitudes *and* were linguistically competent. In effect, what is wanted is an account of the behaviour sustained by competence. The first filter provides a general formula that takes a description of a speaker's attitudes as input and delivers a description of the behaviour that a speaker with those attitudes would exhibit if she were linguistically competent. The formula is this. The speaker would exhibit the behaviour of someone with the same range of attitudes *and* ordinary knowledge of a semantic theory. A diagrammatic representation of the filter should involve the following components: two speakers, the speakers' (shared) attitudes, the neural basis of the first speaker's competence, the second speakers' ordinary knowledge of a semantic theory, and, finally, the speakers' equivalent behaviours.

How does Campbell argue against the first filter? Is his argument convincing? Compare the filter view with the minimal view of the relation between competence and semantic theory – i.e., knowledge of a semantic theory suffices for competence. Are they the same view? If not, how do they differ? Explain the second filter ($\boxed{f}\mapsto$). How does Campbell argue against it? Do Campbell's arguments support, or rely on, (P3)?

A knowledge-based account

From $\boxed{g}\mapsto$, Campbell develops an argument in favour of his view of competence. The argument involves an inference to best explanation. Campbell assembles a list of five claims about competence and argues that *cognitivism* – on which competence resides in (a) (tacit or ordinary) knowledge of (b) semantic axioms – supplies the best explanation of their truth. Assessment of his argument therefore turns on two factors. (i) Are the claims true? (ii) If they are, does cognitivism best explain their truth, or do other views provide equally good accounts?

Campbell's claims are presented from $\boxed{g}\mapsto$ to $\boxed{i}\mapsto$ and $\boxed{j}\mapsto$ to $\boxed{l}\mapsto$ List them. Do they seem initially plausible? Do they seem to support one or another aspect of cognitivism ((a) or (b))?

The two key claims are the following. (I) A semantic theory should be compositional ($\boxed{g}\mapsto$). (II) Perceiving a sentence as meaning what it does *essentially* (*necessarily*) involves perceiving the sentence as having a certain structure ($\boxed{h}\mapsto$). Three subsidiary claims, supposed to help explain (I) on the assumption of cognitivism, are the following. (III) Competent speakers are able to explain the meanings of words. (IV) Speakers are able to comprehend solitary words as elliptical for full sentences ($\boxed{j}\mapsto$ to $\boxed{k}\mapsto$). (V) Acquiring (/losing) competence with a sentence is associated with acquiring (/losing) competence with other sentences involving the same words ($\boxed{k}\mapsto$ to $\boxed{l}\mapsto$).

We have come across (V) before, in the form of the *Mirror Constraint* discussed by Wright ([i]→).[3] We have also encountered Campbell's argument, from [l]→ to [n]→, against the capacity of an *innocent* view to explain compositionality (I) in Wright ([h]→ to [k]→). Campbell accepts that innocent views can potentially explain these facts ([m]→ to [n]→) – though, as we'll see, he thinks that the cognitivist account is superior.

> Read [k]→ to [n]→. Compare Wright's argument. What response does Campbell offer on behalf of innocent views? Is the response satisfactory? Is another response available?

From [j]→ to [k]→, Campbell presents (III) and (IV) and argues, there and from [o]→, that cognitivism can better explain their truth than the innocent view.

> Read [j]→ to [k]→ and [o]→ to [p]→. State (III) and (IV) in your own words. Should (III) and (IV) be explained by a theory of competence – i.e., is either an essential element of competence? How does cognitivism explain them? Can an analogous explanation be given from the perspective of an innocent view? If so, what is it? If not, why not?

Since Campbell allows that an innocent view can explain (I) – and since (III)– (V) are of secondary importance – it is crucial to his argument that the cognitivist explanation is superior. His argument for its superiority is based on the ability of cognitivism to explain (II), that perception of structure is *essential* to perception of meaning. Campbell argues that (II) is true from [h]→ to [i]→. From [i]→ to [j]→, he argues that a straightforward cognitivist explanation is available. From [l]→ to [m]→ and [n]→ to [o]→, he argues that no explanation is available on an innocent view.

> Carefully explain each of the three components of Campbell's argument in your own words. You will need to break each component into smaller steps. Note that the third component relies on a principle like (P3) about the relation between neural and psychological explanations. Does the first component justify the claim that perception of meaning would be *impossible* in the absence of perception of structure? If not, can you think of a way in which this claim might be justified? Is Campbell's argument that an innocent view is unable to explain (II) convincing?

---

[3] The constraint derives, through Martin Davies, from the suggestion of Gareth Evans (1981). Evans's paper was a response to an earlier version of Wright's argument (1981). See the reading list on Tacit Knowledge and Compositionality.

One approach to the last question is the following. If the suggestion made at the end of the commentary on Wright is viable, an adequate motivation for compositionality is supplied by interrelations that obtain amongst the semantic facts. It is agreed that knowledge of what 'Bill smokes' means together with knowledge of what 'George drinks' means puts one in a position to know what 'Bill drinks' means. The suggested explanation is that the facts known – the facts that 'Bill smokes' and 'George drinks' mean what they do – guarantee the fact one is in a position to know – the fact that 'Bill drinks' means what it does. If that is right, the semantic facts are themselves (in this sense) structured. Plausibly, a consequence of this is that perception of semantic facts must be perception of those facts as structured. Just as an adequate perception of the structured fact that Bill is next to George must involve a perception of its constituents (Bill and George), an adequate perception of the fact that 'Bill smokes' means what it does must involve a perception of its constituents (what 'Bill' and 'smokes' mean).[4]

Recall that one of Dummett's reasons for rejecting an ordinary knowledge view was a worry about circularity ($\boxed{k}\mapsto$ to $\boxed{l}\mapsto$ in Dummett). From $\boxed{p}\mapsto$, Campbell supplies a useful explanation of Dummett's worry, and he responds on behalf of cognitivism.

> Check your table of views. Has Campbell succeeded in eliminating his rivals?

Conclusion

In this chapter we have explored further the nature of linguistic competence and its relation to semantic theory. We began with Chomsky's view, on which semantic theory aims to characterize what speakers know about meaning. He takes speakers to be related to the rules that generate the theory's descriptions of sentences – semantic axioms. We saw, however, that some obscurity attends Chomsky's view of the relation involved. One natural reading has it that Chomsky views competence as a tacit form of ordinary knowledge. But an equally natural reading has it that Chomsky views competence as residing in (something like) neural structure. On the latter reading, Chomsky is an innocent theorist.

Dummett holds that competence resides in implicit knowledge of the axioms of a semantic theory. His arguments for that view involve considerations that seem to militate against Chomsky. Dummett's argument from the communicability of sense threatens to undermine the conjunction of Chomsky's view of competence, on which its behavioural expression may be imperfect,

---

[4]   For more discussion see the reading list on Linguistic Competence and Knowledge.

with the view that competence determines communicable facts. It is of some urgency, therefore, that a supporter of Chomsky provides a satisfying response. Returning the favour, a friend of Dummett must answer Chomsky's argument for disassociation of ability and competence.

Finally, Campbell holds that speakers have (either tacit or ordinary) knowledge of semantic axioms. As well as objections to Dummett, Campbell presents objections to two innocent views, Gareth Evans's neural structure view and John McDowell's perceptual view. It is incumbent on supporters of those views to answer his charges.

We face an embarrassment of riches, both theories and arguments. Your first task is to work through the arguments to see whether they eliminate some of the theories. Your second task is to begin developing your own arguments and theories. Your eventual aim – ambitious as it sounds – is to reduce the available theories to one. What is left will be *your* view of the nature of competence.

5

Meaning and Compositionality

Introduction

Consider the sentence: 'The man peeled the yellow fruit and watched the woman smoke a cigarette'. Probably, you have never come across that sentence before. But you are able, immediately, to understand it; you know what would be the case if the sentence were true. You are able also to understand countless other new sentences. How are you able to accomplish that feat? An answer that we have come across before is that the meanings of phrases and sentences are determined by the meanings of the words that make them up and the way those words are put together. The answer, in other words, is that language is *compositional*. We shall consider this in more detail in this chapter.

In studying the texts in the last two chapters, we have had to think about the relation between three components of an account of meaning. The first component is a statement of the semantic facts, which reveals the properties of words that make them the meaningful things they are. We saw that these facts might be stated as facts about truth-conditions, for instance that 'Bill smokes' is true in English if and only if Bill smokes. The second component is an account of what it is for words to have the semantic properties they do. For example, we might take the semantic properties of 'Bill' and 'smokes' to depend on the way such sentences as 'Bill smokes' are used by English speakers. The third component is an account of speakers' linguistic competence, their knowledge of language.

We have considered some reasons for thinking that the second component may rest on the third: the semantic facts may be as they are because of what speakers know. However that may be, the three components in any account will have to fit together with one another. And we might think that our account of the status of semantic facts should reveal how knowledge of those facts could sponsor the range of abilities possessed by competent speakers. In this chapter, we consider in some more detail how the first component of an account – the characterization of the semantic facts themselves – is affected if we do think this. The focus here is on speakers' ability to figure out the meanings of new sentences. In what follows, we shall investigate whether the idea that languages are compositional dictates a particular sort of account of the semantic facts. The aim will be to deepen our understanding of accounts of meaning by seeing in more detail how they might help to explain how words combine to determine the meanings of sentences.

Most theorists hold that explaining speakers' ability to understand novel sentences requires a compositionalist account of the semantic facts, so that the semantic facts about phrases and sentences are seen to derive from the semantic facts about words and modes of combination. Developing such an account involves specifying stable properties of individual words, properties that words can contribute to all the larger structures in which they occur. And it involves specifying how putting words with those properties together into phrases and sentences can determine the semantic properties of the larger structures. The idea here is that 'smokes' makes the same semantic contribution to 'Bill smokes', 'George smokes', 'Bill smokes quickly', 'George smokes quickly in the kitchen', and so forth. If we could say what that contribution is, and how the contribution is made, we would be in a position to explain the compositionality of language. We would be in a position to explain how a grasp of the semantic properties of a relatively small number of words, and ways of combining them, might enable speakers to understand the enormous number of phrases and sentences in which those words are found.

Two questions to consider here are the following. (I) Does the compositionality of semantic facts impose requirements that some accounts of those facts are unable to meet? (II) Does compositionality impose the *only* explanatory burden on semantic theory, or are there other requirements to be met in addition? What should we expect an adequate semantic theory to achieve?

Introduction to Horwich

Paul Horwich is John H. Kornblith Family Chair in the Philosophy of Science and Value at City University New York. He has taught previously at Massachusetts Institute of Technology and at University College London. His work on the philosophy of science includes *Probability and Evidence* (1982) and *Asymmetries in Time* (1987). His latest philosophical project, begun in *Truth* (1990) and continued in *Meaning* (1998), from which this reading is extracted, aims to address a range of philosophical problems by showing them to rest on mistaken views of what a solution is required to do, of the facts an account must explain. The views Horwich targets involve thinking of the facts about truth and meaning as, somehow, substantive. Hence they take those facts to call for the sort of explanation which we give to substantive facts elsewhere, for example, in science. Horwich refers to such views as inflationary, since they involve (in his opinion) an inflated view of their subject matter. He wants to replace them with deflationary views, which, instead of explaining the facts, show the aim of explaining them to be misdirected.

In this extract, Horwich turns his attention to meaning, in particular to questions about how sentence meanings are built from word meanings. Two things to ask yourself are the following. (1) What does Horwich think the compositionality of meaning amounts to? (2) How does he want to explain compositionality so conceived?

Paul Horwich, 'The Composition of Meanings' (extracts from Ch. 7 of *Meaning*)

The title is intended to suggest a pair of related problems: first, the issue of how the meanings of sentences are built out of the meanings of their constituent words; and second, the issue of what sort of stuff meaning is, how it is created, which of an expression's underlying properties give it the particular meaning it has. My focus here is going to be on the connection between these two issues: on the question, roughly speaking, of what meanings must be like in order to be compositional. Or, more precisely, what constraint is placed on an account of the underlying nature of meaning properties by acknowledging that the meanings of complex expressions are typically engendered by the meanings of their parts? My aim will be to answer this question, first, by giving a general, deflationary account of what it is to understand a *sentence*; second, by showing how this account yields an exceedingly simple explanation of how such understanding arises; and third, by concluding that the compositionality of meaning imposes no constraint at all on how the meaning properties of *words* are constituted.

[a]→   Let me start with an example. Presumably our understanding of the sentence 'dogs bark' arises somehow from our understanding of its components and our appreciation of how they are combined. That is to say, 'dogs bark' somehow gets its meaning (or, at least, one of its meanings) from the meanings of the two words 'dog' and 'bark', from the meaning of the generalization schema '*n*s *v*', and from the fact that the sentence results from placing those words in that schema in a certain order. However, as Davidson was the first to emphasize, it is not possible to produce a strict logical deduction of what 'dogs bark' means from these more basic facts alone.[1] So a question arises as to which further premises are required. What assumptions about the character of meaning should be added in order to obtain an explanation of the meaning of the sentence on the basis of the meanings of its words?

    The answer that I would like to suggest derives from the following simple idea, which is the basic thesis presented here: namely, that understanding one of one's own complex expressions (non-idiomatically) is, by definition, nothing over and above understanding its parts and knowing how they are combined. In other words, once one has worked out how a certain sentence is constructed from primitive elements, and provided one knows the meanings of those elements, then, automatically and without further ado, one qualifies as understanding the sentence. No further work is required; no further process needs to be involved, leading from those initial conditions to the state of understanding the sentence. For all we have in mind when we speak of understanding a complex expression of our own language is that those conditions (of understanding its words and being aware of their mode of combination) are satisfied.

    If this is correct, then the fact that 'dogs bark' means what it does – or, as I will put it (using the convention of capitalizing an English expression to obtain a name of its meaning), the fact that 'dogs bark' means DOGS BARK – is constituted by whatever is the complex fact regarding its mode of construction and the meanings of its constituents.[2] This turns out to be the fact that the sentence results from

---

[1]   D. Davidson (1984), Essay 2.

[2]   Let me be more explicit about the route from my assumption about what it is to understand a complex expression to my conclusion about how its meaning is constituted. Suppose that understanding a complex of one's own language is (as I assume) identified with the state of understanding its parts and appreciating how they are put together. Then, understanding 'dogs bark' (i.e. knowing what it means) is constituted by knowing both

[b]→ what its parts mean and how they are combined. But these items of knowledge are implicit: someone knows (fully) what an expression means when what it means in his idiolect is the same as what it means in the community language. Therefore, the fact that

putting words meaning what 'dog' and 'bark' mean, into a schema meaning what '*ns v*' means: that is (employing my convention for referring to meanings), the fact that it results from putting words whose meanings are DOG and BARK into a schema whose meaning is NS V. Thus the meaning property

x means DOGS BARK

consists in what I shall call the 'construction property'

x results from putting terms whose meanings are DOG and BARK, in that order, into a schema whose meaning is NS V.

Just as being water consists in being made of H_2O, and just as redness consists in reflecting certain wavelengths of light, so the meaning property of 'dogs bark' consists in its construction property.[3]

This constitution thesis, I would like to suggest, provides the answer to our initial question: it is the missing premise that we need in order to show how the meaning of 'dogs bark' is engendered. And whatever its defects may turn out to be, it has at least the virtue that it does indeed allow the meaning of 'dogs bark' to be deduced from, and explained by, the meanings of its parts and its method of construction. For, given that

---

'dogs bark' means what it does (in language L) is constituted by the facts regarding how it is composed from primitives and what those primitives mean (in language L). Jim Higginbotham has argued (in conversation) that the mode of construction of a sentence may itself have a meaning which contributes to the meaning of the whole sentence; in which case our understanding the sentence would require more than simply understanding the words in it and seeing how they have been combined. It seems to me, however, that any so-called 'method of combination' which intuitively has a meaning (for example, predication or conjunction or 'ns v') can be regarded as a schematic constituent of the sentence. Thus we can make it a matter of stipulation that no meaning attaches to the procedures by which these and other constituents may be combined. Note, moreover, that even if Higginbotham's suggestion were correct, this would not have a substantial effect on the deflationary position advanced here. Our constitution thesis would have to be revised slightly to say that the meaning of a sentence consists in its mode of construction having a certain meaning and its constituents having certain meanings. But the explanation of compositionality would then be no less trivial. And it would be equally clear that compositionality cannot constrain how the meaning properties of words are constituted.

[3] As indicated, the general idea of 'property S being constituted by property U' is a very familiar one. It obtains, roughly speaking, when S and U are coextensional, and when facts about S are explained by this coextensionality. I think it best not to equate the relation of property constitution with that of property identity, but nothing here hinges on preserving this distinction.

'dog' means DOG,
'bark' means BARK,
'*ns v*' means NS V,[4]

and

'dogs bark' results from putting the terms 'dog' and 'bark' in the schema '*ns v*',

it logically follows that

'dogs bark' results from putting terms meaning DOG and BARK in a schema meaning NS V,

which, given our extra premise, then yields

'dogs bark' means DOGS BARK

– just what we wanted to explain.[5]

---

[4] Strictly speaking, meaning facts have the form, 'S's expression k means E' – since one and the same sound type, k, may be meant differently by different people, depending on their language. However, since I am concerned with what is meant by the expressions of a single, arbitrarily selected speaker S, explicit reference to the speaker is suppressed for the sake of ease of exposition. Thus I write '"dog" means DOG' instead of 'S's word "dog" means DOG'; and I ask which property 'u(x)' constitutes the meaning property 'x means E', rather than asking which property 'u(S, x)' constitutes the meaning property 'S's expression x means E'.

[5] One might suspect that

'dogs bark' means DOGS BARK

cannot really be what we want to explain because, given our convention for naming meanings, it amounts to little more than

'dogs bark' means what 'dogs bark' means,

which seems too obvious to be the item of knowledge that constitutes understanding. In order to assuage this concern, note the following points. First, although it is obvious, the fact at issue is none the less subject to substantive explanation; for we can show how 'dogs bark' comes to have the property that constitutes 'x means DOGS BARK'. Second, it is far from unusual to give substantive explanations of facts which exhibit the same appearance of triviality: e.g. that the man elected was the man elected, that the colour of blood is the colour of blood, and so on. Third, despite its obviousness, this may well be the fact about 'dogs bark' whose knowledge coincides with understanding that sentence. No doubt explicit knowledge of it is irrelevant – neither necessary nor sufficient for understanding; but we might suppose that when that fact holds of a given speaker (in virtue of his expression 'dogs bark' having the appropriate construction property), then it qualifies as implicitly known by that speaker, and it is such

Moreover, it seems fairly clear how to generalize this example. Consider an arbitrary complex expression 'e', and suppose that it is constructed by combining certain primitive terms (some of which are schemata) in a certain order. That is,

'e' is the result of applying combinatorial procedure P to the primitives $\langle 'w_1', \ldots, 'w_n' \rangle$

My proposal is that the meaning property of 'e' – namely, 'x means E' – is constituted by the construction property

x results from applying procedure P to primitives whose meanings are $\langle W_1, \ldots, W_n \rangle$

(where W_1 is the meaning of 'w_1', etc.). Assuming this constitution thesis, it is clear how, paralleling the reasoning for 'dogs bark', we can explain why 'e' means what it does from the facts about what its primitive constituents mean and from the fact about how it is constructed from those primitives. The great simplicity of such an account is what justifies the constitution thesis (by 'inference to the best explanation').

This strategy deserves to be called 'deflationary', for it shows that the compositionality of meaning is much easier to explain than we have often been led to believe. It would not seem to be the case, as contended by Davidson and his many followers, that compositionality dictates an explication of meaning properties in terms of reference and truth conditions. Indeed, since our explanation did not involve any assumptions about how the meaning properties of the primitives are constituted, it would seem that compositionality per se provides absolutely no constraint upon, or insight into, the underlying nature of meaning.

[...]

Reference

Davidson, D. (1984). *Inquiries into Truth and Interpretation* (Oxford: Clarendon Press).

---

implicit knowledge that constitutes understanding. And fourth, even the more familiar formulations of what needs to be explained – e.g. that 'dogs bark' expresses the proposition that dogs bark, or that 'dogs bark' is true if and only if dogs bark – focus on facts that are no less obvious.

Commentary on Horwich

In this commentary, we shall look at three elements in Horwich's account: (A) his account of semantic facts; (B) his view of linguistic competence; and (C) his treatment of the compositionality requirement.

(A) *Semantic facts*

Horwich thinks that the appropriate way to characterize the semantic properties of words is by stating the meanings of those words rather than, say, their truth-conditions. He represents the meaning of an expression by capitalizing the expression. For example, (1)'s meaning is represented in (2).

(1) Beware of the dog
(2) BEWARE OF THE DOG

How can (2) represent (1)'s meaning? Horwich's answer is that his use of capitalizing an expression means: whatever *this* expression means. Thus, (3) is to be read as roughly equivalent with (4):

(3) 'Beware of the dog' means BEWARE OF THE DOG
(4) 'Beware of the dog' means what 'beware of the dog' means

A concern we might have with this way of representing meaning is that someone could know that (4) is correct without, thereby, understanding 'beware of the dog'. The response to that concern is that the capacity of (3) to represent to us the meaning of 'beware of the dog' presupposes our understanding of the capitalized expression on the right-hand side. Because we know the meaning of 'beware of the dog', (3) enables us to recognize the association of that meaning with the expression 'beware of the dog'.[1] But what is it to understand – to know the meaning of – 'beware of the dog'?

(B) *Linguistic competence and implicit knowledge*

Horwich takes understanding to reside in what he calls *implicit knowledge* of meaning.

Read Horwich's footnote from [b]→. What does he mean by 'implicit knowledge'?

---

[1] See Chapter 2 on Alston for a similar approach.

One unfamiliar notion here is *idiolect*. An *idiolect* is the language of a particular speaker. Some philosophers allow that a speaker's idiolect might come apart from the language spoken in her community. For example, because I use 'livid' as if it meant *red-faced with anger*, while 'livid' means in English *white-faced with anger*, it might be held that my idiolect is distinct from English.

Let's reconstruct slightly and distinguish implicit knowledge of an idiolect and implicit knowledge of a 'community language', say, English. Then someone implicitly knows the meaning of an expression in her idiolect by virtue of the fact that her use of the expression sustains its possession of a meaning. She has implicit knowledge of the meaning of an expression in English when her use of the expression coincides with the way the expression is used in English. So, someone has implicit knowledge of a language just in case their uses of bits of the language furnish them with meaning. And understanding a language is just having implicit knowledge of it.

(C) *Compositionality*

Between $\boxed{a}\!\!\rightarrow$ and $\boxed{c}\!\!\rightarrow$, Horwich explains the compositionality requirement. He acknowledges that, on one understanding of the requirement, his account of semantic facts is unable to satisfy it. But he thinks that, so understood, the requirement is misconceived.

> Read from $\boxed{a}\!\!\rightarrow$ to $\boxed{c}\!\!\rightarrow$. What is the requirement that Horwich's account is unable to satisfy? What is the requirement that Horwich thinks his account is able to satisfy?

From a statement of the meanings of words and the ways they are combined in sentences, one cannot *deduce* the meaning of the sentence. So, knowing (5), (6), and (7) does not put one in a position to deduce (8):

(5) 'dogs' means DOGS
(6) 'bark' means BARK
(7) The syntactic structure 'noun(+plural)–verb' means NOUN (+PLURAL)–VERB
(8) 'dogs bark' means DOGS BARK

But we take it that knowing the meanings of words and the way they are combined in a sentence *does* put one in a position to know the sentence's meaning. So (5)–(7) might appear inadequate as representations of meaning.

Horwich's response is to supplement (5)–(7) with the claim that the facts they express *constitute* the fact expressed in (8). Although one would not be in a position to work out (8) from (5)–(7), the requirement that the semantic facts should put one in a position to work this out is misconceived. When we recognize that understanding 'dogs bark' amounts to furnishing 'dogs bark' with a meaning, there is no longer a need to explain how speakers arrive at their understanding by drawing out consequences of their understanding of 'dogs', 'bark', and the way they are combined. All that is required is that the facts cited in (5) to (7) suffice for (8). So, Horwich's view of understanding is a crucial element in his account of compositionality.[2]

The next two readings are critical responses to Horwich. Before reading them, spend some time developing your own view of the strengths and weaknesses of Horwich's account.

Introduction to Higginbotham

James Higginbotham is Professor of Philosophy at the University of Southern California. He is a leading exponent of a certain view of semantics and semantic competence, founded in the work of Davidson and of Chomsky. In his view, semantic competence resides in tacit knowledge of a truth-theory. In the extract, Higginbotham develops a line of argument from Davidson's paper, 'Truth and Meaning',[3] in order to defend one aspect of his view – the use of a truth-theoretical representation of meanings. He uses the argument to expose what he sees as the benefits of Davidson's view of semantic theory and the defects of Horwich's treatment of the composition of meanings.

Three questions to consider are the following. (1) What is Higginbotham's argument for the superiority of a truth-theoretic account? (2) Does Higginbotham's argument rely on assumptions about understanding with which Horwich disagrees? (3) If so, does that vitiate the argument's force?

James Higginbotham, 'A Perspective on Truth and Meaning' (extracts)

Donald Davidson's article 'Truth and Meaning' (Davidson 1967), and several others that followed it, were major instruments in clearing the way for a scientific and philosophical project that continues to this day, of attempting to account systematically for the combinatorial semantic properties of given human languages: to show, in his words, how the meaning of a construction in a language depends upon the meanings of its parts. (The lexicon, comprising the meanings of

---

[2] For discussion of compositionality see the reading list on Compositionality and Meaning.
[3] In D. Davidson, *Inquiries into Truth and Interpretation* (Oxford: Clarendon Press, 1984).

the primitive parts, or more precisely of those that have separately stated meanings rather than being taken up syncategorematically, comes in only for minor discussion.) For this purpose, Davidson argued, the construction of a theory of truth for a language was both necessary and sufficient. And not just for this purpose, indeed; for he argued also that knowing possession of a correct theory of truth for a language would enable one to understand its speakers.

Davidson's path to his conclusions is widely known, and I will not review it here. But it will be important for my discussion to distinguish the purely analytical project of exposing the combinatorial structure of language from the more philosophical issue of the relations of a successful theory of language, however arrived at, to the understanding exhibited by its speakers. In each case there is a question of necessity, and a question of sufficiency. We thus have four theses linking meaning and truth: is a theory of truth a necessary component of a theory of meaning? is it sufficient? is a theory of truth a necessary component of a theory of understanding? and, is it sufficient?

Over the years, all four of these theses have been criticized, refined, and criticized again; and it would be unfortunate if nothing had been learned in the process. In this article I will take them up, in a particular order, concentrating upon the more abstract considerations. I will argue that the position of referential semantics, in the current state of the subject, is undiminished. At the same time, as the role of contextual information in human communication has come to be better appreciated and understood, and as the lexical and combinatorial devices of human language have been more deeply explored, we are, I believe, in a much better position than we were some years ago to see what a full theory of the workings of language might look like, and how far it may, even must, draw upon resources that are not themselves linguistic.

On the question of the relations of the deliverances of semantic theory to the psychological states of speakers, a possible answer, which I will assume here, is that the theory gives the knowledge that speakers actually have, in virtue of which they are able to understand what is said to them, or plan their own speech, or engage in any of the myriad applications that are available to any normal native speaker of a human language. The things that native speakers know, and that they know them, enter explanations of their behaviour (and not just linguistic behaviour) in the usual way; that is, they serve as premises from which deductive or defeasible inferences are drawn, given other knowledge and other psychological states. In short, I am supposing that semantic theory aspires to be a theory of semantic competence in the sense of that notion derived from Chomsky.

Theories of competence have been regarded with deep misgiving; but I will not here enter upon the issues that have grown up around conceptions of tacit, implicit, or even unconscious knowledge. Davidson himself did not say that a person, to whom a correct theory of meaning applies, knows that, or any other theory. Rather, as he remarks in the introduction to Davidson (1984), there may be for all that we can tell nothing at all such that we are linguistically competent because we know it. In another formulation, he remarks that a correct semantic theory for S should have the property that one who did know it, and knew that it was correct, could (in principle) use it to interpret S; but nothing is said about the relation of the theory to any knowledge on the part of some actual interpreter of S. Of course, if the theory is correct, then as Davidson puts it in (1986: 438), 'some mechanism in the interpreter must correspond to the theory'; but in Davidson's view this remark would add nothing to the thesis that the theory is in fact correct.

If we assume a specific view of the nature of our semantic capacities (that they derive from knowledge), the questions of the necessity and the sufficiency of a theory of truth for a theory of understanding take on a particular form, and it is natural to ask whether this form may prejudice the issues, perhaps in favour of assigning a significant role to the referential conception; but such prejudice as there is may equally attend Davidson's more modest formulation above. I hope, therefore, that making the assumption will not sacrifice generality. Finally, instead of speaking exclusively of truth, I will generally use the wider vocabulary of reference.

I. Is Reference Necessary?

b⟶ If conditions on reference and truth are necessary for the exposition of the lexicon and the combinatorics of a language, then they must be necessary for understanding as well; for by hypothesis it is in virtue of knowing the lexicon and combinatorics that speakers achieve understanding. The converse does not follow; that is, it may be possible to give the interpretation of the lexicon and the interpretations of the various combinatorial devices of a language without recourse to the concepts of reference and truth, and still not possible that a grasp of these interpretations should confer understanding on a speaker. Theories of meaning that are not finitely axiomatizable, for example those that state outright the meaning of every sentence by using that very sentence, already illustrate the point.

Some care is required in setting up our questions, because we possess a ready-made vocabulary for the phenomenon of understanding itself, namely the very vocabulary that uses conceptions such as 'knowing what was meant,' 'getting the point,' and so on. In this vocabulary, we can express pseudo-theories of understanding, saying for instance that to understand the sentence 'Connecticut is south of Massachusetts' you need to know precisely that it means that Connecticut is south of Massachusetts, or that it is used, or to be used, to say that Connecticut is south of Massachusetts; and in these formulations there is no intrusion of the concept of truth, or the other concepts of the theory of reference. Moreover, empirical manifestations of understanding, or misunderstanding, can be described in the same vocabulary. There remains the truism that expressions that diverge in the referential dimension must also diverge in meaning: but this observation of itself does not advance the issue.

As Davidson observed, however, a significant entering wedge appears when we ask what a humanly manageable theory of understanding must involve. If it must have a finite basis, comprising a finite lexicon and a finite set of combinatorial principles, with each of which are associated meanings, or conditions on meaning, then, given the unbounded nature of lexical and phrasal combinations, what is assigned as meaning or condition of understanding of a lexical item or combinatorial mode will have the following properties:

First, the meaning of a lexical item (a word, or a part of words appearing as an affix, a 'bound morpheme' in the classical sense) must accompany it through each of the infinitely many sentences in which it appears. A single item may have many meanings, but their totality must be finite (in practice, not very large), so that the relevant conception of meaning must respect the finiteness condition in any case.

Second, whatever is advanced as meaning or condition of understanding must be sufficiently flexible as to apply to all categories of expression. In this regard one may think of the different types of meaning attached to predicates, singular terms, quantifiers, connectives; but the scope extends to tenses, aspectual morphemes, adverbials of various sorts, and many others.

Third, it must be possible to express the combinatorics of the language in terms of the relevant concept of meaning; and this combinatorics must have the property that whoever knows the meanings of the parts and the combinatorial principle is in a position to derive the meaning of the whole.

Fourth, it must have the property that reasoning that speakers engage in within the language can be shown to be generally correct, and their knowledge of its correctness stems from their understanding of the language.

Referential semantics, as customarily practised, can satisfy all of the above, over a fairly wide stretch of human language. The elements to which reference is relative, the parameters of evaluation, have undergone various expansions, notably including the parameter of possible worlds, and the idea, originally due to Robert Stalnaker, that the active context of a discourse (represented, for him, by a set of possible worlds, constituting the assumptions of the participants) should be a parameter as well, for the determination of presuppositions and even the nature of the proposition uttered. These expansions in no way alter the fundamental dimensions of the referential theory.

d⟶ The assumption that semantics is referential, however, can be, and has been, questioned on the grounds that reference, satisfaction, and truth should be understood in a way that is 'minimalist' in the sense of Horwich (1990) or 'deflationist' in the sense of Field (1994) (so that they tell us nothing about meaning), and that meaning is constituted, not by conditions on reference, but by concepts expressed (where what concept a linguistic item expresses is derived in some way from its use, manifesting our practical abilities). A recent locus of this alternative is work by Paul Horwich. I will relay what I take to be Horwich's position, based on discussion with him, and convey where, if my summary is correct, my disagreement would come. Whether I have him right or not, I think that the view that I will consider, and the rejoinder to it, deserve to be spelled out.

Assume, then, that concepts are associated with expressions, and that combinations of concepts give rise to other concepts, where some features of use determine what concept a lexical element expresses, and the effect of a given mode of combination. Assume that the lexicon and set of combinatorial modes is finite, and that concepts are sufficiently well described as to type that they may cover all of the various categories of a language. As for reasoning within the language, Horwich (1990) argues that the minimalist position can generalize over patterns of inference in the standard way. There remains an obscurity at the beginning, since we are not told very much about what concepts are (they are not, for example, individuated in terms of reference). But the crucial issue is whether the combinatorics is forthcoming.

e⟶ Meaning, however understood, must be compositional; that is, it must be seen to satisfy the general principle that the meaning of an expression is a function of the meanings of its parts and their mode of combination. The combinatorics of meaning is concerned with interpreting the notion of a 'mode of combination,' and with spelling out the cases that actually occur. Without loss of generality we can assume a version of compositionality that may be called *strictly local*; whether it is generally true or not, it certainly marks the default case.

Suppose that we are looking at a syntactic structure $Z = X - Y$, and that the meaning of whatever occupies X (the conditions on X's reference, on the referential conception) and of whatever occupies Y are known. The points X, Y, and Z will come with certain formal information (in the form, for instance, of syntactic features). Then the thesis of strict locality is that the meaning, or range of possible meanings, of Z is strictly determined once for all by the formal information at X, Y, and Z, and the meanings of X and Y. The thesis implies, then, that further information about how the meanings of X and Y were arrived at is not relevant to the meaning of Z, and furthermore that the contribution of Z to any larger structure W within which it may occur is independent of the nature of W.

The configuration $Z = X - Y$, together with the formal features (identifying, say, X as a Noun, Y as a Verb, and Z as a Sentence) constitutes a syntactic *schema*, to which a condition on interpretation is attached, by hypothesis. An *instance* of the schema is obtained by filling in X and Y with appropriate linguistic material. Let the schema be that of predication, illustrated by simple sentences such as 'Fido barks'. We know how to associate truth-conditions with expressions falling under this schema, but the interest here is whether, by simply endowing the schema with a meaning of its own, we can express the combinatorics of this simple, and strictly local, case of compositionality without bringing truth-conditions into it.

Suppose that (in virtue of whatever phenomena) we have fixed on the concepts expressed by the subject and predicate; say, that 'Fido' expresses FIDO (a certain individual concept) and 'barks' expresses BARKS. Then, the thought is, the meaning of the predication schema yields as the meaning of Z, the sequence 'Fido barks' with grammatical description as given by the syntax, the proposition FIDO BARKS. More generally:

if S is an instance '*a* Vs' of the predication schema, the concept c_1 is the meaning of the instance of *a*, and c_2 is the meaning of the instance of V, then the meaning of S is (the proposition that) $c_1 c_2$

What we have just said for predication would be applied *mutatis mutandis* across the board, throughout the various types of constructions: the meaning GREEN DOOR of 'green door' will be the result of applying the schema governing Adjective+Noun to GREEN and

DOOR; and so on. Compositionality, in the strictly local form, is therefore satisfied.

Notice that Horwich (or at least my version of his views) does not deny the thesis that the theory of meaning may be studied as the theory of a human competence. As such, this theory would have to explain how one may know the meaning of a complex expression given that one knows the meanings of its parts and their mode of combination; and in fact it purports to do just that, by means of the general condition above, for example, on combining concepts under the schema of predication.

$f \rightarrow$ However, as a theory of how you know what 'Fido barks' means, what that condition gives is unsatisfactory, since it does not determine what the meaning of the predication schema, or any of its instances, in fact is. This can be seen from the fact that a person who knew that 'Fido' means FIDO and 'barks' means BARKS, and apprehended the general statement above governing the predication schema would not in virtue of that come to know what the meaning of 'Fido barks' is, unless he already grasped that the latter is to be predicated of the former, which it was precisely the intention by means of that formula to convey. (The schema was *called* 'predication' in the formula, but that it was predication played no role in the formula.) But the meaning of 'Fido barks' must be specified as involving c_2 in the role of predicate of c_1, for we are juxtaposing names of concepts not by way of listing them, but by way of indicating certain propositions, in which c_2 is predicated of c_2.

In sum, one cannot bring another to understand the semantic effect that a mode of combination has on an ensemble of concepts simply by reproducing the linguistic specification of that mode. We know that FIDO BARKS is the proposition delivered by applying the predication schema to FIDO and BARKS (in that order); or alternatively, by applying BARKS to FIDO. But about the meaning of 'Fido barks' we know only that the schema yields FIDO BARKS as value, given FIDO and BARKS; and that does not tell us what proposition FIDO BARKS may be.

The above disquisition is intended as an echo of a swift remark in Davidson (1967), rejecting the proposal that the meaning of the sentence 'Theaetetus flies' can be given as the value of the meaning of 'flies' for the meaning of 'Theaetetus' as argument. Davidson writes:

> The vacuity of this answer is obvious. We wanted to know what the meaning of 'Theaetetus flies' is; it is no good to be told that it is the meaning of 'Theaetetus flies'. (Davidson 1984: 20)

– or, we may add, that it is THEAETETUS FLIES.

g↦ By way of contrast, compare how the interpretation of modes of combination, and the schema of predication in particular, proceed according to
the account of meaning in terms of knowledge of reference. We assume that the native speaker knows

> 'Fido' refers to Fido;
> 'barks' is true of $x \leftrightarrow x$ barks; and
> If S is an instance of 'a Vs', the instance of 'a' refers to y, and the instance of V is true of $x \leftrightarrow F(x)$, then S is true if and only if $F(y)$.

Knowledge of all these (and of the fact that 'Fido barks' is an instance of 'a Vs', where the instance of 'a' is 'Fido' and that of V is 'barks') is sufficient to enable the deduction concluding that 'Fido barks' is true if and only if Fido barks – which, on the referential conception, is part of what the native speaker knows in knowing the meaning of the sentence.
[...]
   I conclude that attempts such as that I am attributing to Horwich have obscured the point that a combinatorial semantic principle, if it is to confer knowledge of the meaning of an expression on the basis of knowledge of the meanings of its parts, cannot take the form envisaged. It is like an equation in two unknowns; we know that the meaning of the predication schema is such that it delivers FIDO BARKS given FIDO and BARKS; and we know that FIDO BARKS is the value of the predication schema for those arguments; but from this single principle we don't know what the predication schema signifies, or what proposition FIDO BARKS may be.
   I have dwelt at length on one 'minimalist' attempt to state a theory of understanding meeting the conditions that I have identified. If only a referential conception of meaning can satisfy these conditions, then grasp of reference and truth is a necessary condition for understanding. But a demonstration of this necessity is by its nature forbidding, because it would have to be shown that nothing at all that does not incorporate reference and truth could in principle be satisfactory.
[...]

References

Davidson, D. (1967). 'Truth and Meaning', *Synthèse* 17: 304–23. Reprinted in D. Davidson, *Inquiries into Truth and Interpretation* (Oxford: Clarendon Press, 1984).

Davidson, D. (1986). 'A Nice Derangement of Epitaphs', in *Truth and Interpretation*, ed. E. Lepore (London: Blackwell).

Field, H. (1994). 'Deflationist Views of Meaning and Content', *Mind* 103: 249–85.

Horwich, P. (1990). *Truth* (Oxford: Oxford University Press).

Commentary on Higginbotham

Semantic theory and semantic competence

From $\boxed{a} \mapsto$ to $\boxed{b} \mapsto$ Higginbotham explains his view of the relation between semantic theory and semantic competence, and contrasts his view with Davidson's.

> What is Higginbotham's view? Where is it located on our taxonomy? How does it differ from Davidson's view? Is either view the same as Horwich's? If not, how do the views differ?

Higginbotham's view is that competent speakers know a semantic theory. But he claims that his argument is going to depend only on the weaker view that a semantic theory must state something knowledge of which would suffice for competence. His aim is to argue that Horwich's account fails to meet the weaker condition: knowing what it states would not suffice for understanding. So, on either view, Horwich's account of semantic facts will not serve as a theory of understanding, a theory of what competent speakers know. The importance of this is brought out as follows. Horwich's account of semantic facts makes no appeal to notions from the theory of reference – notions like reference, satisfaction, and truth. It might, then, be thought that an account could do without those notions. Higginbotham's argument is directed against that thought. On his view, a semantic theory involving notions from the theory of reference is an essential component of an adequate theory of linguistic competence.

Combinatorics

Higginbotham uses the notion of combinatorics as a label for the machinery deployed within a semantic theory to derive meanings of wholes from meanings of parts. From $\boxed{b} \mapsto$ to $\boxed{d} \mapsto$ he argues that viewing a semantic theory as a component in a theory of competence places substantive constraints on the combinatorics.

Paragraph $\boxed{d} \mapsto$ contains two claims. (1) If appeal to referential notions is a necessary feature of a semantic theory, those notions are also essential to a theory of competence. (2) It does not follow from the fact that a semantic theory provides an association of sentences and their meanings that it can play the required role in a theory of competence.[1]

From $\boxed{c}\!\!\mapsto$ to $\boxed{d}\!\!\mapsto$, Higginbotham explains the additional constraints imposed on combinatorics by the need to fit a semantic theory with a theory of competence.

> Explain the additional constraints which Higginbotham introduces from $\boxed{c}\!\!\mapsto$ to $\boxed{d}\!\!\mapsto$.

From $\boxed{d}\!\!\mapsto$ to $\boxed{f}\!\!\mapsto$ Higginbotham presents Horwich's position. This involves, at $\boxed{e}\!\!\mapsto$, explaining a version of compositionality that is strictly local. There are two reasons why Higginbotham gets us to think about this version: first, to provide a clear example of what the compositionality constraint might amount to; second, to present a requirement on an account of combinatorics, on which more below.

> Work through Higginbotham's explanation of the notion of *strict locality*. It will be helpful to use an example, involving a noun for '*X*', a verb for '*Y*', and a sentence composed from '*X*' and '*Y*' for '*Z*'. Try to think up cases where the relation between sentences and their constituents is not strictly local. How might such failures potentially conflict with the facts about understanding that appeal to compositionality is supposed to illuminate?

Higginbotham allows that combinatorics in Horwich's style work when a thesis of strict locality is in place. However, he does not think that combinatorics in Horwich's style can underwrite an account of competence. He argues this from $\boxed{f}\!\!\mapsto$. A satisfactory statement of combinatorics will explain how the configuration of sentence constituents plays a role in determining the meaning of the sentence. That means it must contain a general principle, applicable to all structures of the form '$Z = X - Y$', that takes the meanings of '*X*' and '*Y*' as inputs, and delivers the meaning of '*Z*' as output. If it fails to contain such a general principle, the semantic theory will fail to meet a minimal requirement: it will not supply, in a humanly comprehensible form, a statement of information knowledge of which would suffice for understanding.

In paragraph $\boxed{f}\!\!\mapsto$, Higginbotham says that in the case of 'Fido barks' we are required to explain the effect of putting an element with the meaning of 'Fido' together with an element with the meaning of 'barks' in that configuration. As he explains, we want an account of that effect that distinguishes

---

[1] It is worthwhile comparing claim (1) with Soames's discussion and claim (2) with the claim Wright makes about the non-compositional semantic theory he presents in his argument against Foster (both can be found in Chapter 3).

it from the effect of other configurations, for example a list such as 'Fido, the property of barking'. The problem of saying how the elements in a sentence combine to express a proposition rather than forming a mere list is sometimes known as the problem of the unity of the proposition.

> Think about how you might explain the difference between 'Fido barks' and 'Fido, the property of barking'. Do you end up appealing to the idea that, in the former, 'barks' is *applied to* or said to be *true of* Fido?

Higginbotham claims that on Horwich's view no explanation of the difference is forthcoming. At ⌈g⌋→, Higginbotham explains how appeal to a truth-theory provides a neat explanation of the effect of predicating 'barks' of Fido (i.e., of the reference of 'Fido').[2]

> Think about how the truth-theoretic account works. Compare its explanation with your own attempts. Compare it with Horwich's account. Do you agree with Higginbotham that Horwich's account fails to meet the minimal requirement on an account of combinatorics suitable to a theory of competence? Do you think Horwich's account meets his own requirements on an account of competence? Does your answer support Horwich's account, or undermine his vision of an account of competence?

Introduction to Pietroski

Paul Pietroski is Professor of Philosophy and Linguistics at the University of Maryland. His many publications in the philosophies of mind and language include the books *Causing Actions* (2000) and *Events and Semantic Architecture* (2004).

In the paper reprinted here, Pietroski lists some of the facts he thinks a semantic theory should explain. Since many of them are beyond the purview of Horwich's account, Pietroski argues that Horwich's account is unsatisfactory. Pietroski does not here present detailed accounts of the facts he cites (though he has proposed accounts elsewhere). His present aim is just to convince you that there is a range of interesting facts, potentially in the domain of semantic theorizing, but left unaccountable by Horwich. As in reading Chomsky, you should spend time reflecting on Pietroski's examples and his characterizations of them.[3]

---

[2]   For further discussion of this issue see the reading list on Compositionality and Meaning.
[3]   For more detail, see the reading list on Semantic Theories for Natural Language.

Paul Pietroski, 'The Undeflated Domain of Semantics'

[a] → It is, I suppose, a truism that an adequate theory of meaning for a natural language L will associate each sentence of L with its meaning. But the converse does not hold. A theory that associates each sentence with its meaning is *not*, by virtue of that fact, an adequate theory of meaning. For it is also a truism that a semantic theory should explain the (interesting and explicable) semantic facts. And one cannot decree that the relevant facts are all reportable with instances of schemata like 'S means that p' or 'S, by virtue of its meaning, is true iff p'. Investigation suggests that there is *much* more for semanticists to explain: natural languages exhibit synonymies, ambiguities, and entailments; for any string of words, there are endlessly many meanings it cannot have; there are semantic generalizations, including cross-linguistic generalizations, that go uncaptured and unexplained by merely associating sentences with their meanings; *etc.* Initially, one might think these facts are "peripheral" and can thus be ignored if the aim is to explain why sentences mean what they do. But the study of natural language suggests otherwise. (One can't tell, in advance of investigation, which facts are peripheral to a given domain. It was initially tempting to think that one could ignore falling bodies, and the tides, if the aim was to explain why planets move as they do.)

We *find out* what a theory of meaning can and should explain by *doing* semantics. We start by trying to explain a range of facts pretheoretically regarded as semantic; and then we see where inquiry leads. One can specify trivial algorithms that associate each sentence of a language with its meaning, without deploying the theoretical apparatus that semanticists standardly deploy. But confusion about the aims of semantics – and failure to consider its successes – is easily transformed into skepticism about the need for nontrivial theories of the sort that semanticists try to offer. So I will be stressing that facts like those reported with

(1) 'Dogs bark' means that dogs bark

reflect the tip of an iceberg.

Another truism is that speakers of English understand English sentences. If you know English, then modulo performance limitations, you can associate each sentence of English with its meaning. But it doesn't follow that if you can associate each sentence of English with its meaning, you thereby understand English (or its sentences) – at least not if understanding is taken to be the natural phenomenon exhibited by native speakers. Speakers of a language recognize various synonymies, ambiguities, and entailments; they know what certain strings of words cannot mean; they acquire semantic knowledge at a characteristic (and quick) pace across linguistic environments; *etc.* Investigation suggests that these capacities are not peripheral. When a speaker of English grasps the meaning of 'Dogs bark', she does so by exercising a competence that lets her do more than simply discern the meanings of English sentences. Describing the nature of this competence, and how speakers exercise it, is a matter for empirical investigation. So one cannot decree that understanding a sentence S is simply a matter of figuring out what S means – or figuring this out by some stipulated method.

1. Horwich (1997, 1998) advocates the following thesis – page references are to Horwich (1997):

> Understanding one of one's own complex expressions (nonidiomatically) is, by definition, nothing over and above understanding its parts and knowing how they are combined (p. 504).

> If 'one has worked out how a certain sentence is constructed from primitive syntactic elements', then 'provided one knows the meanings of those elements' one understands the sentence automatically and without further ado... No further work is required; no further process needs to be involved, leading from these initial conditions to the state of understanding the sentence (p. 504).

Correlatively, the fact reported with (1) – or using Horwich's convention of 'capitalizing an English expression to obtain a name of its meaning', the fact that 'dogs bark' means DOGS BARK – is 'constituted by whatever is the fact regarding its mode of construction and the meanings of its constituents'. According to Horwich, this is the fact that the sentence 'results from putting words meaning what "dog" and "bark" mean into a schema meaning what "*ns v*" means' (p. 505).

Horwich uses '*ns v*' to refer to the sentential schema '*noun*(+plural) *verb*'; and while I'm not entirely sure what 'what "*ns v*" means' means, the idea is that the meaning of any sentence that instantiates the schema consists in (i) its having the syntax in question and (ii) its words, which instantiate parts of the schema in a certain order, having the meanings they do. Thus, he writes:

...the meaning property

   x means DOGS BARK

consists in what I shall call the "construction property"

   x results from putting terms whose meanings are DOG and
BARK, in that order, into a schema whose meaning is *NS V*
(p. 505).

I have quoted at length because this is an audaciously simple – and so
audaciously strong – thesis about the meanings of natural language
sentences (and what it is to understand a sentence).

1.1 In a footnote (citing Jim Higginbotham), Horwich considers
the possibility that the syntax of a sentence S may itself make a
substantive contribution to the meaning of S. If this is so, then
understanding S would require more than 'simply understanding the
words in it and seeing how they have been combined'. But according
to Horwich,

> any so-called "method of combination" that intuitively has a
> meaning (for example, predication or conjunction or '*ns v*') can
> be regarded as a schematic *constituent* of the sentence. Thus, we
> can make it a matter of stipulation that no meaning attaches to
> the procedures by which these and other constituents may be
> combined (n. 2, p. 505).

I have three objections to this reply.

   First, I don't see how the *syntax* of a sentence can be regarded as a
constituent of a sentence. Consider

(2) John ran slowly

whose syntax is roughly as follows: $[_S [_{NP}$ John$][_{VP} [_V$ ran$]$
$[_{Adv}$ *slowly*$]]]$. If someone says that combining 'ran' with 'slowly'
signifies a certain semantic operation, over and above the meanings
of the words combined, I don't see how one can gloss this suggestion
by saying that the relevant aspect of natural language syntax –
$[_{VP} [_V \cdots][_{Adv} \cdots]]$ – is a constituent of (2).

   Second, the available evidence suggests that Horwich is wrong. A
large and growing body of work suggests that the meaning of (2)
should be represented along the lines of

(2M) $\exists e[$Agent$(e,$ John$)$ & Ran(e) & Slow$(e)]$

where 'Ran' and 'Slow' are predicates of events and 'Agent' expresses a *thematic* relation that holds between an event done by someone (or something) and the relevant person (or thing).[1] If this is correct, then a natural thought is that the conjunctive aspects of (2M), indicated by the ampersands, are reflected by the syntactic structure of (2). On this view, natural language concatenation is a way of expressing *predicate-conjunction*; see Pietroski (2002, 2004) for defense and further discussion. But perhaps natural language syntax corresponds instead to *function-application*, as in familiar views deriving from the work of Frege (1891) and Montague (1970). This works nicely for sentences like

(3) John ran

involving just predicates and arguments.[2] Though sentences involving adjuncts, like (2) and

(4) The doctor from Chicago is from Chicago

present a challenge. The two tokens of 'from Chicago' in (4) cannot express functions of the same type: the first token combines with 'doctor' to form a complex unary predicate; the second token *is* a unary predicate. Thus, some sort of *type-shifting* is required; and it is hardly obvious that (if this semantic approach is correct) speakers appreciate the semantic effect of type-shifting, in sentences with adjuncts, simply by appreciating the syntax of such sentences. Indeed, a standard thought is that type-shifting reflects agrammatical aspects of meaning due to the intrusion of extralinguistic cognitive factors into (what is fundamentally) a function-argument semantics. One might, however, adopt a mixed view: some but not all syntax corresponds to function-application; see Heim and Kratzer (1998). In any case, questions about the semantic contribution of syntax are subtle and hard.

$\boxed{e} \mapsto$ Third, and most importantly, this is not a matter for *stipulation*. One has to *find out* what natural language syntax contributes to the meanings of natural language expressions. One may as well stipulate that no meaning attaches to auxiliary verbs, or words beginning with

---

[1]   See Castañeda's (1967) comment on Davidson (1967); see also Higginbotham (1983, 1985), Taylor (1985), Parsons (1990), Schein (1993), Larson and Segal (1995).

[2]   If one associates 'ran' with a function (say from individuals to truth-values) and 'John' with an entity in the domain of that function, while associating (3) with the value of the relevant function given the relevant entity as argument, one is effectively associating concatenation with function-application. Thus, one might replace (2M) and (3M) with '[Slowly(Ran)]John' and 'Ran(John)'. But even this "minimal" contribution by syntax does not correspond to a *constituent* of (3).

'q'. As Horwich notes, one could modify his thesis by saying that 'the meaning of a sentence consists in its mode of constitution having a certain meaning and its constituents having certain meanings' (p. 505). But this raises the question, which lies at the heart of compositional semantics, of *which* meanings various aspects of syntax have. (And correlatively, which *types* of meanings words have.) Horwich seems to think he can sidestep such questions by saying that a given mode of combination means what it does: $[_{vp} [_v \ldots][_{adv} \ldots]]$ means $[_{VP} [_V \ldots][_{ADV} \ldots]]$. But if we just homophonically report the meanings of constituents and syntax, then unsurprisingly, we fail to explain the facts that motivate adoption of more substantive proposals.

[f] → Horwich-style theories provide no explanation for the *many* entailment patterns that semanticists regularly discuss. If every dog barked, and Fido is a dog, then Fido barked. But the fact that 'every dog barked' means what it does, because of what its constituents mean and how they are arranged, does *not* help us explain why (speakers know that) this sentence is true iff {x:dog(x)} ⊆ {x: barked(x)}. Without some such (nonhomophonic and substantive) representation of what the quantified sentence means, we cannot capture what seems to be a striking relation between meaning and implication. Saying that 'every' means EVERY just doesn't do it. We need a theory that spells out *why* the quantified sentence is true iff a subset relation holds between the set of things that satisfy 'dog' and the set of things that satisfy 'bark'. One could go on for weeks. If Pat boiled the soup, the soup boiled. If John thinks that Bob likes himself, John thinks that Bob likes *Bob*; cf. 'John thinks that Bob likes him'. If every kid swam, every tall kid swam; whereas if most kids swam, it doesn't follow that most tall kids swam. If every kid is a kid who swam, every kid swam. Why? And how do speakers know such things?[3]

So far as I can tell, Horwich is committed to denying that these facts are due to the meanings of the natural language sentences; although since he never mentions such facts, it is a little difficult to know what his view is. One can introduce a technical term 'meaning*' and stipulate that certain facts are not due to the meanings* of sentences. But then the question is whether the notion of meaning* is of any interest. Either way, work is required: one has to show that the facts are not, *pace* standard theories, best explained as reflections of

---

[3]   Horwich (1998) discusses analyticity without considering such examples. Note that even if 'x boiled y' contains the word 'cause' covertly, which seems unlikely, the crucial question remains: why does $[_S[_{NP} \ldots][_{VP}(\mathbf{cause})[_{XP} \ldots]]]$ imply $[_{XP} \ldots]$? The last inference pattern holds for all natural language determiners; but we can easily invent determiners for which it doesn't. While 'only' is not a determiner, it illustrates the point: only boys are boys who swam; but it hardly follows that only boys swam. See Larson and Segal (1995) for discussion.

meanings; or one has to show that the notion of meaning* is the theoretical notion we should deploy in this domain.

g⊢→ **1.2** Semanticists also try to account for certain *contrasts* in meaning; and a Horwich-style semantics will not help us account for the interesting facts that have been discovered. Consider the following sentences, variants of which are discussed by Higginbotham (1983) and Vlach (1983):

(5) I heard Pat sing
(6) I heard Pat sang.

In (5), where the embedded verb is untensed, 'Pat' occupies a semantically transparent position; if Pat *is* Chris, and (5) is true, then I heard Chris sing. But (6) is truth-conditionally equivalent to

(7) I heard that Pat sang

in which 'Pat' occupies a semantically opaque position. Why? Obviously, (5) and (6) differ syntactically: the former has an untensed embedded clause, while the latter has a tensed embedded clause (and probably a covert complementizer). But why is this difference correlated with such a significant semantic difference? It does no good to say that the arrangement of words in (5) means what it means, and similarly for (6). We want to know why these sentences have different *kinds* of meanings; and the first step is to provide *illuminating* representations of what they do mean. One wonders if Horwich thinks the opacity of (7) can be explained by saying that 'that Pat sang' means THAT PAT SANG. For if more explanation than this is required, I don't see how his proposal provides it – or even allows for it.

Or consider cases of ambiguity. The string of words in

(8) You cannot stop a philosopher with a theory

can support (at least) two different meanings, much like

(9) I saw the philosopher with binoculars.

The two meanings of (8) are correlated with different syntactic structures, as indicated below

(8a) <stop{a [philosopher (with a theory)]}>
(8b) {[stop(a philosopher)](with a theory)}.

But why do these different arrangements of the words in (8) have *different* meanings? Why is one reading roughly synonymous with 'stop a philosopher *who has* a theory', while the other is roughly synonymous with 'stop a philosopher *by using* a theory'. Merely saying that (8a) means 8A, while (8b) means 8B doesn't tell us why 8A ≠ 8B. But this is a crucial part of what is to be explained. The force of the point increases exponentially with a multiply ambiguous string of words like

(10) I can duck and hide whenever visiting relatives might scare me.

Cases of *non*ambiguity illustrate the flip side of the same point. Speakers of English cannot use

(11) Was the child who lost kept crying

to ask whether the child who *was* lost kept crying. Instead, (11) can only be used to ask whether (perversely) the child who lost *was* kept crying. The standard explanation is that the syntax of (11) involves a covert trace of 'was' between 'lost' and 'kept'; and since natural languages do not permit extraction of auxiliary verbs out of a relative clause, (11) cannot be the result of moving 'was' from a position between 'who' and 'lost'.[4] But this raises a question. Why *doesn't* the structure indicated by

(11a) Was$_i$ [$_S$ [$_{NP}$ the child who lost][$_{VP}$ t$_i$ kept crying]]]

support the impermissible meaning? Why does the relevant sentential frame have the meaning it does, as opposed to other possible meanings – like the perfectly coherent meaning that (11) cannot exhibit? If our semantic theory has the consequence that the VP in (11a) is satisfied by an individual x iff x was kept crying, and that this severely constrains what (11a) can mean, we have at least the beginning of an answer; but not so, if we simply say that the sentential frame means what it does. Similar questions arise with respect to many of Chomsky's famous examples. Consider

(12) John ate an apple
(13) John ate

---

4 Very young children are sensitive to this constraint. For discussion, and a review of other psycholinguistic data that bear on semantic theories, see Crain and Pietroski (2001).

(14) John is too clever to catch a fish
(15) John is too clever to catch

Why *can't* (15) mean that John is too clever to catch something or other? Why does it have to mean, on *dis*analogy with (13), that John is too clever for us to catch him? Saying that (14) and (15) mean what they do doesn't even describe – much less explain – the facts of interest here.

Continuing with the golden oldies, the contrast exhibited by

(16) John is eager to please
(17) John is easy to please

is especially striking. While (16) can only mean that John is eager that *he* please relevant parties, (17) can only mean that it is easy for relevant parties to please John. This suggests the following syntactic structures, with italicized items and coindexing representing covert elements and cointerpretation:

(18) John$_i$ is [eager [e_i to please e_j]]
(19) John$_j$ is [easy [e_i to please e_j]]

Presumably, 'eager' and 'easy' differ semantically in ways that explain (in conjunction with various syntactic facts) why 'John' cannot be the object of the embedded sentence in (18), while 'John' cannot be the subject of the embedded sentence in (19). And presumably, 'ready' differs yet again, since

(20) John is ready to eat

is ambiguous. But what are the relevant facts about the meanings of 'eager' and 'easy' (and 'ready')? It does no good to say that 'eager' means EAGER and 'easy' means EASY. If these are trivial claims – 'eager' and 'easy' mean what they do – then Horwich's theses about meaning (and understanding) imply that the facts just illustrated are *not* reflections of the meanings of sentences like (18) and (19). In which case, an alternative explanation of the facts is owed. On the other hand, if it takes work to specify the meanings of 'eager' and 'easy' in ways that help explain the (nondisquotational) semantic facts, then a 'theory' that reports these meanings by simply capitalizing the verbs is inadequate.

References

Castañeda, H. (1967). 'Comments', in *The Logic of Decision and Action*, ed. N. Rescher (Pittsburgh: University of Pittsburgh Press).

Crain, S. and Pietroski, P. (2001). 'Nature, Nurture, and Universal Grammar', *Linguistics and Philosophy* 24: 139–86.

Davidson, D. (1967). 'The Logical Form of Action Sentences', in *The Logic of Decision and Action* (1967); reprinted in Davidson, *Essays on Actions and Events* (Oxford: Clarendon Press, 1984).

Frege, G. (1891). 'Function and Concept', in *Translations from the Philosophical Writings of Gottlob Frege*, trans. P. Geach and M. Black (Oxford: Blackwell, 1979).

Heim, I. and Kratzer, A. (1998). *Semantics in Generative Grammar* (Oxford: Blackwell).

Higginbotham, J. (1983). 'The Logical Form of Perceptual Reports', *Journal of Philosophy* 80: 100–27.

Higginbotham, J. (1985). 'On Semantics', *Linguistic Inquiry* 16: 547–93.

Horwich, P. (1997). 'The Composition of Meanings', *Philosophical Review* 106: 503–32.

Horwich, P. (1998). *Meaning* (Oxford: Oxford University Press).

Larson, R. and Segal, G. (1995). *Knowledge of Meaning* (Cambridge, Mass.: MIT Press).

Montague, R. (1970). 'English as a Formal Language'. Reprinted in his *Formal Philosophy* (New Haven: Yale University Press, 1974).

Parsons, T. (1990). *Events in the Semantics of English* (Cambridge, Mass.: MIT Press).

Pietroski, P. (2002). 'Function and Concatenation', in *Logical Form and Language*, ed. G. Preyer and G. Peter (Oxford: Oxford University Press).

Pietroski, P. (2004). *Events and Semantic Architecture* (Oxford: Oxford University Press).

Schein, B. (1993). *Events and Plurals*. (Cambridge, Mass.: MIT Press).

Taylor, B. (1985). *Modes of Occurrence* (Oxford: Blackwell).

Vlach, F. (1983). 'On Situation Semantics for Perception', *Synthèse* 54: 129–52.

Commentary on Pietroski

Adequacy conditions

From [a]→ to [b]→, Pietroski outlines his view of what an adequate semantic theory might achieve. One thing an adequate theory might do is to explain *crosslinguistic generalizations*. These are generalizations about more than one language, sometimes about all natural languages.

Think about how the existence of such generalizations might interact with Chomsky's view of Universal Grammar (UG).

On Pietroski's view, there is much that we might expect a semantic theory to explain. But not every theory that associates expressions with their meanings provides the sort of explanation we want. For example, we saw in Wright that some semantic theories fail to capture interrelations among semantic facts that competent speakers are able to appreciate.

How does Pietroski think that the boundary of the range of facts amenable to semantic theorizing is to be determined?

The semantic contribution made by syntax

From $\boxed{b}\mapsto$ to $\boxed{g}\mapsto$, Pietroski presents what he takes to be the core of Horwich's account and makes three objections. The objections concern the manner in which Horwich wants to account for the semantic contribution made by syntactic configurations. So Pietroski's claims contra Horwich are in line with Higginbotham's.

Read $\boxed{c}\mapsto$ to $\boxed{f}\mapsto$. State Pietroski's three objections to Horwich's view of the semantic contribution made by modes of combination.

Since the objections are compressed, and involve some unfamiliar notions, this is difficult. Four unfamiliar notions are (A) concatenation, (B) predicate-conjunction, (C) function-application, and (D) type-shifting.

A. *Concatenation* is a *syntactic* notion: two words are said to be concatenated when they are joined or linked, i.e. spoken or written next to one another.

B. *Predicate-conjunction* is a *semantic* notion. Just as sentences can be joined together with 'and' to arrive at a conjunction, so can predicates. A predicate conjunction, then, is a complex predicate, having the same semantic role – roughly, of applying to things – as a simple predicate. The '&'s in Pietroski's (2M) are a mark of predicate conjunction. Thus, according to the semanticists who represent the meaning of (2) using (2M), the concatenation of 'ran' and 'slowly' corresponds at the semantic level to a conjunction of two predicates.

C. Frege introduced the idea that modes of semantic combination could be modelled on *function-argument* analysis. A *function* is a mapping from *arguments* to *values*. Consider the function expressed by '+3', which a mathematician might write '$f(x) = x + 3$'. This is a function that yields the value 7 for the argument 4, the value 8 for the argument 5, and so on. Frege expanded the notion of a function to allow for arguments and values other than numbers. Following his idea, predicates can be treated as functions from objects to truth-values, where a truth-value is one or other of the abstract objects The True or The False. So, for instance, 'is a doctor' can be treated as expressing a function that delivers the value The True when its argument is a doctor, and the value The False when its argument is not a doctor.

D. We specify the *type* of a function by saying what sorts of inputs (arguments) and outputs (values) it has. We have seen that predicates like 'is a doctor' may be thought to correspond to functions from objects to truth-values. Some functions have functions as their arguments. So there is a second type of predicate-function, which takes predicate-functions of the first type as arguments and delivers functions of the first type as output. That is one way of treating the predicate 'from Chicago' in 'Bill is a doctor from Chicago'. On this way of thinking, the function corresponding to 'from Chicago' takes the function corresponding to 'is a doctor' as input, and delivers the function corresponding to 'is a doctor from Chicago' as output. When the type of function to which an expression corresponds changes from one occurrence to another, the expression is said to be *type-shifting*. For example (ignoring the copular 'is'), 'from Chicago' might be treated in this way. Sometimes it expresses a function from objects to truth-values, for instance in 'Bill is from Chicago'; sometimes it expresses a function FROM functions from objects to truth-values TO functions from objects to truth-values, for instance in 'Bill is a doctor from Chicago'. By contrast, a predicate-conjunction view might treat 'from Chicago' as functioning in the same way in all occurrences. On this view, 'Bill is a doctor from Chicago' would be treated as 'Bill is a doctor *and* is from Chicago'.

Pietroski's first objection, from [c]⊢→, is that he finds one of Horwich's suggestions unintelligible. The suggestion is that the semantic effect of the configuration of 'ran' and 'slowly' involved in 'John ran slowly' may be captured by viewing the configuration itself as a *constituent* of the sentence, in effect as another *word*.

We might try pressing Pietroski's objection a little harder. Suppose that the configuration of 'ran' and 'slowly' was taken to be a constituent. Then, it seems, we could enquire about the effects of *its* configuration with the other constituents. There is presumably a difference between a list naming the constituents of a sentence, now taken to include the configurational constituent, and the result of *configuring* those constituents. But, if so, the difference cannot be captured by treating the configuration of those elements as itself another constituent.

Pietroski's second objection, from [d]⊢→, is that Horwich makes questions about combinatorics easy, though actually they are difficult. There is a dispute about the correct treatment of 'John ran slowly', but if Horwich were right, there would be no dispute.

> On the face of it, this objection might seem to beg the question at issue, by simply assuming that we must take a reference-based approach to semantic theory. Is there a way of understanding Pietroski's objection on which it is not question begging?

Pietroski's third objection, from $\boxed{e}\mapsto$, derives from the second. The fact that apparently rational dispute arises over the proper treatment of configurational effects on sentence-meaning suggests that we are not entitled simply to stipulate a view of those effects.

From $\boxed{f}\mapsto$, Pietroski presents some more facts that a semantic theory might be expected to explain, involving the lexical semantics of *determiners* or *quantifiers*, expressions like 'the', 'every', 'some', and 'most' that combine with nouns, as in 'the politician', 'every politician', 'most politicians'. The facts he cites involve *entailment* relations between sentences.

For present purposes, we can assume that a sentence entails another just in case the truth of the first sentence guarantees the truth of the second. A truth-conditional semantic theory might explain such connections between sentences (/the absence of such connections) by showing that the conditions in which the first sentence would be true suffice (/fail to suffice) for conditions in which the second sentence would be true. That account would depend, in turn, on an account of the truth-relevant (referential) properties of constituents and their configurations.

Pietroski claims that Horwich's representations of meaning fail to illuminate the facts about entailment. The pressing question for Horwich is whether the facts about entailment are sometimes *semantic* facts – that is, whether it is the job of a *semantic* theory to illuminate those facts. Given that there are semantic theories that appear to do the work done by Horwich's account *and* also to explain some entailments, it is difficult to see how a denial of the semantic status of entailments could be motivated.

From $\boxed{g}\mapsto$ Pietroski develops this line of objection. He presents a number of examples of contrasts among the meaning of sentences, ambiguities, and failures of ambiguity. Let's take a very simple example. Why don't we understand (1) as meaning the same as (2)?

(1) George loves Bill
(2) Bill loves George

Standard approaches to such examples involve something like the following pattern of explanation. First, an account is given of the semantic contribution made by syntactic configurations like that in (1) and (2). For our purposes, (3) will serve:

(3) A sentence configured thus: [Name [Predicate]] is true in English iff the object to which the name refers satisfies the predicate

Given its truth conditions, this requires us to view (1) as configured syntactically thus:

(4) [Name George [Predicate loves Bill]]

Given that 'George' refers in English to George and an object satisfies 'loves Bill' in English iff it loves Bill, we can now derive (5):

(5) 'George loves Bill' is true in English iff George loves Bill

We must now explain why (2) does not have that meaning, why (6) is false.

(6) 'Bill loves George' is true in English iff George loves Bill

In order for (6) to be true, given (3), one of the following hypotheses has to be true.

(H1) An object satisfies 'loves Bill' in English iff it is *loved by* Bill.
(H2) (2) is configured syntactically thus: [Name George [Predicate loves Bill]]

So long as it can be fixed – as is plausible – that neither (H1) nor (H2) is stated in (or derivable from) our syntactic and semantic theories, those theories serve to explain why (1) cannot mean the same as (2). Crucially, the standard form of explanation relies on hypotheses about syntactic configurations *and* hypotheses about their semantic effects, as in (3). So a view, like Horwich's, that refuses to explain the semantic impact of configurations, is unable to underwrite the standard form of explanation. Accounting in detail for the difference between (1) and (2) will be more involved than this. Accounting satisfactorily for many of the examples Pietroski mentions is an ongoing task. But the standard approach at least provides a model of how accounts are to be developed through balancing our syntactic and semantic theories.[1]

Work carefully through Pietroski's examples. Note: *cointerpretation* means (roughly) co-reference. Do your intuitions about meaning match Pietroski's? Think about how, in broad terms, the standard approach might be applied to the examples.

---

[1] See reading lists on Semantic Theories for Natural Language, and Syntactic Theory.

Conclusion

In this chapter, we have critically examined a deflationist approach to the first component of an account of meaning, a statement of the semantic facts. The examination of this approach has achieved four main things. First, it has suggested the shape an alternative to Davidson's account of a statement of meaning might take. Second, reflection on the contrast between Davidson's approach and the alternative has served to illuminate some of the strengths of Davidson's. Third, it has provided another opportunity to consider the relations between different elements in an overall account of meaning. As we have seen, Horwich's account of statements of meaning-facts and their determinants seems to depend on his view that linguistic competence is a mere reflex of those facts, not a system of knowledge for which a substantive additional characterization might be sought. A more robust view of competence – for example, Higginbotham's view – imposes additional requirements on an exposition of the semantic facts. The fourth purpose has been to put on display some of the facts a semantic theory may be required to explain, and the kind of explanation that can be offered.

We're now in a position to appreciate the importance of Davidson's question: Can a theory of truth be given for natural language? To the extent that facts of the sort Higginbotham and Pietroski cite are semantic facts, an adequate semantic theory must be able to capture those facts. So, we need an account of the facts, not only for its intrinsic interest, but because being able to sustain an account is a necessary condition on adequacy.[2]

---

[2]   For more discussion, see the reading list on Semantic Theories for Natural Language.

6

Non-literal Meaning

Introduction

Consider a use of language that might be thought of as a paradigm case from the semantic theorist's point of view. A person comes out with the words, 'It's raining here'; she asserts (or states[1]) that it's raining where she is; and that is all that she does. This counts as a paradigm case because what the speaker does with her words is only what an indicative sentence such as 'It's raining here' appears to be semantically fitted to do.[2] If all uses of language conformed to this paradigm, the philosopher of language would have a relatively easy life. Language use would be accounted for by providing (a) theories of meaning of the kind we have been looking at in the last three chapters, and (b) an account of the speech acts that sentences are fitted for such as we looked at in Chapter 2. But of course there are many uses of language that don't conform to the paradigm. We shall think about some of these in the present chapter, under the head of 'non-literal' meaning.

---

[1]   The word 'assert' is used much more widely nowadays than J. L. Austin's word 'state'; but they mean much the same. When he complained about philosophers' concentration on *statements*, Austin was encouraging us to look beyond the semantic theorists' paradigm.

[2]   A couple of complications: (a) A semantic theorist will have to take a view about what non-indicative sentences of various kinds are fitted to do: imperatives are fitted for giving orders, interrogatives for asking questions, etc. In this chapter, as elsewhere in this book, the focus is mainly on indicatives. But non-indicatives, like indicatives, can be used to do something other than that which they are 'fitted' for doing. ('Can you reach the salt?', an example in Chapter 2, illustrates this.) (b) A semantic theory will treat the word 'here' (in 'It's raining here') as having its reference fixed in context. Different notions of context are distinguished in the Conclusion to this chapter.

Philosophers of language are apt to think of the semantic facts as the facts about what words *literally* mean. So a person is thought of as speaking non-literally if she directly communicates something other than that which the words she uses mean according to a semantic theory. In the ordinary sense of the word 'non-literal', speaking non-literally is a matter of making use of one or another figure of speech. Since a person who uses a figure of speech usually does mean something other than what her words literally mean, the philosophers' sense of 'non-literal' is obviously connected with the ordinary one. But a large range of phenomena potentially falls under the head of 'non-literalness' in the philosophers' sense. You will get a feel for some of these in reading the pieces in the present chapter. In the rest of this Introduction, we can connect them with the theorizing we started to consider in the Conclusion to Chapter 2.

There we noted one kind of example in which we have to move beyond the semantic theorist's paradigm – an example in which an illocutionary act is performed indirectly. Cases of this sort, in which the speaker uses a sentence that means one thing but she means a different thing by using it, are extremely common. Imagine circumstances in which Jane replies to the question, 'Would you like to go for a walk?' by saying, 'It's raining', and thereby conveys that she would not like to go for a walk. Jane then does more with her words than to assert what they are fitted to assert. Still, in cases of this sort, no radical departure from the semantic theorist's paradigm appears to be called for. For even though Jane means more than what her words do, her words themselves can be taken quite literally.[3] What we apparently need, in order to account for such cases, is some general explanation of how speakers can mean, and be taken by their hearers to mean, something which is not simply conveyed in their words. We shall come to one such general account in introducing Bach's paper below.

In examples of different sorts, something funny appears to be going on with the words themselves. For instance, Fred says, 'That's the icing on the cake', in a context in which there is manifestly no icing and no cake that he could be alluding to. Now we would seem to be definitely in the realm of non-literalness, on anyone's account. And we can see why there is trouble for the semantic theorist's paradigm. According to the paradigm, an utterance of a sentence means that p when a correct theory treats it as true if and only if p, and thus treats it as fit for asserting that p. But here what the speaker's utterance means requires for its truth something about some cake. Although Fred got something across with the utterance (we might imagine a hearer who knew exactly what he meant), he doesn't seem to have asserted anything whose truth requires something about some cake. The usual connection between meaning of words and content of assertion appears to break down.

---

[3]   Though even here, as we shall see when it comes to Bach, there might be a question whether Jane had literally said that it was raining *where she was*.

How should we account for the breakdown? Evidently we need to make use of the distinction between the standing meaning of words and how those words are *used* on a particular occasion. But what exactly is a speaker doing, if she is not asserting that which her sentence literally means? And how is she able to do what she does?

The main focus of the first two papers in this chapter is on the metaphorical use of language. The third piece we have included here is about 'loose talk', which its author, Bach, subsumes under the head of non-literalness. By the end of the chapter, you will come to see that because philosophers have different views from one another about the domain of semantics, they disagree with one another about exactly how much falls under the head of the non-literal. As you read, you should be aware that the demands imposed on theorists who want to give a systematic account of language use may affect their view of what is literal. You should think about what you are inclined to mean when you say that someone has spoken *literally*.

Introduction to Bergmann

Merrie Bergmann is an Associate Professor of Computer Science at Smith College in Massachusetts, where she also teaches in the Philosophy Department and the Logic Program. She specializes in computational linguistics, logic, and philosophy of logic and language, and is co-author of *The Logic Book* (3rd edn, 1998).

In her paper, Bergmann claims that metaphorical language can perfectly well be used in making assertions, even though in cases of metaphor the usual connection between the literal meaning of words and the content of assertion appears to break down. Bergmann supports this claim with an account of just what it is that a speaker may assert when using metaphor. As you read, think up examples of metaphorical language of your own; think about how they would be treated on Bergmann's account; and consider whether you find the treatment plausible.

Merrie Bergmann, 'Metaphorical Assertions'

Metaphors can be used, and used successfully, to make assertions. The claim that there is such a use of metaphor seems obvious enough, and many authors have treated it as such. Yet the claim is incompatible with, even flatly denied by, numerous other accounts of the 'nature' of metaphor. Although the antagonists hail from diverse philosophical quarters, they share a concern with one aspect of metaphor: this is the 'richness,' or the 'pregnancy' or 'expansiveness' of metaphor. [...] The claim that metaphors are rich means that they invite many readings, or suggest many things, and diverse ones.

There are those who maintain outright that the richness of metaphor precludes its use in the making of assertions. And there are those who stop short of this conclusion but nevertheless maintain that because of their richness, what we say when we use metaphors is in some way different in kind from what can be said literally: for example, we use metaphors to say things that are 'wildly' or 'mythically' true.*

In this paper, I provide a theoretical account of the assertive use of metaphor. One of the consequences of the account is this: not only is the richness of metaphor compatible with its use in making assertions; but in addition our assessments of the richness of metaphors are based on the workings of the same linguistic mechanism which enables us to make and understand specific assertions with metaphors. Once this mechanism is understood, there is no need to maintain that the contents of metaphorical assertions, or their truth-values, are different in kind from those of literal assertions.

II

My claim is that the author of a metaphor can use that metaphor to assert something, and can do so with success. In this section I provide a theoretical account of this linguistic act. First, I characterize the assertive use of metaphor; and second, I explain what is involved in the success of this use of language. For even when an author intends to assert something with metaphor, the communicative enterprise, just like any other attempt at communication, may fail. Some of the reasons for failure are peculiar to metaphor, but others are not.

[...] I do not maintain that metaphors are *always* used to make assertions. The account that follows paves the way for a theoretical description of other uses of metaphor as well. For although I develop an account of the assertive use, I characterize metaphor independently of any particular illocutionary force.

To simplify matters, I focus on assertive metaphors that occur in conversational contexts. What counts as a metaphor, and what we

---

*   **Editors' note:** In a passage cut from the present reprinting, Bergmann says that the richness of metaphors makes a certain conclusion tempting – a conclusion expressed by Davidson in a passage that Bergmann quotes. This quoted passage and Bergmann's response to it are presented in the paper by Davies – next in this chapter.

should regard the metaphor as doing, both involve questions of use. Asking of a sentence itself – say, 'Smith is a Communist' – whether it is a metaphor is like asking of the sentence itself whether it is a lie, or whether it is a warning or an insult. In each case the question is illegitimate. What we can legitimately ask is whether the sentence is, on a particular occasion, being used as a metaphor. And an answer to this question relies on recognizing, or assuming, something about the *intentions* of the person who uses the sentence.[1] The sentence 'Smith is a Communist' is not itself either literal or metaphorical; it may be used either way.

But the classification of a sentence as a metaphor does not settle the other questions of use. The uses of a sentence as a metaphor and as a lie are not mutually exclusive; and so it is with metaphor and warning, metaphor and criticizing, metaphor and asserting. Concerning lying, it suffices to note that metaphor may be used with or without intent to deceive. And when we decide that a sentence is a metaphor we are not classifying it according to illocutionary force. Here we have three dimensions of use, distinguished from one another by the sorting criterion that operates within each dimension: sincerity (truth-telling or lying), purpose (illocutionary force), and manner: the systematic relation between the words used and the content of the illocutionary act. Identification of a sentence as metaphor is classification according to manner, and manner may be literal, metaphoric, ironic, hyperbolic, and so on. In the case of the assertive metaphor, then, we must make two distinct identifications as to use: the sentence is being used *as* a metaphor, and *to* assert.

Further, when a sentence is used as a metaphor with the intention of assertion, various propositions may be intended or conveyed, depending on the author and the context. The point of 'Smith is a Communist' used as a metaphor may be to assert that Smith is unpatriotic, that Smith advocates abolition of the nuclear family, or that Smith opposes religious freedom. [...]

Whereas a proposition represents the world as being a certain way, an act of asserting a proposition is an act of saying that the world *is* the way the proposition represents it as being.[2] When language is used literally to assert a proposition, there is an intimate connection between the words used and the proposition asserted: the words literally *express* the proposition. Or, to put it another way, the proposition is the

---

[1]   The nonexclusive contrast with lying is Davidson (1978). The inadequacies of purely semantic characterizations of metaphor are discussed in Bergmann (1979), in Cohen, 'Notes on Metaphor,' and in Loewenberg (1975).

[2]   Cf. Stalnaker (1978).

meaning of the sentence used.[3] But a person who uses a sentence metaphorically does not use it to assert the proposition that is literally expressed by the sentence. In the case of assertive metaphor, we must distinguish between sentence meaning and speaker's meaning.[4]

[b]→ If the use is to count as *metaphor*, however, rather than as some other figure like irony or even as nonsense, a particular sort of relation must hold between the sentence used and the proposition asserted. What is distinctive of all metaphorical uses of language (whether the purpose is to assert or to do something else) is that the content of what is communicated is a *direct* function of salient characteristics associated with (at least) part of the expression – rather than of the literal meaning of that part. The concept of a salient characteristic associated with an expression is a technical one [. . .]. Here I'll just give examples for some simple sorts of expressions.[5]

Characteristics include properties and relations. *Salience* of characteristics is partially a function of commonplaces and stereotypes. The salient characteristics of a thing include those characteristics which we would typically list on the spot if asked to state what we believe is *distinctive* of that thing.[6] So the salient characteristics associated with a name include properties that are commonly attributed to the thing

---

[3] Strictly speaking, this needs qualification of a sort that need not concern us here: qualification concerning, for example, ambiguity and the use of indexicals.

[4] I agree with Davidson on this point:

> Once we understand a metaphor we can call what we grasp the 'metaphorical truth' and (up to a point) say what the 'metaphorical meaning' is. But simply to lodge this meaning in the metaphor is like explaining why a pill puts you to sleep by saying it has a dormative power. Literal meaning and literal truth conditions can be assigned to words and sentences apart from particular contexts of use. This is why adverting to them has genuine explanatory power. (Davidson 1978, p. 31)

The fact that an expression can be used as a metaphor does not point to, or create, an *ambiguity* in the expression. When metaphors die, to be sure, we may be left with new ambiguities. But that is the point of calling a metaphor 'dead' – it has become common currency.

[5] The concept of salience has appeared now in several accounts of metaphor. In particular, I am indebted to the work of Andrew Ortony for detailed discussions of this concept. See his (1976), in Ortony (1979).

[6] The 'distinctive' part is important. Israel Scheffler (1979) has pointed out that an account of metaphor that appeals to commonplaces with no restrictions will allow unacceptable interpretations of metaphors:

> That wolves are larger than mushrooms is not only true but also commonly held to be true by laymen within our culture. These laymen also normally hold that wolves have eyes, occupy space and have weight; they are persuaded that no wolf is a tree or an umbrella or identical with Mount Everest. Does [such an account] then imply that to call men wolves is to say that men too are larger than mushrooms, have eyes, and so forth? (*Beyond the Letter*, p. 114)

named (perhaps incorrectly). Salient characteristics associated with the name 'Einstein' include the properties of being a scientist, and of being brilliant. In virtue of these characteristics, I may use 'John is an Einstein' to say that John is a brilliant scientist. The proposition I have asserted is then a function of the literal meaning of 'John' and of salient characteristics associated with 'Einstein'. I may also use 'Einstein' to *refer* to John, if he is a brilliant scientist: 'Einstein is on his lunch break'.

The salient characteristics associated with a common noun or intransitive verb include properties commonly believed to be characteristic of the things – possible or actual – the noun or verb applies to, properties that are part of the stereotype of that sort of thing. [...] One salient characteristic associated with 'encyclopaedia' is the property of being a source of information. Thus I can use 'Marie is an encyclopaedia' to attribute that property to Marie, to assert that Marie knows lots of things. A salient characteristic associated with 'smile' is benevolence and consequently I can use 'Uncle George was smiling at us when he wrote his will' to assert that Uncle George decided to leave us something after all. The salient characteristics associated with a transitive verb include relations that are commonly thought to hold between things standing in the relation literally expressed by the verb. A salient characteristic associated with 'cook' is the relation *prepare*. Thus I can assert that Roger has become a poet by saying 'Roger is cooking poems these days'.[7]

Salience is also sensitive to context – to matters of ongoing concern, information that has just been shared. Thus the salient characteristics associated with a name also include properties that, in the context in which the name is used, have been made conspicuous by some means or other. A certain context may bring the property of being eccentric to the status of a salient characteristic associated with 'Einstein' – for example, one in which I have just been telling anecdotes (mostly false) about Einstein. In such a context, 'John is an Einstein' may be used to assert the proposition that John is eccentric, as well as (or instead of) the proposition that he is a brilliant scientist. Or perhaps you have been complaining about the exorbitant price you just paid for a cord of wood, lamenting that you will now have to watch your budget

---

[7] Sometimes the salient characteristics we associate with a general expression such as a common noun or a verb are characteristics thought typical or distinctive of some prominent subclass of the extension of the word. Consider 'He had a green thought.' I can't think of any distinctive characteristics associated with the entire collection of green things, save that they are green. In interpreting the sentence as metaphor we may focus on a subcollection of green things – plants, perhaps, or unripe fruit. Then we have the characteristics on the one hand of growing, or thriving; and on the other of being immature or underdeveloped.

closely. I pick up on this when the conversation turns to my new refrigerator, saying 'That refrigerator is *my* cord of wood' to indicate that it, too, was expensive and that I will be on a tight budget as well.

I want to stress that properties or relations may be *ephemerally* rather than eternally salient. By telling anecdotes about Einstein I have managed to make eccentricity a salient characteristic of the man; but tomorrow this may be forgotten. And what is salient for one person may not be salient for another. A third party who did not hear your complaint will not understand why I called my refrigerator, rather than my electric space heater, a 'cord of wood'.

Salience, then, is context-dependent. And a context, when the understanding of metaphor is at issue, is a context for a person. We may think of the context that a person brings to the interpretation of a metaphor as the set of prominent beliefs that determine salience-beliefs that may vary from person to person and from situation to situation. The context includes the linguistic exchange in which the metaphor occurs – what propositions have been asserted, what the topics are.[8] The context also includes background knowledge about parties to the conversation. [. . .]

What can be said in favor of accepting the salience relation as the basis for determining the content of metaphorical assertions? It works. Take an assertive metaphor, and take what you assume is the content of the metaphor – and you will find that content *is* determined by salient characteristics you associate with expressions in the metaphor. Moreover, the account based on salience corresponds nicely to what we do when we set out to *explicate* metaphors. A typical way to explicate 'Life is a game' as a metaphor about life is to draw attention to our beliefs about what characteristics are distinctive of games and to attribute these characteristics to life.[9]

Now we may state the conditions for success in the case of assertive metaphor. First, the audience must recognize the author's utterance as metaphor. [. . .] Second, the audience must recognize the author's utterance as an assertion. And third, the audience must properly identify the proposition the author intended to assert. [. . .]

---

[8] This includes the topics of the metaphorical sentence. Although I do not ordinarily take their lacking consciousness as a distinctive property of vegetables, in the context of the sentence 'John's grandfather is a vegetable' the property does become a prominent, noticeable characteristic. (The example is Andrew Ortony's.)

[9] I should also add, for those who have qualms about resting an account of metaphor on the context-sensitive concept of salience, that statements of comparison and counterfactual statements are in the same boat as metaphor in this respect. See David Lewis (1973), pp. 91–5 and 114–17; and (1979), pp. 466–7. [. . .]

The responsibility for the success of a metaphorical assertion is the author's; he or she must ensure that the audience can figure out what proposition is being asserted. [...] Principles of cooperative discourse are in effect here as well as in literal discourse. This is just as one would expect, if metaphors can be used to make assertions.

III

Finally, I shall use my account to address some important issues in the literature on metaphor [...].

$\boxed{c} \rightarrow$

1. *The salience relation distinguishes metaphor from other tropes.* The relations involved in figuration differ from trope to trope. For example, the relation in irony is one of inversion: what is meant is the *opposite* of what is literally expressed; the relation in hyperbole is one of exaggeration: what is literally expressed is an exaggeration of what is meant. In this paper, the examples I have given are cases of 'pure' metaphor – the use of the expression involves only the figure of metaphor. Metaphor does not interfere with other tropes or figures; but it should not be *confused* with them. 'You are the cream in my coffee' may be used at once ironically and metaphorically; 'It's the Empire State Building' may involve both metaphor and hyperbole.[10]

2. *Understanding metaphor requires more than understanding word meaning.* A while back, various attempts were made to show how metaphorical 'meanings' could be generated on the basis of deleted selection restrictions of semantic features (components of literal meanings). Thus L. Jonathan Cohen and Avishai Margalit write:

> The metaphorical meanings of a word or phrase in a natural language are all contained, as it were, within its literal meaning or meanings. They are reached by removing any restrictions in relation to certain variables from the appropriate section or sections of its semantical hypothesis. For example, *baby* has as one of its metaphorical meanings the sense of *very small of its kind*: cf. *baby airplane* as against *baby daughter*. Here it is

---

[10] And some dead metaphors may not, when live, have been pure ones. On this point see Goodman (1968), pp. 76–7.

obviously the age and human/animal/artificial/etc. variables that are being treated as if they imposed no restriction, while a restriction of size is still retained. Or if this is considered an example of already dead metaphor, consider *That old man is a baby*, where on the most straightforward interpretation the age and size variables are presumably being treated as if they imposed no restriction, and other attributes of babies are being ascribed, such as mental incapacity. (Cohen and Margalit 1972, p. 735)

⌐d⌐→ Such a theory requires a broad conception of literal meanings – most of us wouldn't normally think of mental incapacity as contributing to the literal meaning of 'baby'. This objection has been raised often enough.

But there is a more severe problem with the theory. For ephemerally salient characteristics may not be commonplace at all; yet, as I have suggested, they can play an important role in the interpretation of metaphors. Consider:

John: Look at how blue the sky is today!
Joe: Sure is. What a great colour... and not a cloud in sight. When the sky is that blue, the air seems fresher... crisper... it really makes you feel good.
John: Yeah, it sure is a good feeling. Like everything's gonna be great, when the sky is that blue.
Joe: Mmm... Hey – even the news report was blue today for a change – lotsa good stuff.

What has happened during this brief exchange is that 'blue', which under somewhat conventional usage has the associated salient characteristic sad or depressing, has picked up a very different associated characteristic: one that will likely be lost shortly in John's and Joe's conceptual schemes. In basing my account of assertive metaphor on the concept of associated salient characteristics I have developed a theory that is sensitive to those interpretations which clearly rest on context rather than on lexical knowledge, as well as to those interpretations which are dependent on community-wide beliefs.[11]

---

[11]   Ted Cohen has argued in his (1975) that because what a metaphor 'means' is not a function of its literal meaning, metaphorical meaning is therefore not rule-governed and is hence unpredictable. I have been arguing that interpretation of metaphor *is* rule-governed; but the output depends on salience determined by the context as well as on literal meanings. It is this reliance on *context*, rather than the lack of a rule, that makes for unpredictability: as what is salient changes, so do the interpretations we read into metaphors.

3. *A metaphor used assertively may not admit of simple paraphrase.* The claim has often been made that metaphors are not paraphrasable in literal language. Sometimes the claim is trivial, as when we are then told that even literal expressions cannot be paraphrased. When it is not trivial, the claim takes one of three forms:

> (i) There is a lexical gap in our vocabulary; there are some things that can be said by metaphor for which we have no literal words.
>
> (ii) No literal paraphrase can capture the suggestiveness of a metaphor.
>
> (iii) No literal paraphrase can give the 'insight' a metaphor gives.[12]

I shall comment on (ii) and (iii) below; it is (i) that interests me here. My theory is consistent with both (i) and its denial.

It is important to distinguish two versions of the gap mentioned in (i):

> (ia) There is some proposition that, given the available resources of our language, is not literally expressed by any sentence or set of sentences.

I have not seen any convincing example supporting the existence of a gap of this sort that has been successfully plugged by a *metaphor*. Stipulation and theoretical introduction of terms, as in scientific inquiry, may fill such gaps – but this is not metaphor.

> (ib) There is some meaning of a nonpropositional sort that, given the available resources of our language, is not literally expressed by any single word.

This claim seems to be true. For example, I know of no single word that means the same as what 'brilliant and eccentric scientist' literally expresses. Yet, under appropriate circumstances, this may be a metaphorical interpretation of 'an Einstein'.

4. *There is no one answer to the question 'Why do we use metaphors?'* Although I have focused on the use of metaphor in making assertions, we must not forget that metaphors can be

---

[12]   The first form has been attributed to Aristotle (the *Poetics*); an example of the second is found in Stevenson (1944); and an example of the third is found in Black (1955).

used nonassertively: for example, we may question or command with metaphors. But even when the use of a metaphor *is* assertive, there may be purposes beyond that of conveying a proposition. The metaphor may be used for aesthetic reasons (it conjures up a pleasing or disturbing image), or rhetorical ones (an expression in the metaphor has strong emotive connotations). Or the metaphor may be used because it is believed to be rich, to be fecund, or to have considerable organizing power.

f⟶ A metaphor is *fecund* if it suggests other, related, metaphors. [...]

A metaphor has *organizing power* if it influences our orientation toward a subject matter. [...] The organizing power of a metaphor concerns the *directedness* and *restrictedness* of what it suggests. A metaphor may highlight certain aspects of a subject while obscuring others. Here, I think, is the heuristic value in thinking of the understanding of certain metaphors as being akin to 'seeing-as': metaphors sometimes give us a new orientation toward a familiar subject matter, making us revise, ignore, or even forget, the beliefs that went along with the old orientation.[13]

5. *Our assessments of the richness of metaphors are based on the workings of the same linguistic mechanism that enables us to make specific assertions with metaphor.* The mechanism is, of course, the manner of metaphor: the salience relation between the expression used and the content of what is communicated.

A metaphor is rich if it is one that causes us to notice many things. Richness is not something inherent in a metaphor; rather our judgments as to richness are based on the effects the metaphor has on us. Our perceptions of the richness of a metaphor, like those of fecundity and organizing power, may vary with time and with concentration.

Take 'John is a child' as metaphor. I may use this to assert that John is naïve, but it may cause you to notice (and I may have intended this) that John has other, perhaps less salient, characteristics of children: he is small, he giggles a lot. If I had just said 'John is naïve' you would probably not, as a result of my utterance, notice these other things about John. In this sense, the literal paraphrase of my assertion does not have the suggestive power of the metaphor I used.

What you are noticing are salient characteristics associated with 'child'. I have already explained how salience can vary from context to context, and this is true whether the point of metaphor is assertion,

---

[13] There is extensive discussion of what I have called the *organizing power* of metaphor in Lakoff and Johnson (1980).

heuristic guidance, or poetry. But there is another way in which salience won't stay fixed. Namely, the act of dwelling on a metaphor long enough, teasing out all that it can 'mean', will affect salience of characteristics associated with component expressions. Specifically, if we repeatedly ask of a metaphor 'What else might it mean?', after the propositions based on some highly salient characteristics have been noted we may begin to notice, or to focus upon, characteristics that initially were not salient – and this very focusing raises the salience of those characteristics.

Thus, it is not surprising, to echo Davidson, that when we dwell on a metaphor we realize that there is no end to what it can 'mean'. And here we find one of the makings of poetry. For the poetic context invites us to dwell, to go beyond the immediately salient. But the poetic metaphor does not differ from the street variety in kind, for both do their work through salient characteristics. The difference lies in the practice rather than in the principle, in the ways we allow or disallow the immediate context to determine salience and hence interpretations. The underlying mechanism is the same in both cases. And it is reliance on this mechanism, rather than the purpose for which an expression is used – be it simple assertion, the sharing of profound insight, or poetry – that makes a linguistic act a metaphorical one.

References

Bergmann, Merrie (1979). 'Metaphor and Formal Semantics', *Poetics* 8: 213–30.

Black, Max (1955). 'Metaphor', *Proceedings of the Aristotelian Society 55*.

Cohen, L. Jonathan and Margalit, Avishai (1972). 'The Role of Inductive Reasoning in the Interpretation of Metaphor', in *Semantics of Natural Language*, ed. Donald Davidson and Gilbert Harman (Dordrecht: D. Reidel).

Cohen, Ted (1975). 'Figurative Speech and Figurative Acts', *Journal of Philosophy* 72: 669–84.

Davidson, Donald (1978). 'What Metaphors Mean', *Critical Inquiry* 5: 31–47.

Goodman, Nelson (1968). *Languages of Art* (New York: Bobbs Merrill).

Lakoff George and Johnson, Mark (1980). *Metaphors We Live By* (Chicago: University of Chicago Press).

Lewis, David (1973). *Counterfactuals* (Cambridge, Mass.: Harvard University Press.

Lewis, David (1979). 'Counterfactual Dependence and Time's Arrow', *Noûs* 13: 466–7.

Loewenberg, Ina (1975). 'Identifying Metaphors', *Foundations of Language* 12: 315–38.

Ortony, Andrew (1976). 'Beyond Literal Similarity', *Psychological Review* 86: 161–80.

Ortony, Andrew (1979). 'The Role of Similarity in Similes and Metaphors', in *Metaphor and Thought*, ed. A. Ortony (New York: Cambridge University Press), pp. 186–201.

Scheffler, Israel (1979). *Beyond the Letter: A Philosophical Inquiry into Ambiguity, Vagueness and Metaphor in Language* (London: Routledge and Kegan Paul).

Stalnaker, R. (1978). 'Assertion', *Syntax and Semantics 9*.

Stevenson, Charles L. (1944). *Ethics and Language* (New Haven: Yale University Press.

Commentary on Bergmann

In this commentary, we shall pick up on some of the main ideas in Bergmann's paper.

By using the notion of *manner*, Bergmann shows how her treatment of metaphor fits in with a treatment of other figures of speech.

> What does Bergmann mean by saying that metaphor is a manner of use? See $\boxed{a}\!\!\mapsto$.

The manner in which words are used concerns the relation between the words and the content of the speaker's illocutionary act. Different sorts of figurative manner correspond to different sorts of discrepancy between what the speaker's sentence means and what the speaker means by it. See $\boxed{c}\!\!\mapsto$, and consider some examples of irony and hyperbole (exaggeration).

> What does a speaker making a metaphorical assertion assert according to Bergmann? See from $\boxed{b}\!\!\mapsto$ to the end of section II.

Take a case where a speaker says '*a* is F', using '*a*' literally and 'F' metaphorically. ('Marie is an encyclopaedia' would be an example.) Then Bergmann will tell us that what the speaker asserts is that '*a* is G' where 'G' specifies the salient characteristics which in the context are associated with 'F' ('is very knowledgeable', as it might be).

> Why does Bergmann think of different kinds of salient characteristics as associated with different parts of speech?

The salient characteristics associated with a word used metaphorically depend upon what the word literally means (as well as upon the context). Evidently words from different semantic categories – i.e. different parts of speech – have

different sorts of meaning. So Bergmann needs to show how salient characteristics get to be associated with words in different categories. The salient
characteristics associated with a proper name derive from the thing the name
names; the salient characteristics of a transitive verb derive from the relation
between things that the verb expresses; and so on. In the 'Marie is an
encyclopaedia' example, the salient characteristics derive from properties of
things to which the predicate 'is an encyclopaedia' applies.

> What objections does Bergmann find with Cohen and Margalit's account
> of metaphor? Are they good objections? (See [d] $\rightarrow$ following.)

Bergmann notes an oft-made objection to Cohen and Margalit's theory that
metaphorical meanings are 'contained within literal meaning'. If the theory is
to work, literal meanings have to be conceived extremely broadly. The objection (which Bergmann herself doesn't spell out) will presumably be that literal
meanings would have to be conceived so broadly that the theory will have
nothing at all specific to say about metaphorical meaning and thus do very
little to illuminate the phenomenon of metaphor.

The real problem with this theory, as far as Bergmann is concerned, is that it
fails to account for the context-dependence of metaphor.

> See whether you can construct an example which, like Bergmann's John-
> and-Joe example, shows that a word may be imbued with a metaphorical
> meaning in a specific context which would not be predictable except by
> someone having very detailed knowledge of the context.

Bergmann's account (in terms of salient characteristics) is an account of the
literal content of the assertion made by a speaker who uses a metaphor in an
assertion. So she would seem to be committed to the claim that anything said
by a metaphor can be said using words literally.

> How does Bergmann support her denial that there are things that can be
> said by metaphor for which there are no literal words? See [e] $\rightarrow$.

Bergmann's strategy is to separate the claim that she needs to deny from
others with which it might be confused and whose denial is consistent with
her theory. Her (ia) is the claim that would make trouble for her if it were true.
And she says that there are 'no convincing examples'.

> Suppose that someone who used a metaphor was asked to say what they
> had said using only literal language, and that they responded that this was
> impossible. This person *thinks* they have said something that can only be
> said using their metaphor. Are they wrong?

The answer isn't obvious! The example makes us think about how we should use the word 'say'. Presumably Bergmann would hold that the metaphor user's reluctance to allow that they could have *said* (and thus asserted) what they did using literal language stems from the fact that they could not have done *everything* that they did by using the metaphor if they had used only literal language.

> What more – besides making an assertion – can there be to the use of a metaphor, according to Bergmann? See ⌐f⌐ → following.

Metaphors can be used to conjure up images, to add emotional tone, to be suggestive, to get us to notice things, to reorient us to a subject matter, to revise our beliefs, and so on.

The fact that all these various things can be done by speakers using metaphors might seem to be in tension with Bergmann's account of them. According to that account, a metaphor is used to assert some definite content (that Marie is extensively knowledgeable, or whatever it might be). But when we think of metaphors as conjuring up images (say), it is easy to think of them as not having any definite content. You should consider whether there is a real difficulty here for Bergmann's account. Davies has something to say about this.

Introduction to Davies

Martin Davies took up his present position as Professor of Philosophy in the Research School of Social Sciences at the Australian National University in 2000. He is also an Adjunct Professor at the Macquarie Centre for Cognitive Science at Macquarie University in Sydney. He is author of *Meaning, Quantification and Necessity* (1980), and co-editor of many collections, most recently, with Max Coltheart, of *Pathologies of Belief* (2000). His many published articles cover topics in philosophy of logic and language, philosophy of mind and psychology, and epistemology.

Davies treats metaphor in section II of the paper we reprint. He has things to say not only about Bergmann's account of it, but also Davidson's,[1] Searle's, and Black's. In reading Davies closely, you will be helped in thinking about what is really at issue between the different accounts. Davies employs the notion of what a speaker 's-means' at various places. Davies's 's-meaning' is one notion of speaker meaning, as Grice conceived that (see Commentary on Searle in Chapter 2). For a speaker to s-mean something, as Davies defines

---

[1]   Davidson's 1978 paper, 'What Metaphors Mean', is reprinted in various places: see reading list on Metaphor. Davies refers to the reprinting in Platts, whereas Bergmann's references are to the original.

this, she must intend that the audience believe it. As you read Davies and consider various metaphors, you should ask yourself what, if anything, a speaker using the metaphor would intend: what effect would the speaker have on her audience if she had employed the metaphor successfully?

Section I of Davies's paper is mainly concerned with idiom. It touches also on other phenomena that raise questions for semantic theorists. In considering these questions, you will need to think some more about the axioms of the sort of semantic theory introduced in Chapter 3. You might want to refer back to the section 'Theories of truth as semantic theories' in the Commentary on Davidson there.

Martin Davies, 'Idiom and Metaphor'

0. The philosopher of language begins with the literal use of language. He tries to give an elucidation of the notion of literal meaning, perhaps in terms of conventions and speakers' intentions. And he tries to give an account of the way in which the literal meaning of a complete sentence depends upon the semantic properties of its constituent words and modes of combination. In attempting this, he has to address questions about abstract, theoretical semantics, and about the psychological reality of the dependence of meanings of wholes upon meanings of parts.

The literal use with which the philosopher of language begins is only a fragment of our total linguistic practice; and, in fact, it is something of an idealisation even of that fragment. Surveying the broader totality, the philosopher of language is bound, sooner or later, to cast an eye towards the literary, rather than the literal, use of language, and to have something to say about (roughly speaking) poetry. And if it is true that 'The metaphor is to poetry what the proposition is to logic',[1] then he will do well to focus attention on the concept of metaphor.

I shall be concerned with metaphor in the second part of this paper. Recent years have seen a massive increase in the philosophical literature on the topic, but my aim will be modest. I want to make some comments on the accounts of metaphor offered by Max Black, Donald Davidson, John Searle, and most recently Merrie Bergmann. I label the accounts of Searle and Bergmann 'proposition theories', and contrast them with Davidson's, which I label an 'image theory'. As for the difference between Davidson and Black, I shall suggest that there may be less to it than meets the eye.

---

[1]   Preminger (1974), p. 494.

In the first part of the paper I shall be concerned with idiom. This is not because I think, as some theorists have apparently thought, that metaphor is 'a species of' idiom.[2] On the contrary, getting clear about what idiom is, is a way of getting clear about what metaphor is not.

I

1. Idiom is certainly an obstacle to word-by-word translation. The French phrase 'avoir raison' has to be translated into English as 'to be right', not as 'to have reason'. Someone might suggest that this fact about translation goes to the heart of the notion of idiom: an idiom is a phrase which cannot be correctly translated on the basis of translation of its syntactically distinguished constituent words and modes of combination. One feature of such a definition would be that whether a phrase in one language is an idiom could only be determined relative to some chosen second language. Thus, 'avoir raison' would be an idiom in French relative to English, but not relative to Spanish ('tener razón') or to Italian ('avere ragione'), for example. This would be a counter-intuitive feature of the definition. Intuition proclaims simply that the French phrase is an idiom, and that there are corresponding idioms in Spanish and Italian, but not in English.

2. What then is an idiom? Roughly, it is a phrase (or sentence) which is conventionally used with a meaning different from its constructed literal meaning (if it has one). If the phrase does have a constructed literal meaning, it will thus be ambiguous. In a systematic semantic theory there will be a theorem specifying the constructed literal meaning: a theorem derived in a certain canonical way from axioms specifying the semantic properties of the phrase's constituent words and modes of combination. And there will be a separate axiom specifying the idiomatic meaning of the phrase. An idiom has no semantic structure; rather, it is a semantic primitive.[3]
[...]

5. The idiomatic meaning of an idiom cannot be worked out by rational inductive means (cannot be 'projected') from the semantic properties of the constituent words and modes of combination alone. But it may be that, given general non-semantic knowledge, one could work out what the idiom might well mean; and one could come to see

---

[2] See Scheffler (1979), p. 83, discussing the intuitionistic approach to metaphor.
[3] Here and in the next two paragraphs, I follow the terminology of Davies (1981), Chapters 3 and 4.

its idiomatic meaning as unsurprising, or felicitous, or apt. Relevant knowledge might include knowledge of phonetics, knowledge of literature, and general knowledge about how the world works. [...]

6. No particular interest would attach to a taxonomy of apt idioms. But some interest does attach to the class of semantically apt idioms: syntactically complex expressions whose meanings are not determined by the semantic properties of their constituent words and modes of combination, but whose meanings can be seen as somehow felicitous given the semantic properties of their constituents. This class is itself somewhat heterogeneous.

In an earlier paper, I considered words beginning with the 'hydro-' prefix and claimed that they should be regarded as semantically unstructured (1981, p. 141). The semantic properties of 'hydro-' and 'phobia', for example, determine at most that 'hydrophobia' applies to a phobia having something to do with water. I should now add, what was already implicit there, that the syntactically complex 'hydrophobia' is semantically apt. Given some general knowledge about the way the world works, in particular about water and about phobias, we can see its meaning as unsurprising.

7. Similar remarks apply to combinations like 'carpet sweeper' and 'vacuum cleaner'. The meanings of these phrases cannot be worked out from the semantic properties of their constituent words and modes of combination alone: a carpet sweeper sweeps carpets but a vacuum cleaner does not clean vacuums, it cleans by means of a vacuum. But again, given some general knowledge about the way the world works, we can see their meanings as unsurprising.

Considerations such as these can help to remove the unease that may be felt over simply classifying such syntactically complex expressions as semantically unstructured (that is, as semantic primitives). And we can add that there is no reason to suppose that the boundary between mere semantic aptness and genuine semantic structure is absolutely sharp.

8. The semantic aptness of an idiom may be of a rather different kind. It may be that the meaning of the idiom is related to the meaning that is determined by the semantic properties of its constituents in a way appropriate to some figurative use of language; appropriate to metaphor, for example.[4] Typically, of course, such an idiom will be the conventionalised residue of a genuinely figurative use of language.

---

[4] Nothing in the present paper is supposed to depend upon sharp distinctions amongst metaphor, metonymy, and synecdoche, for example. I do assume, however, that metaphor is distinguished from simile.

Consider the sentence 'He burnt his fingers', and assume that it is an idiom, as I have characterised that notion. A semantic theory for English will have a separate axiom for the syntactically complex expression 'burn one's fingers' specifying its idiomatic meaning: to incur harm by meddling. Full understanders of English normally use the idiom with the primary intention that the audience should believe that a certain person incurred harm by meddling, and intend that this primary intention should be recognised (in part) simply by the audience's recognition that the expression is regularly used to 'get across' such a proposition. This is just to say that the expression is treated as an idiom.

Such use of the expression is quite consistent with the speaker's, and the audience's, appreciating that it is a commonplace that burning one's fingers is (often) a case of incurring harm by meddling. Speaker and audience may both appreciate the semantic aptness of the idiom; they may both recognise the relation between the idiomatic meaning and the constructed literal meaning. And it may be common knowledge between them that all this is so.

But if all this is common knowledge between them, then a different use of the expression is possible. The speaker may still have the primary intention that the audience should believe that a certain person incurred harm by meddling, but intend that this primary intention should be recognised (in part) (a) by the audience's recognition of the literal meaning of the sentence, (b) by the audience's recognition that the utterance is not to be interpreted literally (that is, that he is not intended to believe that the person burnt his fingers), and (c) by the audience's recognition of the relation between burning one's fingers and incurring harm by meddling.

In this case there is no idiom, but a metaphorical use of a sentence with its constructed literal meaning. In this use, in contrast with the idiomatic use, the semantic properties of the constituents of the sentence are cognitively crucial.

Idiom and metaphor are disjoint, but this latter kind of semantically apt idiom lies close to the interface.

II

9. In the example that we just considered, where there is no idiom, the speaker (strictly and literally) *says* one thing and *means* (that is, utterer's occasion means, or *s-means*) something else. According to one type of account, this is quite generally what happens in metaphor. Thus, for example, John Searle restricts attention to subject-predicate cases in which a speaker utters a sentence 'S is P' and thereby s-means that S is R, and continues

> [T]he problem of metaphor is to try to get a characterisation of the relations between the three sets, S, P, and R, together with a specification of other information and principles used by speakers and hearers, so as to explain how it is possible to utter 'S is P' and mean 'S is R'. (Searle 1979, p. 98)[5]

Searle goes on to provide some principles of metaphorical interpretation. For present purposes it will suffice to say that the idea is not very different from Black's suggestion that being R should be a commonplace associated with being P.

Merrie Bergmann gives a somewhat similar account.

> [A] person who uses a sentence metaphorically does not use it to assert the proposition that is *literally expressed by the sentence*. In the case of assertive metaphor, we must distinguish between *sentence meaning* and *speaker's meaning*. What is distinctive of all metaphorical uses of language . . . is that the content of what is communicated is a direct function of salient characteristics associated with (at least) part of the expression. (1982, p. 234)

As presented so far, these accounts may not seem to answer to the open-endedness and richness of metaphor. They seem to deal only with the most prosaic of prosaic metaphor: we might say, only with metaphor that is well placed to slide into idiom. But Searle does address the open-endedness of metaphor.

> A speaker says S is P, but means metaphorically an indefinite range of meanings, S is R_1, S is R_2, etc. (1979, *p*. 122)

And it is one of Bergmann's principal claims that the richness of metaphor can be accounted for without any shift in her fundamental position.

> [I]f we repeatedly ask of a metaphor 'What *else* might it mean?', after the propositions based on some highly salient characteristics have been noted we may begin to notice, or to *focus upon*, characteristics that initially were not salient and this very focusing raises the salience of those characteristics. (1982, p. 245)

---

[5] For Searle's principles of metaphorical interpretation, see pp. 113–20. And for a discussion of some of the refinements needed here, see Scheffler (1979), pp. 110–18.

10. Early in her paper, Bergmann quotes a passage from Donald Davidson.

> It should make us suspect the theory that it is so hard to decide, even in the case of the simplest metaphors, exactly what the cognitive
> content [proposition? MD] is supposed to be ... [I]n fact, there is no limit to what a metaphor calls to our attention ... When we try to say what a metaphor 'means', we soon realise there is no end to what we want to mention. (Davidson 1978, at p. 252 in Platts ed. 1980)

And she goes on in reply:

⬚f→
> The fact that metaphors 'generate' further and further readings does not, however, conflict with the claim that an author can successfully use a metaphor to convey a fairly specific cognitive content. (Bergman 1982, p. 231)

Surely she is right about that. But it does not fully answer Davidson's point, particularly the point Davidson made in the sentences omitted from the quotation.

> If what the metaphor makes us notice were finite in scope and propositional in nature, this would not in itself make trouble ...
> [M]uch of what we are caused to notice is not propositional in character. (Davidson, op. cit.)

I label Searle's and Bergmann's accounts 'proposition theories'. What brings Davidson's account into conflict with them is that he denies that the content of a metaphor is exhaustively (let alone finitely) propositional.

⬚g→ I have already mentioned that Searle's and Bergman's accounts are in some ways similar to Max Black's seminal account. Yet it seems to me very unclear whether Black and Davidson are in serious disagreement. In the next four sections I shall concentrate on similarities between Black's and Davidson's accounts. Then, with a view to helping clarify Davidson's position (or my version of it) I shall look at the apparent disagreements. In the final three sections I shall return to the difference between proposition theories and Davidson's account.

11. Famously, Black said that a metaphor 'organises our view' of a subject. He said that the principal subject is 'seen through' the metaphorical expression. Nor must we neglect the shifts in attitude that regularly result from the use of metaphorical language ... to call a man a wolf is to support and reinforce dislogistic attitudes. (Black 1955, at p. 461 in Margolis ed. 1978)

Those claims do not sound very different from the following points made by Davidson.

> Metaphor makes us see one thing as another.
> How many facts or propositions are conveyed by a photograph? ...
> Bad question. ... Words are the wrong currency to exchange for a picture.
> [M]uch of what we are caused to notice is not propositional in character. (Davidson op. cit., pp. 252–3.)

They do not sound *very* different; but there are differences that are worth noting. Black says that the use of a metaphor may support certain attitudes, and I take it that dyslogistic or eulogistic attitudes are not in general propositional. But when Davidson wants to give an example of a non-propositional component of the content of a metaphor, he does not choose an attitude but a case of imaging: 'When the metaphor "He was burned up" was active, we would have pictured fire in the eyes or smoke coming out of the ears' (ibid. p. 244). Thus, we might say that Davidson's is the more radical departure from proposition theories.

12. It will be helpful to consider first a case of organisation, or rather reorganisation, of our view of some subject, that is achieved by a literal, rather than a metaphorical, use of language. Suppose that Malcolm has been universally regarded as a pillar of probity and integrity; in short, as a good man. Suppose now that you are informed that Malcolm is a thief; he stole a large sum of money. Surely your view of Malcolm is radically reorganised. You do not merely add the property of being a thief to the properties you predicate of Malcolm and subtract such properties as may clash with this addition. Amongst the properties you still predicate of Malcolm, weightings and interrelations are changed. And behaviour once interpreted as the product of one attitude may now be interpreted quite differently.

The new piece of information may bring with it countless changes, not only in beliefs, but in other propositional attitudes, in non-propositional attitudes, and in images as well.[6]

Your view of Malcolm is so radically reorganised because you *see him as* (or *think of him as*) a thief. This complex cognitive/imaginative activity is centred on, and informed by, your coming to believe that Malcolm is, indeed, a thief. Certainly there is more to seeing Malcolm as a thief than just woodenly believing that he is a thief. But none of this suggests that your informer's sentence, 'Malcolm is a thief' had, in the context, any meaning other than its strict and literal meaning. The speaker said one thing and s-meant it. His utterance produced a massively complex result. But still his words 'mean what the words, in their most literal interpretation mean, and nothing more' (Davidson op. cit., p. 238).

13. Davidson's suggestion is that this same kind of organisation, or reorganisation, of our view of some subject (or indeed of the world) is what is achieved by metaphor. But, of course, seeing Malcolm as something he is not, say a wolf, is a more complicated matter than seeing him as something he is (e.g. a thief). For crucially, one does not come to believe that Malcolm is (literally) a wolf.

If one sees Malcolm as, or thinks of Malcolm as, a wolf then one does come to believe many other things of Malcolm (such as that he is fierce). And talk of predicating properties from a system of associated commonplaces can be regarded as providing a partial specification of some of the changes in propositional attitude which partly constitute the reorganised view of Malcolm. But such talk leaves out a good deal. For example, it leaves out everything about weightings and interrelations which are the result of the system of commonplaces being associated with the notion of a wolf. Thus Black himself wrote:

> [T]he set of literal statements so obtained will not have the same power to inform and enlighten as the original...the implications, previously left for a suitable reader to educe for himself, with a nice feeling for their relative priorities and degrees of importance, are now presented explicitly as though having equal weight. (1955, at p. 464 in Margolis ed. 1978)

It also leaves out everything about propositional attitudes other than belief, about attitudes that are not propositional, and about images.

---

[6] Cf. P. F. Strawson (1974), p. 53: 'Non-actual perceptions are in a sense represented in, alive in, the present perception.'

This fact has not escaped Black. In a later paper, after discussing the example 'Marriage is a zero-sum game', he wrote

> Such a heavy-handed analysis of course neglects the ambience of the secondary subject, the suggestions and valuations that necessarily attach themselves to a game-theory view of marriage, and thereby suffuse the receiver's perception of it. (Black 1979a, p. 30)

And at the end of that paper he compared metaphors with other 'cognitive devices [charts, maps, graphs, pictorial diagrams, photographs, "realistic" paintings] for *showing* "how things are", devices that need not be perceived as mere substitutes for bundles of statement of fact' (1979a, p. 41).

14. The reorganisation of view that is achieved in a metaphorical use of 'Malcolm is a wolf' is in many respects like that achieved in a literal use of 'Malcolm is a thief'. But the crucial difference remains. In the metaphorical use the speaker does not intend that the audience should believe that Malcolm is a wolf.

According to Searle and Bergmann, for example, the speaker intends that the audience should believe some proposition or propositions *other than* that Malcolm is a wolf. According to Davidson, 'Metaphor makes us see one thing as another by making some literal statement that inspires or prompts the insight' (Davidson op. cit., p. 253). That is, the speaker intends that the audience should see Malcolm as a wolf or (more long-windedly) should see the world as one in which *Malcolm is a wolf*. If seeing the world as one in which...can be regarded as an attitude towards a proposition, then we can capture the contrast between the two accounts this way. For Searle and Bergmann: *same attitude, different proposition*. For Davidson: *different attitude, same proposition*. Perhaps this attenuates the notion of a propositional attitude too much. But we can still mark the contrast. For Searle and Bergmann, the audience does something usual with a proposition *other than* the proposition literally expressed. For Davidson, the audience does something *un*usual with the proposition that is literally expressed.[7]

---

[7] The non-propositional attitudes which are part of seeing the world a certain way may well be centred directly on the proposition that Malcolm is a wolf rather than on any proposition that is believed. Also, Christopher Janaway has pointed out that if we focus on the belief that Malcolm is fierce, say, and ask why he should be called a wolf, rather than a tiger or a bear, there may be no answer available other than that Malcolm's fierceness is the fierceness of a wolf.

Perhaps if one is to see Malcolm as a wolf one must believe him to be treacherous, for example. Perhaps that is common knowledge between speaker and audience, and perhaps sufficient further conditions are met for us to say that the speaker s-meant (*inter alia*) that Malcolm is treacherous. Nevertheless, his intentions in s-meaning various particular propositions will never add up to his primary intention in using the metaphor: the intention that his audience should be inspired or prompted to see Malcolm as a wolf.

A metaphorical use of 'Malcolm is a wolf', like a literal use of 'Malcolm is a thief', may produce a massively complex result, and perhaps in this case there is just room for the idea that the speaker may say one thing and s-mean another (or several others). But it is not difficult to see why someone holding such a view as I have been outlining would say that 'metaphors mean what the words, in their most literal interpretation, mean, and nothing more' (Davidson op. cit., p. 238).[8]

15. I have been concentrating on similarities between Black's and Davidson's accounts. But Davidson's account – as expressed by him – has drawn a reply from Black which is not wholly taken up with pointing to the similarities between their views (Black 1979b). Before moving to some final, general thoughts about metaphor, I want to make some comments that are relevant to Black's reply, and which may help to clarify Davidson's position.

In a case of outright (literal) assertion, a speaker may begin with a belief and intend that the audience should end up believing the same.[9] In believing the proposition that p the speaker does not merely entertain the proposition that p, or wonder whether p, or see the humour in the idea that p, or... Let us say that *he affirms that p in thought*. He may then utter a sentence with the primary intention that the audience end up sharing his belief, and thereby assert that p.

Similarly, in a case of serious use of metaphor, a speaker may begin with a view of the world as one in which q say, and intend that the audience should end up seeing the world as one in which q. In thinking of the world in that way the speaker does not merely entertain the possibility of seeing the world a certain way, or wonder whether to see it that way, or see the humour in the idea of seeing it

---

[8]   Even on Davidson's view, it can be allowed that the speaker says that Malcolm is a wolf and s-means that the audience is to see Malcolm as a wolf. But this is not what people have had in mind when they have said that in metaphor a speaker says one thing and means another.

[9]   If an utterance of s is to be an assertion that p, then I require that s (literally) mean that p and that the speaker's primary intention be that the audience should believe that p. Asserting that p is a special case of saying that p.

that way, or...Let us say that he *metaphorically affirms that q in thought*. He may then utter a sentence with the primary intention that the audience end up sharing his view of the world, and thereby, let us say, *metaphorically assert that q* (cf. Black 1979b, pp. 182–85). To introduce terminology is not, of course, to provide a substantive theory, and certainly this terminology is not intended to bear any explanatory weight. Metaphorically affirming that *q* in thought is not believing that *q*; and correlatively, metaphorically asserting that *q* is not asserting that *q*. Perhaps, we can say a little more: the thought that *q* must be entertained, and further it 'must strike me as in some way right or appropriate' (Scruton 1982, p. 90; see also p. 98).

Black credits Davidson with the view that

> (A) The producer of a metaphorical statement says nothing more than what is meant when the sentence he uses is taken literally.

He later goes on

> One might suppose that since Davidson regards the sentence used in a metaphorical statement as preserving its ordinary literal meaning, he might take its user to be asserting at least one supposed fact...But...what metaphorical statements, taken literally, assert is nearly always plainly false and absurd. Thus, (A) should be understood to mean that a metaphor producer is 'saying' *nothing at all*. (1979b, p. 186)

Much of the problem here seems to be terminological. Davidson regards the sentence as preserving its literal meaning and as being used to perform a *saying*, but not an *assertion*. In sincere assertion one aims at the truth; and, of course, metaphorical statements are apt to be (literally) false. But it does not follow that the metaphor producer *says* nothing at all: what he says is just what the sentence literally means. Sayings are truth-*evaluable*, and assertion is the norm for sayings, but it does not follow that for all sayings falsehood is a fault. Some sayings, and in particular what we have called metaphorical assertions, are not aimed at the truth. In a sincere metaphorical assertion the speaker aims at that which stands to seeing the world a certain way as truth stands to believing the world to be a certain way. A particular way of seeing the world may be insightful or unilluminating, appropriate or inappropriate, rich or barren. By a natural extension of our terminology, we could call the aim of sincere metaphorical assertion *metaphorical truth*. But, once again, the mere introduction of terminology provides no philosophical explanation.

Finally, Black says, regarding the assignment of meaning to metaphors

> A metaphor may indeed convey a 'vision' or 'view'... but this is compatible with its also saying things that are correct or incorrect, illuminating or misleading, and so on. (1979b, p. 192)

Davidson need not deny that sharing a 'vision' or 'view' may be sharing something which is itself illuminating or misleading, or even metaphorically true or false. Nor need he deny that it may involve *inter alia* sharing beliefs which may be correct or incorrect, indeed may be literally true or false. But what Davidson would be concerned to deny is that from the contents of those beliefs we can in general construct something which deserves to be called the content or meaning of the metaphor. Those propositional contents no more exhaust the significance of the metaphor than does having those beliefs constitute having the vision.

16. Let us now focus upon the two kinds of theory of metaphor. I have labelled theories such as Searle's and Bergmann's 'proposition theories'. I label theories such as Davidson's 'image theories'. Could it be that the two kinds of theory apply to two kinds of metaphor? The proposition theory seems to fit what is called prosaic (low-energy) metaphor, the kind of metaphor that at its lowest energy extreme shades into mere idiom. On the other hand, the image theory seems to fit what is called poetic, essential (high-energy) metaphor. Thus, for example, according to the proposition theory, metaphor is in principle paraphrasable; and prosaic metaphor is often reckoned to be paraphrasable. On the other hand, it is no part of the image theory that metaphor is in general paraphrasable; and poetic metaphor is indeed often reckoned to defy paraphrase – hence, *essential* metaphor.

Consider now one of Bergmann's examples.

> One salient characteristic associated with 'encyclopedia' is the property of being a source of information. Thus I can use 'Marie is an encyclopedia'... to assert that Marie knows lots of things. (Bergman 1982, pp. 235–6)

What happens here is that we hold fixed our conception of the world as it really is, and seek to interpret the language used metaphorically, employing various principles (such as those articulated by Searle) to arrive at a proposition that fits the world as it really is. To speak very intuitively and inexactly: the metaphorical language is interpretatively construed downwards to fit the real world.

I should like to compare this with an example from Samuel R. Levin (1979, pp. 132–3). He invites us to consider the following lines by Emily Dickinson.

> The mountain sat upon the plain
> In his eternal chair,
> His observation omnifold,
> His inquest everywhere.
> The seasons prayed around his knees,
> Like children round a sire:
> Grandfather of the days is he,
> Of dawn the ancestor.

According to the proposition theory, we again seek to interpret the language used metaphorically, so as to arrive at propositions that fit the world as it really is (in this case, describe the mountain as it really is). Thus, perhaps, the first two lines express metaphorically the proposition that the mountain was located in a certain place and had been there for some time. And one can work through the remaining lines.

Levin contrasts this account of what happens in the poet and in her audience with another account. Thus, according to the proposition theory

> Emily Dickinson experienced a rather ordinary vision, or conception – that of a mountain's being high and old – and proceeded to make an interesting if unspectacular poem out of that conception by contriving to express it in an extraordinary arrangement of language.

While in contrast

> If we invert the approach, we countenance a world in which the mountain has the properties attributed to him: he actually sits on an eternal chair...On this view it is not the language that is remarkable, it is the conception.

To speak very intuitively and inexactly: the world is imaginatively construed upwards to fit the metaphorical language.

None of this is to deny that if the poet addresses an audience concerning a particular mountain, then the audience, having shared a certain vision, is in the end able to arrive at beliefs about the real world. What Levin says is that we need to modulate the images described in the poem into such as make sense given our knowledge of facts in the actual world. (1979, p. 133)

But what is important for present purposes is Levin's picture of something which happens in the user of the metaphor and in the audience, and which is quite unlike anything admitted by the proposition theory.

17. Suppose we agree that the two kinds of theory apply to two kinds of metaphor. Is it then an illusion that metaphor is a unified phenomenon, ranging from the almost dead metaphors that are scarcely different from idioms, through prosaic metaphors, and on to essential poetic metaphors? I think that it is not an illusion, for to the extent that the proposition theory is correct it seems to be a special case of the image theory.

A metaphor may be, in Black's terminology, not very *resonant*: it does not 'support a high degree of implicative elaboration' (Black 1979a, p. 27). One sees, or thinks of, one thing as another, but the imagination is scarcely engaged. Thinking of A as B is hardly distinguishable from believing that A is C, D, and E. The proposition theory would give an adequate description of the use of such a metaphor.

In general, seeing one thing as another involves a complex of propositional and non-propositional attitudes and elements which are not attitudes at all; in general, but not without exception. Perhaps an exceptional case is provided by what Black regards as an 'unfortunate example' of metaphor: 'Richard is a lion' (Black 1955, at p. 456 in Margolis ed. 1978). Perhaps thinking of Richard as a lion just comes to believing Richard to be brave. (Or perhaps there is a sub-community of speakers of English whose imaginations are so disposed that for them there is no difference: those who have read too many papers on metaphor.)

Of course, none of this refutes the image theory. The image theory applies quite generally, but for cases towards the prosaic end of the spectrum the proposition theory, with its more meagre conceptual resources, is also adequate.

18. Davidson wrote

Metaphor makes us see one thing as another by making some literal statement that inspires or prompts the insight ... *in most cases* what the metaphor prompts or inspires is not entirely, or even at all, recognition of some truth or fact. (Davidson op. cit., p. 253, my emphasis)

With that I have agreed. But I should also agree with Black that any account along these lines is thus far seriously deficient. What we urgently need is

> clarification of what it means to say that in metaphor one thing is thought of (or viewed) *as* another thing. ... [W]e lack an adequate account of metaphorical thought. (Black 1979b, p. 192)[10]

And perhaps we can add that what we lack is not something to be furnished by empirical psychology, but by the philosophy of mind, taking as its starting point the concept of imagination.[11]

References

Bergmann, Merrie (1982). 'Metaphorical Assertions', *Philosophical Review* 91: 229–45. [An edited version is reprinted above.]

Black, Max (1955). 'Metaphor', *Proceedings of the Aristotelian Society 55*. Reprinted in M. Black, *Models and Metaphors* (Cornell University Press, 1962), and also in Margolis ed. (1978).

Black, Max (1979a). 'More about Metaphor', in Ortony ed. (1979), pp. 19–43.

Black, Max (1979b). 'How Metaphors Work: A Reply to Donald Davidson', in Sacks ed. (1979), pp. 181–92.

Davidson, D. (1978). 'What Metaphors Mean', *Critical Inquiry 5*. Page references are to the reprinting in M. Platts (ed.), *Reference, Truth and Reality* (Routledge and Kegan Paul, 1980).

Davies, Martin K. (1981). *Meaning, Quantification, Necessity: Themes in Philosophical Logic* (Routledge and Kegan Paul).

Davies, Martin K. (1994). 'Meaning, Structure and Understanding', *Synthese* 48.

Levin, S. R. (1979). 'Standard Approaches to Metaphor and a Proposal for Literary Metaphor', in Ortony ed. (1979), pp. 124–36.

Margolis, J., ed. (1978). *Philosophy Looks at the Arts* (Temple University Press).

Ortony, A., ed. (1979). *Metaphor and Thought* (Cambridge University Press). [Editors' note: this is the first edition of Ortony (1993), cited in the reading list on Metaphor.]

Preminger, A., ed. (1974). *Princeton Encyclopedia of Poetry and Poetics* (Princeton).

Sacks, Sheldon, ed. (1979). *On Metaphor* (University of Chicago Press).

Scheffler, I. (1979). *Beyond the Letter* (Routledge and Kegan Paul).

---

[10] But see again Scruton op. cit., Chapters 7 and 8, for some steps in the right direction.

[11] I am grateful to Christopher Janaway, Colin McGinn, David Murray, Mark Platts, Mark Sainsbury, and Roger Scruton for comments on an earlier version of this paper. In part I, I am indebted to Lloyd Humberstone, and at §7 and the start of §12 to Mark Sainsbury.

Scruton, R. (1982). *Art and Imagination: A Study in the Philosophy of Mind* (Routledge and Kegan Paul).

Searle, John R. (1979). 'Metaphor' in Ortony ed. (1979).

Strawson, P. F. (1974). 'Imagination and Perception', *in Freedom and Resentment and Other Essays* (Methuen).

Commentary on Davies

I

Semantic theories of the sort introduced in Chapter 3 provide the background against which Davies's remarks about idioms and word combinations are set.

> What does Davies mean by (a) 'constructed literal meaning', and (b) 'semantic primitive' (see [a]→ and [b]→)?

The constructed literal meaning of an expression is specified by the axioms of a semantic theory. Remember that such axioms concern (i) words' semantic properties, and (ii) their ways of combining with one another. If an expression – whether a word or a phrase – is a primitive, semantically speaking, then a single axiom specifies its semantic property, so that the expression is not treated as having components in combination with one another.

Davies points out that semantic theories apparently need to employ more axioms than we would think if we supposed that there was one axiom for each unambiguous word. The example of idioms makes this rather obvious.

> Why does Davies think we might feel 'unease' at treating phrases made up of more than one word as semantic primitives? (See [c]→)

Inasmuch as semantic theories are thought to record speakers' competence, each axiom of a semantic theory might be taken to correspond to an element in speakers' competence. And one might think that any speaker who understood the words 'carpet' and 'sweeper' (for instance) would be in a position, just on the basis of that competence, to understand 'carpet sweeper'. So one might think that 'carpet sweeper' is not a semantic primitive. Davies's point is that even when a semantic theory does not record the way in which two words combine but instead treats their combination as a primitive, still 'general knowledge of the way the world works' can make it predictable what the combination means.

> Consider: 'book case', 'book mark', 'book shelf', 'bookshop', 'bookworm'. Does a semantic theory need a separate axiom for each of these?

The answer isn't obvious, although presumably 'bookworm' is a sort of idiom. There is plenty to think about here: you should try to say what considerations are relevant to the answer. (Think, for instance, about other English nouns that are found in combinations with the word 'case', others found with 'mark' etc.) When Davies says that the distinction between semantic aptness and genuine semantic structure is not absolutely sharp, he allows that there may be borderline cases; so it isn't surprising if you feel undecided about some of these five.

Davies thinks of the phenomena of idiom and metaphor as shading off into one another. But he thinks that there is a definite distinction between them.

What distinguishes a metaphor from an idiom in Davies's view? (See $\boxed{d} \rightarrow$.)

Davies thinks that the speaker who uses a metaphor does not intend that a hearer should come to believe the literal content of the sentence she utters. In other words (given Davies's own view of what is required for assertion), a speaker using a metaphor does not assert what her sentence literally means. A speaker comes out with sentence s, which, according to a semantic theory for her language, means that p; but the speaker does not assert that p – not if they speak metaphorically.

II

When it comes to metaphor, one might see Davies as engaging in a project of reconciliation: he hopes to minimize the amount of disagreement between various authors. He doesn't classify Black's theory as either a proposition theory or an image theory: from the point of view of Davies's dialectics, Black's would seem to be a sort of intermediate theory. It has much in common with the theories of Searle and Bergmann, and, Davies thinks, it has more in common with Davidson's theory than Black himself allows. For the commonalities of Davidson with Searle and Bergmann, see $\boxed{e} \rightarrow$ and $\boxed{g} \rightarrow$, and for the commonality with Black, see §15, especially from $\boxed{h} \rightarrow$.

Rather than follow the details of Davies's argument, let us compare and contrast the two main theories of metaphor as Davies presents them. We shall think of these as theories in the philosophy of language now, and set to one side the important questions Davies raises at the end about what the philosopher of mind can tell us about metaphorical thought and the use of imagination.

What can proposition theories (such as Bergmann's) and image theories (such as Davidson's) agree about, in Davies's view?

We saw that in marking the contrast between idiom and metaphor, Davies makes the claim that a speaker using a metaphor does not assert what her sentence literally means. This claim is never put into question. So we can say that both theories, in Davies's view, agree that

(1)   Someone who uses a sentence meant metaphorically does not *assert* that which is literally expressed by her sentence.

Two further points of agreement emerge in Davies's discussion:

(2)   Metaphors can be enormously suggestive, so that a speaker using a metaphor brings to notice a great number of things, some of which are not 'propositional in character'.
(3)   Someone who comes out with a sentence, using it metaphorically, may *say* what the sentence literally says.

Let us consider (2) and (3) further. As for (2), we saw that Bergmann explicitly endorsed it in her article above. And Davies notes that Bergmann doesn't disagree with Davidson about it: see ⬚f⬚↦. As for (3), this is the point which, according to Davies, Black is wrong to think that Davidson cannot allow (see from ⬚h⬚↦ again). What Davidson *can* allow is that where the sentence used by the metaphorical speaker means (literally) that *p*, the speaker *says* that *p*. Bergmann, in her paper, sometimes uses the word 'say' simply as a variant on 'assert'. But we obviously need to distinguish between saying and asserting here, in order to sort out the issues. When 'say that' is not equivalent to 'assert that', it has sometimes been called 'saying in the thin sense': in this sense, one can say something without putting it forward as true. This is how 'say' is used in (3): the notion of 'saying' there relates a speaker to what Bergmann calls 'the proposition that is literally expressed by the [speaker's] sentence'. And it seems that Bergmann might go along with point (3) as we are now taking it. (Ask yourself whether you think she does.)

What do proposition theories and image theories disagree about?

One disagreement seems to be about *how* a speaker who speaks metaphorically can bring to notice the various things she does. According to the proposition theory, the speaker asserts something. Let us say she asserts – – –. If we imagine that the speaker uses the sentence *s*, and that according to a good semantic theory a speaker who uses *s* says that *p*, then the proposition theory will provide us with an account of how to get from *p* to – – –, i.e. of how to fill in the blanks '– – –'. (This is what Bergmann's account, cast in terms of salient characteristics, is designed to do.) According to the image theory, by contrast, in saying that *p*, there is nothing literal and propositional that the speaker asserts: we cannot fill in the blanks. A hearer who understands a metaphorical utterance goes in for an inventive construal of what the utterance literally means; and this is not a matter of uncovering some proposition that the speaker asserted.

> Do you agree with Davies that 'to the extent that the proposition theory is correct it is a special case of the image theory'? (See [i]→.) Should we endorse the view that results from Davies's reconciliation?

If Davies is right, then the image theory applies across the board; and there is a range of cases ('low energy' ones) to which the proposition theory applies and is not in conflict with the image theory.

> Consider examples of metaphors. It's a good idea to listen and look out for them, so that you can think about concrete, fully contextualized examples. Consider what, if anything, you would say that the speaker had asserted.

You may find yourself agreeing with Bergmann about some examples. If so, then ask yourself how a speaker's assertion of something literal is connected with the suggestiveness of the metaphor they use. This question seems to be relevant to the dispute between Davidson and Bergmann. Davidson might allow that there was nothing terribly wrong in thinking that, in some low-energy cases, a speaker had asserted something literal; but he might claim that in taking the speaker to have asserted something, we do not get any real explanation of how the speaker's words impacted on the hearer. If that claim were right, then asserting something literal could seem to be one by-product of some uses of metaphor, rather than the topic for a theory of metaphor. And in that case, even if there were examples that could be described along the lines of Bergmann's theory, Bergmann's theory and Davidson's theory might appear to be in actual conflict. Davidson denied that there are rules that govern the grasp of metaphor, whereas Bergmann's account of salient characteristics can seem like an attempt to state such rules.

You may find yourself thinking, about some cases, that the speaker using a metaphor actually made an assertion whose content is given in the words she used. For example, you might think that even if Ann has used the sentence 'Smith is a Communist' metaphorically, still Ann has asserted that Smith is a Communist. (On this view, one evidently can't report what Ann asserted without speaking metaphorically oneself.) If this is your view, then you will doubt whether an account of metaphor has any use for the idea of the proposition which a semantic theory stated in abstraction from particular pieces of speech assigns to the sentence uttered by Ann. The point of assertion is to get across some truth. And the truth in question, which Ann asserts in our example on the view we are now considering, is not that proposition. It cannot be that proposition, since, given that we have a case of metaphor, that proposition – that Smith is (*literally*) a Communist – is likely to be false.

In sorting out the various views of metaphor, we distinguished between asserting and 'saying in the thin sense'. This idea of saying appears to be called into question now. What a speaker says in the thin sense was supposed to be the proposition literally expressed by the speaker's sentence. But if one thinks that Ann has asserted that Smith is a Communist (although Ann knows that Smith isn't *literally* a Communist), then one will resist the idea that there is anything which is always expressed by the sentence 'Smith is a Communist' – something expressed both when it is used literally and when it is used by Ann speaking metaphorically.[1] More generally, one will doubt whether the semantic theorist should work with the idea of '*the* proposition that is literally expressed by the speaker's sentence'. If one believes that a speaker using a metaphor can make an assertion whose content is simply carried by their sentence as it is used on the particular occasion, then one will very likely think of the speaker as creating new (non-literal, non-conventional) senses for their words.[2]

> Is it plausible that, with speakers' help, words can take on new senses; or should we think that a semantic theory suffices to tell us the sense of a speaker's words, whatever the speaker's specific intentions?

If you think that, with speakers' help, words can take on new senses in new contexts, then you may seem to be on the side of Humpty Dumpty when he said 'When *I* use a word, it means just what I choose it to mean' (see Commentary on Locke in Chapter 1). But Humpty Dumpty appears to have thought that he could make his choices of word-meaning independently of what his hearer might take him to mean, whereas a philosopher who advocates a place for the contextual-determination of words' senses is likely to want to introduce this into an account of what is *communicated*. They won't reject the whole idea of words' possession of standing meaning-properties (as Humpty Dumpty appears to have done): they will think that speakers' intentions are recognizable by hearers on the basis of their general interpretive abilities as well as their knowledge of the standing meaning-properties of speakers' words. (Notice that Davidson apparently thinks this: he denies that there are rules that govern the grasp of metaphors, thinking that sentences with their 'literal' or standard meanings can be used to give rise to new insights. And even in Bergmann's account, given her insistence that it may be only *in a specific context* that a word is imbued with a metaphorical meaning,

---

[1]   There were actually two ideas which informed the putative thin sense of 'say': (a) that if a speaker uses a sentence which a good semantic theory tells us means that p, then the speaker typically *says* that p; (b) a speaker may *say* something without representing it as true. Even if we give up the idea that there is any sense of 'say' according to which we should endorse (a), we might still hold that there is a sense of 'say' to which (b) applies.

[2]   Bezuidenhout defends an account of the kind gestured at here: see the reading list on Metaphor.

speakers' intentions presumably have a major role to play in determining what may be conveyed by a word when it is used metaphorically.)

The question raised here (in the exercise in the box above) is the subject of current debate. And it won't be resolved by thinking just about metaphor. We shall encounter another aspect of it under the head of 'loose talk', where we shall see once again that the notion of 'what is said' is one that opposing theorists fight over. And we shall return to a related question in the Conclusion to this chapter. In the meantime, you can start to see what may be at issue between philosophers of language, who take opposite sides, by reflecting on this question yourself.[3]

Introduction to Bach

Kent Bach teaches philosophy at San Francisco State University in California. He is co-author with Robert Harnish of *Linguistic Meaning and Speech Acts* (1978), and author of *Thought and Reference* (1988). His many papers over the years argue for a distinctive position in philosophy of language, which has the general shape of a position that Grice put onto the philosophical stage. The paper we reprint is no exception. In order to introduce it, we shall outline the Gricean background.

In Chapter 2, we saw that Grice made use of a notion of what a *speaker* (as opposed to a sentence) means. Grice had a theory about how a speaker can, in particular circumstances, mean very much more than what the sentence she uses mean. Grice's theory takes off from the thought that normal conversation is a joint venture. Speakers want to be understood, and hearers seek to understand; to this extent, they are involved with one another in a co-operative exercise. Other things being equal, speakers and hearers assume that they are using words with shared meaning. Grice gives an account of what a speaker *means* that takes it for granted that what a speaker *says* is given by the literal, conventional, meaning of her words.[4] The sort of co-operativeness that his theory is specifically concerned with, then, is a matter not of shared linguistic meaning, but of shared principles which enable interpretation. Grice's idea is to think of speakers as adhering to various conversational maxims, which are bound to be in place, and known by hearers to be in place, given that speakers and hearers want to co-operate with one another. Examples of such maxims are: Your contribution to the conversation should be truthful, and just as informative as the hearer needs it to be; it should be clearly expressed; it should be relevant; and so on. Grice

---

[3] Reading lists on Language and Convention, on Intention-based Semantics, and on Context and Meaning are all relevant here.

[4] Whether this can always be taken for granted was something that we considered questioning at the end of the Commentary on Davies.

thinks that a speaker who means something that she doesn't say openly disobeys some conversational maxim.

We can see how this works by looking at a couple of examples. In an example in this chapter's Introduction, Jane replies to the question 'Would you like to go for a walk?' by saying 'It's raining'. Here Jane is not speaking relevantly unless the state of the weather can be supposed to have a bearing on what she has just been asked. Provided her questioner is in a position to know that Jane isn't likely to want to go for a walk in the rain, Jane, by saying that it's raining, implies that she does not want to go for a walk. In Grice's technical use, this is something that Jane *conversationally implicates*.[5] Consider an example of a different sort. John comes out with the words 'You're a fine friend', addressing someone who has evidently behaved in an unfriendly manner. What John says is glaringly false; and the person John is speaking to, recognizing that the maxim of truthfulness is flouted, can know that John means exactly the opposite of what he says. Thus John implicates that the person he is addressing is *not* a fine friend.

In reading Bach you will see that he disagrees with Grice on several points. But these are matters of relative detail. Like Grice's account of conversational implicature, Bach's account of conversational impli*c*iture is designed to show how it is that what speakers mean can be different from what they say, and thus to uphold the tenet that there is a notion of what a speaker says according to which they say no more and no less than what their words mean. Notice that in Bach's view, in order to think about what a speaker *says*, one needs to make use of the notion of *literal* truth/falsehood.

Kent Bach, 'Speaking Loosely: Sentence Non-literality'

This paper concerns a linguistic phenomenon so pervasive that it hardly ever gets mentioned, much less labelled, at least by theorists. Perhaps that's the most interesting thing about it. It's a perfectly familiar phenomenon, describable as 'speaking loosely.' But it's a particular way of speaking loosely, not to be confused with other kinds, like exaggeration and understatement. It's a special kind of non-literal use.

---

[5]   Conversational implicature, in Grice's terms, is non-conventional. Grice also gave an account of conventional implicature, which treated words like 'but', 'even', and 'too'. Such words appear to have rule-governed meanings, but appear not to make truth-conditional contributions to the sentences in which they figure. See Grice (1975) in the reading list on Context and Meaning.

Words don't have non-literal meanings (it is redundant to describe the meanings they do have as their literal meanings), but they can be used in non-literal ways. You speak nonliterally when you say one thing and mean something else instead.[1] In familiar cases, such as metaphor and metonymy, particular expressions are used nonliterally. Such uses are commonly described as 'figurative.' But there's a different phenomenon, which I call 'sentence nonliterality,' as opposed to *constituent* nonliterality. Here a whole sentence is used nonliterally, without any of its constituent expressions being so used.

Figurative speech is easily recognized as such. If I call someone an ape, a dog, or a pig, presumably I'm not describing him literally as an animal of any of those sorts. Similarly, if I comment on the behaviour of a know-it-all by saying, 'The brain is pontificating again,' presumably I am using 'the brain' to refer to a certain person. Brains, those chunks of gray matter in people's heads, don't pontificate; people do. I could add to the metaphorical mix by saying that, instead of 'pontificating', the brain is mouthing off (or spouting off) again. When I say such a thing, it is obvious to my audience that I don't mean it literally, and they can easily figure out what I do mean. It is equally obvious to us theorists. Matters are different with sentence nonliterality. That is one reason why it's not a widely recognized phenomenon, at least not by theorists. But ordinary communicators have no problem with it. You can verify its pervasiveness by looking at any newspaper or magazine article or eavesdropping on any conversation, but in the discussion to follow I will have to use isolated sentences to illustrate this phenomenon.

Sentence Non-literality

[a] → We hardly ever mean exactly what we say. It's not that we generally speak figuratively or that we're generally insincere (these are different ways of not meaning what one says). Rather, we commonly speak loosely, by omitting words that could have made what we meant more explicit, and we let our audience fill in the gaps. Language works far more efficiently when we do that. Literalism can have its virtues, like when we're drawing up a contract or programming a computer, but

---

[1] You speak indirectly when you mean one thing and mean something else as well. This can occur when you say one thing and mean not only that but something else as well. It is possible to speak both nonliterally and indirectly in the same breath (Bach and Harnish 1979, pp. 71ff.). You might use 'I'm sure the cat likes having its tail pulled' to assert nonliterally that it doesn't and indirectly to ask your listener to stop pulling its tail.

we generally opt for efficiency over explicitness. In most conversation, though, spelling things out is not only unnecessary, it just slows things down. It is often misleading too, insofar as it guards against something that doesn't need to be guarded against.

Let's start with some examples. Suppose I graciously tell my guest, 'There's beer in the fridge.' He opens the fridge and, contrary to what we both expected, finds not a single can or bottle but merely a small puddle of beer at the bottom of the fridge. I may have inadvertently misled him, but did I say something false? It seems not: there *was* some beer in the fridge.

A baseball fan is glued to the tube during the course of a historic World Series between the Red Sox and the Cubs. The teams are tied at three games apiece. His wife is losing patience with him and, not knowing that the Series is best of seven, wants to know how much more baseball she'll have to put up with. He assures her, 'They'll play only one more game.' Since they will meet again in interleague play the following season, what he said was not really true, but that's not what he meant.

An assistant professor at Harvard, worried that she won't get tenure, seeks the advice of a senior colleague. He assures her, without the slightest intention to mislead, 'You'll be out of here if you don't publish at least five more articles in the next two years.' She publishes seven more articles over the next two years, all in top journals, but is denied tenure anyway. Even so, what her senior colleague said to her was true. After all, publish or perish does not preclude publish and perish.

It's not hard to see what's going on in these examples. The speaker says something but means some qualified version of that. In each case, the speaker failed to make explicit part of what he meant. I could have said to my friend, 'There's beer *to drink* in the fridge.' The baseball fan could have said to his wife, 'The Red Sox and the Cubs will play only one more game *in the current World Series*.' And the professor could have said, 'You won't get promoted if you don't publish at least five more articles in the next two years, *but you will if you do*.' In each of the above examples, the speaker could have made fully explicit what he was trying to convey by including the italicized material (or its equivalent – the exact words don't matter) in his utterance. Usually we don't have to, of course, since ordinarily we can rely on our audience's ability to figure out the intended qualification.

Using sentences non-literally in this way is so common that we tend neither to be aware of doing it nor to think of it as not literal when others do it. But we do it all the time (as I did just then – I left out *when we speak)*. Rather than insert extra words into our utterances in order to make fully explicit what we mean, we allow our listeners to read things into what we say. Even though we may not intuitively think of this phenomenon as nonliterality, because no specific words are being used figuratively, it is a way of not being literal. For the speaker says one thing but intends to convey something distinct from that.

Using sentences as if we included words or phrases that are not there clearly is a kind of nonliterality, for what the speaker is trying to convey in these examples is not the proposition, as compositionally determined, that is expressed by the sentence. Consider the following example:

(1) Rick and Ann are engaged.

Someone who utters (1) is not *saying* that they are engaged to each other, any more than he would be saying this with 'Rick and his sister Ann are engaged.' Rather, this is implicit in what he is saying or, more precisely, in his saying of it.[2] That it is not part of what is said is clear from the fact that it passes Grice's test of cancellability: it may be taken back without contradiction. For example, there is no contradiction in saying, 'Rick and Ann are engaged, but not to each other.'

If leaving words out is a kind of non-literality and, more specifically, a kind of loose talk, how does it differ from other kinds? Sometimes we describe using vague expressions as speaking loosely, though this might better be described as speaking roughly. If you say, 'It's a long way to Tucumcari,' you're not being precise but still mean what you're saying (you're in Albuquerque and don't know just how far Tucumcari is from there). Then there are exaggeration and understatement. In both cases, you're distorting the truth for effect, either by stretching it or compressing it. You describe *Parsifal* as an 'interminable opera' or Tiger Woods as a 'good golfer.' You're using 'interminable' to mean very long and 'good' to mean great. But the kind of loose talk we're concerned with is not a matter of using vague

---

[2]   Here I am alluding to Grice's point that what a speaker implicates in saying what he says is carried not by what he says but by his saying it (1989, p. 39). His point suggests a way of drawing the semantic–pragmatic distinction (see Bach 1999 for details). Semantic information is information encoded in what is uttered – these are stable linguistic features of the sentence – together with any extralinguistic information that provides (semantic) values to context-sensitive expressions in what is uttered. Pragmatic information is (extralinguistic) information that arises from an actual act of utterance. Whereas semantic information is encoded in what is uttered, pragmatic information is generated by, or at least made relevant by, the act of uttering it. The act of producing the utterance exploits the information encoded but by its very performance creates new or otherwise invoked extralinguistic information. . . .

terms or of using particular words or phrases nonliterally, but simply a matter of leaving words out. So, for example, if you say 'I haven't eaten' you don't include *dinner today* or anything of the sort. If you say 'Everyone must wear a costume' you don't include *who comes to my upcoming party*. And if you say 'Tigers have stripes' you don't include *normal* (or *non-albino*).

These examples illustrate what I call conversational 'impliciture,' as opposed to Grice's 'implicature.' Implic-a-ture is an indirect constative speech act, whereby one says and means one thing and thereby asserts something else in addition.[3] In implic-i-ture, one says something but does not mean that; rather, what one means includes an implicit qualification on what one says, something that one could have made explicit but didn't.[4]

It might seem that the qualification implicit in an utterance involves a non-literal use of some particular constituent. Consider, for example, the case of using an obviously incomplete definite description. If a drama buff says to her husband, 'The play will start in an hour,' to refer to some particular play, say the one that they plan to attend that evening, it might seem that she is using 'the play' nonliterally, say for 'the play we plan to attend tonight.' If that is true, this is despite the fact that she is using its constituent words literally – she means *the* by 'the' and *play* by 'play.' It is true that if she had said, 'The play we plan to attend tonight will start in an hour,' she would have, by attaching a relative clause to 'the play,' made fully explicit what she meant. But this doesn't show that she meant 'the play we plan to attend tonight' by the phrase 'the play.' At most it shows that she was using 'the play' to refer to the play she and her husband planned to attend that night. The non-literality is not attributable to any particular constituent of the sentence being used.

This phenomenon I am calling sentence non-literality seems pretty straightforward, but there are objections to how I characterize it. We will take up [...] such objections, but first we should take a closer look at what is going on in examples like the ones above. We can break this question down into two parts: what is the relation between what the speaker says and what the speaker means, and how does the audience figure it out?

[3] Grice also regarded figurative speech, such as metaphor and metonymy, as implicature, even though in these cases the speaker says one thing and means something else instead. Actually, Grice held that in speaking nonliterally one 'makes as if to say' something (1989, p. 30) but does not really say it. Here he seems to have conflated saying with stating or asserting. In my opinion, he should not have classified figurative speech as implicature (Bach 1994a, pp. 143–4).

[4] In all the cases we will consider, the sentence that is uttered expresses a complete proposition...A more controversial species of impliciture involves sentences which, though syntactically complete, are semantically incomplete – they do not express a complete proposition....

The Relation between the Explicit and the Implicit

The implicitures involved in sentence non-literality goes beyond what is said, but unlike implicatures, which are additional propositions separate from what is said, implicitures involve an unexpressed qualification on what is said. They are not a case of conveying one proposition and indirectly conveying another. Grice himself occasionally alluded to what I am calling implic-i-ture, as when he remarked that it is often 'unnecessary to put in . . . qualificatory words' (1989, p. 44). Although he did describe such cases as implic-a-tures, he appeared to have something distinctive in mind: 'strengthening one's meaning by achieving a *superimposed* implicature' (p. 48; my emphasis). But what did he mean by 'strengthening'? In our examples, what is the relation between what is said and what is conveyed?[5] The relation might seem to be logical, such that what is said is entailed by what is conveyed, as in the following examples:

(2) Jack and Jill went up the hill.
(3) Jack went to the cliff and jumped.
(4) Jill got married and became pregnant.

In each case, let's assume, the speaker means something more specific than the proposition expressed by the sentence being uttered, to wit:

(2+) Jack and Jill went up the hill *together.*
(3+) Jack went to the cliff and jumped *off the cliff.*
(4+) Jill got married and *then* became pregnant.

The italicized material, not actually uttered, indicates the implicit qualification on what the speaker said. Now in what way does this implicit qualification strengthen what is said? Since in these examples its result, the impliciture, entails what is said, the strengthening might seem to be logical in character. But that can't be right, because precisely the same phenomenon occurs when the sentences in question are negated. For example, if the speaker uttered (~2) in order to convey (~2+),

(~2) Jack and Jill did not go up the hill.
(~2+) Jack and Jill did not go up the hill *together.*

---

[5] What is conveyed is what the speaker means, i.e. attempts to communicate, in saying what he says. I use 'what is conveyed' rather than 'what is meant' because the latter can include what the sentence means as well as what the speaker means in uttering it.

the relation between what was said and what was conveyed would be the same, even though in this case the entailment is in the other direction.

[d]→ The relation between (2) and (2+), as well as that between their negations, involves what may be called *conceptual* strengthening, in that what is implicit is additional conceptual material, whether or not it logically strengthens the proposition in question that is expressed by the sentence actually uttered. That it is not logical strengthening is clear from the fact that an implicit qualification can be logically redundant. Take the following example:

(5) Jay has three cars.

Since (5) is true just in case Jay has at least three cars, adding 'at least' would not make any logical difference. But it could make a pragmatic difference. For normally an utterance of (5) conveys that Jay has exactly three cars, even though the sentence does not literally mean that (it is true even if Jay has more than three cars). In some circumstances, though, you could use (5) to mean merely that Jay has at least three cars, say if you were explaining why Jay is subject to a special parking fee (for owners of three or more cars). So it would make a pragmatic difference to include the words 'at least' in your utterance. Including them leaves open the possibility that Jay has more than three cars. Though logically redundant, it is not pragmatically redundant.

The pragmatic phenomenon just noted illustrates an important point about the difference between implicit and explicit qualifications. Although expressly making the qualification, in this case with *at least,* would enable the speaker to make fully explicit what he was trying to convey, expressly making it could result in conveying something else as well. In the above case, expressly including the words *at least* forestalls the normal way of taking the utterance without them. You then convey that Jay could just as well have more than three cars as exactly three. And, in circumstances where an utterance of (5) would normally, though not literally, convey that Jay has exactly three cars, say in answer to the question 'How many cars does John have?', including *exactly* expressly would foreclose the possibility

[e]→ that he has more than three.

A more far-reaching point is that some sentences, given what they mean, cannot readily be used literally. This should not seem problematic, for there are many propositions that people are unlikely ever to intend to convey. That shouldn't suggest that there aren't sentences that literally express those propositions. To see how some sentences are hard to use in a strictly literal way, consider and compare the following pair:

(6) Dennis got herpes and had sex.
(6′) Dennis had sex and got herpes.

These two sentences are logically equivalent, but it is hard to use them in the same way. An utterance of (6) is likely to be taken to convey that during a certain period Dennis got herpes and that *during that period* had sex. Reverse the order and matters are different: an utterance of (6′) is likely to be taken to convey that Dennis had sex (on a certain occasion) *and then, as a result of that*, got herpes. It is hard for an utterance of either sentence to convey the bare conjunction that they both literally express. Even if you uttered (6′), say, and followed it with, 'not that his getting herpes had anything had to do with his having sex,' thereby cancelling the impliciture that he got herpes as the result of having sex, you would be taken to be precluding the possibility that he did. The bare conjunction does not preclude this.

Recognizing Implicitures

In examples such as we have considered, how is what is meant recognized, and reasonably expected to be recognized? Implicitures are like implicatures, insofar as they too exploit what Grice called 'maxims' of conversation. He proposed a general Cooperative Principle and specific maxims – of 'quality, quantity, relation [relevance], and manner' (1989, pp. 26ff.) – to account for the rationale and success of conversational implicatures. The speaker intends his audience to figure out what he is conveying, and the audience figures that out, by way of recognizing what would be violation of a maxim if the utterance were taken at face value. On the supposition that the speaker is being cooperative, in particular that he is trying to convey something, which requires that his communicative intention be evident from what he is saying under the circumstances, the audience figures out what he is trying to convey.

Grice seems to be basically right about this, but it is arguable that being cooperative (at least in making constative utterances) consists simply in being truthful and relevant, hence that there is no need for four separate maxims. For example, observing the maxim of quantity is just being relevantly informative. Also, the maxims might better be thought of as presumptions, for it is on the presumption that the speaker is being truthful and relevant (and intends to be taken to be) that the hearer figures out what the speaker means in saying what he says.[6]

At any rate, it might seem that implicitures are like Gricean quality implicatures, whereby the audience recognizes what the speaker is trying to convey by drawing an inference from the obvious falsity of what the speaker is saying.[7] This is initially plausible with these examples,

(7) I haven't taken a bath.
(8) I have nothing to do.

The sentences are likely to be literally false (evaluated relative to the identity of the speaker and the time of their utterance), and are likely to be used in a more restrictive way. You'd probably use (7) to mean you hadn't taken a bath that day, and (8) to convey to your boss that you had no assigned work to do. However, it's not the obvious falsity of the sentences that matters, for in the same circumstances, utterances of the positive sentences,

(7') I have taken a bath.
(8') I have something to do.

would likely be made and be taken with the same implicit qualifications. But these sentences are very likely to be literally true. So the implicitures in question should not be understood on the model of quality implicatures.

Besides, the sentences in most of our earlier examples were obviously true, not obviously false. In each case, what triggers the hearer's search for something other than what is said is not its obvious falsity but its lack of relevant specificity. As with any non-literal utterance, with sentence non-literality the audience is to recognize that the speaker couldn't plausibly be taken to mean exactly what he said. Assuming that the speaker is trying to communicate something and is therefore trying to make what he means evident, the audience has to

---

[6] See Bach and Harnish (1979, pp. 62–5). We propose replacing Grice's Cooperative Principle with a 'Communicative Presumption,' to the effect that whenever someone says something to someone, he intends to be communicating something (p. 12). Grice's Principle is too strong, since communicators need be cooperative only to the extent that they make, and may be presumed to be making, their communicative intentions evident. Their intentions in other respects may be obscure, deceptive, or downright malicious.

[7] The obvious falsity of a metaphor is sometimes thought to be what triggers the hearer's inference to what the speaker means. But that can't be right, as is clear from 'No man is an island,' which is obviously true.

find some salient connection between what is said and what is meant. Generally speaking, that involves finding some way of taking the utterance that is pertinent to the current purposes of the conversation. Of course, this is not to say precisely how, in any given case, the hearer figures out just what that is. That is a difficult and unanswered question for the psychology of communication.

Possible Objections

Let's call the view that utterances like the ones considered above are not literal the sentence non-literality account (SLA). SLA entails that what is said in such an utterance does not include what I am calling the implicit qualification. This is because the implicit qualification does not correspond to any constituent of the sentence. Here I'm assuming that what is said must satisfy what I'll call the 'Syntactic Correlation Constraint,' as expressed by Grice's stipulation that what is said must correspond to 'the elements of [the sentence], their order, and their syntactic character' (1989, p. 87). What is said is determined compositionally by the semantic contents of the constituents ('elements') of the sentence as a function of their syntactic relationship.[8] Where there is lexical ambiguity, this compositional determination is relative to a given set of readings of the ambiguous terms, and because of the presence of tense and sometimes indexicals, what is said in the utterance of a given sentence is not independent of the context in which it is used. In short, what is said is the semantic content of the sentence relative to that context.[9] But it is independent of the speaker's communicative intention. In effect, the Syntactic Correlation Constraint says that every constituent of a proposition expressed by a sentence corresponds to a constituent of the sentence. The Syntactic Correlation Constraint entails that if any element of what the speaker intends to convey does not correspond to any element of the sentence he is uttering, it is not part of what he is *saying*. Of course it may correspond to what he is asserting, but I am not using 'say' to mean *assert*. In the jargon of speech act theory, saying is locutionary, not illocutionary. All of our examples and, it seems, much of everyday speech, involves conveying more than what one says, by using sentences nonliterally.

[8]   I defend this strict conception of what is said in Bach (2001).
[9]   Notice that I do not speak of the semantic contents of *utterances*. If 'utterance' means what is uttered, then an utterance is just a sentence. And if 'utterance' means an act of uttering, then the content of an utterance is really the content of the speaker's communicative intention, which can depart in various ways from semantic content.

SLA assumes that the implicit qualification on an utterance does not correspond to any constituent of the sentence being uttered. Also, it seems to presuppose that every such utterance has a determinate qualification, which the hearer must identify if he is to figure out what the speaker is trying to convey. Moreover, SLA may seem to require that the hearer can figure out what the speaker means only by consciously reasoning that the speaker could not mean merely what he is saying. Finally, it may seem that the Syntactic Correlation Constraint, which the SLA presupposes, does violence to our intuitions about what is said. These points suggest certain possible objections:

1. What is allegedly implicit is really the value of a covert variable.*
2. What is implicit is not always determinate.
3. Hearers don't make inferences of the sort SLA requires.
4. SLA is counterintuitive – the utterances under discussion seem perfectly literal.

[...]

Objection 2: What is implicit is not determinate

It might be objected that by using specific words or phrases to represent the implicit qualifications in our examples, SLA implausibly requires that the speaker must have meant something determinate, and that in order to understand him his audience had to figure out just what this was.

If the objection is that the audience must figure out the exact words the speaker had in mind but didn't use, surely that would be too strong a requirement. But SLA doesn't require that. Indeed, I was careful to describe the implicit qualification involved in sentence non-literality as what the speaker could have made explicit if he had included certain words *or their equivalents*. The exact words don't matter. But what counts as equivalent here?

So perhaps the objection is that it is not determinate what the implicit qualification is, not how it is expressed. I'll grant the point

---

* **Editors' note:** We have cut the passage in which Bach formulates and replies to this objection. The claim made by Objection 1 is that cases which Bach treats as cases of loose talk are cases in which there is more which determines what is said by the speaker than meets the eye (or ear): a theorist will postulate covert syntactic elements in the speaker's sentence, so that the literal content of the sentence is more specific than shows up on the surface. What Bach characterizes as a kind of non-literal use is better understood on the model of using indexicals, according to this Objection. We explain the idea of indexicality in the Conclusion to this chapter.

but deny it's an objection. Consider (7) again. In saying 'I haven't taken a bath,' the speaker might mean that he hasn't taken a bath that day or that he hasn't taken one lately or that he hasn't taken one since he last worked out or whatever, but for normal purposes of communication it doesn't matter precisely what he means, or whether the hearer identifies precisely that. Indeed, he might not mean any one thing precisely, and be quite prepared to concede that he didn't mean some one of those things as opposed to any of the others.

Objection 3: Hearers don't make inferences of the sort SLA requires

The objection here is that when people hear utterances of sentences like the ones we've discussed, they don't first compute the bare, unqualified proposition expressed by the sentence and then, after deciding that the speaker couldn't plausibly be taken to mean that, infer that he means some implicitly qualified version of that.

Let's grant the psychological claim underlying the objection. The question is whether SLA requires what the objection says it requires. In fact, SLA does not require that the hearers must compute the bare propositions. It concerns the semantics of sentences, not the psychology of understanding utterances of them. Moreover, all the objection suggests is that hearers can infer what a speaker is communicating without first identifying what the speaker is saying. But SLA is not committed to an account of the temporal order or other details of the process of understanding. For all it says, hearers can identify implicit qualifications on the fly, without having first to figure out the semantic content of the entire sentence.[10]

Besides, even if a hearer doesn't explicitly represent the proposition literally expressed by a sentence, hence does not explicitly reject it as the one that is meant, still he makes the *implicit* assumption that it is not what is meant. Implicit assumptions are an essential ingredient in default reasoning in general (Bach 1984) and in the process of understanding utterances in particular. Communicative reasoning, like default reasoning in general, is a case of jumping to conclusions without consciously taking into account all alternatives or all relevant considerations. Even so, to be warranted such reasoning must be sensitive to

[10] The sentence has its semantic content independently of whether the hearer has to ascertain that content before figuring out what the speaker means. Its semantic content, the proposition it literally expresses, is the information available to the hearer simply in virtue of hearing the sentence and quite apart from any question of what the speaker intends to be communicating. How the hearer exploits that information is another matter. For further discussion of this and related issues see Bach and Harnish 1979, especially pp. 91–3.

□⟼ such considerations. This means that such considerations can play a dispositional role even when they do not play an explicit role. They lurk in the background, so to speak, waiting to be taken into account when worth considering.

Objection 4: SLA is counterintuitive

The objection here is that the utterances under discussion seem perfectly literal. Accordingly, SLA disregards ordinary intuitions about the truth or falsity, hence about the content, of what is said. For example, it seems that sentence (7), 'I haven't taken a bath,' as uttered on a certain day, is true if the speaker hasn't taken a bath that day, although on SLA it is false if he has ever taken a bath. This is counter-

m⟼ intuitive.[11] In this and the other cases, I claim, what the speaker means is distinct from he says, since what he means includes an implicit qualification on what he says. Of course what the speaker *means* is true, but that includes the implicit qualification provided by *today*, which is not present in the sentence.[12] However, people's intuitions tend not to be sensitive to the difference, at least not until they're sensitized. That's because they tend to ignore the Syntactic Correlation Constraint on what is said.

It is easy to sensitize people's intuitions to this constraint. One way

n⟼ is to get them to appreciate Grice's cancellability test for what is not said. Just present them with sentences like (2)–(4), followed by cancellations of the implicit qualification, as in (2xx)–(4xx),

(2xx) Jack and Jill went up the hill but not together.
(3xx) Jack went to the cliff and jumped but not off the cliff.
(4xx) Jill got married and became pregnant but not in that order.

---

[11] Gibbs and Moise (1997) devised some experiments that purport to show that people's intuitions about what is said tend to include implicit qualifications. I could discuss Gibbs and Moise's experiments in detail, but suffice it to say that their research tested for the wrong thing. [... They] assumed that what people *say* about what is said is strongly indicative of what *is* said. They really tested for how people apply the word 'say' and the phrase 'what is said.' Little was established about what is said, much less about the cognitive processes whereby people understand utterances. Moreover, Nicolle and Clark (1999) have experimentally challenged Gibbs and Moise's findings [...].

[12] Recanati (1989) even formulates a principle, the Availability Principle, which prescribes that intuitions about what is said be 'preserved' in our theorizing. But he needs to explain why the intuitions he takes to concern what is said really do concern that, as well as why we should be confident in their accuracy.

and see if they sense a contradiction or just a clarification. Or ask them to compare what is said with *explicitly* qualified versions of (2), (3), or (4) to what is said with sentences (2), (3), and (4) themselves:

(2eq) Jack and Jill went up the hill together.
(2)   Jack and Jill went up the hill.
(3eq) Jack went to the cliff and jumped off the cliff.
(3)   Jack and Jill are engaged.
(4eq) Jill got married and then became pregnant.
(4)   Jill got married and became pregnant.

They are likely to say that the explicitly qualified utterances say something not said with the original ones.

These considerations aside, why should we be confident in the accuracy of people's untutored intuitions about what is or is not literally expressed by a sentence? To be sure, we have a perfectly good handle on what our words mean, on how they are put together into sentences, hence on what our sentences mean. Who could deny that competent speakers have such knowledge? But this is not theoretical knowledge. Even so, Grice regarded it 'as a sort of paradox [that] if we, as speakers, have the requisite knowledge of the conventional meaning of sentences we employ to implicate, when uttering them, something the implication of which depends on the conventional meaning in question, how can we, as theorists, have difficulty with respect to just those cases in deciding where conventional meaning ends and implicature begins?' (1989, p. 49). Grice's paradox may seem especially troubling if it is supposed, as it often is, that accounting for our ordinary judgments, our 'intuitions,' about the truth-conditions of sentences is the central aim of semantics.

This worry is unfounded. It is the central aim of semantics to account for semantic facts, not intuitions. People's spontaneous judgments or 'intuitions' provide data for semantics, but it is an open question to what extent they reveal semantic facts and should therefore be explained rather than explained away. Since they are often responsive to non-semantic information, to what is implicit in what is said, they should not be given too much weight.

Besides, these intuitions don't seem to play a role in ordinary communication. In the course of speaking and listening to one another, we generally don't consciously reflect on the semantic content of the sentences we hear or on what is said in their utterance. We are focused on what we are communicating and on what is being communicated to us, not on what is being said. Moreover, we don't have to be able to make accurate judgments about what information is semantic and what is not in order to be sensitive to semantic information. To take intuitions overly seriously in our theorizing about what is said would be like relying on the intuitions of unsophisticated moviegoers about the effects of editing on a film. Although people's cinematic experience is dramatically affected by cuts and camera angles, there is no reason to suppose that their intuitions are reliable about these effects or about how they are produced. Intuitions about what is said may be similarly insensitive to the difference between the contribution that is made by the semantic content of a sentence and that made by extra-linguistic factors to what an utterance communicates. So, I conclude, what worried Grice was not a real paradox.

[...]

Summing Up

I have tried to make a case for the existence of the phenomenon of sentence nonliterality. I have sketched how it works but really did nothing more than invoke Grice's well-known theory of conversation. Neither it nor I can explain in detail how people manage to convey more than what their sentences mean and how their listeners manage to understand them. That, I conceded, is a matter for the psychology of communication. Short of that, the most interesting thing about the phenomenon of sentence non-literality is, as I suggested at the outset, that it is so pervasive that it gets no theoretical attention. Here are a few more examples (with likely implicit qualifications in brackets) to illustrate how prosaic it is:

(12) Helen poured some wine [intentionally].
(13) Helen spilled some wine [unintentionally].
(14) Roy has always been an honest judge [since he's been a judge].
(15) The stroke victim is not going to die [from that stroke].
(16) Dr. Atkins is not [what I would describe as] a physician but a quack.

As I also suggested, you can verify the pervasiveness of sentence non-literality by looking at any newspaper or magazine article or eavesdropping on any conversation. You may find that to be much more interesting than theorizing about it.

References

Bach, Kent (1984). 'Default Reasoning: Jumping to Conclusions and Knowing When to Think Twice,' *Pacific Philosophical Quarterly* 65: 37–58.

Bach, Kent (1994a). 'Conversational Impliciture,' *Mind & Language* 9: 124–62.

Bach, Kent (1994b). *Thought and Reference*, paperback ed., revised with postscript. Oxford: Oxford University Press.

Bach, Kent (1995). 'Standardization vs. Conventionalization,' *Linguistics and Philosophy* 18: 677–86.

Bach, Kent (1999). 'The Semantics–Pragmatics Distinction: What It is and Why It Matters.' In Ken Turner (ed.), *The Semantics–Pragmatics Interface from Different Points of View*. Oxford: Elsevier, pp. 65–84.

Bach, Kent (2001). 'You Don't Say?,' *Synthese* 127: 11–31.

Bach, Kent and Robert M. Harnish (1979). *Linguistic Communication and Speech Acts*. Cambridge, MA: MIT Press.

Gibbs, Raymond and Jessica Moise (1997). 'Pragmatics in Understanding What is Said,' *Cognition* 62: 51–74.

Grice. Paul (1989). *Studies in the Way of Words*. Cambridge, MA: Harvard University Press.

Nicolle, Steve and Billy Clark (1999). 'Experimental Pragmatics and What is Said: A Response to Gibbs and Moise,' *Cognition* 69: 337–54.

Recanati, François (1989). 'The Pragmatics of What is Said,' *Mind & Language* 4: 295–329.

Commentary on Bach

In this Commentary, we shall highlight some of Bach's main points, and then look critically at some of the responses Bach makes to the objections to his account that he envisages.

State in your own words what Bach means by 'sentence nonliterality'. Read from [a]↦ to [b]↦.

Whenever a speaker or writer leaves out words that would come into an explicit statement of what they mean, there is a case of sentence non-literality.

What is Grice's Cancellability Test for implicatures? See [c]↦ and [n]↦.

If we say something, we are, as it were, committed to it: we can't in the same breath say the opposite – not without contradicting ourselves. However, if our utterance makes a conversational implicature, then we can take this back without contradicting ourselves. Taking it back is cancelling it. Grice proposed cancellability as a test for what is implicated, i.e. for implicatures. It is also a test for impli*ci*tures. Here it serves to distinguish between what the speaker says and what is implicit in, and conveyed by, her saying of it.

> What is the distinction between propositional strengthening and conceptual strengthening? Read from $\boxed{d}\mapsto$ to $\boxed{e}\mapsto$.

A sentence is conceptually strengthened when words are added to it. A sentence is logically strengthened when it is changed so that the proposition it expresses carries entailments not carried by the original. Bach wants us to notice that cases of sentence non-literality are sometimes cases where the speaker means something logically stronger, sometimes cases where they mean something logically weaker, than what they say.

> How do speakers manage to mean something they don't say? Read from $\boxed{f}\mapsto$ to $\boxed{g}\mapsto$.

The kind of mechanism at work is just like that postulated by Grice in his theory of conversational implicature. A hearer, guided by the presumption that the speaker is being co-operative, and recognizing that the speaker could not plausibly be taken to mean exactly what they said, is in a position to know what it must be that the speaker actually means in saying what they do.

> State Bach's Syntactic Correlation Constraint in your own words. (See $\boxed{g}\mapsto$.)

According to the Constraint, the meaning of a sentence – and thus what the speaker says in using a sentence – is compositionally determined by the meanings of the constituents in their context, and determined in a way that is predictable from how those constituents fit together syntactically.

> Is it a problem for Bach that a speaker may not mean anything determinate? Read from $\boxed{i}\mapsto$ to $\boxed{j}\mapsto$.

Bach wants to allow that indeed there need not be any precise thing that the speaker meant: several precise things, each as good as any other, might be used in stating explicitly what the speaker meant. Suppose we accept this. Then perhaps the objection will be that if we are allowed to say that there is nothing precise that the speaker meant, why should we not say that there is nothing precise that the speaker *said*? (If we say this, then we probably offend against the Syntactic Correlation Constraint as Bach formulates this. But someone who objects to Bach's account may want to know why that Constraint should be held sacred. They may doubt the presumed connection between what a speaker *says* and what the speaker's sentence means.)

Is it an objection that hearers don't seem to make the sorts of inferences that they are postulated as making on Bach's account? Read from $\boxed{k} \mapsto$ to $\boxed{l} \mapsto$.

Ordinary speakers don't ordinarily think of themselves as using what a speaker said as a starting point for figuring out what they meant. Bach makes two points with a view to persuading us that there can be figuring out on the part of hearers of the sort his account requires. First, his account leaves it open what exactly goes on psychologically in the process of understanding. Secondly, although a hearer must work with an assumption about what the speaker said, this can be an implicit assumption that need not play an active role in arriving at knowledge of what the speaker meant. Do you find this plausible? Bach's view may now seem to be that an account of how language works is one thing, and an account of how linguistic communication works is another thing. Do you think that this is his view? Does such a view seem acceptable?

Does Bach satisfactorily deal with the objection that his account is counter-intuitive? Read from $\boxed{m} \mapsto$ to $\boxed{o} \mapsto$.

You may have been somewhat surprised initially by Bach's claim that 'we hardly ever mean exactly what we say'. If you were surprised, then that is because you seldom, if ever, notice any discrepancy between what you say and what you mean in the kinds of case that concern Bach. Bach acknowledges this. But he thinks that the discrepancies are ones to which we can become sensitive by thinking about examples, and learning to apply the Cancellability Test. And he sees no reason why speakers should have reliable intuitions about how they do what they do with language. Still, what Bach's opponents will want to know is why the notion of what is said is so important, if speakers are not aware of what they say, and are able to communicate as they do without being sensitive to what they say. Towards the end of the Commentary on Davies, we saw how someone might arrive at the view (in connection with metaphorical language) that there is nothing which counts as what the speaker said excepting for something partly determined by the speaker's particular intentions in the context in which she spoke. Someone who holds that view evidently has no use for Bach's notion of what is said. They may hope to describe cases that Bach subsumes under 'sentence non-literality' by making use only of an intuitive notion of what is said.

Conclusion

Thinking about metaphor and about the pervasiveness of loose talk makes us aware of how very often a speaker means and conveys something that wouldn't be predictable given just the sentence she uttered and a semantic theory which treated her sentence in abstraction. What a speaker means depends on much more than the meaning of her sentence itself. It depends, we might find ourselves saying, upon the *context* in which her sentence is used. Well, this has to be right, if we simply mean by 'context' absolutely everything that might be relevant to deciding what a speaker meant beyond what a semantic theory tells us about her sentence. But the notion of context has a theoretical use in the study of language. And we should look at this now. Understanding this notion of context is necessary for becoming clearer about the different views there are about what is literally said.

If we did use 'context' simply as a label for everything that is relevant to what a speaker means beyond what a semantic theory tells us, then semantic theory itself would have no use for the notion of context. But everyone agrees that context does have a use there. Consider the words 'I am tired'. You don't know what proposition is expressed by those words until you know who says them. If Guy says 'I am tired', then the truth of what he says depends upon whether Guy is tired. A piece of contextual information – in this example, information about who the speaker is – is needed to determine the truth-conditional content of an utterance of the sentence. Where contextual information plays this role, we have so-called indexicality.[1] Not only the speaker, but also the time (consider for example 'now' and tensed-sentences spoken at different times), and the location (consider for example 'here' uttered in different places) are elements of the context in which the sentence is uttered. Contextual elements have a place in semantic theory in these cases. It seems right that they should: intuitively, it is part of the conventional meaning of words like 'I' and 'now' and 'here' that their reference is fixed in context. (Notice that Davidson incorporated context by treating sentences *as spoken* by a particular person at a particular time. For instance, from Chapter 3: ' "Es regnet" is true-in-German when spoken by x at time t if and only if it is raining near x a t.')

Even if we stick with this narrow, semantic notion of context, it is controversial exactly how much it can be used to explain. Some semantic theorists believe that it covers much more than Bach says it does. Among these are theorists who hold that there are covert syntactic elements in sentences – that some expressions are 'unarticulated but understood'.[2] They think these

---

[1]   The readings in the list on Indexicals are concerned with expressions whose reference is fixed in context.

[2]   They are the theorists who make the objection to Bach mentioned in our Editors' Note to his text at p.296.

unarticulated expressions may have their reference fixed by elements of context that belong in semantic theory. But even though they make much more use of the semantic theorists' notion of context than Bach does, they agree with him that semantics is the determinant of what we literally say. And they agree with him that insofar as semantics is often not a determinant of what we mean, that is because we have communicative skills that enable us to work out what we mean on the basis of what our sentences literally say. Like Bach, they think that the theorist's first task is to account for what sentences literally say.

Some people doubt that our communicative skills can be cleanly separated from our ability to know what our sentences literally say. These are the people who have no use for Bach's notion of *what is said*. Even when allowance has been made for context in the narrow semantic sense, they doubt whether there is any such thing as the proposition expressed by a sentence that should be characterized independently of what speakers actually do when they use sentences. They may say that illocutionary acts, not sentences, are the primary bearers of content. Any actual speech act takes place in a set of circumstances. And what determines the content of what the speaker has done can be any of a broad range of facts about the circumstances in which they use their words, including their intentions at the time. If we call these circumstances 'the context', then we are now giving 'context' a very much broader sense than the narrow semantic one. And if we think of context in this broad sense as a determinant of meaning, then we are on the side of those who say that language cannot be isolated as a semantic system divorced from the conditions in which speech takes place.

Those who think that we cannot attribute a content to what a speaker does unless we treat the speaker's words in context in the broad sense take issue with the dominant position among philosophers of language today, of which Bach is one representative. According to the dominant position, natural language sentences (taken in their context, in the narrow semantic sense) must be attributed a truth-conditional content independently of what the speaker actually means, and dependent only on the words she uses and their mode of composition. An enormous range of considerations can be brought to bear in thinking about whether the dominant position is sustainable. However, thinking about the phenomena we have looked at in Chapter 2 and in this one should give you a sense of what the issue is about.[3]

We started this book by saying how easy it is to speak and understand. What is difficult is to know what counts as a correct theoretical account of speech and understanding. Even at the end of the book, we don't expect that you'll find it easy to know this. But we hope that you'll have discovered some ways of thinking about it.

---

[3] Many of the readings in the list on Context and Meaning are concerned with this issue.

Further Reading

The first list below contains some useful multi-authored collections of papers. The abbreviations shown in parentheses there are used in subsequent lists.

In each of the subsequent lists, readings that we would recommend to someone starting out on the topic are in **bold type**. The first three lists are on Chomsky's, Davidson's, and Dummett's philosophies of language. The remaining ones are all referred to in footnotes in the commentary: they are arranged in six clusters, corresponding to the chapters in which reference to them was first made.

1 Definite Descriptions
  Indexicals
  Indirect Speech and Propositional Attitude Ascriptions
  Language and Convention
  Proper Names
2 Intention-based Semantics
  Non-indicatives
  Performatives and Speech Acts
3 Radical Interpretation and the Principle of Charity
  Semantic Theories for Natural Language
  Tacit Knowledge and Compositionality
  Tarski's Truth-theoretic Machinery
  Truth-theories and Understanding
4 Computational Psychology
  Innate Knowledge and 'Poverty of Stimulus'
  Linguistic Competence and Knowledge
  Perceptual Views of Linguistic Competence

Syntactic Theory
Tacit Knowledge: Its Nature
5 Compositionality and Meaning
6 Context and Meaning
Metaphor

Anthologies

Davis, S., ed. (1991). *Pragmatics: A Reader* (Oxford: Oxford University Press). [DAVIS]

Evans, G. and McDowell, J., eds (1975). *Truth and Meaning: Essays in Semantics* (Oxford: Clarendon Press). [EVANS and McDOWELL]

Geirsson, H. and Losonsky, M., eds (1996). *Readings in Language and Mind* (Oxford: Blackwell). [GEIRSSON AND LOSONSKY]

Hale, B. and Wright, C., eds (1998). *A Companion to the Philosophy of Language* (Oxford: Blackwell). [HALE AND WRIGHT]

Harnish, R. M., ed. (1994). *Basic Topics in the Philosophy of Language* (London: Harvester Wheatsheaf). [HARNISH]

Katz, J. J., ed. (1985). *The Philosophy of Linguistics* (Oxford: Oxford University Press). [KATZ]

Ludlow, P., ed. (1997). *Readings in the Philosophy of Language* (Cambridge, MA: MIT Press). [LUDLOW]

Martinich, A. P., ed. (1996). *The Philosophy of Language*, 3rd edn (Oxford: Oxford University Press). [MARTINICH]

Moore, A. W., ed. (1993). *Meaning and Reference* (Oxford: Oxford University Press). [MOORE]

Nye, A., ed. (1998). *Philosophy of Language: The Big Questions* (Oxford: Blackwell). [NYE]

Platts, M., ed. (1980). *Reference, Truth and Reality: Essays on the Philosophy of Language* (London: Routledge & Kegan Paul). [PLATTS]

Richard, M., ed. (2003). *Meaning* (Oxford: Blackwell). [RICHARD]

Chomsky, Davidson, Dummett: Philosophies of Language

Chomsky's Philosophy of Language

Antony, L. M. and Hornstein, N., eds (2003). *Chomsky and His Critics* (Oxford: Blackwell).

Chomsky, N. (1975). *Reflections on Language* (New York: Pantheon).

Chomsky, N. (1980). *Rules and Representations* (Oxford: Blackwell).

Chomsky, N. (1986). *Knowledge of Language: Its Nature, Origins, and Use* (New York: Praeger). (The Chomsky text herein is taken from Ch. 1 of this book.)

Chomsky, N. (2000). *New Horizons in the Study of Language and Mind* (Cambridge: Cambridge University Press).

Collins, J. (2003). 'Language: a Dialogue', *Richmond Journal of Philosophy* 1/ 5: 18–24.

D'Agostino, F. (1986). *Chomsky's System of Ideas* (Oxford: Clarendon Press).

George, A., ed. (1989). *Reflections on Chomsky* (Oxford: Blackwell).

Kasher, A., ed. (1991). *The Chomskyan Turn* (Oxford: Blackwell).

McGilvray, J. (1999). *Chomsky: Language, Mind, and Politics* (Cambridge: Polity Press).

Smith, N. (2004). *Chomsky: Ideas and Ideals* **(Cambridge: Cambridge University Press, 2nd edition).**

Davidson's Philosophy of Language

Davidson, D. (1967). 'Truth and Meaning', *Synthèse* 17: 304–23. Reprinted in his *Inquiries into Truth and Interpretation*. Also in HARNISH, GEIRSSON AND LOSONSKY, MARTINICH, and MOORE.

Davidson, D. (1984). *Inquiries into Truth and Interpretation* (Oxford: Clarendon Press). (The Davidson text herein can be found in this book.)

Davidson, D. (1990). 'The Structure and Content of Truth', *Journal of Philosophy* 87: 279–328.

Davies, M. (1981). *Meaning, Quantification, Necessity: Themes in Philosophical Logic* (London: Routledge & Kegan Paul).

Evans, G. and McDowell, J. (1976). 'Introduction', in EVANS AND MCDOWELL.

Evine, S. (1991). *Donald Davidson* **(Cambridge: Polity Press).**

Hahn, L. E., ed. (1999). *The Philosophy of Donald Davidson* (Chicago and LaSalle, IL: Open Court).

Joseph, M. (2004). *Donald Davidson* (Chesham: Acumen).

Lepore, E., ed. (1989). *Truth and Interpretation: Perspectives on the Philosophy of Donald Davidson* (Oxford: Blackwell).

Ludwig, K., ed. (2003). *Donald Davidson* (Cambridge: Cambridge University Press).

Platts, M. (1997). *Ways of Meaning: An Introduction to a Philosophy of Language,* **2nd edition (Cambridge, MA: MIT Press).**

Ramberg, B. (1989). *Donald Davidson's Philosophy of Language: An Introduction* (Oxford: Blackwell).

Wiggins, D. (1998). 'Meaning and Truth Conditions: from Frege's Grand Design to Davidson's', in HALE AND WRIGHT.

Dummett's Philosophy of Language

Dummett, M. A. E. (1973). *Frege: Philosophy of Language* (London: Duckworth).

Dummett, M. A. E. (1993). First ten essays in *Seas of Language* (Oxford: Clarendon Press). (The Dummett text herein can be found in this book.)

Heck, R., ed. (1997). *Language, Thought, and Logic: Essays in Honour of Michael Dummett* (Oxford: Oxford University Press).

McGuinness, B. and Oliveri, G., eds (1994). *The Philosophy of Michael Dummett* (Dordrecht: Martinus Nijhoff).

Taylor, B., ed. (1987). *Michael Dummett: Contributions to Philosophy* (Dordrecht: Martinus Nijhoff).

Weiss, B. (2002). *Michael Dummett* **(Chesham: Acumen).**

Chapter 1

Definite Descriptions

Bezuidenhout, A. (1997). 'Pragmatics, Semantic Underdetermination and the Referential/Attributive Distinction', *Mind* 106: 375–409.

Davis, M. (1981). Ch. VII of *Meaning, Quantification, Necessity: Themes in Philosophical Logic* (London: Routledge & Kegan Paul).

Donnellan, K. (1966). 'Reference and Definite Descriptions', *Philosophical Review* 77: 203–15. Reprinted in DAVIS, LUDLOW, and MARTINICH.

Kripke, S. (1977). 'Speaker's Reference and Semantic Reference', in *Studies in the Philosophy of Language* (1977), ed. P. French, T. Uehling, and H. Wettstein (Midwest Studies in Philosophy). Reprinted in DAVIS, HARNISH, LUDLOW, and MARTINICH.

Larson, R. and Segal, G. (1995). Ch. 9 of *Knowledge of Meaning: An Introduction to Semantic Theory* **(Cambridge, MA: MIT Press).**

Neale, S. (1990). *Descriptions* **(Cambridge, MA: MIT Press).**

Reimer, M. and Bezuidenhout, A., eds (2004) *Descriptions and Beyond* (Oxford: Clarendon Press).

Russell, B. (1905). 'On Denoting', *Mind* 14: 479–93. Reprinted in his *Logic and Knowledge: Essays 1901–1950*, ed. R. C. Marsh (London: Allen & Unwin, 1956). Also in HARNISH and NYE.

Sainsbury, R. M. (1992). pp. 77–86, 'Philosophical Logic §1', in *Philosophy: A Guide Through the Subject,* **ed. A. C. Grayling (Oxford: Oxford University Press).**

Strawson, P. F. (1950). 'On Referring', *Mind* 59: 269–86. Reprinted in his *Logico-Linguistic Papers* (Aldershot: Ashgate, 1971/2004). Also in LUDLOW and MOORE.

Indexicals

Evans, G. (1985). 'Understanding Demonstratives', in his *Collected Papers* (Oxford: Clarendon Press). Reprinted in Ludlow, and in Yourgrau (ed.), cited below.

Kaplan, D. (1989). 'Demonstratives', in *Themes from Kaplan*, ed. J. Almog, J. Perry, and H. Wettstein (Oxford: Oxford University Press), and in HARNISH.

Larson, R. and Segal, G. (1995). Ch. 6 of *Knowledge of Meaning: An Introduction to Semantic Theory* **(Cambridge, MA: MIT Press).**

Perry, J. (1998). 'Indexicals and Demonstratives', in HALE AND WRIGHT.

Taylor, B. (1980). 'Truth Theory for Indexical Languages', in PLATTS.

Yourgrau, P., ed. (1990). *Demonstratives* (Oxford: Oxford University Press).

Indirect Speech and Propositional Attitude Ascriptions

Burge, T. (1986). 'On Davidson's "Saying That" ', in *Truth and Interpretation: Perspectives on the Philosophy of Donald Davidson*, ed. E. Lepore (Oxford: Blackwell).

Crimmins, M. (1992). Chs 1, 5, and 6 of *Talk about Belief* (Cambridge, MA: MIT Press).

Davidson, D. (1968). 'On Saying That', *Synthèse* 19: 130–46. Reprinted in his *Inquiries into Truth and Interpretation* (Oxford: Clarendon Press, 1984). Also in LUDLOW and MARTINICH.

Dummett, M. (1973). *Frege: Philosophy of Language* (London: Duckworth, reprinted 1981), Ch. 9, 'Indirect Reference'.

Forbes, G. (1990). 'The Indispensability of *Sinn*', *Philosophical Review* 99: 535–63.

Higginbotham, J. (1986). 'Linguistic Theory and Davidson's Programme in Semantics', in *Truth and Interpretation: Perspectives on the Philosophy of Donald Davidson*, ed. E. Lepore (Oxford: Blackwell).

Kripke, S. (1979). 'A Puzzle about Belief', in *Meaning and Use*, ed. A. Margalit (Dordrecht: D. Reidel). Reprinted in Salmon and Soames, cited below. Also in LUDLOW.

Quine, W. V. O. (1960). §30 of *Word and Object* (Boston, MA: MIT Press). Reprinted in HARNISH.

Rumfitt, I. (1993). 'Content and Context: The Paratactic Theory Revisited and Revised', *Mind* 102: 429–54.

Salmon, N. and Soames, S., eds (1988). Introduction to *Propositions and Attitudes* (Oxford: Oxford University Press).

Segal, G. (1989). 'A Preference for Sense and Reference', *Journal of Philosophy* 86: 73–89.

Language and Convention

Avramides, A. (1998). 'Intention and Convention', in HALE AND WRIGHT.

Burge, T. (1975). 'On Knowledge and Convention', *Philosophical Review* 84: 249–55.

Davidson, D. (1984). 'Communication and Convention', *Synthèse* 59: 3–17. Reprinted in his *Inquiries into Truth and Interpretation* (Oxford: Clarendon Press, 1984).

Davidson, D. (1986). 'A Nice Derangement of Epitaphs', in *Philosophical Grounds of Rationality*, ed. R. Grandy and R. Warner (Oxford: Oxford University Press), pp. 156–74. Reprinted in *Truth and Interpretation: Perspectives on the Philosophy of Donald Davidson*, ed. E. Lepore (Oxford: Blackwell, 1986). Also in MARTINICH.

Laurence, S. (1996). 'A Chomskian Alternative to Convention Based Semantics', *Mind* 105: 269–301.

Lewis, D. K. (1969). *Convention: A Philosophical Study* (Cambridge, MA: Harvard University Press).

Lewis, D. K. (1975). 'Languages and Language', in *Minnesota Studies in the Philosophy of Science*, vol. VII, ed. K. Gunderson (Minnesota: University of Minnesota Press). Reprinted in his *Philosophical Papers I* (Oxford: Oxford University Press, 1983).

Proper Names

Bach, K. (1987). *Thought and Reference* (Oxford: Clarendon Press).

Burge, T. (1973). 'Reference and Proper Names', *Journal of Philosophy* 70: 425–39. Reprinted in LUDLOW.

Davies, M. (1981). Ch. V of *Meaning, Quantification, Necessity: Themes in Philosophical Logic* (London: Routledge & Kegan Paul).

Evans, G. (1973). 'The Causal Theory of Proper Names', *Proceedings of the Aristotelian Society* 47: 187–208. Reprinted in his *Collected Papers* (Oxford: Clarendon Press, 1985). Also in LUDLOW and MOORE.

Evans, G. (1982). Ch. 11 of *The Varieties of Reference*, ed. J. McDowell (Oxford: Clarendon Press).

Kripke, S. (1980). *Naming and Necessity* (Oxford: Blackwell).

McCulloch, G. (1989). *The Game of the Name: Introducing Logic, Language, and Mind* (Oxford: Clarendon Press).

McDowell, J. (1977). 'On the Sense and Reference of a Proper Name', *Mind* 86: 159–68. Reprinted in his *Meaning, Knowledge, and Reality* (Cambridge, MA: Harvard University Press, 1998). Also in MOORE and PLATTS.

Recanati, F. (1993). *Direct Reference: From Thought to Language* (Oxford: Blackwell).

Sainsbury, R. M. (1992). 'Philosophical Logic §1', pp. 65–77, in *Philosophy: A Guide Through the Subject*, ed. A. C. Grayling (Oxford: Oxford University Press).

Chapter 2

Intention-based Semantics

Avramides, A. (1989). *Meaning and Mind: An Examination of a Gricean Account of Meaning* (Cambridge, MA: MIT Press).

Avramides, A. (1998). 'Intention and Convention', in HALE AND WRIGHT.

Grice, H. P. (1989). Part I of *Studies in the Way of Words* (Cambridge, MA: Harvard University Press).

Rumfitt, I. (1995). 'Truth Conditions and Communication', *Mind* 104: 827–62.

Schiffer, S. (1972). *Meaning* (Oxford: Clarendon Press).

Strawson, P. F. (1964). 'Intention and Convention in Speech Acts', *Philosophical Review* 73: 439–60. Reprinted in his *Logico-Linguistic Papers* (Aldershot: Ashgate, 2004).

Travis, C. (1991). 'The Annals of Analysis', *Mind* 100: 237–64.

Non-indicatives

Davidson, D. (1979). 'Moods and Performances', in *Meaning and Use*, ed. A. Margalit (Dordrecht: D. Reidel). Reprinted in *Inquiries into Truth and Interpretation* (Oxford: Clarendon Press, 1984).

Dummett, M. A. E. (1993). 'Mood, Force and Convention', in his *Seas of Language* (Oxford: Clarendon Press).

Hornsby, J. (1986). 'A Note on Non-Indicatives', *Mind* 95: 92–9.

Segal, G. (1990). 'In the Mood for a Semantic Theory', *Proceedings of the Aristotelian Society* 91: 103–18.

Wilson, D. and Sperber, D. (1988). 'Mood and the Analysis of Non-Declarative Sentences', in *Human Agency: Language, Duty and Value*, ed. J. Dancy, J. Moravcsik, and C. Taylor (Stanford, CA: Stanford University Press). Reprinted in *Pragmatics: Critical Concepts*, vol. II, ed. A. Kasher (London: Routledge, 1998).

Performatives and Speech Acts

Austin, J. L. (1962). *How to Do Things with Words* (Oxford: Clarendon Press).

Bach, K. and Harnish R. M. (1992). 'How Performatives Really Work', *Linguistics and Philosophy* 15: 93–110.

Heal, J. (1974). 'Explicit Performative Utterances and Statements', *Philosophical Quarterly* 24: 106–21.

Lemmon, E. J. (1962). 'On Sentences Verifiable by their Use', *Analysis* 22: 86–9.

Searle, J. R. (1989). 'How Performatives Work', *Linguistics and Philosophy* 12: 535–58. Reprinted in Harnish.

Tsohatzidis, S. L., ed. (1994). *Foundations of Speech Act Theory: Philosophical and Linguistic Perspectives* (London: Routledge).

Warnock, G. J. (1973). 'Some Types of Performative Utterance', in *Essays on J. L. Austin*, ed. I. Berlin et al. (Oxford: Clarendon Press).

Chapter 3

Radical Interpretation and the Principle of Charity

Burge, T. (1999). 'Comprehension and Interpretation', in *The Philosophy of Donald Davidson*, ed. L. E. Hahn (Chicago and LaSalle, IL: Open Court).

Evans, G. (1975). 'Identity and Predication', *Journal of Philosophy* 72: 343–63. Reprinted in his *Collected Papers* (Oxford: Clarendon Press, 1985).

Heal, J. (1998). 'Radical Interpretation', in Hale and Wright.

Quine, W. V. O. (1960). Ch. 2 of *Word and Object* (Cambridge, MA: MIT Press).

Rawling, P. (2003). 'Radical Interpretation', in Ludwig.

Sainsbury, M. (1980). 'Understanding and Theories of Meaning', *Proceedings of the Aristotelian Society* 80: 127–44.

Semantic Theories for Natural Language

Heim, I. and Kratzer, A. (1998). *Semantics in Generative Grammar* (Oxford: Blackwell).

Higginbotham, J. (1985). 'On Semantics', *Linguistic Inquiry* 16: 547–93.

Higginbotham, J. (1986). 'Linguistic Theory and Davidson's Program', in *Truth and Interpretation: Perspectives on the Philosophy of Donald Davidson*, ed. E. Lepore (Oxford: Blackwell).

Larson, R. and Segal, G. (1995). *Knowledge of Meaning: An Introduction to Semantic Theory* (Cambridge, MA: MIT Press).

Lewis, D. K. (1970). 'General Semantics', *Synthèse* 22: 18–67. Reprinted in *Semantics of Natural Language*, ed. D. Davidson and G. Harman (Dordrecht: D. Reidel, 1972), and in his *Philosophical Papers I* (Oxford: Oxford University Press, 1983).

Platts, M. (1997). *Ways of Meaning: An Introduction to a Philosophy of Language*, 2nd edition (Cambridge, MA: MIT Press).

Tacit Knowledge and Compositionality

Davies, M. (1987). 'Tacit Knowledge and Semantic Theory: Can a 5% Difference Matter?', *Mind* 96: 441–62.

Evans, G. (1981). 'Semantic Theory and Tacit Knowledge', in *Wittgenstein: To Follow a Rule*, ed. S. Holtzman and C. H. Leich (London: Routledge & Kegan Paul). Reprinted in his *Collected Papers* (Oxford: Clarendon Press, 1985).

Fricker, E. (1983). 'Semantic Structure and Speakers' Understanding', *Proceedings of the Aristotelian Society* 83: 49–66.

Miller, A. (1998). 'Tacit Knowledge', in HALE AND WRIGHT.

Wright, C. (1981). 'Rule-Following, Objectivity and the Theory of Meaning', in *Wittgenstein: To Follow a Rule*, ed. S. Holtzman and C. H. Leich (London: Routledge & Kegan Paul).

Tarski's Truth-theoretic Machinery

Davies, M. (1981). Chs II and VI of *Meaning, Quantification, Necessity: Themes in Philosophical Logic* (London: Routledge & Kegan Paul).

Larson, R. and Segal, G. (1995). *Knowledge of Meaning: An Introduction to Semantic Theory* (Cambridge, MA: MIT Press).

McDowell, J. (1997). 'Physicalism and Primitive Denotation: Field on Tarski', in PLATTS.

Platts, M. (1997). *Ways of Meaning: An Introduction to a Philosophy of Language*, 2nd edition (Cambridge, MA: MIT Press).

Soames, S. (1999). *Understanding Truth* (Oxford: Oxford University Press).

Tarski, A. (1944). 'The Semantic Conception of Truth and the Foundations of Semantics', *Philosophy and Phenomenological Research* 4: 341–75. Reprinted in HARNISH, GEIRSSON AND LOSONSKY, MARTINICH, and NYE.

Tarski, A. (1956). 'The Concept of Truth in Formalized Languages', in his *Logic Semantics, Metamathematics* (Oxford: Clarendon Press).

Truth-theories and Understanding

Davidson, D. (1976). 'Reply to Foster', in EVANS AND MCDOWELL. Reprinted in his *Inquiries into Truth and Interpretation* (Oxford: Clarendon Press, 1984).

Davies, M. (1981). Ch. IV of *Meaning, Quantification, Necessity: Themes in Philosophical Logic* (London: Routledge & Kegan Paul).

Foster, J. A. (1976). 'Meaning and Truth Theory', in EVANS AND MCDOWELL.

Higginbotham, J. (1989). 'Knowledge of Reference', in *Reflections on Chomsky*, ed. A. George (Oxford: Blackwell).

Higginbotham, J. (1992). 'Truth and Understanding', *Philosophical Studies* 65: 3, 3–16. Reprinted in RICHARD.

Hornsby, J. (1989). 'Semantic Innocence and Psychological Understanding', in *Philosophical Perspectives* 3, ed. J. E. Tomberlin. Reprinted in her *Simple Mindedness: In Defense of a Naïve Naturalism in the Philosophy of Mind* (Cambridge, MA: Harvard University Press, 1997).

Lepore, E. and Ludwig, K. (2003). 'Truth and Meaning', in LUDWIG.

Loar, B. (1976). 'Two Theories of Meaning', in EVANS AND MCDOWELL.

Segal, G. (1999). 'How a Truth Theory Can Do Duty as a Theory of Meaning', in *Donald Davidson: Truth, Meaning, and Knowledge*, ed. U. M. Zeglen (London: Routledge).

Chapter 4

Computational Psychology

Crane, T. (2003). *The Mechanical Mind*, 2nd edition (London: Routledge).

Cummins, R. (1983). *The Nature of Psychological Explanation* (Cambridge, MA: MIT Press).

Fodor, J. A. (1968). *Psychological Explanation* (Cambridge, MA: MIT Press).

Fodor, J. A. (1975). *The Language of Thought* (New York: Crowell).

Harnish, R. M. (2002). *Minds, Brains, Computers: An Historical Introduction to the Foundations of Cognitive Science* (Oxford: Blackwell).

Pylyshyn, Z. (1983). *Computation and Cognition* (Cambridge, MA: MIT Press).

Innate Knowledge and 'Poverty of Stimulus'

Cowie, F. (1999). *What's Within: Nativism Reconsidered* (Oxford: Oxford University Press).

Crain, S. and Pietroski, P. (2001). 'Nature, Nurture, and Universal Grammar', *Linguistics and Philosophy* 24:139–86.

Fodor, J. A. (2001). 'Doing without What's Within: Fiona Cowie's Critique of Nativism', *Mind* 110: 99–148.

Griffiths, P. E. (2002). 'What is Innateness?', *The Monist* 85: 70–85.

Laurence, S. and Margolis, E. (2001). 'The Poverty of the Stimulus Argument', *British Journal for the Philosophy of Science* 52: 217–76.

Pinker, S. (1995). Chs 1, 2, 8, and 13 of *The Language Instinct* (London: Penguin Books).

Stich, S. P., ed. (1975). *Innate Ideas* (Los Angeles: University of California Press).

Linguistic Competence and Knowledge

Barber, A., ed. (2003). *Epistemology of Language* (Oxford: Oxford University Press).

Devitt, M. and Sterelny, K. (1989). 'What's Wrong with the Right View?', *Philosophical Perspectives* 3 (Philosophy of Mind and Action Theory): 497–531.

Fisher, J. (1974). 'Knowledge of Rules', *Review of Metaphysics* 28: 237–60.

Pettit, D. (2002). 'Why Knowledge is Unnecessary for Understanding Language', *Mind* 111: 519–50.

Schiffer, S. (1987). *Remnants of Meaning* (Cambridge, MA: MIT Press).

Smith, B. C. (1992). 'Understanding Language', *Proceedings of the Aristotelian Society* 92: 109–41.

Stich, S. P. (1971). 'What Every Speaker Knows', *The Philosophical Review* 80: 476–96.

Weiss, B. (2003). 'Knowledge of Meaning', *Proceedings of the Aristotelian Society* 104: 75–92.

Perceptual Views of Linguistic Competence

Fodor, J. A. (1983). *The Modularity of Mind* (Cambridge, MA: MIT Press).

Fricker, E. (2003). 'Understanding and Knowledge of What is Said', in *Epistemology of Language*, ed. A. Barber (Oxford: Oxford University Press).

Higginbotham, J. (1987). 'The Autonomy of Syntax and Semantics', in *Modularity in Knowledge Representation and Natural Language Understanding*, ed. J. Garfield (Cambridge, MA: MIT Press).

Hunter, D. (1998). 'Belief and Understanding', *Philosophy and Phenomenological Research* 58: 559–80.

McDowell, J. (1980). 'Meaning, Communication and Knowledge', in *Philosophical Subjects*, ed. Z. Van Straaten (Oxford: Oxford University Press). Reprinted in his *Meaning, Knowledge, and Reality* (Cambridge, MA: Harvard University Press, 1998).

McDowell, J. (1987). 'In Defence of Modesty', in TAYLOR. Reprinted in his *Meaning, Knowledge, and Reality* (Cambridge, MA: Harvard University Press, 1998).

Syntactic Theory

Adger, D. (2003). *Core Syntax: A Minimalist Approach* (Oxford: Oxford University Press).

Haegeman, L. (1994). *Introduction to Government and Binding Theory*, 2nd edition (Oxford: Blackwell).

Napoli, D. J. (1993). *Syntax: Theory and Problems* (Oxford: Oxford University Press).

Radford, A. (1997). *Syntactic Theory and the Structure of English: A Minimalist Approach* (Cambridge: Cambridge University Press).

Tacit Knowledge: Its Nature

Collins, J. (2004). 'Faculty Disputes', *Mind & Language* 19: 503–33.

Davies, M. (1989). 'Tacit Knowledge and Subdoxastic States', in *Reflections on Chomsky*, ed. A. George (Oxford: Blackwell).

Fodor J. A. (1981). 'Some Notes on What Linguistics is About', in *Readings in the Philosophy of Psychology*, vol. II (1985), ed. N. Block (Cambridge, MA: Harvard University Press). Reprinted in KATZ.

Rey, G. (2003). 'Intentional Content and Chomskyan Linguistics', in *Epistemology of Language*, ed. A. Barber (Oxford: Oxford University Press).

Stich, S. (1972). 'Grammar, Psychology, and Indeterminacy', *Journal of Philosophy* 79: 799–818. Reprinted in KATZ.

Stich, S. (1978). 'Beliefs and Subdoxastic States', *Philosophy of Science* 45: 499–518.

Chapter 5

Compositionality and Meaning

Fodor, J. A. and Lepore, E. (2002). *The Compositionality Papers* (Oxford: Oxford University Press).

Gibson, M. I. (2003). *From Naming to Saying: The Unity of the Proposition* (Oxford: Blackwell).

Horwich, P. (1997). 'The Composition of Meanings', *Philosophical Review* 106: 503–32.

Larson, R. and Segal, G. (1995). Ch. 3 of *Knowledge of Meaning: An Introduction to Semantic Theory* (Cambridge, MA: MIT Press).

Pagin, P. (1997) 'Is Compositionality Compatible with Holism?', *Mind & Language* 12: 11–33.

Schiffer, S. (1987). *Remnants of Meaning* (Cambridge, MA: MIT Press).

Chapter 6

Context and Meaning

Bach, K. (2001). 'You Don't Say?', *Synthèse* 128: 15–44.

Carston, R. (2002). *Thoughts and Utterances: The Pragmatics of Explicit Communication* (Oxford: Blackwell).

Grice, H. P. (1975). 'Logic and Conversation', in *Syntax and Semantics*, Vol. 3, *Speech Acts*. Reprinted in his *Studies in the Way of Words* (Cambridge, MA: Harvard University Press, 1989). Also in HARNISH.

Higginbotham, J. (1988). 'Contexts, Models, and Meanings: A Note on the Data of Semantics', in *Mental Representations: The Interface Between Language and Reality*, ed. R. Kempson (Cambridge: Cambridge University Press).

Recanati, F. (1994). 'Contextualism and Anti-contextualism in the Philosophy of Language', in *Foundations of Speech Act Theory: Philosophical and Linguistic Perspectives*, ed. S. L. Tsohatzidis (London: Routledge).

Recanati, F. (2004). *Literal Meaning* (Cambridge: Cambridge University Press).

Searle, J. R. (1978). 'Literal Meaning', *Erkenntnis* 13: 207–24. Reprinted in his *Expression and Meaning* (Cambridge: Cambridge University Press, 1979).

Sperber, D. and Wilson, D. (1986). *Relevance: Communication and Cognition* (Oxford: Basil Blackwell).

Stanley, J. and Szabó, Z. (2000). 'On Quantifier Domain Restriction', *Mind & Language* 15: 219–61.

Travis, C. (1985) 'On What is Strictly Speaking True', *Canadian Journal of Philosophy* 15: 187–229.

Travis, C. (1998). 'Pragmatics', in HALE AND WRIGHT.

Waismann, F. (1951). 'Verifiability', in *Logic and Language*, 1st series, ed. A. Flew (Oxford: Blackwell).

Metaphor

Bezuidenhout, A. (2001). 'Metaphor and What is Said', in French and Wettstein, cited below.

Black, M. (1979). 'How Metaphors Work: a Reply to Davidson', in *On Metaphor*, ed. S. Sacks (Chicago: University of Chicago Press).

Cooper, D. (1986). *Metaphor* (Oxford: Basil Blackwell).

Davidson, D. (1978). 'What Metaphors Mean', in *Critical Inquiry* 5: 31–47. Reprinted in his *Inquiries into Truth and Interpretation* (Oxford: Clarendon Press, 1984). Also in DAVIS, MARTINICH, and PLATTS.

French P. and Wettstein H. K., eds (2001). *Figurative Language* (Oxford: Blackwell). (*Midwest Studies in Philosophy XXV.*)

Moran, R. (1998). 'Metaphor', in HALE AND WRIGHT.

Ortony, A., ed. (1993). *Metaphor and Thought*, 2nd edition (Cambridge: Cambridge University Press).

Searle, J. R. (1979). 'Metaphor', in Ortony, ed. (cited above; first appeared in first edition). Reprinted in MARTINICH.

Index